POWER SHIFT

D1555875

Energy transitions are fundamental to achieving a zero-carbon economy. This book explains the urgently needed transition in energy systems from the perspective of the global political economy. It develops an historical, global, political and ecological account of key features of energy transitions: from their production and financing, to how they are governed and mobilised. Informed by direct engagement in projects of energy transition, the book provides an accessible account of the real-world dilemmas in accelerating transitions to a low-carbon economy. As well as changes to technology, markets, institutions and behaviours, *Power Shift* shows that shifts in power relations between and within countries, and across social groups and political actors, are required if the world is to move onto a more sustainable path. Using contemporary and historical case studies to explore energy transitions, it will be of interest to students and researchers across disciplines, policymakers and activists.

PETER NEWELL is Professor of International Relations at the University of Sussex and Research Director of the Rapid Transition Alliance. He has worked on the political economy of energy transitions and climate change for over 25 years. His books include *Climate for Change* (Cambridge University Press, 2000), *Governing Climate Change* (Routledge, 2010 with Harriet Bulkeley), *Climate Capitalism* (Cambridge University Press, 2010 with Matthew Paterson) and *Global Green Politics* (Cambridge University Press, 2019).

POWER SHIFT

The Global Political Economy of Energy Transitions

PETER NEWELL

University of Sussex

CAMBRIDGE
UNIVERSITY PRESS

CAMBRIDGE
UNIVERSITY PRESS

University Printing House, Cambridge CB2 8BS, United Kingdom

One Liberty Plaza, 20th Floor, New York, NY 10006, USA

477 Williamstown Road, Port Melbourne, VIC 3207, Australia

314–321, 3rd Floor, Plot 3, Splendor Forum, Jasola District Centre,
New Delhi – 110025, India

79 Anson Road, #06–04/06, Singapore 079906

Cambridge University Press is part of the University of Cambridge.

It furthers the University's mission by disseminating knowledge in the pursuit of
education, learning, and research at the highest international levels of excellence.

www.cambridge.org
Information on this title: www.cambridge.org/9781108832854
DOI: 10.1017/9781108966184

First published 2021

A catalogue record for this publication is available from the British Library.

ISBN 978-1-108-83285-4 Hardback
ISBN 978-1-108-96582-8 Paperback

Contents

Figures

Tables

Preface

This book brings an innovative interdisciplinary approach to the pressing question of how to accelerate transitions towards a lower- or zero-carbon economy. With commitments from governments and the private sector falling well short of what is required to avert dangerous climate change, the question of how to accelerate and deepen the decarbonisation of the global economy is an urgent one. This implies not only an analysis of the political work of assembling actors and social forces in favour of accelerating moves towards a lower-carbon economy, but also the more difficult task, perhaps, of undoing incumbent power organised around the fossil fuel complex: disassembling the high-carbon economy in order to realise the objectives of the Paris Agreement on climate change.

By introducing neglected global, political, historical and ecological dimensions, the book provides a richer account of the necessary enabling conditions and political processes required for the sorts of transformations in energy production and consumption, including shifts in institutions, finance, infrastructure, technology and broader social and cultural changes that are now imperative for tackling climate change. It does so by combining empirical and theoretical work on technology and innovation studies with history and (international) political economy and ecology to analyse when and how such transformations have occurred before, or are emerging in embryonic form in today's world, and how far insights about them can shed light on our current predicament in relation to the need to rapidly and fairly decarbonise the global economy. This improves upon our understanding of the politics and prospects of delivering such an energy transformation on the scale now required to tackle climate change, while addressing energy poverty and enhancing energy security: the so-called energy trilemma. It also challenges the predominantly apolitical and largely national focus of many theories of socio-technical transition, the ahistorical approach of most policy discussions and the ecological blindness of much contemporary thinking about energy.

Acknowledgements

The preparation of this book began shortly before the release of the 2018 IPCC SR15 report, which spoke of the need for 'transformative systemic change' to address global heating. Headlines ran that we had twelve years to save the planet. I completed the book in 2020 amid a global pandemic caused by Covid-19. This led to dramatic shifts in the global energy system with oil prices plummeting, aircraft grounded and many companies going bankrupt. Attention to the crisis also, however, meant that efforts to tackle climate change took more of a back seat, despite calls to make sure that the recovery was a 'green' one and for governments to 'build back better'. In fact, amid wave after wave of bailouts for fossil fuel incumbents, it is clear that the rush to resume business as usual means that an opportunity to reset systems of transport and energy provision, for example, has, for the most part, been lost. It is a timely reminder, nevertheless, that, for all our models, historical insights and theoretical frameworks, unpredicted events bring new challenges and opportunities to an ever-shifting political terrain.

The writing of this book was supported by an ISRF (Independent Social Research Foundation) Political Economy Fellowship, which brought me relief from teaching duties. I am hugely indebted to the foundation for its support for this project. The book draws on empirical material and conceptual insights accumulated over more than ten years of working on energy transitions, and the additional fifteen years before that in the field of international climate politics. I am grateful to funders of that research, which include the Economic and Social Research Council (ESRC), the Climate and Development Knowledge Network (CDKN), the International Development Research Centre (IDRC), Climate KIC, the United Nations Development Programme (UNDP) and the KR Foundation. Much of the research which informs the book has benefited from collaborations I have been lucky enough to have with friends and colleagues including Lucy Baker, Harriet Bulkeley, Phil Johnstone, Josh Kirshner, Richard Lane, Abigail Martin,

Acknowledgements xiii

Dustin Mulvaney, Matthew Paterson, Jon Phillips, Marcus Power, Adrian Smith and Benjamin Sovacool.

During the writing of this book, I also benefited greatly from the energy, enthusiasm and wisdom of the Rapid Transition Alliance team, for which I serve as research director. Andrew Simms, in particular, has been a source of continual insight and inspiration. I am also indebted to fellow board members and colleagues at Greenpeace UK and colleagues across the University of Sussex, which provides such a supportive and critical intellectual fulcrum for work on energy transitions and global political economy. It has been a pleasure, once again, to work with Matt Lloyd and colleagues at Cambridge University Press in bringing the manuscript to publication and I appreciate the help of Freddie Daley in preparing the manuscript for submission.

On a personal level, I am ever grateful to the best friend anyone could have, Rahul Moodgal, and to my family in the UK and Argentina for their love, support and understanding, especially my parents Helen and Brian and my wife Lucila.

I dedicate this book to my children Ana and Camilo.

Abbreviations

ADEPT	Association of Directors of Environment, Economy, Planning and Transport
AI	artificial intelligence
CACE	Council Action in the Climate Emergency
CAfE	Community Action for Energy
CARES	Community and Renewable Energy Scheme (Scotland)
CAT	Centre for Alternative Technology
CBI	Climate Bonds Initiative
CCRIF	Caribbean Catastrophe Risk Insurance Facility
CCS	carbon capture and storage
CDKN	Climate and Development Knowledge Network
CDM	Clean Development Mechanism
CDP	Carbon Disclosure Project
CERs	certified emissions reductions
CERES	Coalition for Environmentally Responsible Economies
CEFC	Clean Energy Finance Corporation (Australia)
C-FACT	Corporate Finance Approach to Climate Targets
CIF	climate investment funds
CIFF	children's investment fund and foundation
CO_2	carbon dioxide
CORSIA	Carbon Offsetting and Reduction Scheme for International Aviation
CPRE	Council for the Protection of Rural England
CRA	climate risk assessments
CRERAL	Cooperativa Regional de Eletrificação Rural do Alto Uruguai Ltda (Brazil)
CSI	climate stabilisation intensity
CSR	corporate social responsibility
DIY	do-it-yourself

ECT	Energy Charter Treaty
EITI	Extractive Industries Transparency Initiative
ETS	Emissions Trading Scheme
ETSU	Energy Technology Support Unit (UK)
EU	European Union
EV	electric vehicle
GATS	General Agreement on Trade in Services
GCF	Green Climate Fund
GEF	Global Environment Facility
GEEREF	Global Energy Efficiency and Renewable Energy Fund
GEVA	greenhouse gas emissions per unit of value added
GGON	Global Gas and Oil Network
GHG	greenhouse gases
GIB	green investment bank
G7	Group of Seven most industrialised countries
G20	Group of Twenty most industrialised countries
IAM	integrated assessment model
ICAO	International Civil Aviation Organisation
ICAP	International Carbon Action Partnership
ICCT	International Council on Clean Transportation.
IEA	International Energy Agency
IFC	International Finance Corporation
IISD	International Institute for Sustainable Development
ILO	International Labour Organization
IMF	International Monetary Fund
IPCC	Intergovernmental Panel on Climate Change
IPE	international political economy
IR	international relations
IRENA	International Renewable Energy Agency
JSW	Jastrzębska Spółka Węglowa
KfW	Kreditanstalt für Wiederaufbau (Germany)
LDCs	least-developed countries
LNG	liquefied natural gas
MDBs	multilateral development banks
MEC	minerals-energy complex
MLP	Multi-Level Perspective
MNRE	Ministry of New and Renewable Energy (India)
MoEF	Ministry of Environment and Forests (India)
MRV	monitoring, reporting and verification

NAFTA	North American Free Trade Area
NETS	negative emissions technologies
NFFO	Non-fossil Fuel Obligation
NIMBY	not in my back yard
NOPE	not on Planet Earth
NYC	New York City
OECD	Organisation for Economic Co-operation and Development
OPEC	Organization of the Petroleum Exporting Countries
PCS	Public Commercial and Service (trade union)
PIDG	Private Infrastructure Development Group
PPP	public–private partnership
R&D	research and development
REEEP	Renewable Energy and Energy Efficiency Partnership
SBTs	science-based targets
SDGs	Sustainable Development Goals
SEC	Securities and Exchange Commission
SHS	solar home system
SIBS	state investment banks
SREP	Scaling up Renewable Energy Programme
STS	science and technology studies
TUC	Trades Union Conference
UK	United Kingdom
UKEF	United Kingdom Export Finance
UNDP	United Nations Development Programme
UNEP	United Nations Environment Programme
UNESCO	UN Educational, Social and Cultural Organisation
UNFCCC	United Nations Framework Convention on Climate Change
USA	United States of America
WBCSD	World Business Council for Sustainable Development
WCI	World Coal Institute
WEF	World Economic Forum
WEO	World Energy Outlook
WHO	World Health Organization
WRI	World Resources Institute
WTO	World Trade Organization

1

Introduction

The question of whether and how we can collectively steer our economy and society onto a lower carbon development trajectory is among the most pressing that the world currently faces. Runaway climate change threatens the very habitability of the earth: systematically undoing progress made in advancing the human condition and rendering impossible the achievement of the Sustainable Development Goals (SDGs) agreed in 2015. But despite rhetorical embrace of the concept and need for transition by governments, businesses and international organisations, critical applied analysis of what a dramatic shift in the structures of production and consumption, and, more challengingly, the (re)alignments of political and economic power that would be required to achieve and sustain a low or zero carbon economy would imply, is sorely lacking. The need for fundamental transformations in the way we produce, consume and distribute energy is glaringly obvious, despite painfully slow progress in the shift away from our fossil-fuel dominated world. A series of factors conspire to make the need for deeper transformations and nearer-term energy transitions acute and urgent. Today's energy system is not fit for purpose on a number of grounds.

Firstly, there is the growing threat of climate change and the need to drastically and rapidly decarbonise energy systems which continue to be heavily reliant on fossil fuels. If, as a global community, we are serious about keeping warming below 2°C (let alone 1.5°C), large swathes of existing reserves of fossil fuels will have to remain in the ground un-burned (McGlade and Ekins 2015). Even to keep warming below 2°C, 80 per cent of coal, oil and gas reserves are now un-burnable (Carbon Tracker Initiative 2013). Carbon embedded in existing fossil fuel production will take the world far beyond safe climate limits (SEI et al. 2019). Yet money is still being funnelled into extracting more, with US$50 billion going towards new oil and gas projects alone. Doubts concerning the scale of non-existent negative emissions technologies (Keary 2016) and the limited development of carbon capture and storage built into models mean that the proportion of un-burnable reserves may be even higher (Anderson and Peters 2016).

The latest findings of the Special Report of the IPCC SR15 call for carbon to be cut overall by 45 per cent by 2030 and for investments in fossil fuel extraction and unabated power generation to fall by up to US$0.85 trillion over 2016–50 and unabated (without CCS) coal to zero by 2030 (IPCC 2018), while the Paris Agreement calls for net zero emissions by 2050. For this to be achievable, emissions of greenhouse gases (GHGs) needed to peak by 2020 with the gap closed by 2030 (UNEP 2018). SR15 makes very clear that staying below a 1.5°C warming limit cannot be achieved through business-as-usual economics, politics and behaviours. Limiting warming to 1.5°C requires 'transformative systemic change', involving the upscaling and acceleration of far-reaching climate mitigation across regions and sectors. Even assuming full implementation of unconditional nationally determined contributions (NDCs) and a continuation of climate action similar to that of the existing NDCs, global average temperature will increase by 2.9–3.4°C above pre-industrial levels (UNEP 2018). This implies catastrophic consequences, especially for many of the world's poorest and most vulnerable populations that have contributed least to GHG emissions.

While transitions are underway in various countries, limiting warming to 1.5°C will require a greater scale and pace of change to transform energy, land, urban and industrial systems globally. Progress is being made, but not fast enough. There is an urgent need for more rapid and deeper transitions to limit warming to 1.5°C. Such transitions have been observed in the past within specific sectors and technologies. But the geographical and economic scales at which the required rates of change in the energy, land, urban, infrastructure and industrial systems would now need to take place are larger and have no direct documented historic precedent (IPCC 2018). We are in many ways in uncharted territory, therefore.

But we can use historical examples to inform our understanding of the likelihood and possibility of rapid change of the sort required to steer the global economy onto a 1.5°C compatible pathway. It is also the case that never before have we faced a pressing need for transformation of complex social systems to ensure planetary survival. Even managing threats of nuclear apocalypse is down to inter-state diplomacy and bargaining, albeit with important pressure from social movements. But they do not imply change at every level of society in terms of all aspects of production and consumption, as is required for energy transformations. The omnipresence of energy in all aspects of human life poses particular challenges to our ability to reorganise energy systems in the face of climate change.

Climate change is not, of course, the only environmental driver of the need for energy system reform. The global health crisis caused by air pollution from cars and pollutants from fossil-fuelled power stations adds another significant dimension to the crisis. Globally, there are 7 million premature deaths annually from exposure to air pollution (one in eight of total global deaths), dubbed the world's 'silent killer' by the World Health Organization (WHO). Indoor air pollution, largely from wood-burning stoves, is responsible for 3.3 million deaths per year in low- and middle-income countries in the South-East Asia and Western Pacific regions alone (WHO 2014).

Secondly, there is the ongoing challenge of energy security. States continue to fulfil their growing energy needs through a range of geopolitical strategies, from diplomacy and multilateralism to violence and war. This makes energy an issue of high politics. As Moran and Russell (2009: 2) note:

It is in the energy sector that strategic planners now find it easiest to imagine major states reconsidering their reluctance to use force against each other. 'Energy security' is now deemed so central to 'national security' that threats to the former are liable to be reflectively interpreted as threats to the latter. In a world in which territorial disputes, ideological competition, ethnic irredentism and even nuclear proliferation all seem capable of being normalized in ways that constrain the actual use of military force, a crisis in the global energy supply stands out as the last all-weather *casus belli* when the moment comes to hypothesize worst case scenarios.

They continue: 'The possibility that access to energy resources may become an object of armed struggle is almost incontestably the single most alarming prospect facing the international system today. The political stability of advanced societies and the continued prospects for economic and social improvement in developing countries are both irreducibly dependent on avoiding such a conflict' (Moran and Russell 2009: 2). And yet nurturing and inflating that possibility (fuelling 'petroleum anxiety' (Klare 2009)) provides a useful way for the military establishment to secure for itself additional resources such that 'the possibility of war to seize or defend energy resources provides a much-needed rationale for preserving the heavy conventional forces that still consume the lion's share of defense spending around the world' (Moran and Russell 2009: 2). An analysis of the exercise of incumbent power in shaping and resisting energy pathways needs, therefore, to consider the key role of the military (Johnstone and Newell 2018; Cox et al. 2016).

At the time of writing, the threat posed to energy security of regimes in places as diverse as Iran and Venezuela is being invoked by military actors as a reason to enhance their role in those regions through covert and overt means. Disruptions by terrorist organisations such as Al-Queda to key energy infrastructures, such as oil and gas pipelines, also form part of this complex geopolitical mosaic where between 1990 and 2005 alone there were more than 330 terrorist attacks against oil and gas facilities (Haynes 2009). At the same time, energy resources can be mobilised as an alternative to the use of force: wielding the 'energy weapon' obviates the need for military ones (Moran and Russell 2009).

The militarisation of energy resource management necessarily permeates the politics of competing energy transition pathways and responses to climate crises around securing borders, disaster risk management and policing migrant flows, where the spaces and infrastructures of the rich are secured from the poor and dispossessed in conditions of accelerated climate disruption. In this sense, militarism is often mobilised to protect the 'secure' and their assets and not the dispossessed, who in their role as migrants and refugees are constructed as threats to security (Buxton and Hayes 2016). For example, McDonald (2013: 46) reveals how a 2003 Pentagon report proposed that some states 'might seek to develop more effective border control strategies to ensure that large populations displaced by manifestations of climate change (whether rising sea levels or extreme weather events) could be kept on the other side of the national border' such that 'people displaced by environmental disasters or environmental stress may be positioned as threats to the security of the state rather than as those in need of being secured'. In their book *The Secure and the Dispossessed*, Buxton and Hayes (2016) show 'how the military and corporations plan to maintain control in a world reshaped by climate change. With one eye on the scientific evidence and the other on their global assets, dystopian preparations by the powerful are already fuelling militarised responses to the unfolding climate crises.' This is unlikely to form the basis of a progressive or effective response to global climate change. Dominant framings come from actors with a stake in protecting or expanding expenditure in their sector who benefit from threat proliferation which justifies their existence and, indeed, growth. The pitch to policymakers is around climate adaptation and their ability to secure assets and infrastructures and protect borders.

There have also been shifts in who provides energy security with the privatisation of security services and the reliance on market actors to secure energy supplies. This blurring of public/private and security/economy challenges traditional state-centric understandings of energy security (Buzan 1994). As we will see in Chapter 5 on 'governing' energy transitions, there is an ideological component to this. Moran and Russell (2009: 5) suggest: 'The fact that strong states have been prepared to trust their energy security to the workings of international markets is testimony to their faith in the efficiency of those markets and to their belief that the costs of war aimed at controlling energy resources would be so great as to outweigh the benefits.' This builds on the classic liberal peace doctrine of Doyle (1986), which suggests that economic interdependence reduces the prospects of war by heightening the mutual costs that would be incurred by the use of force. Of relevance to our concern here with energy transitions is the (contestable) claim that it was the 'market' that during the industrial revolution 'was asked to escort Western civilization across the rickety, fog-shrouded bridge that connected its agrarian, wood-fuelled past to an industrial, fossil-fuelled future' (Moran and Russell 2009: 5). It is an open question whether 'the market' will be the principal mechanism of the transition away from the fossil-fuelled economy that the industrial revolution brought into being.

The relationship runs both ways, however, given that the 'international energy market has always rested on the possibility that major market participants might be required to use force to defend or manage its operation' (Moran and Russell 2009: 9). The issue is not just the inter-state politics of energy security, however. Everyday insecurity is also produced through extractivism as usual and its attendant violence. Land acquisition, including 'green grabs' of land for biofuel development (Borras et al. 2010; Harnesk and Brogaard 2017), renewable extractivism (Dunlap 2018), population displacement, pollution and ill-health are just some of the impacts of energy developments that poorer communities the world over are routinely exposed to (Newell and Mulvaney 2013). Export-led extractivism has led to intense social conflict and violence across the globe, as a glance at a world map of environmental justice and resource conflicts makes clear (EJOLT 2020). Violence and exchange, hand in hand.

The shifting geopolitics of energy have, nevertheless, reconfigured the ways in which states seek to provide energy security for their citizens and industries. Whether it is reducing imports of oil in India by adopting a 'solar mission', the USA's embrace of fracking to reduce oil imports from the Middle East, or the problems created by Europe's dependence on gas from Russia, in terms of an ability to stand up to geopolitical manoeuvres by the Putin regime in Ukraine and Crimea, energy is high politics and it was ever thus (Yergin 1991). In many contexts, moves towards lower carbon pathways are primarily driven by such preoccupations with energy security, especially where climate change alone may have less salience as a driver (Schmitz 2017; Kuzemko 2013).

Thirdly, energy poverty. With more than one billion people still lacking access to electricity, this is a critical issue. The 2030 Agenda for Sustainable Development has as one of its main SDGs to 'ensure universal access to affordable, reliable, sustainable and modern energy services for all' (SDG7). According to the United Nations, progress towards SDG7's ambition of access to affordable, reliable, sustainable and modern energy for all has now reached nearly 89 per cent of the global population. This leaves around a billion people without access to electricity (IEA et al. 2020). The SE4All initiative calls ambitiously for universal access to sustainable energy by 2030 (SE4All 2019). Delivering electricity services to nearly half a billion poor and marginal people in the least developed countries (LDCs) is particularly challenging given how tightly energy access is related to other development challenges. Energy is crucial for achieving almost all of the SDGs: from eradicating poverty through advancements in health, education, water supply and industrialisation, to combating climate change. To date, however, 41 per cent of the world's population still cooks with polluting fuel and stove combinations, more than 80 per cent of the current final energy consumption relates to non-renewable energy sources, and the lack of laws on renewable energy within and across countries remains an obstacle to faster deployment of renewables. These net global figures also disguise huge disparities within and across countries and regions (IEA 2019).

Something that is often not afforded sufficient attention in discussions which frame the issue in terms of an energy trilemma is that global energy transitions will have to be socially just transitions in a number of ways. One of these is to ensure that the maldistribution of finance, technology and innovation in the global energy economy towards large industries and economies and towards richer citizens is redressed to meet the needs of those living in energy poverty. This is especially so where there are constraints on supply and there is a need for richer consumers to relinquish ecological and carbon space to poorer groups to meet their basic needs and to pursue pathways out of energy poverty. If low carbon energy access is the goal, as reflected in the ambition of initiatives such as SE4All, then there is a need to design more de-centralised, needs-focused and inclusive energy systems, attentive not just to hardware and financing gaps but to the multiple forms of exclusion that poorer groups experience from a range of services including those around energy (Casillas and Kammen 2010; Ockwell and Byrne 2017). This would imply and necessitate a shift in power too, where the central organisation of energy systems often reflects and reinforces elite power, leading to patterns of clientelism and rent seeking which frustrate attempts to democratise energy systems and increase their access and affordability (Newell and Phillips 2016). Energy poverty is not just a phenomenon that affects marginalised communities in the global South. Fuel poverty blights many communities, even those living in richer parts of the world where choices have to be routinely made between heating the home or eating because families cannot afford to do both (Bridge et al. 2018a). Poor insulation and lack of building regulations regarding energy conservation compound this situation.

Addressing the goals of energy security, energy poverty and climate mitigation simultaneously produces a complex series of energy 'trilemmas' (WEC 2012). For example, subsidies are provided to poorer communities for kerosene (ostensibly to alleviate energy poverty), but these lock in dependence on fossil fuels, building political constituencies that come to depend on their continuation (Skovgaard and van Asselt 2018). Likewise, fracking has been embraced by countries like the USA as a 'lower carbon' way of enhancing energy security. But while it may be less carbon-intensive than coal and oil, it is still a fossil fuel that further locks in dependency on their use while crowding out alternatives and creating other problems such as water contamination and earth tremors (Tomain 2017). Similarly, biofuels have been embraced by some countries, especially Brazil, but can exacerbate the poverty of those whose land is acquired for their cultivation or of poorer consumers who see the price of maize rise because of demand for grains associated with biofuel expansion resulting in 'tortilla riots' (Smith 2000). As Watts (2007) puts it more polemically, '[t]he cars of the rich are now rivalling the bellies of the poor for corn, cane and edible oils'.

Some definitions of 'green energy policy' are both broad and under-specific when applied to 'any policy measure aimed at aligning the structure of a country's energy sector with the needs of sustainable development within established planetary boundaries' (Pegels et al. 2018: 26). But they also fail to provide an account of the politics of managing the conflicts and competing choices over how to reconcile shifts in the energy sector with broader social and developmental goals. Whether and how these goals can be achieved, by whom and under what conditions are first and foremost political questions. They are political because they affect some groups more than others, and have distributional consequences, and are ridden with issues of justice and differentiated responsibility. Introducing classic political economy questions, Abramsky (2010: 10) asks: 'Who will bring the transition about and for what purpose? Who will benefit and at whose expense?'

Indeed, attempts to reorganise energy systems by decarbonising them need to start with an acknowledgement that it is the 1 per cent of the population that is disproportionately responsible for GHG emissions (Kenner 2019) and just 90 companies that have generated more than two-thirds of emissions since the industrial revolution (Heede 2014). Discussions about how to justly allocate remaining carbon space within and between countries and across competing social needs need to be cognisant of these historical and ongoing disparities and injustices. Whose energy needs are met, how and at what and whose expense? They are political questions because social groups are frequently included and excluded from decision-making about energy futures by design, or by default, on grounds of class, gender and race, for example, due to political marginalisation or barriers of (technical, scientific, economic or legal) expertise that are erected to delimit engagement. They raise issues of participation, representation and democracy. Whose interests are represented, whose voice is heard, who speaks for whom and whose knowledge counts? They are also political because they are ecological. They determine whether energy needs are met in ways congruent or incompatible with sustaining life on earth: polluting some environments and not others. Are energy pathways low carbon or resource intensive in terms of inputs, production processes and waste? Because of the fundamental and close relationship between energy and growth, a theme to which we will return throughout the book, efforts to reorder energy systems and which may even imply or require different approaches to the pursuit of growth and well-being are deeply contested by incumbent actors that have expanded and profited from growth-oriented economies served by (thus far) cheap fossil fuels and legitimated by a pervasive modernist ideology that growth is infinite.

Emphasising these deeper political questions is not to say that technology is unimportant, nor cost and price signals, nor culture and society. They clearly are. But these too are political, even if not acknowledged as such in mainstream policy debates. Who decides which technologies should be supported with finance, policy, research and development, what level energy prices or carbon taxes should be set at, or which cultural changes should be promoted and whose cultures should change are questions of politics. They reflect power and uneven social relations which seek to keep difficult and contested energy policy choices on a manageable terrain, controllable by incumbent actors. Power is exercised in determining which questions can be posed and the basis on which they will be debated (if at all). I argue that Gramsci's (1971) notion of 'trasformismo' usefully describes the political attempt to manage this terrain: to ensure that politics and policy reinforce a market liberal approach to transitions *within* capitalism as opposed to more sweeping transformations of it (Newell 2018). None of these things are immune from political contestation or devoid of power relations and the sorts of social conflict that run through all other areas of human life. It is these aspects that I focus on here.

This challenges dominant conceptions regarding technology and progress, for example, where investment in the former is assumed and asserted to be a prerequisite to the latter. This is a conviction which Hornborg (2013: 48) suggests 'has for at least two centuries been fundamental to dominant conceptions of history, development and modernization', overlooking the fact that 'technological progress has been the privilege of affluent elites and the very existence of the new technology has relied on the appropriation of resources from an increasingly impoverished periphery'. Think of the links between steam technology in nineteenth-century Britain and the Atlantic slave trade, or, more generally and contemporarily, the ways in which embodied labour and resources from poorer parts of the world are extracted through uneven exchange (Patel and Moore 2017). This underscores the need to ensure that both the social justice and sustainability of new waves of technological venture feature centrally in our analysis.

Not only are energy transitions political; they are also historical because, as Abramsky (2010:10) puts it:

Today's energy patterns are the cumulative product of hundreds of years of historical development. The energy system is the outcome of many different social relationships through which human beings organise themselves in order to live, sustain and reproduce themselves over time. The energy system is intimately intertwined with the expansion of the social, economic and political relations of which it is a part.

He is right to further propose that '[s]truggles for control of energy (broadly along the lines of interstate, interfirm, and inter (and intra) class struggles) have had a crucial impact on the historical development of capitalism as a global set of social relations' (Abramsky 2010: 10). A green history of the world (Ponting 2007) would suggest that energy is a key factor in the rise and fall of previous civilisations and empires and underpins the ascendancy of key contender states such as China and Russia (Hill 2004). Hornborg (2013: 42) notes, for example: 'Agrarian empires were also ultimately dependent on the productivity of solar energy processed by plants, animals and humans and they too generally acknowledged (and in fact often worshipped) the sun.' What we have come to call land and labour are in fact the ultimate energy resources, as well as the sources of all wealth, as Marx pointed out in *Capital* (Marx 1974).

Energy transitions are also ecological because they imply resource extraction, throughput, exchange and disposal. They necessarily and inevitably reorder natures, produce new geographies and landscapes and constitute, as well as reflect, socio-natures which shape their social and environmental sustainability. They produce new circuits of extraction, exchange and consumption which play an important part in determining the very possibility of life on earth. The ecologies of energy transition form a key element of the analysis in this book, therefore.

1.1 The Argument

The essential argument advanced in this book is that climate change (re)presents, amongst other things, a legitimacy crisis for contemporary global capitalism, though not just global capitalism. Energy transitions form one site of struggle in this broader terrain. In intended and direct as well as unintended and indirect ways, climate change draws attention to, highlights and amplifies a series of tensions and contradictions that inhere in the project of industrialism.

This is apparent, firstly, in the inability to maintain levels of required capitalist growth while safeguarding a climate system fit for human existence. The best analysis available suggests that the conventional pursuit of growth in OECD (Organisation for Economic Co-operation and Development) countries cannot be squared with halting warming at 2°C, 3°C or even 4°C (Simms 2010). Tellingly, it was only in the wake of the financial crisis that in May 2009, the International Energy Agency (IEA) reported for the first time since 1945 that global demand for electricity was expected to fall. The same has occurred in the wake of the coronavirus pandemic which has shut down factories and severed global supply chains

(IEA 2020a). Abramsky (2010: 7) suggests: 'Only unintended de-growth had had the effect that years of international regulation sought to achieve.' For sure, there are sites of decarbonisation and some de-linking of emissions from growth in specific sectors at particular moments in time (Newell and Lane 2018). But Jevon's paradox – the fact that resource savings in a growth-oriented economy tend to get reinvested in more consumption – outweighs the effects of these incremental gains (Brockway et al. 2017). 'All the energy-efficient technologies in the world, though crucial to any long-term solution, cannot, *on their own*, square the circle by reducing the total emissions of a system whose survival is based on continual expansion' (Abramsky 2010: 8). And yet the drumbeat of support for the mantra of 'green growth' continues from governments, economists and international institutions such as the OECD (2011) and the World Bank (2012).

Secondly, these contradictions are manifest in a system which, through wage labour, ties the welfare of workers to such an irrevocably unsustainable project. This ensures resistance to systemic change which, while it might offer the long-term prospect of increasing both social justice and environmental sustainability, in the short term pits, a powerful and wide-ranging incumbency complex against a viable future for humankind. We see this in debates about 'just transitions', explored further in what follows, and in the role of some trade unions and 'astro-turf' organisations in mobilising workers and communities against international climate agreements such as Paris or Kyoto, or national-level climate policies such as carbon taxes or emissions trading that have provided bitter battlegrounds in places such as France and Australia (Hudson 2018). The ironic effect of this cumulative resistance to more ambitious action is to commit us to a warming world in which the livelihoods of the poorest and the most marginal will be most exposed to harm.

Thirdly, the contradictions are further magnified by the need to reverse centuries of extraction and exploitation by capitalist elites in the global North (with ample collaboration from elites in the global South), so that expansion of economic activity in parts of the world afflicted by extreme poverty can be accommodated by corresponding cuts in production and consumption in the global North consistent with remaining global carbon budgets that would keep the world the right side of a 1.5°C or even 2°C threshold of warming. This is the starting point for ideas about 'contraction and convergence' (GCI 2018) or the Greenhouse Development Rights framework (GDR 2018) or 'doughnut economics' (Raworth 2017) that seek to square efforts to meet basic human development needs with respect for planetary boundaries. But in a world economy characterised by uneven development and patterns of systematic exploitation of periphery countries by the core, this presents a full-frontal threat to capitalism as we know it and as it has been practised for the last two centuries. It implies both more just allocations of responsibility for action going forward, as well as proper acknowledgement of accumulated carbon debts and the corresponding need for compensation for poorer countries. The global politics of uneven exchange and patterns of exploitation between core and periphery are deeply woven into the politics of energy transitions. Rather than addressing contemporary and historical inequities, the preference on the part of transnational elites has been to employ spatial and temporal fixes to displace solutions onto poorer regions of the world and into the future in order to outsource the painful politics of disruption and avoid threats to near-term capital accumulation.

The issue is clearly not just inter-state social conflict. Energy and its provision and distribution at times brings into sharp relief, at other times merely exacerbates, social conflicts and inequalities. Who and what is energy for? Many conflicts are over the maldistribution of energy and competition between industrial and social uses, urban and rural, rich and poor. The DESERTEC project that was touted as providing cheap and clean solar power for the whole of Europe was premised on erecting huge solar power farms across the Saharan desert in Northern Africa to meet the energy needs of wealthier European citizens (Newell et al. 2011). Opposition to wind farms often comes from the fact not that communities are opposed to the form of energy per se, but that they do not get to benefit from the electricity generated by the wind turbines. Patterns of energy access are often deeply racialised (Newell 2020a), as McDonald's (2009) work in South Africa shows, as well as often heavily gendered, especially in rural settings (Winther et al. 2017). Energy transitions are shaped by, and have to navigate, these deeply entrenched inequalities. If they are to succeed in being just as well as sustainable, energy transitions will need to help address these social cleavages.

To see off the evident and pressing need for transformation, in which energy is at the heart because of its relationship to growth, states and corporations have engaged in a project of what Gramsci (1971) called *trasformismo*, to accommodate the threat posed by climate change to the legitimacy of the economic system and the political systems and governance structures set up to steer it and manage its contradictions (Newell 2018). This is apparent in attempts to deflect, delegitimise and downplay calls for reduced consumption and production and more sustainable and inclusive models of economic development, and for redistribution, by focusing on the need for more: for more technology and finance, more markets and better pricing systems, enforceable property rights and enabling conditions for a new round of accumulation. It is apparent in claims by fossil fuel incumbents that their industries are vital to meeting the needs of the poor (WCA 2021), overlooking the fact that the majority of large energy consumers are other businesses and richer consumers, since many of the poorest people in society are either not connected to the grid in large parts of the global South or living in fuel poverty in the North, or in claims that climate change measures will hit the poor hardest, overlooking the fact that poorer groups are the most vulnerable to the effects of climate change.

1.2 The Approach

The premise of this book is that much of the policy debate so far, as well as existing academic scholarship reviewed earlier, has failed to provide a fuller *political* analysis of historical precedents of when organised large-scale sociotechnical and economic change has occurred in the past and what lessons might be deduced for the current challenge of drastically and rapidly decarbonising the global economy. It is precisely such a political and historical analysis of transition that is proposed here. This requires the novel fusion of insights from technology and innovation studies, history, economics and international political economy (IPE) and ecology about how rapid shifts in systems of production and consumption can occur and be accelerated by political action. This is vital to appreciating the political enabling conditions for the much-feted new industrial or energy revolution now required to tackle climate change and enhance energy security. Rather than focus just on technology or finance in isolation, however, this project addresses the neglected political, historical and ecological dimensions of energy transitions. It seeks to revisit examples of previous transitions primarily told through the lens of socio-technical configurations, without sufficient attention to power and politics, and in so doing provide a more politically inflected account.

Simultaneously historicising, politicising, globalising and ecologising the study of energy transitions is no easy task. But it is nevertheless an important one. Bringing the four dimensions together firstly seeks to address the fact that historical work on transitions, of which there is a great deal in terms of specific case studies of sociotechnical transitions, is often insufficiently attentive to politics and political economy and often overlooks the ecological dimensions of transitions, especially beyond the narrow parameters of the case in question. Secondly, work on the politics and political economy of transitions, given its more contemporary nature, often underplays historical dimensions and is similarly negligent when it comes to the ecological aspects of transitions. Thirdly, work on the environmental impacts and implications of energy transitions, because of its basis in engineering, modelling and technology and innovation studies for the most part, is neither very historical in orientation, since it is often largely future oriented, nor explicitly political in terms of the competing actors, interests and uneven social outcomes implied by different scenarios and pathways.

The approach taken is highly interdisciplinary, drawing on insights from innovation studies on sociotechnical transitions (Geels 2005; Loorbach 2007), historical economics (Perez 2002, 2013; Pearson and Foxon 2012) and theoretical and conceptual insights from IPE (Cox 1987; Rupert 1995), political economy more broadly (Koch 2012; Malm 2016), as well as political ecology (Robbins 2004; Lawhon and Murphy 2012) to guide the empirical enquiry by highlighting key historical moments, actors and initiatives that warrant further investigation. The selection of examples referred to in the book is guided by the desire to illustrate their potential relevance to key aspects of contemporary debates about energy transitions in terms of who will produce what, where the finance will come from, how they will be governed and what the politics of mobilisation will look like. This locates contemporary developments as part of longer historical processes which need to be revisited in order to understand precedents for disruption, change and the realignment of economies, technologies and politics, as well as the (re)production of incumbent power. It highlights contradictions at the heart of capitalism, which compromises its ability to engage effectively in the sorts of energy transitions now required and the forms of politics to which it gives rise: both as the politics of *trasformismo* in order to manage those contradictions, and the politics of dissent and counter-movements which seek to contest the framings, practices and politics of orthodox transitions as part of a more ambitious project of transformation.

In this way, the book seeks to locate energy transitions as part of a necessary broader project of political, ecological and economic transformation comparable in many ways to the double-movements that Polanyi (1957 [1944]) described that sought to re-embed the market economy in frameworks of social and democratic control, though hopefully, in this case, with a more positive and lasting outcome. This is not about containing threats to the legitimacy of capitalism through incremental improvements and concessions to social and environmental movements or improving its governance. It is more about a redefinition and redirection of the purpose and orientation of the economy towards the needs (including for energy) of the majority of humans and non-humans on the planet. The German Advisory Council on Global Change has argued that the transformation towards a low carbon, sustainable global economic system should be radical, on a par indeed with the two great transformations that mankind has encountered so far: the prehistoric Neolithic settlement and the transformation of agrarian into industrial societies (WBGU 2013). The report also points to an important distinction in that the first two great transformations were natural, evolutionary processes, while the shift towards a new sustainability paradigm needs to be predominantly a planned, policy-induced process, though I would argue here that social mobilisation will also be critical. Who sets the terms of such a shift is a pressing question.

Though the discussion is divided into chapters on each of the key dimensions of transition - producing, financing, governing and mobilising – in practice, of course, they are intimately connected, as Figure 1.1 makes clear.

The research upon which the book builds draws on research projects, consultancy work and policy and activist engagements undertaken principally over the last ten years. This involved research projects on the governance of clean development in India, Argentina and South Africa (with a particular focus on the energy sector), work on the role of rising powers (China, India and Brazil) in energy transitions in South Africa and Mozambique, a project on the political economy of 'climate compatible development' in Kenya and consultancy work on, respectively, climate justice, pursuing clean energy equitably, the politics of rapid transitions, scaling behaviour change and supply-side climate policies.

These projects were conducted using a mix of methodologies including historical analysis to uncover the political conflicts and negotiations that attended previous major social-technical changes in energy systems, off-the-record conversations, informal networking and semi-structured interviews conducted over a number of years with key contemporary actors involved in both financing and delivering low carbon solutions, and those involved in the political work of assembling alliances, networks and associations that are seeking to build a low carbon economy. This includes informants in government, international organisations, business and civil society. It has also involved a large degree of participant observation in spaces, arenas and debates concerned with the political economies of energy transition. Over the course of the writing of the book, these range from direct participation in protests, media work and the organisation of local citizens' assemblies to respond to the climate emergency, through to involvement in national-level policy debates and strategy discussions with major campaigning organisations and funders of innovation and technology, consultancy work for donors, as well as the organisation of events and dialogues with business actors and governments involved in the UN climate negotiations.

The research undertaken for this book benefitted from my role as co-founder of the Rapid Transition Alliance, an initiative to source and share what I call 'evidence-based hope' among researchers and practitioners about the possibility of rapid transitions, from contemporary and historical examples across regions and sectors of the world.[1] This has involved meetings and discussions, media work and research and advocacy on the theme of transitions with a range of state (local and national), corporate and civil society actors. The contacts I have made, the observations I have been able to make, and the processes and spaces I have had the opportunity to access as a result of involvement in this initiative have yielded insights that inform much of what is contained in the book. Hence, though not

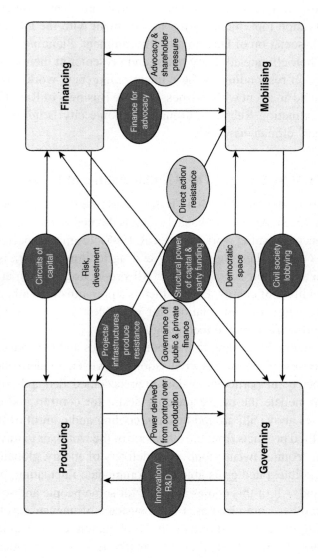

Figure 1.1 A map of some of the connections between the different elements of transition covered in the book

always explicitly highlighted in the chapters that follow, their presence is felt and informs many of the insights and conclusions that follow. These insights have been further enhanced by my experience of serving as a board member for Greenpeace UK and Carbon Market Watch in Brussels, two organisations engaged in different ways with a variety of aspects of the political economy of transition and ongoing debates about how best to accelerate energy transitions. Three other forms that participant observation took included my involvement with the UK local council group ADEPT (Association of Directors of Environment, Planning and Transport) as a member of their climate advisory board and presenter at their workshop with business partners on responding to the climate emergency, work with the group Carbon Trust around an event with business on 'The Business of Rapid Transition'[2] and work with Extinction Rebellion around my home city Brighton and Hove's plans for a citizens' climate assembly.

1.3 Why Energy? The Peculiar Politics of Energy

Energy is central to modern life. It is rightly described as the lifeblood of the economy (Huber 2013). At its most basic level it is defined as the ability to do work or the means of accomplishing work (Rosa et al. 1988). From transport and mobility to cooking and cooling, heating, industry and agriculture, energy is intimately linked to all economic and social activity. All production, movement and work implies the expenditure of energy. Energy then is a prerequisite to all other types of development and innovation in relation, for example, to agriculture, the use of water, industry, infrastructure and technology.

   The need to generate heat, light, to transport ourselves and to produce goods and services characterises all of human civilisation. However, modern industrial and contemporary society in particular makes unprecedented demands of its energy systems to accommodate the ever-expanding desire for comfort and convenience of its richer classes above all; around heating, cooling and control of homes, to be able to consume food products from the other side of the world, or to travel long-haul for holidays. This requires twenty-four/seven delivery of energy, globally connected infrastructures and integrated grids able to accommodate fluctuating, but generally increasing, demand. All of this comes at a cost for some people and some environments more than others, premised as it is on systems of uneven development and exchange. Meeting these demands eats into the remaining ecological space that, if equity had anything to do with it, should be reserved for poorer under-consuming classes. And it comes at a time when, in the face of climate change, we need to radically reduce levels of energy consumption and meet energy needs in different ways and do so within (unprecedentedly) short periods of time (IPCC 2018). This is not to imply that these shifts are driven by ever more consumerist and materialist societies, though that is part of the story (Kasser 2016). The restlessness of capital and the need for ever-increasing returns require these increases in demand to feed profits, searching out new markets and outlets for investment in energy-hungry technologies and infrastructures. This is why, in many energy projections, the role of conservation, efficiency and demand-side measures is often so neglected. The assumption is that demand will continue to increase, and we need to find new resource frontiers, develop new technologies and build new infrastructures to meet that demand.

The fact that its provision is currently organised in such environmentally unsustainable and socially detrimental and uneven ways presents huge challenges for transforming energy systems, therefore. There is a particularly close relationship not only among energy, electricity and capitalism (Di Muzio 2015; Di Muzio and Ovadia 2016), but also between energy and industrialism. For much of modern history, energy systems have been organised around fire (Patterson 2015): burning oil for transport, gas to heat homes, oil to power industry, biomass to warm schools and hospitals. Increasingly, there is a move towards electrification – of trains and cars, of homes – as well as shifts towards more localised forms of (micro) energy generation less dependent on centralised infrastructures, pipelines and utilities to service energy needs which some describe as the 'democratisation of energy' (Tomain 2017).

The advent of the 2015 SDGs establishes a stand-alone SDG for energy focused on energy access, as was noted already. But there is also one for climate change and, as many people have pointed out, our ability to successfully address many of the SDGs will be undermined unless we get a grip on climate change (Ansuategi et al. 2015). The fact that the SDGs are both universal and indivisible creates both challenges and opportunities for accelerating more transformative energy transitions. On the one hand, there is scope to address energy more ecologically, holistically and synergistically, looking at its role in what is often referred to as the nexus of water-energy-food and opening up the possibility for more circular and life-cycle thinking. On the other hand, despite the trade-offs and contradictions that will emerge from attempting to deliver simultaneously on all the SDGs, the tendency to date, and the likelihood going forward, is that these tensions will be obscured amid pressure to act and report on the SDGs in rather tick-box terms where, despite some concessions and modifications, overriding political priorities of industrial growth will not be compromised.

1.4 Continuity and Change in the Study of Energy

Though many accounts achieve this feat, the history of the world to date cannot be meaningfully or accurately told without reference to the energy which has powered, enabled and frustrated the accumulation of power and the pursuit of social and economic ambitions over centuries (Yergin 1991; Smil 1994; Lohmann and Hildyard 2014). Early sociological work on energy took as given that energy is largely responsible for material differences between societies, and sought to develop grand theories to explain how and why some societies achieve greater material output than others (Spencer 1980), such that 'the ability to harness more and more energy to production lay at the foundation of the evolution of societies' (Rosa et al. 1988: 150). Early anthropological writing also suggested that levels of cultural development vary according to the amount of energy per capita harnessed and put to work, such that the evolution of culture was dependent upon degrees of energy intensification (White 1943). White (cited in Strauss et al. 2013: 17) wrote of a fuel revolution thus:

By the beginning of the eighteenth century . . . cultural development had gone just about as far as it could on the basis of animate energy and wind and water; it could not advance appreciably farther without tapping new sources of energy. Herein lies the significance of the revolutionary achievement of harnessing the energy of fossil fuels. Vast amounts of energy were locked up in the earth's crust in the form of coal, oil and gas. The development of steam and internal combustion engines was the means of harnessing and utilizing these energies into ever increasing amounts. And the new technology was extended into all phases of life: into industry, transportation by land and by water, aviation and into the arts of war as well as those of peace.

Hence, in these (bio-)'energetics' approaches, the social advances and differences in levels of development could be accounted for by energy: the more consumed, the more advanced the society, where success was determined by the ability of societies to extract 'cumulative surpluses' from converting energy into productive purposes (Carver 1924) and the technological efficiency of its conversion. Buchan (1972: 163) wrote: '[D]evelopments in the use of energy . . . have shaped the course of modern history more than other forms of technological change', a point underscored by Clark (1990: 1) arguing in his political economy account of world energy in the twentieth century that it was 'no coincidence that several nations reached industrial maturity at the close of the nineteenth century simultaneously with the emergence of increasingly sophisticated energy systems'. In a similar vein, it has been suggested that 'the Darwinian struggle for existence is really a competition for available energy' (Rees 2020: 3). Ecologists such as Lotka (1922) formulated the 'maximum power principle' which suggests that successful systems are those that evolve in ways that maximise their use of available energy per unit time in the performance of useful work (growth, self-maintenance and reproduction). 'In the Anthropocene', Rees (2020: 3) suggests, 'no other species comes close to challenging humanity's energy hegemony'.

Such (bio-)energetic accounts are clearly problematic on numerous grounds, including the fact that very poor societies are in aggregate higher, but hugely unequal, energy consumers and the fact that energy interdependencies mean that levels of development and under-development are relational. Subsequent critiques of what I would call 'modernist' approaches to development (following Rostow's (1960) stages of economic development) and ideas about the 'energy ladder' (van der Kroon et al. 2013) drew attention to the limits of energy consumption. In particular, they referenced the second law of thermodynamics that energy, unlike materials, cannot be recycled such that there are inevitable limits to available useable energy (Altvater 2006; Soddy 1912). This line of critique was further developed by broader critiques of growth of which energy was just one element (Georgescu-Roegen 1971). This claim was, and in most quarters of the policy and corporate establishment still is, seen as heresy. It challenged the unquestioned, but deeply questionable, line of logic that because 'energy was essential to economic growth and since economic growth represented improvements in societal well-being, it was but a short step to infer that energy growth was essential to societal well-being' (Rosa et al. 1988: 158). This has stood up despite evidence that increased energy consumption above a certain level does not increase welfare and the same goes for growth. In echoes of the 'spirit level' argument (Wilkinson and Pickett 2009), and sharing the view of Buttel (1979) and others, Rosa et al. (1988: 159) show that

while a threshold level of high energy consumption is probably necessary for a society to achieve industrialisation and modernity, once achieved, there is wide latitude in the amount of energy needed to sustain a high standard of living. Moreover, given that latitude industrial societies could choose slowed-growth energy policies without great fear of negative, long-term consequences to overall welfare.

This speaks to the much neglected need to address both supply-side policy (Erickson et al. 2018) which sets production limits, and demand-side policy, which has an explicit aim of reducing energy consumption (Green and Dennis 2018). It turns on its head the historical and ongoing assumption that increases in per capita energy use are a reliable and tenable indicator of progress, rather than providing a barometer of resource depletion on a finite planet.

Suggestive of the inevitability of transformation, either planned and nurtured or imposed and reactive, energy limits in this rendition imply crises for modern societies. As Rosa et al. (1988: 153) put it, 'since sustained periods of economic growth shaped the character of modern industrial societies, physical limitations on future growth portend fundamental changes in that character'. In part, this implies a shift in the concentration and organisation of power, the central theme of this book, since 'social power evolves and becomes more concentrated as the harnessing of energy increases' (Rosa et al. 1988: 153). We will see in Chapter 6 in relation to discussions about community energy and democratising energy that part of the rationale is the desire to take back control of energy systems and to share the determination of collective energy futures. For the very same reason, unsurprisingly, incumbent actors alert to this potential threat resist such moves.

Though I have described them here in terms of historical debates about energy and society, their contemporary relevance could not be clearer. Because of the second law of thermodynamics, the organised and massive scale waste of energy cannot carry on indefinitely, even if it is powerfully driven by capitalist growth imperatives. In that sense, as other work on rebound effects and the limits of just scaling up renewable energy technologies within conventional productivist frameworks has shown (Zehner 2012), massive technological fixes, which form the dominant response to previous energy crises, will not solve and will almost certainly exacerbate the challenges we currently face. As Lovins (1977) argued, 'soft energy paths' imply a complete restructuring not just of energy supply systems, but of society itself. Entrenched assumptions that have sedimented into ideologies of development progress, espoused and backed with institutional and material power by states and global institutions, about the key to development being the presumed abundance of inexpensive, easily accessible and available energy resources, increasingly run up against the reality of 'un-burnable' fossil fuels and natural and social limits to extraction. The crisis we currently face results from a long history of failure to acknowledge the prospect of resource depletion, years of active climate denial and a reluctance to consider energy efficiency, conservation and reductions in energy demand.

Occasionally, such complacency is shaken by shocks to the system such as the 1974 oil embargo crisis or the Iranian revolution. Regarding the former, as Rosa et al. (1988: 160) suggest: 'With a stroke of the OPEC pen in 1973 the complacency of assuming forever expensive, plentiful secure energy supplies was all but shattered.' They continue: 'The embargo also sparked a fundamental shift in the definition of energy supply, from a solely technological problem to a bundle of social ones' (Rosa et al. 1988: 164). It is hard to over-state the rupture it caused. Odell (1981: 240) suggests that the prospect of reduced and uncertain supply of oil 'served to undermine the planning and policies of all western governments and so make it impossible for them to sustain the rising expectations of their populations for continued development'. As well as giving rise to the creation of the IEA as a means to co-ordinate the strategies of rich oil-importing countries, it also heightened interest in energy conservation and renewable energy, while also opening the way for a renaissance of nuclear energy and renewed efforts to develop domestic energy sources. In France, for example, just three months after the embargo, the

French government decided to raise the share of electricity produced by nuclear plants from 8 per cent to 70 per cent by 1985 and the Japanese government announced a fifteen-fold increase in their nuclear-generating capacity (Hammarlund 1976: 183). Energy crises can also often usher in shifts in social values and attitudes towards energy, around conservation in the wake of the OPEC crisis, or the delegitimisation in some quarters of fossil fuels in light of the climate crisis, or strong social reactions to nuclear crises in the wake of the Chernobyl and Fukushima disasters.

Indeed, shifts in the study of energy and energy systems are often driven by crises. Interest in the study of energy peaked in the wake of the above-described OPEC crisis, and from the early 2000s interest returned in the form of concern about dependence on oil from the Middle East, the theatre of wars in 1991 and then again in 2003. The current wave of interest in energy transitions is likewise prompted in large part by the climate crisis and the clear need for rapid transitions away from fossil fuels and deeper transformations in systems of energy provision underscored by the Paris Agreement and recent IPCC reports (IPCC 2018). The question is whether the climate crisis, which perhaps poses less of a threat to immediate access to supply or ownership regimes than the OPEC crisis, or is yet to manifest itself in steep price rises, can trigger another such shift in global energy policy. Rosa et al. (1988) draw an interesting and potentially important distinction between a 'crisis' and a 'predicament', where crisis refers to a rapidly deteriorating situation that can lead to near-term disaster, whereas predicament refers to a chronic problem that requires continuous attention. Crises come and go, often related to issue attention cycles, while predicaments persist unless resolved and since the current situation is characterised by powerful incumbency and 'slow violence' (Nixon 2011) for poorer populations, the prospects of its resolution can appear remote indeed.

1.5 Energy as a Change in State

Energy is intimately entwined not only with modern history and the world economy, but also with the form and practice of statecraft and international relations. Whether it is energy diplomacy and statecraft or electricity provision and the extension of the grid as a shorthand for modernity and delivering development (Gore 2017), energy often serves as both the end and the means of statecraft. Strauss et al. (2013: 12) note: 'Ensuring access to continued supplies of energy and other resources is one of the central functions of centralized political systems. Shortages of energy – blackouts and queues for gasoline – quickly become political problems and often have political antecedents.'

Energy is also implicated in violent politics (Watts 2008), imperialism (Bromley 1991) and changing balances of power, for example, brought about by the shift in power in the world oil regime that occurred as producing and exporting nations took control over the supply and price of oil through collective action. It is often claimed that it is in the Middle East that the importance of the relationship between oil and world politics is clearest (Odell 1981). Yet claims of oil companies serving as agents of US imperialism were levelled by many Latin American countries in the 1970s in the era of dependence thinking leading to expropriations and the estab-lishment of state-owned companies such as Petróbras in Brazil or in other cases the downfall of leaders such as Perón in Argentina. As Odell (1981: 223) notes:

The international companies, moreover, effectively organised their activities around the world behind the guarantee of security offered by the political and/or military presences of the United States and the United Kingdom, which between them provided the home base for six and a half of the seven international oil companies (with the remaining half – the Royal Dutch part of Shell – domiciled in the Netherlands).

The protection afforded by states also means that, in exchange, demands can be made of companies in the pursuit of foreign policy goals such that oil companies were asked not to charge for the oil they sold to what was Western Europe as part of the Marshall Plan. Resources can also help build identities and forge regional alliances. As Odell (1981: 204) argues, echoing the point above about how energy co-operation, at times, also provides the means of avoiding war:

[A]s a result of the economic and political advantages that oil revenues could buy, there would be an Arab Middle East with an enhanced cohesion and a more significant geo-political potential among the power blocs of the world. This was achieved in 1973, when it became somewhat ironic to find the commodity which originally helped to divide the region into the spheres of influence of competing outside powers ... emerging to provide the means whereby greater regional cohesion and strength between the Arab nations became a reality.

Though, as Hornborg (2013: 42) suggests, 'the particular way in which access to energy is significant for the economy seems to escape economics as a discipline', as ecological economists have focused our attention on flows of energy production and consumption in the global economy (Georgescu-Roegen 1971): the patterns of ecologically uneven exchange in both contemporary settings and historically accu-mulated carbon and other debts (Simms 2005). This seeks to challenge the modern world view, propelled by large-scale fossil fuel use of 'unlimited good', of a world beyond constraints (Hornborg 2013: 46). Others, such as Bellamy Foster (1999), have employed ideas of a 'metabolic rift' occurring as a result of the way that energy is produced and consumed under capitalism (drawing on Marx's under-standing of the rupture in the metabolic interaction between humanity and the rest of nature emanating from capitalist production (Marx 1981)).

Energy systems are always in flux and being reconfigured to (re)align with shifting sites of production, patterns of consumer demand, the availability of finance, opportunities for the construction of infrastructures, changing political priorities and ecological shocks. They are constituted by assemblages of moving parts which create opportunities for disruption, change and alternatives. In many ways, transitions in energy systems are just one element or site of contestation in the broader relationship between energy and society. Sociological literature on energy and society (Rosa et al. 1988) and the cultures of energy studied by anthropologists (Strauss et al. 2013; Boyer 2014), are useful in comprehending this. The starting point is that 'energy, though fundamentally a physical variable, penetrates significantly into almost all facets of the social world. Life-styles, broad patterns of communication and interaction, collective activities and key features of social structure and change are conditioned by the availability of energy, the technical means for converting energy into useable forms, and the ways energy is ultimately used' (Rosa et al. 1988: 14). For anthropologists, meanwhile, '[a]n anthropology of energy must shuttle back and forth among laws of physics, opportunities and constraints of ecological systems, and processes of culture' (Strauss et al. 2013: 12).

As we will see, though literature on transitions purports to account for sociotechnical transitions, work in that tradition sometimes offers a narrow and impoverished notion of what counts as the social and the political. While increasingly attending to a particular view of governance, it often has less to say about collective mobilisation, social hierarchies and inequalities and networks of power and questions of identity. Yet there are earlier bodies of research that can be usefully drawn upon to fill some of these gaps. Lewis Mumford's (1967 [1934]) work introduced the importance of social values to the study of energy, characterising key eras in terms of the relationship between dominant energy sources and technologies and predominant social values. For example, the ecotechnic epoch was dominated by water and wood, the paleotechnic with a coal-based energy system and the neotechnic resting on electricity-based energy systems. Cottrell (1955) also explored the multiple dimensions of social, political and even psychological change which accompanied the transition from low to high energy societies implying a 'total transition of society' (Rosa et al. 1988: 153). In recent years, this has given rise to a substantial body of work looking at consumer attitudes and the role of behaviour change led by psychologists (Whitmarsh 2009). It is clear that energy consumption and conservation practices are too complex to be explained by models of economic rationality which assume price signals will be received by utility-maximising and rational individual consumers, or linear attitude-behaviour-change models (Shove 2010). Yet Strauss et al. (2013: 22–3) claim:

There is a startling paucity of analysis of the everyday life of energy: how people view it, appropriate it, use it, conserve it- and why. If our current predicament of energy over-consumption has any chance of being nudged back in the direction of individual restraint and collective, society-wide conservation, changes will have to be made at the community, household and individual levels.

The invisibility of energy has also proven to be a challenge for efforts to change behaviours and energy consumption patterns where usually energy consumption is rendered visible only through meters, bills or receipts at petrol stations, for example, and as citizens we are often poor self-monitors of consumption. The use of smart meters on individual appliances is one attempt to address this characteristic of energy and work on behavioural change shows that improved monitoring and financial incentives to do so can bring down energy consumption. Again, social cleavages are key, with more affluent households investing in energy efficiencies and poorer ones reducing energy use through lifestyle adjustments. But practice theory also points to the way in which technologies, goods and appliances can themselves reshape practices. Wilhite (2013: 64) notes: '[O]nce in place and running in a home, household technologies such as refrigerators, cooking appliances, washing machines and air conditioners bear with them the potential to reshape practices.' This includes the ways in which devices notionally aimed at improving efficiency allow people to increase energy consumption in other domains as part of a rebound effect (Sorrell et al. 2020).

Clearly then, an adequate account of energy transitions has to be able to hone in and out of particular sites of change, moving across scales of governance, regions and sectors and drawing from insights from a range of disciplines. As we will see throughout the book, energy both produces particular types of political economy and is shaped in turn by diverse political and economic systems. This is so because of the materialities and material properties of energy: its lootability (Le Billon 2007); fluidity and transportability (in some cases) and its geographical concentrations (in others). Its value as a resource has a tendency at times to produce a 'resource curse' (Ross 2012), to enable a particular politics of rent-seeking – the desire to exercise control over energy decision-making to extract gains in negotiating contracts (Newell and Phillips 2016) – and sensitivity over its control in trade agreements (Newell 2007).

Energy sources at once embody geophysical properties and social characteristics. But while recognising the agency of nature, it is important not to fall into resource determinism where the availability or material properties of an energy source are assumed to dictate the nature of political orders in a causal or linear way. Around oil, for example, there is often a strong undercurrent of 'orientalist environmental determinism at play in accounts of conflict and international relations in the Middle East' (Hoffmann 2018: 40). Hoffmann's (2018) notion of 'social energy' is helpful here. It treats energy not as biophysical matter, but as an historically and geographically specific set of social relations. Energy is understood, then, 'as a political category, a field of social change and contestation, rather than a limiting biophysical structure' (Hoffmann 2018: 40). This more dialectical understanding helps to de-naturalise dominant energy regimes and assemblages. In this rendition, social energy relations need to be contextualised within 'historically specific forms of power' which include 'technologies of energy extraction, production, consumption, transmission and storage, generated by specific social formations' (Hoffmann 2018: 42).

In this regard, Gavin Bridge's work also usefully unpacks the related processes of resource-making and state-making through analysis of political practices (Bridge 2014). Political imaginaries and work are required to construct energy resources as potential commodities that can be brought into 'commercial life' in terms that are intelligible to market society. Watts (2008) draws a distinction, for example, between oil as an artefact and oil as an artifice. According to Strauss et al. (2013: 19), 'oil exists as a material substance (an artefact) even as its existence serves to create social, political and economic structures (artifices) that organize societies for whom petroleum and its derivatives are foundational'. Transboundary forms of oil governance can be hindered by the fact that 'oil is pretty sneaky stuff, oozing in, around and across borders and making its transparent and forthright management elusive' (Strauss et al. 2013: 30). Hydropower produces its own peculiar politics because of its necessary displacements of human populations and natures, diversions of flows and redrawing of geographical, social and political boundaries (Swyngedouw 2015).

Energy sources also require particular types of infrastructure (Bridge et al. 2018b). Whereas oil can be easily transported, gas needs to be liquefied or transported through pipelines. Therefore, the technological and political challenges are greater for gas than they are for oil (Leal-Arcas 2018). As Ediger and Bowlus (2018: 22) show in writing about the battle for naval supremacy between Britain and Germany, '[o]il affected the outcome of the war itself and changed the nature of warfare. On land, the internal combustion engine powered the tanks, airplanes and transport vehicles of the Allies to victory, whereas the Germans relied on coal-powered railroads, and were unable to marshal resources and troops as efficiently across multiple fronts.' Infused with power relations, infrastructures shape our worlds in all sorts of ways. From transport networks that get us to and from places, pipes that carry our sewage, flood mitigation structures, or 'green infrastructures' in cities, to less tangible structures that shape economies, governance and representation, infrastructures mediate social-environmental interactions and establish knowledge structures. They also create vulnerabilities. Witness the impact on the movement of oil, prices, access and competition and ultimately international relations when the Suez Canal was closed in the Suez war of 1956 and the Six Day War of 1967 (Odell 1981). Or, in a more contemporary context, the challenge of reducing the carbon in food miles when so much food is imported and delivered from farm gate to dinner plate through globalised supply chains, chains which get disrupted by financial as well as increasingly by climatic (and health) shocks. A key question is how we can understand and research infrastructures in ways that question perceptions of them as neutral or passive underlying material structures. This links well to how society-specific resource endowments and constraints partially condition particular pathways to development for nations or particular social classes within them.

Just as the characteristics or materialities of 'technology' contribute to the (re) production of different forms of governmental practice or governmentalities (Johnstone and Newell 2018), so too do particular types of energy require and assume a particular type of state. For example, nuclear energy requires a more militarised state. Quoting Denis Hayes, Hammarlund (1976: 187) suggests: 'The nuclear option requires ... widespread surveillance and police infiltration of all dissident organisations will become social imperatives, as will the deployment if a paramilitary nuclear police force to safeguard every facet of the massive and labyrinthine fissile fuel cycle.' Indeed, concerns around the 'plutonium economy' (Patterson 1984) and the 'nuclear state' (Jungk 1979) highlighted how the security implications of plutonium meant that there was a necessary level of secrecy and non-transparency, due to the nature of the materials being handled, which reduced democratic control.

Energy, then, is high politics. Energy is development. Energy is everywhere. But the ways we organise, produce and consume it are in constant flux and are now undergoing a profound reordering. So, how do we think about energy transitions?

2

Theorising Energy Transitions

Transitions can be thought of as radical shifts in the provision of services such as energy, transport, food and sanitation. They often refer to a change in the state of a system, rather than merely a change in technology or fuel source, for example (Grubler et al. 2016). Indeed, originally the term transition was used by scientists to describe 'phase transitions' of substances going from solid to liquid to gas, that is, a fundamental change in state (Verbong and Loorbach 2012: 6). Applied to the questions of societal responses to sustainability challenges, transitions combine social, economic and technical elements of finance and innovation, technologies, infrastructures, regulation, cultural change and social pressure and seek to disrupt and displace the previous way of doing things. Diverse literatures place different emphasis on which are the primary drivers of transitions and how best to understand them.

Significant emphasis has been placed on modelling work through quantitative energy-environment-economy models, in particular integrated assessment models (IAMs). IAMs are designed to help us understand how human development and societal choices affect each other and the natural world. They are 'integrated' because they combine different strands of knowledge to model human society alongside different parts of the Earth's system (Parson and Fisher-Vanden 1997). IAMs seek to combine knowledge from multiple disciplines in formal integrated representations to inform policymaking, prioritise key uncertainties and advance knowledge of broad system linkages and feedbacks, particularly between socio-economic and biophysical processes. They combine simplified representations of the socio-economic determinants of energy pathways, the atmosphere and impacts on human activities and ecosystems, and potential policies and responses (Parson 1995).

They tend to vary, however, in their conclusions on the scale and direction of the likely macroeconomic impacts of a low carbon transition. The characteristic discrepancies in models' outcomes have been traced to their origins in different macroeconomic theories, most importantly their treatment of technological innovation and finance, by relevant branches of macro-innovation theory: 'equilibrium' and 'non-equilibrium'. While both approaches are rigorous and self-consistent, they frequently yield opposite conclusions about the economic impacts of low carbon policies such as carbon taxes, for example. Model outcomes are mainly determined by their representations of monetary and finance dimensions, and their interactions with investment, innovation and technological change (Mercure et al. 2019). Despite critiques of their limitations as predictive tools or problematic framing assumptions, they continue to underpin policymaking in key areas of energy and climate politics, where the Intergovernmental Panel on Climate Change (IPCC), for example, relies heavily on them in constructing different scenarios for achieving climate goals.

2.1 Sociotechnical Transitions

There is also now a substantive and wide-ranging literature on what are often called *sociotechnical transitions* which often build on, but go beyond, these models. This is a broad umbrella label for a series of literature derived from innovation studies that includes work on strategic niche management and transition management as well as the Multi-Level Perspective (MLP) (see Figure 2.1). Markard et al. (2012) identify four frameworks for transition studies: transition management, strategic niche management, technological innovation systems and the MLP. Early emphasis was on technological innovation systems, while the Dutch school emerged from science and technology studies (STS) and evolutionary economics and sought to combine an understanding of specific technologies with a macro-view of historical change. These seek, in different ways, to identify and explain the necessary social and technical components of a sociotechnical transition (Geels 2005; Geels and Schot 2007; Loorbach 2007). The focus of explanation has widened over time to include STS, economics and, more recently, politics and international relations (IR) (Meadowcroft 2009; Kern 2011; Newell 2018; Kern and Markard 2016; Sovacool 2014; Arent et al. 2017).

At the centre of many current applications of sociotechnical transitions is the popular MLP. Conceptualised as 'major *technological* transformations in the way societal functions such as transportation, communication, housing, feeding, are fulfilled' (Geels 2002: 1257, emphasis added), a great deal of insight into the nature of sociotechnical transitions has been generated through this 'multi-level perspective' on transitions. The MLP explores the interaction of elements of a sociotechnical system across several levels, from a *niche* technology and its supporters seeking to break into a market controlled by incumbent interests,

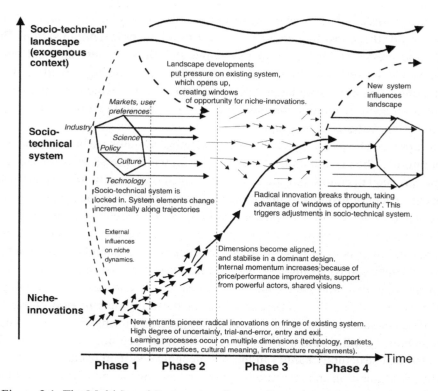

Figure 2.1 The Multi-Level Perspective. Source: Reproduced from Geels (2019).

thought to be part of a *regime* (often assumed to be operating at the national level), up to a series of *landscape* pressures that are often assumed to emanate from the global level (see Figure 2.1).

'Niches' provide a space within which social and technological learning processes and network building can be nurtured to develop alternative forms of sociotechnical configuration. Niche spaces often depend on support from the landscape or the regime to cultivate the economies of scale and scope to become competitive. 'Regimes', in contrast, are made up of the complex of practices, regulatory requirements, institutions and infrastructures required to achieve particular societal functions such as housing, mobility or power. This provides a useful point of departure for thinking about the role of incumbent actors involved in fossil-fuel energy systems whose structural dominance in energy investment and policy shapes the spaces available for developing alternatives. The 'landscape' of a sociotechnical system, meanwhile, is seen as comprising the

structuring forces of ideologies, institutions, discourses and political and economic trends that constitute enduring forms of sociotechnical organisation. These
landscape pressures include climate change and shifts in international energy
markets which exert disruptive pressure upon the regime as the prevailing way of
organising an energy system and its services, the effect of which can be to enable
a transition away from this dominant mode of organisation while creating space
for niche innovations to be supported.

The approach helps to explain how sociotechnical systems are both sustained and
reconfigured. The need to understand the ways in which pressures from above and
below can 'lead to cracks, tensions and windows of opportunity' (Geels 2010: 495)
opens up space for insights from political economy about *who* the agents are in this
process and *how* the forms of power that they exercise are able to bring about or
resist transitions in energy systems. Successful systems are regarded as tending
towards stability, held in place through regimes with 'relatively stable configurations of institutions, techniques and artefacts, as well as rules, practices and
networks that determine the "normal" development and use of technologies'
(Smith et al. 2005: 1493). The operations of these regimes in turn create both
'path dependency' and 'lock-in' (Unruh 2000) to certain forms of dominant energy
sociotechnical configuration, while others remain 'locked out' and marginal. It is
expected that structural changes in the sociotechnical system occur where there is
positive configuration and there are 'alignments' among the three levels resulting in
'transitions'. This means that the ways in which regimes, niches and landscapes
interact will have an effect on the form of transition that unfolds; a plurality of
possible transition pathways can result. Typically, these involve shifts that permit
the increasing influence and development of niches as sociotechnical configurations, and the unsettling, decline and discontinuity of regime configurations. The
successful penetration of a niche development pathway would be indicated not only
by increasing shares of renewables in the energy mix, for example, but also by
greater power for renewable energy actors in the design and development of energy
institutions.

There are a number of limitations, however, with this body of scholarship and its
ability to effectively account for the global political economy of energy transition
and the key dimensions explored in this book. Firstly, there is still a Eurocentric
orientation to much of the theorising about transitions to date, which limits its
ability to account for global experiences or the relationships between transitions.
The Netherlands is the historical epicentre of transition studies in universities such
as Delft, Eindhoven and Utrecht. Because work on sociotechnical transitions has
typically been focused on Europe, it inevitably makes assumptions about the nature
of state capacity, markets, institutions and infrastructural systems that do not hold in

many parts of the world, for example, where state capacity is often weak and institutions are subject to elite capture and lack of resources, or where markets and infrastructural systems are under-developed (Power et al. 2016).

Likewise, European experience, in which access to energy is more or less universal and where structures of energy provision such as electricity and transport are heavily regulated and energy governance has not had to deal with crises such as outages and an outdated grid, is held up as the norm. In contrast, in many parts of the world, energy access is far from universal and there are multiple forms of energy provision operating concurrently, from the large-scale hydroelectricity for heavy industrial use to burning firewood and charcoal for domestic use. Moreover, in Europe, many countries have liberalised their electricity sector whereas, elsewhere, state control over the energy sector remains resolutely in place. In South Africa, for example, there is a monopoly utility in the form of Eskom (Baker et al. 2014). Some scholars have started to study transitions beyond European settings including in countries in Asia (Smits 2009; Berkhout et al. 2009; Mori 2018), Latin America (Howe 2015; Rubio and Folchi 2012) and sub-Saharan Africa (Baker et al. 2014; Power et al. 2016; Newell and Phillips 2016), combined with more interconnected, comparative (Hochstetler and Kostka 2015; Hochstetler 2021), multi-scale and regional or global perspectives on sociotechnical transitions (Truffer 2012) that are of greater relevance for understanding developments in other settings.

Relatedly, Eurocentrism in transition studies can lead to a partial historical understanding of the material and social basis of transitions in terms of the financing, exchange and flows of raw materials that enabled the creation of new infrastructures for energy, transport and housing, for example. Transitions in Europe (and elsewhere) have been prefigured or are often contingent upon both historical (often colonial) and contemporary patterns of extraction and disruption elsewhere (Lennon 2017). The issue is not just extraction and exchange, however, but the reinvestment of profits in energy regimes. The circuits of finance capital by which profits from slavery, plantations and colonial dispossession were first acquired and then recirculated are ripe for analysis regarding the ways in which they were invested in the industrial revolution and a series of major energy infrastructures such as railways (Williams, E. 1994 [1944]; Inikori 1987). It is no coincidence that the industrial revolution was funded by a few people who held the power to issue essentially infinite credit (Heaton 1937) including, of course, to finance the experiments of James Watt, inventor of the steam engine. There is further work to do in foregrounding this pre-history in studies of energy transitions when they unfold in uneven racialised economies (Tilley and Shilliam 2018).

Building on this critique of prevailing Eurocentrism, others have sought to emphasise the importance of different geographies of transition (Bridge et al.

2013). Geographical work has focused on energy poverty and justice (Broto et al. 2017), energy transitions and renewable energy (Power et al. 2016), land grabbing and social oppression linked to large-scale energy investments (Finley-Brook and Thomas 2011), extractive industries (Kirshner and Power 2015) and cultural aspects of new lighting technologies (Kumar 2015). Geographers have provided evidence of how economic, political, social, spatial and technical dynamics shape, enable and constrain energy systems, at various scales. For example, they have shown how large-scale electrification initiatives across polities are refashioning the geographies of statehood in a variety of settings and scales (Power and Kirshner 2018; Gore 2017): in households, by means of new 'smart' subjectivities; through solar and energy-efficient lighting; along development corridors, as a result of the electrification of railway lines and attendant claims to technological prowess by developmental states; and in long-neglected peripheries, through decentralised control over electrification in the 'renewable peripheries' (Calvert 2015).

Secondly, a certain methodological nationalism prevails in transition studies as opposed to a focus on networks, assemblies and landscapes (Newell and Bulkeley 2016). This means, that, as well as the Eurocentrism and failure to capture the diverse and uneven geographies and pre-histories of transition just noted, dominant approaches are often unable to account for the interrelationships between transitions: how national transitions and choices of pathways have global repercussions (Selby 2019). Or how these are often dependent on resourcing or outsourcing solutions to other parts of the world, whether it is the impact of the use of biofuels in transport on land use and access in southern Africa or the rise of electric vehicles (EVs) and their impacts on conflicts over rare earth minerals in parts of central Africa (Sovacool 2019) or the use of carbon offsets for projects in the global South (Newell and Bumpus 2012; Böhm and Dhabi 2009). More generally, transitions literature also has relatively little to say about questions of (geo)politics and diplomacy, or about the political factors that impact on interstate economic relations and domestic and international energy policy choices, despite the emergence of a growing literature on the international political economy of energy (Van de Graaf et al. 2016; Goldthau et al. 2018; Newell 2018; Van de Graaf and Sovacool 2020).

Thirdly, the foregrounding of technology within transitions means that approaches typically place significant emphasis on the ability of 'bottom-up' niche-led innovations to bring about change, but often fail to adequately consider powerful landscape or regime stakeholders such as multinational firms, whose behaviour cannot be easily shaped by the state in many contexts (Newell and Bulkeley 2016). In this sense, there is a need to bring political economy into sociotechnical literature to allow us to understand how, where and why transnational actors shape the regimes, landscapes and niches of energy systems and with what implications. Part of this involves building on emerging strands of work concerned with undoing incumbency and the destabilisation and discontinuity of regimes (Johnstone and Kivimaa 2018; Rogge and Johnstone 2017; Stirling 2018; Kungl 2015; Leipprand and Flachsland 2018). This is critical because unless incumbent regimes are actively and more rapidly disassembled, no amount of support to niche actors will enable energy transitions in line with what is required to meet the goals of the Paris Agreement.

Fourthly, despite a rich body of historical cases of transition (Arranz 2017; Allen 2012; Fouquet 2016a, 2016b; Fouquet and Pearson 2012; Arapostathis and Pearson 2019; Podobnik 1999), the literature often fails to engage with the deeper political enabling environments that have nurtured disruptive change historically and whether relevant insights can be gleaned for today's world. Work on 'deep transitions' has sought to address this gap to some extent by looking at how 'sociotechnical systems are an expression of a limited number of meta-rules that, for the past 250 years, have driven innovation and hence system evolution in a particular direction' (Kanger and Schot 2018: 1045; Johnstone and McLeish 2020). A deep transition is formally defined as a series of connected and sustained fundamental transformations of a wide range of sociotechnical systems in a similar direction. Examples include moves towards increased labour productivity, mechanisation, reliance on fossil fuels, resource-intensity, energy-intensity and reliance on global value chains. The political projects and constellations of power underpinning and driving these shifts warrant further attention, however.

If more political takes on transition histories have been lacking, recent contributions have sought to address the neglect of politics in much mainstream transition literature (Meadowcroft 2009; Geels 2014; Kern 2011; Kuzemko et al. 2016; Arent et al. 2017), seeking to extend the predominantly European and technocratic focus of scholarship on transitions to other areas of the world (Power et al. 2016; Baker et al. 2014; Newell and Phillips 2016) and to pay greater attention to the role of institutions (Kern 2011; Geels 2014). Cherp et al. (2018), meanwhile also develop a 'meta-theoretical' framework that integrates *techno-economic, sociotechnical* and *political* perspectives on national energy transitions. They depict energy transitions as a function of the co-evolution of three types of system: energy flows associated with energy production and consumption coordinated through markets, energy technologies for extracting, utilising and transforming energy, and energy-related policies regulating the socio-political role of energy systems. This is combined with three perspectives: *techno-economic* with its roots in energy systems analysis and economics; *sociotechnical* grounded in sociology of technology, STS and evolutionary economics and focused on knowledge, practices and networks associated with energy technologies; and *political* based in political science addressing systems of political action. They follow Grubler et al.'s (2016) definition of energy transition as a change in the state of an energy system, as opposed to a change in an individual energy technology or fuel source. From the perspective of political economy, the techno-economic and sociotechnical practices, networks and forms of political action are all deeply political, such that the contributions of global political economy (GPE) analysis are not just confined to the latter perspective, as will become clear throughout the book.

The benefit of combining these approaches is to go beyond the insights of techno-economic modelling, through IAMs, for example, to engage with the social and political context in which decision-makers choose one pathway over another. Sociotechnical perspectives help to capture inertia and path dependence, often referred to as 'lock-in' (Unruh 2000), and the role of rules and routines by looking at the configuration of technologies, services, infrastructures and regulations, for example (Schot et al. 2016). The emphasis is very much on the conditions of emergence of new niches and modes of service provision, and less so on how to manage or accelerate the decline of incumbents (Turnheim and Geels 2012). Thinking politically about the economic components of transition can be addressed, in part, by applying ideas about varieties of capitalism to transition studies (Lachapelle and Paterson 2013; Mikler and Harrison 2012; Benney 2019), which helps to get at the diversity of political economies and state-market configurations that shape transition pathways.

The emphasis on politics brings in overdue attention to the state (Meadowcroft 2005; Johnstone and Newell 2018), including both state-centric and state-structural approaches, as well as questions of power (Meadowcroft 2009; Scoones et al. 2015). Work on historical institutionalism adds to this an understanding of how the institutional organisation of the polity and the economy privileges some actors and interests to the exclusion of others (Lockwood et al. 2016), while work on policy paradigms (Andrews-Speed 2016) helps to account for shifting framings and ideologies in politics. Other studies have looked at the role of party politics. For example, a study by Hess and Renner (2019) cautions against assuming an automatic linkage between far-right parties and opposition to energy transition policies and against assuming that far-right parties will oppose all types of energy-transition policy.

But we continue to lack analysis of the deeper politics of transition in terms of the distributions of power and the re-casting of state–market relations required to bring about transformations in energy production and consumption, informed by historical analysis of the conditions in which these have been achieved before and foregrounding questions of (political) ecology relative to the (often assumed) sustainability of different transition pathways. Placing global articulations of power and political economy, history and ecology at the forefront of analysis, as is proposed here, both challenges and goes beyond the useful but narrower focus upon sociotechnical transitions and their governance in the existing literature. It does so by foregrounding the relations of global power that shape particular institutional configurations and sociotechnical possibilities.

2.2 From Transition to Transformation

The word transition implies a shift in state. We transition from life to death and people undergo life transitions such as parenthood and retirement. Economies are said to be 'in transition' – a label applied to formerly Socialist Central and East European economies as they 'transitioned' from socialism to capitalism. There is often an implied direction of change – forward, a profound change from one state of being to another, something intentional and assuming agency – often that of the state or some higher power deriving from a God or deity. This is the case even though many profound transitions in history have been propelled by market and private actors – or social movements. Think about revolutions in IT or mobile phone use, or deep cultural shifts around attitudes towards gender equality, slavery and colonialism in which the state was often a passive, reactive actor or active in obstructing change.

Debates about transition are full of multiple, though often unstated, theories of change. There is a disciplinary dimension to this where economists tend to look at shifts in the prices of commodities and system change as a function of shifts in finance capital (Perez 2002), or the ability to provide (energy) services more cheaply (Fouquet 2016a), while sociologists and psychologists look at cultural shifts and the evolution of social values, norms and practices (Whitmarsh 2009; Shove 2003). The sorts of shifts that IR scholars study include grander geopolitical shifts in world order from the Pax Britannica to the Pax Americana, for example (Cox 1987; Desai 2013). To complicate things, historical processes described by some as transitions are more disruptive and re-constitutive of political, economic and social orders than a reconfiguration of sociotechnical assemblages and probably, therefore, more deserving of the label transformation. For example, in political Marxism, the 'transition debate' concerns the systemic change in a mode of production: the transition from feudalism to capitalism (Wood 2002). Likewise, 'economies in transition' from socialism to capitalism might, in reality, be said to be undergoing profound transformations, in many cases resulting from revolutions. Activists are sometimes more explicit in articulating the transformative nature of their project as one of 'sparking a worldwide energy revolution', for example (Abramsky 2010).

Given the need to challenge the narrow framing of transitions in neo-liberal terms as a realignment of technology, finance, infrastructures and institutions, where business as usual power configurations persist, others prefer the language of transformations to distinguish more discrete realignments of sociotechnical functions and service provision from more disruptive and deeper change that seeks to chart a different direction, pursue different goals and consciously unsettle existing power relations (Newell 2018; Stirling 2014; Scoones et al. 2018). In the case of the former emphasis on transitions, Newell and Martin (2020) refer to a 'plug-and-play' approach to energy transitions where new technologies are adopted and financed, but power and decision-making authority continue to reside with incumbents. These tend to generate and reproduce negative outcomes, socially and environmentally, because the same providers and business models grounded in extractivism are in play. Rather than replacing fossil fuels, renewable energy sources may be 'additive': merely expanding the overall amount of energy that is produced (York and Bell 2019).

Often transitions and transformations are intimately connected. As Gore (2017:9) suggests, 'it is important to distinguish between technical energy transitions and the multiple, contested political and social transformations that underpin those transitions'. But in many ways the language of transformation more accurately describes the scale of the challenge and the need to address power relations which narrow transitions, understood as reconfigurations of sociotechnical practices around key services (mobility, cooking, heating, etc), might not require. Herein lies the tension between the increasingly recognised need for transformation and the ability of incumbent actors to narrow the debate to questions of incremental transition through 'trasformismo' (Newell 2018). Applied to transitions, this refers to the ability to accommodate pressures for more radical and disruptive change and to employ combinations of material, institutional and discursive power to ensure that shifts which do occur in sociotechnical configurations do not disrupt prevailing social relations and distributions of political power. The Gramscian concept of 'trasformismo' describes a process of co-optation that 'serves as a strategy for assimilating and domesticating potentially dangerous ideas by adjusting them to the policies of the dominant coalition and can thereby obstruct the formation of organised opposition to established social and political power' (Cox 1983: 166–7). In the current world order, a combination of ideational, institutional and material sources of power serve to maintain the status quo and accommodate pressures for more far-reaching change, in ways usefully highlighted in work which draws on Antonio Gramsci's insights on hegemony (Cox 1987; Levy and Newell 2002). As laid out in the argument in Chapter 1, such strategies are central to the ability of capitalists to be able to claim that energy challenges and climate crises can be addressed through market society and do not pose a threat to its basic organisation and imperatives.

Typologies can be developed to explain and characterise the different forms transformations take. They can be more state-led; market-led, technology-led or citizen-led, whereby these overlap, compete and reinforce one another in different configurations in different parts of the world (Scoones et al. 2015). This has led some to characterise the competing politics of transitions in terms of pathways – an approach developed by the STEPS centre at Sussex.[1] Here it is suggested: 'In a complex world it is practically and analytically useful to think in terms of systems, describing how changing, interacting social, technological and environmental elements are configured around a given issue.' Pathways then are 'the particular directions in which such systems change over time' (Leach 2010). Central to the pathways approach is a recognition of more than one way of 'framing' – understanding and representing – a system. Framing involves choices about 'which elements of the system to highlight, where its boundaries are and at what scale to view it, as well as subjective and value judgements about it. Particular system-framings often become part of narratives about a problem or issue: simple stories that suggest how systems should develop to bring about particular outcomes or goals.' In this regard, attention to multiple framings and narratives opens up opportunities to advance sustainability debates and connect them more firmly with social justice by revealing the interests, biases and power relations at play. 'Processes of governance mean some narratives and pathways dominate, while others remain marginalised. The claim is then that "lock-in" to a particular powerful narrative and associated pathway can exclude others' (Leach 2010). The normative project of the pathways approach is to 'open up' and make space for more plural and dynamic sustainabilities, challenging dominant narratives and pathways, and highlighting alternatives, including those reflecting the perspectives and priorities of poor and marginalised people in particular settings. But negotiating pathways to sustainability is not just about opening up a plurality of options; it is also about the political process of building pathways which are currently hidden, obscured or suppressed (Leach 2010). How, why and by whom they are obscured or suppressed brings us back to the question of the exercise of incumbent power.

2.3 Political Economies of Transition

We need to understand (i) where power comes from (literally); (ii) how it is held, sustained and reproduced and (iii) how, where and when it might change. Historical materialism affords insights into the relationships among power, production and world order (Cox 1987) and hence affords a more global and historical conceptual-isation of incumbency. Historically specific configurations of geopolitics and institutional constructions of global governance reflect a particular base of produc-tion and an associated set of energy resources. These different historical conjunc-tures have been described in terms of 'petro-market civilisation' (Di Muzio 2012), 'carbon capitalism' (Di Muzio 2015), 'fossil capital' (Malm 2016) and, more specifically and contemporarily at this conjuncture, 'climate capitalism' in a finance-led regime of accumulation (Newell and Paterson 2010). But, as we will see in this chapter, such accounts also afford the possibility of understanding the potential for change at key historical junctures based on a reading of where power lies and which social forces are more dominant as well as weaker.

Political economy analysis also helps to explain the operation of hegemony and interacting sites of power derived from and manifest in material, institutional and discursive sites of power (Levy and Newell 2002). Hegemony, as Gramsci fre-quently underlined, is never complete. Hence a political economy account also requires a focus on the fractures, vulnerabilities, openings for change, resistance and transforming or transcending the current energy order. A political economy approach places questions of states and markets and their interrelationship, and of production, consumption and exchange, centrally. But by placing questions of power centre stage, reflected in patterns of participation and representation, for example, it also invites questions about procedure and distribution and the relation-ship between the two. This provides us with a stronger basis for understanding why energy policy serves some social groups over others and is more responsive to some interests than others. We explore this further in Chapter 5 on governing energy transitions where we look at questions of institutional access, donations to political parties, revolving doors between business and the state, access to the media and sponsorship of advertising and working through cultural spheres of education and the arts to validate the role of fossil fuels in society, as part of a broader notion of civil society that a Gramscian analysis enables.

This last dimension of culture and ideology and 'economic imaginaries' (Jessop 2010) sets a more Gramscian political economy approach apart from other strands of historical materialism and, as we will see in Chapter 6 on mobilising and culturing transitions, is viewed as an important site of struggle in itself. There is a bridge here to cultural political economy (Bulkeley et al. 2016) and the ways in which shifting economic practices and governmentalities can usefully be viewed through cultural lenses. How, for example, 'contemporary forms of carbon govern-ment work through calculative practices that simultaneously totalise (aggregating social practices, overall greenhouse gas emissions) and individualise (producing reflexive subjects actively managing their greenhouse gas practices)' (Paterson and

Stripple 2010: 341). Powerful narratives meanwhile about 'keeping the lights on' and the relationships among energy, employment and growth serve to shut down alternative pathways while legitimating incumbent ones.

2.4 Globalising the Political Economies of Energy Transition

What makes the political economy account developed in this book global is its attention to the global organisation of transitions across space and time. We will discuss the historical dimensions of this next and have already noted the importance of acknowledging the pre-histories of energy transitions. But in the contemporary world, there is a geopolitics and international relations of energy transitions that needs to be attended to. Decisions, choices and pathways cast in one part of the world have global consequences, as discussions of global energy justice make clear (Sovacool and Dworkin 2014). The social and ecological shadows cast, the uneven distribution and displacement of risk across societies, regions and between generations bear testimony to this relational dynamic of interdependence (Choucri 1976). The global production, exchange and distribution of technology, finance, materials and flows and the capture of value reflect and advance existing uneven capitalist relations that are both historically constituted and socially differentiated.

Hence, while there is increasing attention in scholarship on sustainability transitions research to issues of power, politics and governance (Köhler et al. 2019), it currently neglects the potential contribution of critical GPE to understanding the broader political and economic landscapes which shape transition pathways, the global interrelationships between national-level transitions and to an appreciation of the shifting role of the state in a context of globalisation (Newell 2020c). In this book, I make the case for drawing on more critical strands of GPE that have thus far been neglected, to help situate sustainability transitions within particular historical conjunctures: the deeper political projects of reordering the economy that can contribute to work on 'deep transitions' (Kanger and Schot 2018). This can be done through reference to shifts in the stages of capitalism where, for example, an understanding of industrial mass production and consumption can be fruitfully understood in relation to the hegemonic power of the United States (Rupert 1995) linking the geopolitics of security to economic transformations. As Hoffmann (2018) observes, it was not that the invention of the internal combustion engine by a German engineer revolutionised the world economy. 'It was only [through] its mass production within the US capitalist social formation that this innovation became the core of a new industrial age and, eventually […] Fordism informed the constitution of a new global order' (Hoffmann 2018: 42). An account grounded in critical GPE affords an understanding of the historical and contemporary interrelationships between transitions in different parts of the world which reflect the uneven distribution of power in the international system as well as vitally locate the state in a global context in relation to its insertion within the global political economy. The critical GPE scholarship which is most useful in this endeavour deals with the nature of neo-liberalism and the spatial and temporal fixes that are often employed by powerful states to avoid domestic restructuring (Harvey 2003), a dynamic we can clearly see across a variety of sociotechnical transitions, and scholarship on the changing nature of the state in this context (Cox 1993; Jessop 2002).

Firstly, work within critical GPE can help to situate transitions within particular historical conjunctures. This is not just about providing rich histories of transition which existing scholarship has amply attended to, as noted already. Nor is it merely about 'investigating how multiple regime shifts can shape landscape developments and thus societies as a whole' (Köhler et al. 2019: 5). In MLP terms, it is about taking much more seriously ideological and political landscape pressures which bear down on regimes and which may help to explain continuity and commonality among approaches to transitions across sectors even amid the diversity of contexts. Though there is clearly variety across sociotechnical transitions even within the same country, visions and ideologies regarding the role of the state and the private sector permeate across individual transitions through programmes of privatisation, for example, and global reform programmes propagated by multilateral institutions like the World Bank. Work on neo-liberalism and the way it constrains and enables particular transition pathways has an important contribution to make here (Newell and Phillips 2016), or on the growing financialisation of the global economy which brings both challenges and opportunities for transitions (Newell 2018), but where an historical understanding of the power of finance capital is critical (Perez 2002). This provides a more specific account than more general theorisations of capitalism and sustainability transitions (Feola 2019). It affords comparisons across historical periods and regions to look at how dominant ideologies (such as Keynesianism and Fordism) shape what is possible in terms of shifts in production, changes to labour and what are seen as legitimate forms of state intervention. Parallels are often drawn between the industrial revolution which started in England in the late eighteenth century and what is needed today to accelerate transitions to a low carbon economy, or between President Roosevelt's New Deal and a contemporary version of it, but often without sufficient attention to the political context in which they emerged and whether they can be replicated.

A robust GPE analysis could, on the one hand, hone in on particular configurations of power at national level, illustrated, for example, through the application of the idea of a minerals-energy-complex (MEC) to the case of South Africa's energy transition (Baker et al. 2014), but, on the other, then 'scale up' to the geopolitics of transition to understand the significance of China's rise for the financing and governance of transitions, for example. As Köhler et al. (2019: 7) note, there are 'interesting but unexplored questions about how global power shifts (such as from the West to the East) will influence the international politics of transition processes'. The analysis needs to move beyond an assessment of how the rise of BRICS countries impacts on transitions elsewhere (Schmitz 2017; Power et al. 2016) to explore how the very goals, modalities and possibilities of transition might be reimagined in different geopolitical circumstances, making a contribution to forward-looking analysis of emergent transitions.

Secondly, insights from GPE can provide an account of the interrelationships between transitions in different parts of the world as they are constituted historically and made in the present. Energy is imported and exported as part of the routine functioning of the economy. Choices made in one country have direct implications for resource, availability and access elsewhere. Whether it is increased demand for biofuels putting pressure on land that could be used for growing food, or the rush for lithium and other minerals to support expanded demand for renewable energy and electric batteries (Romero 2019), states and corporations displace food, water and energy challenges onto other countries, and often poorer populations in particular (Sovacool 2019). How these trade-offs are resolved, and on whose terms, reflects the exercise of power between states and classes. Critical scholarship on the 'spatial' and 'temporal' fixes that are employed to avoid crises in the core of the global economy by sourcing solutions elsewhere or into the future (Harvey 2003) (through carbon trading, biodiversity offsets, water grabs and the like) is helpful in understanding these dynamics. GPE scholarship on global production networks and value chains (about which more in Chapter 3), meanwhile, can helpfully provide an analysis of how capital employs spatial and temporal fixes to manage crises. This type of approach will help transition scholars to anticipate and engage with the justice dimensions of transitions that are coming to the fore in debates about just transitions (Swilling and Annecke 2012; Morena et al. 2019) and ideas of global energy justice (Sovacool and Dworkin 2014).

Thirdly, GPE scholarship can help to locate the state in a global context in relation to its insertion within the global economy. These issues are core concerns in GPE amid debates about the 'retreat of the state' (Strange 1996) and the degrees of policy space available to developing countries to pursue autonomous development pathways (Wade 2003). These can easily and fruitfully be extended to studies of transitions to better understand the power relationships which impact on emergent transitions in large parts of the majority world in particular, where donors and transnational business actors often play a decisive role in shaping transition trajectories (Power et al. 2016; Newell 2018). To do this effectively, such accounts need to be cognisant of all dimensions of state power (Johnstone and Newell 2018) and not just those to do with technology and innovation or sectoral responsibilities, including military dimensions which many scholars of global politics take as their starting point.

2.5 The International Relations of Energy

Notwithstanding recent literatures in IR on global energy governance (Florini and Sovacool 2009, 2011; Van de Graaf 2013; Goldthau and Witte 2010) and on global climate governance (cf. Bulkeley and Newell 2015; Hoffmann 2011), the global politics and political economy of transition from one energy order to another, as is required to address climate change, have been neglected. Besides a very recent spike in interest (Di Muzio and Ovadia 2016; Van de Graaf et al. 2016; Kuzemko et al. 2018, 2019; Van de Graaf and Sovacool 2020), Susan Strange's invitation in her seminal book on *States and Markets* (1988) to take energy seriously in IPE has not been taken up for the most part by the broader discipline, where a mutual neglect by IPE scholars of questions of energy (beyond oil) and energy transitions in particular, as well as by energy policy scholars of IPE, persists, thereby frustrating a productive cross-pollination of insights. Given the centrality of energy to state power, geopolitics, international economic relations and the global politics of sustainability, this is particularly surprising and problematic.

Energy is the lifeblood of modern society and is central to the contemporary global political economy through its relationship to growth, statehood, militarism and geopolitics (Huber 2013; Bromley 1991; Yergin 1991; Malm 2016; Mitchell 2011; Painter 1986; Labban 2008; Wrigley 2010). In spite of this fact, energy has often been neglected within the discipline of IR. Traditionally its role in international affairs has been reified and naturalised – reduced to the status of material resource external to the state and state formation. Work on what may be broadly described as the political economy of energy has looked at the international politics of energy interdependence (Choucri 1976), and the broader international relations of energy, particularly with regard to energy security (Moran and Russell 2009). In Realist literature, energy is often simply the object of state competition (Ikenberry 1986; Colgan 2013; Hill 2004) and control over energy is one more asset that can be counted towards aggregations of power over other nations. The traditional study of geopolitics falls within a neo-Malthusian or Realist paradigm characterised by what Hoffmann (2018: 43) calls an 'a priori assumed and under-specified competition over territory and scarce resources'. Instead, he calls for a geopolitics of energy which goes beyond the pessimistic expectations of Realists about the inevitability of conflict, the overly optimistic expectations of trade and cooperation by Liberals and Marxists' expectations of neocolonial domination and resource extraction (Hoffmann 2018).

Goldthau and Sitter (2015: 23) note how the major juncture points in world politics over the last four decades reveal the importance of energy in driving events and influencing their trajectories: 'the end of the post-World War II economic boom (a function of OPEC flexing its muscles in 1973), the Iranian revolution in 1978–9 (a reaction to US and UK attempts to keep control over oil-rich Persia), the collapse of Russia in 1998 (a result of low oil prices) eventually bringing Putin to power, or the 2014 Ukraine crisis (which triggered the EU's integration effort towards an energy union)'. It is also the case that the global debt crisis was triggered by the recycling of petrodollars to least developed countries (LDCs) to address balance of payments deficits. Richer countries also sought to offset rising oil bills through expansion of exports such as military hardware and nuclear technology. The exercise of power demonstrated by OPEC countries over the world's oil supply produced a legitimation crisis of sorts for global managers that needed to diffuse calls for a New International Economic Order (NIEO) which included fairer terms of trade and commodity prices, better regulation of transnational corporations (TNCs) and higher levels of aid (Williams, M. 1994). One effect of the oil crisis was then to produce a 'realignment of forces', nudging Western governments towards acceptance of some elements of the NIEO (Odell 1981: 276). Odell (1981: 276) notes: 'The oil exporters' oligopolistic behaviour seems certain to produce a significant effect on other groups of nations hitherto excluded from a "say" in running the system.' Aid and the arms trade were mobilised to ensure access to energy (Hammarlund 1976).

It also had domestic political repercussions on energy choices. Deliberate and active oversight of solar in favour of nuclear in the USA, despite the findings of its own task force and the obvious benefits for LDCs, is explained in relation to the dependence it propagates on Western technology (Hammarlund 1976: 184–5). It also helps to reduce internal tensions: 'Inflationary pressures, unexpected increases in capital costs, long construction delays, and growing public opposition have prompted a wave of cancellations and suspensions by energy utilities. In order to recoup their massive investments and offset higher payments for oil imports, capitalist states have responded by encouraging export sales to the Third World' (Hammarlund 1976: 186). Sales of nuclear technology were promoted through subsidies, no or low interest loans, preferential pricing of fuels and reprocessing services. Particular targets were those authoritarian regimes that 'can more easily ignore cries of public opposition' (Hammarlund 1976: 187). These events can be interpreted in a number of ways.

More liberal political economy accounts show how the history of international energy can be understood only if political, institutional, social and economic factors, all inextricably linked, are attended to. Such accounts focus on nation states and domestic public and private energy companies to furnish a 'primarily institutional and political' account of the political economy of energy (Clark 1990: 4). Wars, depressions and crises, in which energy becomes an additional battleground for inter-state rivalry, form the backbone of the analysis where crises of supply and price determine the rise and fall of power. For example, it shows how an oligopoly of multinational oil companies backed by US and British state power ruled the oil industry for the bulk of the first half of the twentieth century before having its power decentred by an oligopoly of oil-producing states bringing about 'sudden change in energy centres of power and the consequences for production, pricing, national security and so on' (Clark 1990: 6). Clark (1990: 365) concludes his book on *The Political Economy of World Energy* reflecting that the political economy of world energy in the twentieth century suggests that '[t]he world's nations and peoples experienced diverse and complex energy transitions. The locus of national and world power constantly shifted. Power blocs rose and decayed.' Yet it was also attentive to the transformation of (domestic) energy mixes and energy policy formation, reifying the division between domestic and international politics, but suggesting points of engagement with transition debates. Indeed, the book suggests, ahead of its time perhaps, that 'the real energy crisis is one of overconsumption of fossil fuels and inexcusable neglect of renewable energy and conservation' (Clark 1990: 7).

Many such liberal institutionalist accounts, inspired by the framework of transnational relations developed by Nye and Keohane (1972) to understand world politics, were written in the shadow of the OPEC crisis, and so shifts in the oil regime and the politics of cartels and conflict assume centre stage (Choucri 1976; Clark 1990). Recognising that the energy system has undergone transformations that have led to new centres of power emerging globally, many emphasise interdependence whereby even the most powerful countries struggle to exercise unilateral control and the welfare of each country becomes sensitive and vulnerable to the actions of others (Hammarlund 1976: 154; Choucri 1976). This line of thinking came to prominence in the wake of the OPEC crisis of 1974, which exposed the economic insecurity of the capitalist core of the global economy.

The normative project is to build energy co-operation around an energy regime to manage interdependence around shared interests, vulnerabilities and cognisance of structural asymmetries and inequalities in co-ordinating responses (Wilson 2015).

This leads to a paradox: 'No state alone can impose its conception of order or control upon the others. Yet, any successful coordination of behaviour can only be undertaken in the belief that it enhances national autonomy. Only through the pursuit of autonomy is coordination possible politically, and only through some coordination can the dispute over control be resolved' (Choucri 1976: 192). The aim is to meet national energy requirements 'without generating undue economic and political dislocations' (Choucri 1976: 195). Choucri (1976: 211) suggests that 'no matter what sources of energy will be used in the future, in whatever mix or proportion, the management of interdependence will remain the most critical challenge confronting all nations'. In more recent iterations, Liberal perspectives have engaged with the 'regime complex' around energy (Colgan et al. 2012): the interrelations between different actors and institutions active in the energy domain, and the ways and means of strengthening global energy governance (Van de Graaf 2013; Goldthau and Witte 2009; Cherp et al. 2011).

More Marxist-inspired renditions (Bromley 1991; Rees 2001) emphasise energy resources (particularly oil) as the focus of imperialism and exploitation. Bromley (2005: 227) suggests, for example, that '[c]ontrol of oil may be seen as the centre of gravity of US economic hegemony'. Other Marxist accounts have sought to project energy policy scenarios for capitalist society (Hammarlund and Lindberg 1976). Despite some attempts to diversify energy supply, the unwavering commitment to productivist growth necessitates a foreign policy guided by the need to secure and then protect predictable supplies of energy for domestic growth. Though the need to reduce dependence on imports was noted, the logical conclusion that demand needed to be reduced was not heeded. Indeed, most consuming nations increased their dependency on foreign imports in the wake of the oil embargo (Hammarlund 1976). Employing a range of Marxist lenses, recent work by Di Muzio and Ovadia (2016) and Di Muzio (2015) explores the respective relationships among energy, capitalism and world order and energy, social reproduction and world order, in which issues of energy transitions are just one feature (Newell 2016).

Whatever the limitations or historical specificities associated with these diverse literatures within IR and political economy, they have inadvertently helped to provide the basis of a more global, historical and political framework for thinking about transitions. As Choucri (1976: xiii) puts it: 'The energy problem is basically a political one- it emanates from disputes over who controls energy transactions, what the rules of the game will be, who gains and who loses, and at what costs to whom.' Their contribution is to treat energy politically where previously it had been understood as overwhelmingly economic in nature. Despite these advances, however, by way of indictment of the debate about energy in the discipline, Van de Graaf et al. (2016: 4) maintain that Ernest Wilson's (1987: 126) claim that work on the international dimensions of energy is 'largely descriptive, atheoretical and noncumulative' remains valid today. Against this background, how global environmental change and climate change in particular might alter and be changed by global energy politics has received even less attention (Falkner 2014; Kuzemko et al. 2015): an issue I address in each of the following chapters in the section on 'ecologies'. Recent work which seeks to understand how energy transitions impact upon the global political economy promises to address another neglected area of the interface between IPE and energy (Goldthau et al. 2019).

There is clearly, then, an urgent need to bring existing theoretical and conceptual tools from different strands of political economy to bear on the question of transitions to a lower carbon economy, while at the same time revisiting and sensitising these approaches to what is different and unique about energy and its history, ecology and political economy. I argue here that insights from the literature in critical IPE, in particular, can provide a source of clues as to the prospects of steering the forces of human history in more sustainable directions – in particular towards the decarbonisation of the global economy. This serves to highlight vulnerabilities, weak spots and active agents of change that will need to be enrolled in any project of transformation beyond more narrowly conceived sociotechnical transitions. These need to take seriously the centrality of the relationship between energy and growth, energy and statehood and the role of energy in producing different forms of capitalism, as is required again now at this historical moment. The need is urgent because of the mutual neglect of energy questions in (international) political economy and the equally problematic neglect of politics in innovation studies and economic history, which need to be combined to enrich our understanding of which combinations of institutions, actors and social forces, finance and technology are best placed to address these challenges of energy transformation.

Political economy analysis is often strongest and best at explaining why radical change does not come about. With reference to the structural power of key state, corporate and institutional actors and their control over the means of production, their hold over finance and technology in the contemporary global economy and power of elites to project and maintain the status quo as normal and given, it is strongest when explaining why business as usual prevails and radical alternatives are accommodated and diluted, crushed, de-legitimised or ignored (Gill 2008; Levy and Newell 2002). More challenging is to look back historically and infer lessons for the present about when radical, disruptive and socially progressive change has been possible before, and could be again, in the face of sustainability challenges.

In building a GPE account, it is worth speculating what classic political economists such as Smith, Ricardo, Marx, Polanyi and Mill would have made of the debate about energy transitions. Smith (1776 [2014]), rather like many mainstream economists, might be confident that the laws of supply and demand will see to it that price signals will indicate scarcity and that behaviours (and finance) will correspondingly realign. If oil is in scarce supply, prices will go up and producers and consumers will be naturally drawn to other sources. In this regard, a famous bet took place between Paul Ehrlich, author of the book *Population Bomb* (1975) coming from a neo-Malthusian perspective, and the economist Julian Simon. Ehrlich feared that a growth in population would deplete natural resources. Simon counterintuitively argued that population growth would actually make resources more abundant because of long-term changes in income, as well as the impact that technology and human ingenuity would have on the availability of resources. In September 1980, Simon challenged Ehrlich to a bet on resource depletion. Simon told Ehrlich he could choose a group of raw materials that he thought would become less abundant over the next decade. If the real prices of those materials increased over that time, then Ehrlich would win the bet. In the period between September 1980 and September 1990, population rose by 873 million people, and all five commodities that Ehrlich selected declined in real price, with an average drop of 57.6 per cent (Robbins et al. 2010: 29).

Likewise, Smith would have approved of Sir Nicolas Stern's emphasis in his report on *The Economics of Climate Change* that markets can be made to work in combatting climate change (Stern 2006). Stern famously described climate change as the world's greatest market failure. The failure is to internalise externalities. Pricing, therefore, is the answer. This tradition, which dates back to the work of economists such as Coase and Pigou, has lent intellectual weight to much of the drive towards carbon trading and markets. For Ricardo (1817), trade would be key, and he would be fascinated by debates about embedded carbon, trade and energy, the potential for an 'energy' round and the politics of relations between energy exporters and importers (Kassler and Paterson 1997). The need for specialisation and the new divisions of labour in the energy economy (Lachapelle et al. 2017) would also be unsurprising to him, though he would reject ecological critiques of how the narrow pursuit of comparative advantage leads to and justifies damaging forms of internationalised production and exchange (Newell 2012).

Marx would be unsurprised, of course, by capitalism's destructive nature and failure to recognise that all wealth in the end derives from the soil and the worker (Marx 1974: 475). He would look with a combination of awe and horror at the constant disruptions to production and their destabilising effects on the social systems in which production operates. Energy features heavily in Marx's analysis of capitalism and some writers have sought to construct an account of Marx's ecology (Bellamy Foster 1999). Marxists have drawn upon ideas about the 'metabolic rift' and laws of entropy and thermodynamics to counter prevailing economic myths about the role of energy in the economy (Georgescu-Roegen 1971; Altvater 2006). But Marx would also mock debates about a 'just transition' absent of a serious discussion about class struggle and the relationship between capital and labour. He would posit that unless and until the means of production are held by the proletariat, any prospects of a just, let alone sustainable, transition would be remote indeed. He would share Abramsky's view that '[a] discussion of energy cannot be separated from a discussion of capitalism, crisis and class struggle' (Abramsky 2010: 11). He might be more interested in debates about energy democracy and struggles to spark a 'worldwide energy revolution' to re-common energy. He would echo Abramsky's (2010: 10) claim that '[a] class analysis of energy helps to situate the contemporary evolution of the energy sector in general, and the expanding renewable energy sector in particular, within systemic dynamics'. And he would be sympathetic to the claim that 'the transition process to a new energy system is, in effect, the next round of global class struggle over control of the means of production and subsistence' (Abramsky 2010: 10).

But, equally, Marx might be dismayed by the ways in which bosses and trade unions are often uniting in opposition to (ecological and social) transformation, more preoccupied with gaining short-term concessions than moving beyond capitalism. Polanyi (1957 [1944]), meanwhile, would want to see a re-embedding of energy markets within broader frameworks of social control to tame the more destructive elements of market society. This might include better regulation of 'climate capitalism' (Newell and Paterson 2010), or a more ambitious programme of social reform. These insights about the role of shifting historical social forces have informed a range of approaches drawing on different strands of Marxism to understand climate politics (Koch 2012; Mann and Wainwright 2018; Malm 2016) and the carbon economy in particular, and to a lesser extent energy politics (Huber 2013; Di Muzio 2015; Newell 2018).

The deeper, more explicitly political, global and historical analysis proposed here is vital to allowing us to move beyond glib statements about 'green growth' and 'win-win solutions' without probing the conflicts, trade-offs and compromises that are implied by such fundamental restructuring of the economy and the relations of power which will determine which pathway is chosen. The 'incumbent' regime of existing actors and interests that benefit from ongoing reliance on a fossil fuel economy and that have played such a decisive role in the development of capitalism over the last century will not give up their position easily (Newell and Paterson 1998; Newell and Johnstone 2018); nor, in all likelihood, will governments and international institutions that have, so far, shown little appetite for initiating structural change in a context of financial austerity. Since energy use, in particular, is closely correlated with growth, there is tremendous political sensitivity around proposals to transform its provision and distribution.

2.6 Historicising the Political Economy of Energy Transitions

History teaches us nothing but just punishes us for not learning its lessons.
Vasily Kliuuchevsky (quoted in Shmelev and Popov 1989).

As we will see throughout this book, the historical dimension of energy transitions is important for understanding both the evolution and the solidification of lock-in around a fossil fuel complex, but also as a source of insights about disruption (Geels 2018; Kivimaa et al. 2021) and creative or (self)-destruction (Wright and Nyberg 2015). An account of when things have changed as a way of understanding constellations of power and their limits can inform an enquiry into the possibility of accelerating energy transitions at this historical conjuncture. This helps to locate contemporary (and historical) energy transitions as a product of a particular configuration of social and class forces of production. Antonio Gramsci (1971) once said: 'The starting-point of critical elaboration is the consciousness of what one really is, and in "knowing thyself" as a product of the historical processes to date, what has deposited in you an infinity of traces, without leaving an inventory.' As Edward Said (1978: 25) then goes on to observe, '[t]he only available translation inexplicably leaves Gramsci's comment at that, whereas in fact Gramsci's text concludes by saying, "therefore it is imperative at the outset to compile such an inventory"'.

There are then important questions about *when* and *how* transitions can come about, exploring their historical, economic, political, social and cultural enabling conditions. This includes debates about their temporality and whether they can be accelerated and, if so, over what sorts of time frame (Smil 2016; Sovacool 2016; Simms and Newell 2017) as well the spatial (Broto and Baker 2018) and geographical (Bridge et al. 2013) dimensions of transitions noted earlier. As Roberts et al. (2018) note, the obvious need for acceleration has created an urgent debate over whether and how the necessary changes can happen quickly enough. Many scholars offer pessimistic answers. Smil (2016) makes a particularly compelling historical argument that transitions in energy systems are 'long and arduous'. If they are to succeed at mitigating climate change, therefore, the pace of transitions to low carbon energy systems must somehow differ from historical precedent, as the IPCC's (2018) SR15 made very clear. The report argued that such transitions have been observed in the past within specific sectors and technologies, but that the geographical and economic scales at which the required rates of change in the energy, land, urban, infrastructure and industrial systems would now need to take place are larger and have no documented historic precedent (IPCC 2018).

This will require an acceleration of the pace of change. There is some reason for hoping that such an acceleration could be plausible. Past energy transitions have been triggered by a largely emergent combination of policy efforts, economic shifts, technological developments and other factors. While currently ongoing low carbon transitions also benefit from emergent technical, economic and cultural developments, however, they are also being actively pushed by policymakers on an international level, in a way unlike any other energy transition on historical record. Sovacool's (2016) list of ten rapid energy transitions, some of which went from a 1 per cent to a 25 per cent market share in just a few years, shows that this kind of acceleration can achieve impressive results. This has provoked significant debate on whether Sovacool's relatively small-scale examples can have a bearing on the global energy transitions necessary to mitigate climate change (Smil 2016; Grubler et al. 2016).

What, if any, historical precedents are there for the rapid and disruptive change to existing ways of organising the economy, technology, finance, politics and society in ways which brought about positive change that might be useful for analysis and praxis at this historical conjuncture? History provides plenty of examples of violent periods of war, revolution, social upheaval and rapid, but socially regressive transitions (arguably Reganomics and Thatcherism or contemporary alt-right popular politics) involving the reorganisation of the economy and social contracts or rapid lock-in along unsustainable lines (Fordism or the dismantling of rail and urban mass transit systems to build the infrastructures for cars or the rapid expansion of mass aviation). Or of environmentally beneficial rapid transitions undertaken in socially regressive ways such as the 'rapid decarbonisation' transition from coal to gas in the UK in the 1980s (the 'dash for gas') which sparked a miner's strike and widespread social unrest, but was described as 'among the most globally significant of any national decarbonisation' (Pollitt 2012: 135; Turnheim and Geels 2012). The same was true of the Supreme Court ruling in India in 2002 which insisted on a tight timeline for the adoption of compressed natural gas in taxis and rickshaws in Delhi before the infrastructure was in place to meet demand for the alternative fuel, leading to widespread disruption and protest. These examples illustrate both how state power can de-stabilise and deliberately phase out whole sectors of the economy when the will is there to do so, but also the socially regressive ways in which this can be done. So, does history also offer any lessons about the scope for socially positive rapid transformations, a progressive version of Naomi Klein's (2007) 'shock doctrine' perhaps of when crises create opportunities to introduce more ecologically and socially sustainable practices and systems?

Seeking to historicise a discussion of rapid socio-environmental transformations is useful and necessary, therefore, for the reasons given here, but it does bring with it a number of analytical and political challenges. Case selection is often biased towards success, and not the far greater number of failed transitions. In this regard, I follow the recommendation of Fouquet and Pearson (2012: 3) that 'the choice and selection of historical cases ought to be driven by a diagnosis of the type of challenges that we currently face'. Additional challenges include, firstly, seeking to combine rapidity with large-scale transformations. This limits the pool of relevant cases significantly since most transformations in systems such as energy are thought to unfold over decades, if not centuries. Smil (2008: 2) writes that 'all energy transitions have one thing in common: They are prolonged affairs that take decades to accomplish, and the greater the scale of prevailing uses and conversions, the longer the substitutions will take.' On this basis, he cautions against 'unrealistic expectations concerning the pace of future energy transitions' (Smil 2016: 194). The work of Carlota Perez (2002) on finance capital and technological revolutions similarly shows 'waves of creative destruction' rise and break over decades or centuries in terms of unsettling old orders and delivering technological revolutions. Think of the industrial revolution, the age of steam and railways, or Fordism and auto-mobility.

History shows that energy system transitions, in particular, are rare events whose complex and long-drawn-out processes are often decades in the making and can take centuries to fully unfold (Fouquet and Pearson 2012:1), even if there are intense periods of acceleration in the deployment and uptake of particular technologies, as we seeing with solar PV. The fall in the use of biomass and coal and the rise in oil were all transitions that lasted seventy to ninety years. The period in which innovations go from initial commercial success to 2 per cent market share can take over two decades. New systems tend to face the 'lock-in' or 'path dependency' of existing systems. As Smil (2016: 195) points out: 'It's taken between 50 and 70 years for a resource to reach a large penetration. When you look at the money, the infrastructure, the regulation, the technologies, it takes many decades for any fuel source to make a large impact.' Electric vehicles came before petrol cars, while early experiments with solar energy can be dated to the 1950s. He further claims that 'global energy transitions have been always gradual, prolonged affairs', particularly so in large nations whose high levels of per capita energy use and whose massive and expensive infrastructures make it impossible to greatly accelerate their progress even if there is resort to some highly effective interventions (Smil 2016: 195). Fast transitions, when they occur at all, are considered anomalies, limited to countries with very small populations or highly specific contextual circumstances that strictly condition any lessons that can be derived from them. For example, the decision to switch the British Navy's fuel from coal to oil prior to the First World War was a key trigger for the growth of the UK oil industry and, post-Cold War, Cuba's rapid energy shift was the result of loss of access to cheap Soviet oil. In general, the only technologies that go faster are those that are readily substitutable for existing technologies. This time, transitions that take decades or centuries have to be radically accelerated given diminishing available carbon space and that generates a peculiar set of issues and dilemmas.

There are nevertheless challenges to the mainstream view of energy transitions as long, protracted affairs. As Sovacool (2016: 203) notes:

[M]any transitions – at varying scales and sectors – have occurred quite quickly – that is, between a few years and a decade or so, or within a single generation. At smaller scales, the adoption of cook stoves, air conditioners, and flex-fuel vehicles are excellent examples. At the state or national scale, almost complete transitions to oil and electricity in Kuwait, natural gas in the Netherlands, and nuclear electricity in France took only a decade, roughly, to occur. [I produce] ten case studies of energy transitions that, in aggregate, affected almost one billion people and needed only 1–16 years to unfold. Clearly, this evidence suggests that some energy transitions can occur much more quickly than commonly believed.

These disputes among academics about the historical and temporal dimensions of transitions are compounded by the politics of how we define and measure rapidity and how we typologise transitions. Sovacool (2016: 211) gives the example of Brazil's transition to flex-fuel vehicles, which 'arguably, took a year (from the start of the national program to large-scale diffusion), more than twenty years (from the first invention of a FFV in 1980), almost thirty years (from the start of their national ethanol program), or more than eight decades (from the first invention of a Brazilian engine capable of using ethanol in the 1920s)'. Likewise, you can date the introduction of wind turbines to the 1880s and solar PV to 1954 (Fouquet 2016a). In dealing with the temporal dynamics of transitions, there is always a danger of comparing 'apples and oranges' (Grubler et al. 2016), of drawing parallels, for example, between the slow dynamics of 'grand transitions': global primary energy transitions (from one fuel to another) to more rapid national transitions. In the case of the latter, even sceptics such as Smil (2016), concede that rapid transitions over just a few years are possible. The common characteristics of rapid transitions, according to Grubler et al. (2016), are where a new and well-established technology simply substitutes for an old one (clean cookstoves, LPG, FlexFuel cars), where substitute technologies have been previously used in other markets, benefitting from the experience of early adopters and where the scales, either national or sub-national are relatively small, and finally where the technologies offer high tangible benefits for adopters such as health (cookstoves), flexibility (FlexFuels), cost and convenience as well as benefitting from well-designed public policies. These are not representative, they hasten to add, of the more pervasive energy system transitions that have been the focus of historical studies or of the climate and sustainability scenario literature (Grubler et al. 2016). In sum, the duration of transitions increases with complexity, more so when we are talking about 'systems of systems' (Grubler et al. 2016).

Secondly, a note of caution is appropriate about the unintended political consequences of invoking urgency as a criterion for transitions. The demand for rapidity can give rise to a series of 'urgency dilemmas' amid claims about the need to suspend democratic politics as usual. This can take the form of overriding planning decisions (such as that of Lancashire council in the UK against fracking) or speeding them up (to accelerate the adoption of nuclear invoking the urgency of transitioning to a low carbon economy, for example) given the need to accelerate the adoption of technologies labelled low carbon by policy elites. Clarion calls of a 'global emergency', however well intended, can pave the way for 'exceptional' actions, on the part of states in particular, which bypass the need for regular democratic scrutiny. Bromley (2016: 170), for example, argues that 'decision-makers cannot wait for a climate catastrophe to consolidate public opinion and political will, so a way must be found to frame imminent disaster alongside extraordinary interventions that will save the day'. Urgency can be used to trump and supersede political conflict, what has been referred to as 'post-politics' (Swyngedouw 2010) and accelerate the diffusion of controversial technologies (such as geo-engineering or negative emission technologies), or to suspend forms of political engagement that are incompatible with business as usual politics and economics on the basis that we have to 'go with the grain' of existing actors and institutions.

Related to this is the real danger that an emphasis on urgency and, by definition, crisis management frames responses in terms of top-down interventions from elite actors, that is, those with the power, resources and control over finance, production and infrastructures, or that can call upon the coercive powers of the state. For example, the declaration of climate emergencies by local authorities around the world is, on the one hand, a welcome recognition of the gravity of the threat posed by climate change, coming on the back of the IPCC Special Report on 1.5 degrees mentioned earlier (IPCC 2018). Some councils in the UK and France have organised citizen assemblies to deliberate on appropriate local responses. Shifting budgetary priorities and reversing decisions which lock in carbon (cancelling infrastructure developments such as proposed airport expansions, for example) might all be welcome. Providing a blank slate for governments to impose their preferred versions and visions of low carbon futures, however, would be to open the possibility of regressive interventions validated by the emergency.

This scenario potentially diminishes scope for more plural, bottom-up, inclusive and deliberative pathways to sustainability where transformations are cultured and follow an ethic of 'care' rather than 'control' (Stirling 2011, 2014).

A further consideration in case selection is that by consciously cherry-picking from history examples of sudden and disruptive change, we potentially run the risk of reifying and reinforcing disabling accounts of change wherein the key processes and institutions are incumbent ones controlled by powerful actors. The challenge is to recognise this tension and ensure that analogous cultural shifts and contentious politics are included in the analysis, to ensure that we recognise that instances of decisive change and leadership by powerful actors often come on the back of years, if not decades, of cultural change and shifts in values and norms, politics of protest and agitation when explaining and attributing agency. In this regard, Sovacool (2016: 204) quotes O'Connor: 'Big transitions are the sum of many small ones. Looking at overall energy consumption will miss the small-scale changes that are the foundation of the transitions and the cumulative effects of changes in practice.'

Looking for primary drivers of major disruptions inevitably reveals a partial and incomplete picture. Social scientists and historians tend to overlook daily 'micro-disruptions', focusing instead on the 'big bang' of reflective agency (Hopf 2018). It is indeed the case that 'major transitions' are only easily identifiable because of a series of 'minor transitions' that have occurred in a concerted manner. This underscores the point about the confluence of practices of governance, finance, mobilisation and culture as key to enabling the likelihood and probability that transitions can be accelerated. Indeed, actors and their agency need to be looked at in relation to one another rather than in isolation. As Scoones et al. (2015) show, while green transformations can be more state-led, market-led, technology-led or citizen-led, in reality they converge, compete and reinforce one another. This is not a search for a mono-causal big-bang theory of change, therefore. The changes are always multidimensional. As Sovacool (2016: 205) shows: 'In order to counteract path dependence, inertia, and lock-in, scholars looking at transitions theory have argued that truly trans-formative change must be the result of alterations at every level of the system simultaneously' from technology niches to regimes and the broader landscape which shapes them.

Appreciating the tensions inherent in the dynamics of rapid change does not absolve us of the responsibility for engaging concretely, as well as analytically, with the pressing need for accelerating transitions towards sustainability and addressing the consequences and injustices of current patterns of 'slow violence' (Nixon 2011) and near-term anticipated impacts. Likewise, it is critical to acknowledge the grave consequences of failing to adopt a transition pathway compatible in scale and speed with meeting the targets of the Paris Agreement on climate change. These include a world of worsening climatic upheaval, in which positive feedbacks trigger irreversible processes of environmental change whose impacts disproportionally fall on low-income and marginalised groups.

Thirdly, there is the issue of the lack of relevant historical precedents for conscious transitions driven by environmental imperatives. Previous shifts from coal to oil, or around transitions in transportation towards private transport under Fordism, or towards public sanitation systems over open sewers, were driven by the possibility of making more money, producing efficiency gains or dealing with major crises (health and disease with sanitation) in the case of the OPEC oil crisis driving investments in renewable energy and energy efficiency. In Fouquet's (2010) review of fourteen past energy transitions, he finds that for new sources to become dominant, in each case the service it provides has to be cheaper than the incumbent energy source, as well as offer enhanced characteristics (such as ease of use, exclusivity, cleanliness or status). Even if currently not framed this way by incumbent actors, debatably, with sustainability we face the very real prospect of having to produce and consume less, or to invest in pathways that may be less cost-effective, profitable or convenient (at least in the short term) than the alternatives with which they are competing and which, therefore, make them potentially less appealing to investors. Ediger and Bowlus (2018: 2) suggest: 'The two transitions from one dominant source to another – wood to coal and coal to oil – occurred over several decades and when overall energy demand was growing, but energy demand growth is not guaranteed to drive a future transition'.

On the other hand, and more positively, as Kern and Rogge (2016) argue, it is precisely the gravity of the situation we now face with climate change that means historical parallels are less useful regarding the drivers of energy and other transitions, since never before have we faced a situation in which one of the primary rationales for change is planetary survival. Hence politics may trump economics as usual in the context of public backing for more rapid and far-reaching transitions than have been contemplated to date. Kern and Rogge (2016: 13) note:

The key reason for our optimism is that historic energy transitions have not been consciously governed, whereas today a wide range of actors is engaged in active attempts to govern the transition towards low carbon energy systems . . . [T]he 2015 Paris agreement demonstrates a global commitment to move towards a low carbon economy for the first time, thereby signalling the required political will to foster quick transitions and to overcome resistance.

In a report on 'transformation points', the Centre for Alternative Technology (CAT 2019:1) argues:

The Paris Agreement is nothing less than a mandate to transform and move the global energy system into a new state supporting economic prosperity and sustainable development using zero-carbon technologies. System transformations of this scale are possible and have happened before. Mobile phones, for example, soared from virtually zero to almost full coverage in less than two decades. A slower transformation on a much larger scale is already happening in renewable electricity, where the costs of some sources have dropped exponentially over the last two decades, making renewables competitive with incumbent technologies. In this process, a transformation point marks the moment when a previously novel technology, behaviour or market model achieved critical mass, took off, and became the new normal.

The authors argue that zero carbon technology deployment will typically pass through the four following stages: 1) an *initiation phase* where a technology demonstrates feasibility at a project level; 2) a *development phase*, which overcomes the main barriers to adoption by putting certain building blocks in place, then reaches a moment of critical mass (the 'transformation point'), where the previously new state begins to be considered the new norm; 3) a *take-off phase* where the adoption rate increases rapidly before levelling off such that further adoption still requires effort after this point, but this decreases over time until the final phase; 4) a *completion phase* involving continued effort to reach completeness and maximum market penetration. It is notable, however, that, in this framing, transformation is about the enabling conditions for technological take-off and not about disrupting or challenging dominant power relations.

Nevertheless, targeted policies can aid transformation in some countries: To facilitate the transition in the renewable energy sector, a small number of ambitious actors, in particular governments introducing policies such as feed-in tariffs, took the lead, and were followed by a critical mass of early movers (Sterl et al. 2017). Key to reaching the transformation point for mobile phones was the perceived advantage of the new technology, relative ease of access and scalability compared to the incumbent land-line technology (which never penetrated many parts of the world due to high infrastructure costs). The key characteristics of an 'S-curve' of new technology dispersion and adoption are the rate of increase (speed) and the maximum achievable level (scale). Even after the transformation point, some effort (e.g. policy support or financial incentives) may be needed to speed up take-off and completion phases and to avoid sliding back to the old system. Another important characteristic of the S-curve transformation is that the rate of change accelerates. The system changes slowly in the beginning but speeds up over time. To achieve the aim of full decarbonisation, a concerted and far-sighted effort will be needed to initiate the transformation (as has happened in the past for the power sector) and to then keep the transformation going at the necessary speed (Rockström et al. 2017). Resonating with the historical reflections referred to already, one driving force will be the considerable advantages associated with the transformation to a zero carbon society, such as co-benefits in cost, comfort and convenience that are already starting to appear (Carbon Action Tracker 2019).

To put it bluntly, the Stone Age did not end because we ran out of stone. As Ediger and Bowlus (2018: 2) argue: 'The abundance of the new source has not necessarily determined the pace of its adoption, nor has the remaining availability of the existing source necessarily determined the rate of its decline.' Whereas previous transitions were more 'opportunity' driven, the low carbon transition might be more 'problem' or 'threat' driven. Likewise, '[w]hile past transitions may have been rooted in abundance, future ones may involve scarcity' (Sovacool and Geels 2016: 235). The driver may be less the discovery of new fuels, the availability of new services or drops in the cost of technology, though each of these may play an important role. It may rather be the conscious redesign of the economy along lower carbon lines and the managed decline of existing industries, not because they are no longer profitable or able to meet consumer needs, but because they are pushing us beyond ecological limits.

The accelerated and deliberate decline of whole and very powerful industries for reasons of sustainability, as we are witnessing with the demise of coal in particular (Caldecott et al. 2017), suggests that we are entering a new terrain of transition. Transitions are not organic and non-linear, but have to be imagined, designed, financed, constructed and socially accepted. All this requires political work which can set and support the direction of change. In this sense, there is increased scope for what Bromley (2016) calls 'extraordinary interventions'. Drawing parallels with the political and industrial landscape prior to the Second World War, he suggests that the conditions are amenable to increased rapidity in transitions. He notes the fact that research and development (R&D) policies of leading industrial nations are supportive of strategic and rapid innovation, including the increasing popularity of Green New Deals, that there is a support base for strategic intervention across a range of public and private actors, and that zero carbon technologies are already cost-competitive in many jurisdictions.

This transition will also unfold in a more globally integrated world than previous transitions where experimentation, diffusion and collaboration around technology and production are more globally organised and co-ordinated, even if it is a sub-set of states that wield disproportionate power over the direction of change which they can drive, at speed, through the global economy. The falling price and availability of solar PV is a case in point. Unlike previous transitions, it is also more likely that we are looking to a multitude of energy sources to meet different energy needs through different pathways, such that the standard metric of 50 per cent market share for global energy transitions is less relevant. The adage that 'necessity is the mother of all invention' seems more appropriate. And if there is anything which most transition scholars can agree on, it is that transitions are non-linear processes, so surprises and unintended consequences are one of the few things that are certain (Sovacool and Geels 2016). Indeed, Fouquet (2016a) highlights the ability of energy price shocks to create 'tipping points' as well as 'lock-in'. The soaring price of coal drove many countries to invest in hydropower during the First World War, while the oil shocks in the 1970s led many economies to reduce their dependence on oil.

I have noted many of the challenges and limitations associated with trying to project into the future based on a (necessarily selective) reading of the past. The dynamics may be different going forward and questions of sustainability bring with them particular challenges around urgency and the need for a fundamentally different model of economic development that goes beyond replacing one mode of accumulation and regulation for growth, with its associated technologies, flows of finance and models of production, for another. For this reason, as Fouquet and Pearson (2012: 3) put it, 'past energy transitions may not be the best analogies for a future low carbon energy transition'. As Sovacool (2016: 210) suggests: 'Future transitions may also become a social or political priority in ways that previous transitions have not been—that is, previous transitions may have been accidental or circumstantial, whereas future transitions could become more planned and coordinated, or backed by aggressive social movements or progressive government targets.'

For example, unlike earlier transitions driven primarily by price or an abundance of resources, future ones may be driven by scarcity and the unaffordability of resources or stranded assets and un-burnable carbon. In terms of the knowledge base, scientific consensus and broad policy toolkits for addressing these issues that are now available – production tax credits, feed-in tariffs and renewable portfolio standards that can hasten the adoption of preferred technologies – a positive enabling environment may be said to exist. Despite this, transitions may well be incremental, cumulative, messy and multidirectional for the most part. As Sovacool (2016: 211) suggests, 'most energy transitions have been, and will likely continue to be, path dependent rather than revolutionary, cumulative rather than fully substitutive'. But, as I have shown here, this does not exclude the possibility and imperative of rapid disruptive change over shorter time frames where shifts in governance, financing, mobilisation and culture of the sort described above coincide, overlap and drive one another. I concur with Grubler (2012:8): 'History does not preordain the future, but it is the only observational space available from which to draw lessons from and to inform policy models and makers of what it takes to initiate and sustain a much-needed next transition towards sustainability.'

An approach grounded in historical materialism lends a more historical perspective to the debates about precedents for and the possibilities of transitions and transformations in society and the economy, and not just in (re)alignments of technology and social practice. This is consistent with an historical materialist approach to studying an emergent world order 'in terms of its economic, political and socio-cultural dimensions, with a view to its emerging contradictions and limits and the possibilities these imply for different collectivities' (Gill 1993: 16). Gramsci distinguishes this approach to showing how ideas and material conditions are always bound together, from a more reductionist 'historical economism' which reduces all explanations to the material sphere (Gramsci 1971). This approach can build on previous histories of transitions which emphasise factors such as the role of prices, science and human capital (Fouquet and Pearson 2012; Grubler 2012; Pearson and Foxon 2012; Allen 2012). But rather than view the technological and the social context which supported particular transitions in isolation, the emphasis here is on identifying the underlying political, historical and material factors that enable large-scale transformations to take place, which will inform our understanding of the contemporary global politics of energy transitions. This is critical to appreciating the terrain upon which competing social forces will contest the future organisation of the economy in a carbon-constrained world, based on their role in shaping and resisting previous political change and how they have engaged with the challenge of an energy transition to date (Podobnik 2006), given that the scale of the challenge is often likened to that of creating a new global industrial revolution.

2.7 Ecologising the Political Economy of Energy Transitions

Layered upon the globalised and historical account of the political economy of energy transitions described so far in this chapter, we need to bring in an ecological dimension in recognition of the fact that all energy pathways have ecological consequences and their very viability in the long term will be a function of their ecological sustainability. So, what does ecological political economy add to an historical GPE account? If it is to have contemporary value and application, political economy has to be able to speak to the ecological crisis we now face.

Bringing in political ecology can help to ecologise a GPE account of transitions and address its potential to overemphasise economism (Lawhon and Murphy 2012). The core questions that political ecologists ask about access, allocation, property regimes and justice are as pertinent to energy as to other resource arenas where these insights have been applied (Robbins 2004; Peet et al. 2011). Foundations of ecological political economy can be found in the work of Gale and M'Gonigle (2000), Barry (1999), Katz-Rosene and Paterson (2018), Moore (2015b), Bookchin (1980) and Newell (2012, 2019). In its make-up, it often combines elements of different green thinking (social ecological, socialist and Marxist), as well as feminist and Marxist political economy: combining attention to social and historical processes of exclusion and exploitation with a critical account of the state and capitalism in terms of their ability to address ecological crises. Normatively, it finds expression in accounts of a green state (Eckersley 2004; Barry and Eckersley 2005) and a sustainable economy (Trainer 1996).

An ecological approach, certainly one grounded in social ecology (Bookchin 1980), brings with it a more critical view of the state, able to situate the state within broader social relations which tie it to industrialism and militarism in ways which are problematic from the point of view of sustainability. Appreciating the multidimensionality of the state is critical to understanding its imbrication in energy systems closely tied as they are to commercial, accumulation, geopolitical and military strategies (Johnstone and Newell 2018). This challenges the idea of the state as a neutral arbiter of competing energy pathways. Historically speaking, as Conca (2005: 181) notes: 'The emergence of the centralising, industrialising, national state, with its capacity to centralise decision-making, concentrate capital, strip local communities of their historical property rights in nature, supply coercive power and protect elite interests, has been a key social innovation along the road to global planetary peril.'

Going beyond conventional political economy analysis, an ecological approach illustrates why industrialism, and not just capitalism, is problematic ecologically (Newell 2019). It also holds a distinct view of growth as problematic and unsustainable. In this sense, as Dobson (1990: 32) suggests: 'It makes no appreciable difference who owns the means of production if the production process itself is based on the assumption that its development need not be hindered by thoughts of limits to growth.' This challenges some critical accounts of transitions which assume that by changing ownership structures, or even more fundamentally the mode of production, more sustainable energy systems can be created. Green views cast doubt on that idea and would emphasise much more the need for supply-side constraints on production and radical reductions in demand, rather than just diversifying energy options. Such a perspective differs sharply from given assumptions in many literatures on innovation, environmental management and ecological modernisation, for example (Mol 2003), as well as dominant narratives about green growth (OECD 2011).

But it also raises questions about how, for what and by whom the economy should be organised. Applied to energy, it would prioritise sustainability over other traditional energy policy objectives and see it as a sub-set of the larger question of the viability of the system, since energy access and security do not amount to much in a context of runaway climate change. It would also 'ecologise' the study of energy transitions, not viewing them as isolated from, or disembodied from, other ecosystems and ecological cycles such as land, water and air. As we will see in each of the chapters, choices made in one domain imply change and impact upon all other ecological domains, even if siloed policymaking often makes it hard to comprehend, let alone act upon that reality (Royston et al. 2018). This raises issues of policy coherence and integration that I discuss in Chapter 5 on governing transitions and it comes through strongly in discussions of the nexus and linkages among the Sustainable Development Goals (SDGs) (Kuzemko et al. 2018). Methodologically, it is informed by ecological economics and an appreciation of ecological stocks and flows and patterns of uneven exchange which characterise contemporary global energy systems (Söderbaum 2000; Costanza 1991). Because of a strong normative commitment, bringing a (political) ecological perspective to energy transitions raises difficult questions about urgency and rapid change, which I will return to elsewhere in the book, while at the same time being sceptical about state-led and market-led transformations. It operates then as critique, normative vision, as well as contributing to strategic thinking (Newell 2019).

Overall, then, the approach here seeks to simultaneously politicise, historicise, globalise and ecologise energy transitions. The focus throughout the book is on power and politics as manifest in contests over *producing* transitions between labour, the state and different types of (fossil and other) capital; *financing* disruption and creative destruction; *governing* transitions involving the state and non-state as well as transnational actors and global governance institutions; and finally, but critically, *mobilising* and *culturing* transitions through resistance to energy extractivism and energy injustice and through building alternative pathways.

3

Producing Energy Transitions

This chapter shows how production is at the base and centre of energy transitions. How production is financed, governed and resisted determines production pathways and, therefore, the likelihood that transitions are both sustainable and socially just. Conflicts over energy are increasingly central to the global processes of restructuring production. Hence, notwithstanding the increasing financialisation of energy in particular, and the economy in general (discussed further in Chapter 4), production remains key. It seems appropriate, therefore, to start with how, why and for whom energy production is organised at this conjuncture, how we have got here and the challenges this presents for attempts to reorganise it along lower carbon and more socially just lines.

This firstly implies a brief historicisation of the fossil fuel economy, a theme we will return to in each of the chapters, since the fossil fuel complex operates and is sustained by interrelated material, institutional and discursive types of power through assemblages of finance, infrastructure, institutions, social networks and the projection and reinforcement of forms of cultural power. But rather like the geology of fossil fuels, the fossil fuel economy has become ossified through layers of lock-in and stratification of political and economic power built up over hundreds of years (Malm 2016). Dislodging this power and challenging both incumbents (individual actors) and incumbency (the systems and structures which support them), as part of moves to transform energy politics in order to ecologise and democratise them, presents a challenge of staggering proportions. It amounts to undoing a very profitable and (economically at least) successful growth model held in place by the most powerful states and corporations in the global economy, to say nothing of the militaries which back them.

Though new market entrants seeking to produce new forms of energy and using alternative technologies have gained in power and market share over the last fifteen or so years, incumbent power holds firm in many settings reflected in ongoing exploration and extraction of fossil fuels and ever-rising levels of greenhouse gases.

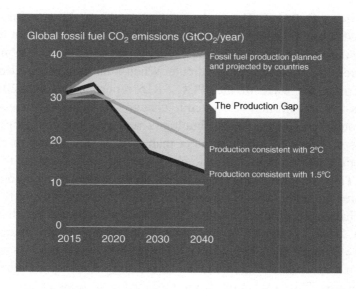

Figure 3.1 The Production Gap report. Source: Adapted, with permission, from SEI et al. (2019).

Currently, global demand for coal, oil and gas are all growing, with fossil fuels accounting for 81 per cent of energy use (IEA 2018). Worryingly, the International Energy Agency (IEA) projects total fossil fuel use rising for decades still to come, surpassing all climate targets (IEA 2018). There has also been a tripling in the pace of oil and gas pipeline building since 1996 (Foster Report 2019). Governments are planning to produce about 50 per cent more fossil fuels by 2030 than would be consistent with a 2°C pathway and 120 per cent more than would be consistent with a 1.5°C pathway (see Figure 3.1). These planned levels of fossil fuel production are inconsistent with the collective climate pledges under the Paris Agreement and, as a consequence, the global production gap is even larger than the already significant global emissions gap (SEI et al. 2019).

Energy transitions have been strongly framed in terms of substituting technologies, building mixes of policies and energy sources to meet rising demand without, to date, taking seriously the idea of restricting supply and production or reducing demand. This is an idea we will return to in Section 3.8 on ecologies of energy production. Despite this, or because of this, there have been recent moves to emphasise the role of supply-side climate change policy (Erickson et al. 2018; Lazarus et al. 2015) including both state-led commitments to leave fossil fuels in the ground and proposals for new international agreements to restrict the proliferation of fossil fuel extraction (Simms and Newell 2018; Newell and Simms

2019; Asheim et al. 2019). These ideas are currently on the margins of debate, however, and solutions which invoke the need to keep fossil fuels in the ground through regulation and law, or to reverse decisions to expand carbon-intensive infrastructures, are often subject to ridicule. When I discussed such ideas with Sir Nicolas Stern in the wake of the IPCC SR15 report in October 2018, which clearly calls for 'transformative, systemic change', he made very clear his view that fuels could be changed, and technologies replaced, but changing the orientation of the economy by anything other than pricing signals and market mechanisms (despite their obvious failure to generate the required change to date) was unrealistic. This excluded even merely reversing the approval of carbon-intensive infrastructures including airport expansions, which interestingly courts in the UK have now challenged in relation to a new runway at London's Heathrow airport (Carrington 2020). In terms of the 'energy hierarchy' (from energy saving, through to efficiency then renewables followed by conventional sources), the emphasis is far more on substitution than on reducing demand or even improving efficiency of use. This is what has been described as a 'plug and play' approach to energy transitions where energy sources and technologies can be substituted and replaced, but overall levels of production and consumption stay the same (Newell and Martin 2020).

I will show in Section 3.1, however (and as discussed in Chapter 2), that although 'grand transitions' in structures of energy production can take hundreds of years (Smil 2016), more rapid transitions in supply and demand are possible and have been achieved in the past (Sovacool 2016) and are unfolding in the present in some sectors and regions (IPCC 2018), pointing to at least the possibility of moving beyond the current impasse. It is the case, however, that there are very few direct historical parallels of the phase-out of energy sources at the speed and scale now required of the Paris Agreement. Many such radical shifts in the past have generally occurred at times of war and economic crisis (the fall in gas production in Russia, the OPEC crisis in the 1970s, the reunification in Germany and the 'wall-fall effect'), to which health crises can now be added to the list, rather than in times of peace or relative economic stability.

If there is to be an energy transition, let alone a transformation of the energy system, not only *how* we produce energy but *for whom* and *for what* will have to dramatically change. Though this is rarely conceded in conventional approaches to transitions that rely on notions of technological substitutability, existing models and ideologies of energy development will have to change. Regarding *who* and *what* energy is for, for example, the need to reduce traditional forms of energy production reliant on fossil fuels will mean that priority will have to be given to nations and classes of people living in energy poverty and those who have consumed far fewer fossil fuels in the past and to whom a sizeable 'carbon debt' is owed by richer countries (Simms 2005). Social over industrial needs may have to take priority in a context of limits, implying a major redistribution of energy access.

Political economy analysis would suggest that with shifts to structures of production come changes to social relations and configurations of power, since the two are closely related (Cox 1987). This indeed is why incumbents fight so hard to protect the structure of production which they benefit and profit from: it forms the basis of their power. More de-centralised and less resource-intensive systems of energy generation, transmission and distribution threaten the power and networks of established actors (Tomain 2017). This is apparent in practices of rent-seeking in energy politics around control of revenue flows and who negotiates major energy contracts: where state elites often jealously guard their power to extract concessions and side-payments from lucrative deals with investors (Sovacool and Brisbois 2019). Democratising and de-centralising energy systems diffuses power at the expense of incumbent actors. Those incumbents are not just corporate energy interests but state officials who often prefer to maintain tight control over the energy system, often through state-owned energy enterprises, and trade unions who prefer centralised bargaining in which they have an established role and a privileged seat at the table, and where the assumption is that larger numbers of jobs can be provided by centralised systems of energy provision. This relates to broader arguments that particular models of energy production and technology use require and imply particular types of politics and certain forms of state practice (Johnstone and Newell 2018). We discuss this further in Chapter 5, particularly in relation to the nuclear state or the reproduction of electric capitalism (McDonald 2009), for example. Hence issues of governance, financing and mobilisation are intimately connected to energy production.

As well as central roles for the state and capital, the question of who produces energy introduces questions of labour. Whose labour produces and adds value to energy and the circulation of rents from energy? Beyond core questions of ownership, there is an army of global labour extracting energy, building infrastructures for its transmission and transportation, policing and securing production sites, as well as generating demand through consumption for the labour of other workers. The provision of 'cheap' energy exacts a high price from labour and the environment, though this is true of some types of labour, in some parts of the world, and some environments more than others (Patel and Moore 2017). Globally and historically 'cheap' labour in colonised parts of the world enabled and powered energy advances in its rich centres and in many ways continues to do so today through processes of uneven exchange, ecologically and economically speaking (Hornborg 1998). Accusations that China is a new 'colonialist' because of the 'new scramble for Africa' in which it is engaged to service its domestic energy needs, often ironically made by former colonisers themselves (Ayers 2013), situate this dynamic in a more contemporary context (The Economist 2008). Decolonising transitions means ensuring that decarbonisation is not achieved in ways which deepen social, racial and historical inequalities as well as addressing past injustices.

Posing the question *for whom* energy is produced raises questions of just transitions and the construction of need. This relates to the argument sketched in Chapter 1 that some elements of the labour movement and capital currently have a common interest in resisting accelerated transitions. An anecdote from a meeting of the UN climate negotiations that I attended as part of this research is revealing in this regard. A roundtable 'debate' on 'just transitions' was taking place at an SB50 meeting in Bonn in Germany in June 2019 involving government representatives, EU officials and trade unions where all the discussion was about process: how to host dialogues involving all stakeholders in managing transitions away from fossil fuels, mainly coal in this instance. So far, so good. But, I asked the panel, since we know that at least 80 per cent of remaining coal reserves need to remain in the ground if countries are to comply with the target of the Paris Agreement (which all of them attending had signed up to do), surely the discussion is bounded: some options in terms of coal futures are no longer viable and should be off the table. And there is a clear deadline to be met to make sure that all of this happens. The silence in the room that followed my question suggested that while the process dimensions of a just transition were up for discussion, notions of limits were clearly not.

Likewise, the needs of the poor are often invoked by oil majors such as ExxonMobil or bodies such as the World Coal Institute to justify continued and expanded fossil fuel use. In a similar vein, 'pursuing clean energy equitably' (Newell et al. 2011) raises questions about the distribution of benefits between those producing energy and hosting energy infrastructures and those that consume the energy. The case of the aborted 'DESERTEC' project is instructive in this regard where the proposal was to set aside large swathes of land in the Saharan desert in North Africa in order to generate solar energy for export to wealthier consumers in Europe (Newell and Mulvaney 2013). Such dynamics emerge in scenarios of 'renewable extractivism' and emerging conflicts over land in relation to wind farms, for example (Zehner 2012; Dunlap 2018), where poorer communities are expected to serve as 'sacrifice' zones for the production of (lower carbon) electricity for wealthy urban centres, as well as around 'green conflict minerals' such as cobalt and lithium mined in the global South for principal use in the global North (Church and Crawford 2018; Sovacool 2019). Around solar, for example, there are processes of land appropriation and dispossession for solar infrastructure development. There is the mining and exploitation of mineral resources (including lithium, cobalt, silver, bauxite) for the production of solar batteries and photovoltaic (PV) modules, and even solar-powered mining operations. Issues of labour arise around working conditions, labour control and discipline at sites of manufacturing in solar supply chains (including PV modules, electronic components), global subcontracting arrangements and off-shoring and forms of unfair, bonded labour and modern slavery. Ecologically, waste from the production of toxic and electronic waste across the life cycle of solar electronic equipment is an issue and there is a politics of solar recycling initiatives (Mulvaney 2013, 2014). Questions of ownership, property rights, wealth and value creation and distribution, central to political economy accounts, run deeply through energy politics and debates about transitions.

3.1 Historicising Energy Production

Historicising energy production is important because the challenges we face today around how to undo and re-make the energy system are not new, even if the drivers of change in the contemporary context take a different form in the shape of climate change, energy security and energy poverty; sometimes referred to as the energy trilemma (Bradshaw 2010, 2013). Indeed, the study of energy transitions is full of case studies of historical shifts in energy production, technology and infrastructure (Allen 2012; Fouquet 2010). If we are to change and transform energy systems, we also need to understand, appreciate and engage with the landscape of power and social relations we encounter today, which results from decades, and centuries in some cases, of gradual lock-in and the sedimentation of networks of power, institutions and structures of financing and production that will not easily be moved. A key challenge for activists then is how to disrupt and challenge this formation while nurturing alternative alliances and bases of power.

Energy, particularly but not exclusively fossil-fuelled energy, is central to the historical evolution of capitalism, especially its industrialisation and globalisation (Altvater 2006). Coal-powered steam engines enabled the factory-based production system which both concentrated and disciplined labour in new ways, and the use of railway and steam ships to extract and transport commodities over longer distances expanded the reach of markets and created new outlets for accumulation and to deal with crises of over-production and under-consumption (Malm 2016). Fossil fuels, according to Hornborg (2013: 46), 'propelled the railways and the steamships with which Britain, frequently using military coercion, organized the metabolic flows of its global empire'. Artificial lighting played a key role in lengthening the working day in order to extract additional surplus value. 'Cheap' energy formed a key tenet of post Second World War growth, helping to consolidate US hegemony globally (Rupert 1995), while mechanisation and automation enabled mass production along Fordist lines, boosting productivity and driving consumer demand which fuelled more growth (Koch 2012).

Energy-intensive agriculture was vital to the 'green revolution' in South Asia and subsequently the global production of 'cheap food', and earlier fossil fuels brought freedom from the constraint of generating energy from the land as a form of energy that did not compete with food production. Hornborg (2013: 56) notes that 'the age of fossil fuels has kept land requirements and energy requirements conceptually distinct, justifying a pervasive trust in limitless economic growth and technological progress', a separation which the advent of biofuels nevertheless brings into question. Meanwhile, nuclear energy has been vital to states' military capabilities, significantly affecting the balance of power in the world (Pearce 2018). The issue is not of course just capitalist production. Lenin famously defined Communism as 'Soviet power plus electrification', such that the Cold War and its rivalry between capitalism and communism is shot through with the politics of energy. More recently, think of the high energy-consuming IT systems that extend the possibility of work and access to labour in unprecedented directions alongside artificial intelligence (AI) and automation. Given the multifarious links between energy and production, it is not hard to see why there is such sensitivity around discussions of limits to production or reorganising production along lower carbon lines.

The configuration of the modern energy system, however, is often dated to the industrial revolution (Malm 2016; Wrigley 2010). This is often highlighted as the starting point of what has been referred to as the Anthropocene when humans were able to unleash such powerful impacts on the environment around them as to constitute a dominant geological force (Steffen et al. 2007). In many ways, the origins of the climate crisis are to be found in the rapid expansion in the use of fossil fuels at the time of the industrial revolution in the late eighteenth century. This was the birth of fossil fuel civilisation, of what Di Muzio refers to as 'petro-market civilisation' (Di Muzio 2012). But, as Andreas Malm has shown in his book *Fossil Capital* (2016), this was not as conventionally assumed, only about coal-fired steam offering a cheaper or more abundant source of energy (Freese 2006); rather, it was about the superior control of labour that it afforded, allowing capital to concentrate production at the most profitable sites and during the most convenient hours. This story is interesting and important not only in terms of how lock-in was created, but also in relation to subsequent narratives that have been constructed about how to 'undo' lock-in and create a new (low carbon) industrial revolution by: (i) creating new sites of accumulation for capital particularly by engaging finance capital; (ii) stimulating and accelerating waves of creative destruction; and (iii) allowing the market to determine which energy sources and technologies should prevail. This is the idea that those energy pathways which are the most efficient, competitive and for which there is greatest demand will win out. It is an account devoid of the politics shaping and constraining such pathways.

Despite the complexity and breadth of the energy system over the centuries, and the undoubted role of multiple distributed agency, the principal architects of human-induced climate change, through their control over production, can be narrowed down quite significantly beyond generic framings of human responsibility for the Anthropocene. For example, just ninety companies have caused two-thirds of man-made global warming emissions including Chevron, Exxon, Shell and BP according to a study by Richard Heede (2014) published in the journal *Climatic Change*. All but seven of the ninety were energy companies producing oil, gas and coal. The remaining seven were cement manufacturers. Notably, some thirty-one of the companies that made the list were state-owned companies such as Saudi Arabia's Saudi Aramco, Russia's Gazprom and Norway's Statoil (now Equinor). So, this is about public and private businesses and the blurred lines and hybridity that characterise the space between them; an issue to which we will return in Chapter 5 on governing energy transitions. More worryingly still, half of the emissions were produced in the last twenty-five years when government and business were well aware of the threat posed by climate change. This is true in relation not only to the increasingly alarming findings of the IPCC, but also to the advice that companies such as Exxon received from their own scientists and advisers as early as 1977 that the continued rise in emissions from fossil fuels would warm the planet. This underlines the need to be more specific about who the 'we' is when referring to generic claims about 'our' responsibility to address climate change, and 'our' energy system when control over production is so heavily concentrated in so few hands.

If the industrial revolution features centrally in accounts of the origins of the fossil fuel complex, we can fast forward to the great acceleration in understanding the expansion and upscaling of the use of fossil fuels. This describes an intensification of resource use globally and across sectors in the post-war world since the 1950s. Steffen et al. (2015) show how broad trends of Fordism, and mass consumerism have intensified and globalised these modes of extraction and exchange. Increases in transportation, fertiliser use, extraction of fossil fuels, the growth of petro-chemicals and plastic set in train many of the trends that have reaped the extensive environmental destruction that we are faced with trying to manage today. The globalisation of the world economy in the 1980s and 1990s then brought with it internationalised systems of production, more mobile and deregulated finance, and waves of trade liberalisation that have locked in an export-oriented, energy-intensive global industrial model of development (Newell 2012). Indeed, half the fossil energy ever used (and half the fossil CO_2 ever produced) has been burned in just the past thirty-five years (Rees 2020). This has had an impact over the nature, depth, speed and form of energy transitions the world over, locking in pathways around extractivism governed by ideologies of comparative advantage and market rule and pursued through the privatisation and concentration of energy systems.

Oil production is particularly important in this account of acceleration and globalisation. That there is a voluminous literature on oil (Choucri 1976; Odell 1981) is unsurprising given that, as Odell (1981:11) suggests, 'it is probably the only international industry that concerns every country in the world'. Of particular interest has been the growing consolidation of oil power among the so-called 'seven sisters' (Odell 1981) where ownership and direction were developed by a small group of countries known as 'international majors', the seven companies that, at that time, controlled up to 80 per cent of oil production in the world outside of North America and the Communist world, while controlling more than 70 per cent of refining capacity and operating more than 50 per cent of international tankers. Of these international majors, five had their headquarters and the overwhelming majority of their shareholders in the USA (Standard Oil, Exxon, Mobil (when they were separate), Chevron and Texaco; the others were Shell and BP). Caldwell and Woolley, for example, writing in 1976, wrote of how oil companies had 'undertaken a quiet revolution in the last decade, during which time they established control over the remaining resources of the world' (p. 111). Of particular concern, was the vulnerability of advanced capitalist nations to the power of the oil giants captured in the title of Raymond Vernon's (1971) book *Sovereignty at Bay*. Many countries viewed control over their oil industries by major companies as a form of economic colonialism leading to limits being imposed on the freedom of oil companies operating in jurisdictions such as Chile, Brazil and Argentina where they were obliged to submit to a degree of state control (Odell 1981).

There is an interesting and significant relationship between energy and growth whose history also dates back in particular to the 1970s (Lane 2015). This is a story about the normalisation of growth as a social goal and GNP as the appropriate metric by which to measure it (Dale 2012; Barry 2018; Schmelzer 2016) in which energy came to play a central role. The exploitation of oil and the simultaneous institutionalisation of energy, understood as a system of interchangeable power sources, were key to the development of the 'growth paradigm'. Energy, largely in the form of oil, provided the material, conceptual and discursive fuel for the newly predominant post-war focus on the growth of national economies measured, defined and made comparable through the newly emergent systems of national accounts and gross national product (GNP) (Newell and Lane 2018). Caldwell and

Woolley (1976: 110) argue: 'If the environmental movement tested assumptions relating to the desirability of unlimited growth, it was the energy crisis that called into question the possibility of continued high growth.' This required political work, in particular by powerful fossil fuel interests, in making the argument that their sector served the interests of 'capital in general' as opposed to a particular fraction of capital (Newell and Paterson 1998) because the provision of cheap energy was central to the growth strategies of all other sectors. As we will see, later attempts to manage and contain critique about the limits to growth have emphasised the scope, contested by many (Mardani et al. 2019), for de-coupling, efficiency savings and the prospects of 'green growth' (OECD 2011).

Caldwell and Woolley (1976: 111) suggest that 'because the political administrative systems of advanced capitalist states are inextricably tied to the dynamic of economic growth and energy consumption, they either fail to adjust to the distributions and conflicts that accompany growth or they experience costly lags in the process of adjusting'. In a statement timeless in its relevance, they continue: 'Growth based assumptions preclude the consideration of alternative policy options and differential participation by energy industry actors results in policy decisions they help to shape.' Some of these problems derive from preferences among leading capitalist states for individual over mass transit and low taxes for industry, protective tariffs and the provision of infrastructure which had the effect of intensifying resource problems. But underpinning such manoeuvres is also a 'devout adherence to the proposition that copious supplies of cheap energy are causally linked to economic growth' (Caldwell and Woolley 1976: 113). A blind commitment to growth and the primacy of productivity focused on supply-side discovery of new resources has meant that the inefficiencies in capital and energy use which growth fosters have been ignored at great cost.

Also ignored has been the extent to which the development of today's energy system was, and continues today, to be imprinted with the legacy of ties to colonialism and extractivism through infrastructures for export, slave labour and the export of energy wealth in general (Abramsky 2010) and from specific peripheries such as the 'open veins' of Latin America described by Galeano (1997) and more recently by Hildyard (2019). Hoffmann (2018: 41) notes: 'Colonisation was quickly followed by post-colonial state building projects, many of which adopted and expanded energy intensive colonial economies.' Historically then, the evolution of the fossil fuel era intersects with a mixture of colonialism (or, more contemporarily, 'CO$_2$ Colonialism', as activists put it, to refer to the acquisition of land in poorer countries to host climate mitigation projects for richer countries reluctant to reduce their own emissions (Bachram 2004)) and patriarchy, producing racialised, class-based and gendered patterns of injustice which climate change exacerbates (Newell 2005b). This is observable in direct impacts and deprivations around impacts on land, loss of livelihood (due to changes in agriculture and loss of water etc.), disruption from extreme weather events, droughts and flooding, and indirectly through green grabs for biofuels (Smith 2000) and dispossession of land for carbon sequestration projects (Leach and Scoones 2015). These dynamics of uneven development form the basis of carbon trading whereby the South provides sites where emissions reductions are cheaper according to certain metrics: what has been referred to as 'accumulation by de-carbonisation' (Bumpus and Liverman 2008).

The history of energy is intertwined with these broader social and political struggles for political independence, democracy and resource sovereignty. Indeed, in ways which should inform contemporary debates about energy transitions, moves between energy sources in previous transitions were driven by the allure of alleged benefits of a new energy source, plus the possibility of bypassing labour resistance. In his book *Carbon Democracy*, Mitchell (2011) shows how the drive away from coal to oil was enabled by the desire to overcome the resistance that workers could mobilise by shutting down infrastructures at ports and mines. Resource curses (Ross 2012; Watts 2008), meanwhile, have enabled elites a degree of immunity from domestic democratic pressures for redistribution and improvements in welfare.

In terms of energy consumption, shifting patterns of demand drive increased production. Although widespread use of fossil fuels began in the nineteenth century, more than half of all the fossil fuels ever consumed have been burned in the period since 1950 (Pirani 2018) consistent with a Fordist model of development (Koch 2012) which was entrenched during the 'great acceleration'. This historical work on energy consumption shows that people consume energy, including fossil fuels, through technological systems that are embedded in social and economic systems. Rather than assuming that aggregate economic development and population increase have been the primary causes of the staggering growth in fossil-fuel consumption since 1950, Pirani (2018) analyses the political, economic and social factors that help to determine levels of fossil-fuel consumption. In particular, he examines industrialisation, especially the expansion of energy-intensive industries such as steel and cement production, changes in the labour process, electrification, urbanisation, motorisation and the rise of consumerism as key to explaining the shifting trajectories of energy consumption.

Although economic growth has been the main source of the relentless rise in the use of fossil fuels, the manner in which societies are organised significantly shapes their levels of energy consumption. Individuals directly consume only relatively small quantities of coal, oil and natural gas, for example, to heat and cool their homes or to power their cars. Most fossil fuels indirectly enter into the production of food, electricity, building materials, machines and consumer goods. But societies differ considerably in how they produce and consume these products reflecting uneven levels of development, geophysical characteristics and different material cultures. Even when individuals consume fossil fuels directly, they do so in a social, economic and technological context over which they often have little control (Pirani 2018) where infrastructures and the organisation of services sharply enable and constrain individual choice (Newell et al. 2015). This brings us back to the importance of broader structures of production emphasised by IPE scholars (Strange 1988).

Even as the service economy has expanded since the 1990s, new demand has driven increased energy production. Firms such as Google and Microsoft, for example, have come in for closer scrutiny for their role in driving demand for carbon-intensive energy use on their platforms and servers. At around 1.5 m tonnes of carbon, the energy usage of the online giant Google is on a par with that of the United Nations (Clark 2011). This includes cryptocurrencies such as Bitcoin. Bitcoin's annual electricity consumption adds up to 45.8 TWh, meaning annual carbon emissions range from 22.0 to 22.9 MtCO2; a level that sits between the emissions produced by the nations of Jordan and Sri Lanka (Stoll et al. 2019). The climate implications of profligate and pervasive use of computing power might undermine low carbon transitions. Conversely, the implementation of ICT solutions in five sectors – buildings, transport, manufacturing, power and 'dematerialisation' of services – has the potential to cut 7.8 metric $GtCO_2$ by 2020, 15 per cent of today's emissions (McKinsey 2008). This is not of course to disregard the role of IT and social media companies in providing space for advertising carbon-intensive products which drive energy demand nor their proffering of AI technologies to help oil and gas exploration as both Google and Amazon do (Newell 2020b). As Hoffmann (2018: 42) concludes, 'the resource use of post war hydro-carbon, automotive and real estate capitalism is more obvious, but by no means more intense than the energy hungry contemporary digital and financial capitalism'. They just move through different circuits of capital.

3.2 Political Economy of Energy Production

Political economy analysis encourages us to ask who wins, who loses, how and why? (Kelsey and Meckling 2018). Applied to energy production, it invites questions about who produces what, where and for whom? There have been historical shifts in views of who and what energy is for, as well as ideas about who produces and 'owns' it (Bremmer and Johnston 2009). As Goldthau (2012: 198) puts it: 'Like almost no other sector, energy reflects changing paradigms. Following a statist approach in which energy services were subject to public provision and administered by state companies, the free market paradigm took over in the 1980s and 1990s, making energy subject to private provision instead. More recently, the world has witnessed a new era of interventionism.' We can see this in decolonisation discourses around energy sovereignty that were prevalent in the late 1960s and 1970s including concerns that the sovereignty of countries was compromised by the power of foreign TNCs (Vernon 1971), expressed in demands for a New International Economic Order, and in more contemporary manifestations of 'resource nationalism' in places such as Iran, Bolivia and Argentina which re-nationalised YPF under President Christina Kirchner. Given its geopolitical and strategic value, energy was traditionally thought of as having to be subject to strong state control in an era of mercantilism (Kuzemko et al. 2018). Neo-mercantilism survives today in various guises (Van de Graaf and Sovacool 2020). Sensitivity around state control over energy continues to manifest itself in discussions of energy chapters in trade treaties (Newell 2007), as well as regional energy charters such as the European Energy Charter and deeply politicised discussions about regional carbon taxes and whether revenues should be collected by bodies higher than the state (Newell and Paterson 1998).

Mapping energy resources globally, it is easy to see why their uneven distribution creates political tension and conflict. There are the politics that flow from the distribution of energy importers and exporters. Kassler and Paterson (1997) describe the different vulnerability of energy exporting nations, as well as the political strategies they have used to delay action on climate change and protect their exports from carbon abatement measures including calls for compensation and the insertion of language in the text of the UNFCCC regarding their special status. Article 4.8, for example, calls for attention to measures that could have an adverse effect on 'countries whose economies are highly dependent on income generated from the production, processing and export, and/or on consumption of fossil fuels and associated energy-intensive products', while Article 4.10 refers to Parties that 'have serious difficulties in switching to alternatives' to fossil fuels. This grouping includes major oil exporters such as Saudi Arabia, Iran, Iraq, Kuwait, Venezuela and Nigeria, developing country oil and gas exporters such as Algeria, Libya, Syria and Indonesia and then industrialised countries such as Australia, Canada, Norway, Russia and Mexico. There are differences here by energy source in terms of vulnerability where since oil is a traded commodity in a global market, changes in supply, demand or price have an immediate impact on all oil suppliers, which is less true for coal and gas because substantial proportions of these are consumed within those countries or within the same region (Kassler and Paterson 1997: 6–7).

But, collectively, this group of countries has used its power to great effect to slow responses to climate change (Depledge 2008) and thereby delay the transition away from fossil fuels.

3.3 The Global Organisation of Incumbent Power

State and corporate power are closely entwined in the global fossil fuel complex. From the Pax Britannica to the Pax America and the rise of Fordism in building US global power and hegemony (Rupert 1995), we discussed in Chapter 1 in broad terms the intimate relationship between production and global power (Cox 1987; Bromley 1991). Energy is one of the pillars of power that Susan Strange describes in her book *States and Markets* (1989), albeit a 'secondary' power structure. Likewise, Ediger and Bowlus (2018: 7) state: 'Coal-powered advances in industrial manufacturing and transportation undergirded the Industrial Revolution and Britain's rise as a global hegemon.' They continue: '[S]ince the advent of fossil fuels, the global hegemon has been the largest or one of the largest producers of the dominant energy source and the leader in producing that source's related technologies – the British with coal from 1815 to 1873 and the United States with oil from 1945 to the present' (Ediger and Bowlus 2018: 7). Likewise, '[h]egemonic Britain led and shaped the global coal industry, but its production peaked in 1913' while '[t]he United States became the global hegemon in 1945 and dominated oil production and oil-related industries and technology until US production peaked in 1970' (Ediger and Bowlus 2018: 23).

In more contemporary contexts, the geopolitics of energy manifests itself in the way in which the fracking boom in the USA is sold as a mean of reducing dependence on Middle Eastern oil, as well as the geopolitics of renewable energy around access to new mining sites (IRENA 2019). Behind the commercial geopolitics of energy, there is always war (Bieler and Morton 2018). Hoffmann (2018: 40) notes how Saudi Arabia's geopolitical ambitions are 'enabled by the abundance of oil and the arms funded by its revenues', enabling it not only to become more interventionist in the region but also to maintain low prices to undermine the revenue and power of its rivals and competitors. War and energy are intimately connected through the way in which energy fuels the conduct of war and securing energy supplies is often a driver of war (Kaldor et al. 2007; Rees 2001). For example, Neale (2001) argues that, pre-9/11, the Clinton government supported the Taliban not only because it wanted peace in Afghanistan but also because of a pipeline. In the 1990s, American oil companies moved into former Soviet oil fields bordering Afghanistan and it became clear that Central Asian oil and gas reserves were much larger than previously thought. Before the collapse of the

Soviet Union, all the pipelines had been built to carry the oil north to Russia and the USA took issue with all the alternatives that were then proposed to run through China, which was an obvious competitor with US capital, or through the Caspian Sea north of Iran towards Chechnya, which Russia controlled. Neale (2001: 46) suggests: 'The US[A] needed a stable government, allied to it and Pakistan, in control of Afghanistan. The Pakistani army and the ISI suggested the Taliban could provide this, and the American government decided they were the best option.' Indeed, preceding this, it was in the wake of the Soviet invasion of Afghanistan that the USA developed the Carter doctrine in 1980 and sought to establish a military presence in the Gulf to protect oil supplies.

In considering the geopolitics of energy transitions, it is important to consider, of course, the military as a driver of shifts in consumption and demand for energy (Yergin 1991). Ediger and Bowlus (2018), for example, illustrate how geopolitics, military decision-making and energy security hastened the transition from oil to coal prior to the First World War. They show how

Britain, Germany and the United States sought to transition their naval fleets from coal to oil to gain a military advantage at sea which created, for the first time, the problem of oil-supply security. Through government-led initiatives to address oil-supply security, vast new supplies of oil came on-line and prices fell, the ideal environment for oil to eclipse coal as the dominant source in the global energy system   *(Ediger and Bowlus 2018: 1).*

They suggest: 'Geopolitics drove governments to enact the transition from coal to oil in the naval sector' (Ediger and Bowlus 2018: 5). What this reveals is how a state-led transition in the military sector paved the way for oil to become dominant in the commercial market. Interestingly, Britain, despite being the largest producer and exporter of coal, made the move to oil, in part because of fears about the warnings of William Stanley Jevons (1906) that efficiency savings might lead to a faster depletion of coal supplies than anticipated and enhanced by the 'oil mania' of Admiral Sir John Fisher, first sea lord (Ediger and Bowlus 2018: 11).

Beneath this general canvas of energy's role in geopolitical reconfigurations, energy is also, of course, used as a direct instrument of foreign policy. Financial, material and military power is used to secure energy access and expand the power of domestic energy industries through international relations. Using official UK Foreign Office data, the non-governmental organisation (NGO) Platform found out that the department's Prosperity Fund financed sixteen strategic projects focused on expanding oil and gas industries in Brazil, China, India, Mexico, the Philippines and Myanmar (Global Witness 2020). Two projects focused on creating a better 'business environment' in China by promoting the UK's approach to shale gas regulations (Markova 2018). UK Export Finance (UKEF), a little-known UK government agency that underwrites loans and insurance to help British firms secure business abroad, was found to be using 97 per cent of its energy budget on fossil fuel projects abroad from 2010 to 2017. Indeed, the group's own report published in June 2019 found that UKEF had spent £2.6 billion in the last five years supporting global energy exports. Of this, £2.5 billion went on fossil fuel projects, with the vast majority in low- and middle-income countries (Baynes 2019). Meanwhile, as part of UK government international development, the Private Infrastructure Development Group (PIDG) spent $750 million (half of its energy budget) on fossil fuels, despite calls from international development organisations urging the UK to stop funding fossil fuels abroad. Some of the projects that PIDG has supported include heavy fuel oil power plants in Senegal and Mali. Investigations showed that between 2010 and 2017 the UK spent $4.6 billion on fossil fuels overseas, across all departments (Global Witness 2020).

Energy statecraft such as this involves creating new sites of accumulation for domestic firms overseas. Trade visits are explicit in this intention. Interviews with government officials in Brazil, as part of some earlier research, revealed the energy statecraft of the Brazilian state using 'commercial diplomacy' and aid to build a global model of biofuels demand and diffusion in trading partners (Power et al. 2016), while other work showed the UK government playing the same role prospecting for opportunities for geothermal companies in Kenya (Newell and Phillips 2016) and Danish officials doing the same for wind energy companies in South Africa (Baker et al. 2014). McDonald (2009) also describes the way in which the South African state operates as a regional hegemon by mobilising its regional influence to create new sites of capital accumulation for energy providers across the African content in a process he describes as 'sub-imperialism', drawing on Bond (2005). He suggests:

In the end, the power grids of today are akin to the railway lines of colonial Africa, lacing the continent with ribbons of steel that have little connection to the social, economic or demographic needs of its people. But instead being driven solely, or largely, by European capital, this particular "scramble" for African resources is being determined primarily by the South African state and South African capital (McDonald 2009: 37).

3.4 Discursive Support to Incumbents

Global incumbency is not just maintained by the exercise of soft and hard forms of material, coercive and institutional forms of power. Discursive power is exercised through the politics of knowledge production: building the case for particular production pathways and the associated political work required to make them appear inevitable and desirable. Energy forecasting is particularly important in this endeavour. Within energy forecasts, demand is always projected to increase, so the essential work of the models is to work out which energy sources and technologies are able to close the energy gap: often foreclosing questions of reducing demand or the adoption of energy efficiency and conservation measures. Though modelling and forecasting have traditionally been thought of as neutral techniques (or technologies of governance) for guiding policy interventions in the energy domain, in reality these forecasts have often been used for partisan purposes to push through, or oppose, energy developments threatening to incumbent interests (Midttun and Baumgartner 1986).

Sometimes the politicisation is subtle; at other times it is more explicit and overt. It can operate at the level of unconscious bias and neglecting to expose basic assumptions to critical discussion. BP's energy scenarios, for example, are often taken as authoritative forecasts of potential oil reserves, without acknowledging that they often reproduce national estimates which are frequently inflated to attract investors and give no account of the actual economics or viability of extraction. At the other end of the spectrum, estimates of the potential of renewable energy produced by Greenpeace for the IPCC were ridiculed at the time, but subsequently turned out to be under-estimates of the potential of renewables. But sometimes the mobilisation of forecasts for political ends is even more explicit. Referring to the case of energy forecasting in France, for example, Midttun and Baumgartner (1986: 226) note: 'By committing Electricité de France both to energy forecasting and to an expansive nuclear production together with a commercial strategy to get rid of the energy surplus, electricity forecasts in France have become virtually self-fulfilling.' As a by-product of this, energy conservation was never seriously modelled. In some instances, the directors of studies are leading innovators and advocates for particular technologies, as happened in Germany in the case of the 'father' of fast-breeder technology (Midttun and Baumgartner 1986).

Such politics are also apparent in the work of international organisations. The IEA 'grand coalition' work with oil majors around the construction of energy scenarios has attracted controversy for the assumptions it makes about energy futures (IEA 2020b). The organisation claims that oil and gas companies have been 'proficient at delivering the fuels that form the bedrock of today's energy system; the question that they now face is whether they can help deliver climate solutions'. The analysis in their report 'highlights that this could be possible if the oil and gas industry takes the necessary steps. As such, it opens a way – which some companies are already following – for the oil and gas industry to engage with the "grand coalition" that the IEA considers essential to tackle climate change' (IEA 2020b). In an earlier move in the key *World Energy Outlook* for 2019, the IEA's 'climate' scenario (Sustainable Development Scenario) left space for at least

US$11 trillion in cumulative upstream oil and gas investment from 2021 to 2050, including more than US$5 trillion developing new oil and gas fields, investments which are clearly incompatible with achieving the goals of the Paris Agreement.

There are several key assumptions which the IEA makes to be able to sustain its position that new investment in oil and gas fields is 'needed'. First, it ignores the 1.5°C goal in its scenarios, including the Sustainable Development Goals (SDGs). In the few pages where it explores higher ambition, the IEA states that under a 1.5C pathway without large-scale negative emission technologies (NETs), 'oil demand would fall sharply through to 2050, following a trajectory closer to the decline in supply from fields already producing today' (IEA 2019). Second, it places great faith in carbon capture and storage (CCS) and negative emissions: it assumes that CCS and negative emissions technologies will suck some excess fossil fuel emissions out of the atmosphere. Ignoring carbon lock-in and assuming that markets neatly take care of excess supply, the IEA (and many other models) start with a cost curve, assuming that projects compete in markets to provide a given level of demand, and that higher-cost projects will immediately shut down as soon as global oil prices sink below their break-even costs. This then makes more space for new development. These cost-curve models disregard lock-in factors, generally assuming that existing assets shut down in a market-optimised, friction-free fashion.[1] If only it were that simple and uncontested.

Particularly at times of crisis of supply (such as around the 1974 oil crisis), or during broader legitimation crises (such as in the wake of the IPCC SR15), forecasts are subject to intense political scrutiny and are often used 'as part of inter-fuel competition for market shares in a contracting market' (Midttun and Baumgartner 1986: 219). It is perhaps unsurprising then that diverse actors have 'projected specific energy futures that would be profitable for themselves, legitimating them by the technological and/or economic rationality implicitly embedded in the modelling apparatus' (Midttun and Baumgartner 1986: 219). This contestation and jockeying for position is then transferred into more explicitly political arenas of negotiation 'where political, administrative and industrial interests compete for cognitive and methodological hegemony over the definition of the energy future through modelling and forecasting' (Midttun and Baumgartner 1986: 219). In this sense, models can best be understood as 'systematic codifications of cognitive and social structures' (Midttun and Baumgartner 1986: 220), performing important legitimating functions for policy elites and corporations in particular. But with their language of objectivity, neutrality and control variables, they provide an attractive (if problematic) route for civil society and other organisations to gain credibility and attention amongst those they are seeking to influence. As Midttun and Baumgartner (1986: 230) note: 'By invading the field of forecasting, the alternative movements gained access to a strategic political tool in a scientifically oriented society.'

By focussing on price signals and exchange rates, making certain assumptions about the performance and diffusion of technologies and rates of growth in the economy, or around levels of electricity consumption (often assumed to double every ten years, for example), positive and self-fulfilling (in so far as they provide a guide to necessary investment and policy support mechanisms) models perform the vital political work of mapping and justifying some pathways and, through neglect and disregard, downplay or undermine other possibilities (Smil 2000). For example, low energy growth scenarios are normally 'presented in sufficiently negative tones to ensure general rejection. The most optimistic view of future electricity consumption was usually adopted instead' (Midttun and Baumgartner 1986: 233). Data has to be selected, parameters defined, and ideal types worked with in order to generate scenarios and forecasts. For example, economists that dominate large-scale social system modelling employ ideal types of behaviour around optimisation through markets in their models. Econometric modelling necessarily stresses the use of price signals as policy options, while overlooking solutions that presuppose reorganisational innovation, limiting the issues that can be analysed and the questions that can be asked about reducing demand or restricting supply, for example. Moreover, despite attempts to serve policy (Parson 1995), discussion of political feasibility is almost entirely missing.

Integrated assessment models (IAMs), which many energy policy communities use, have also attracted criticism (Ayres 1984; Risbey et al. 1996). They can only plug in quantifiable data and indicators and not broader social, cultural and political phenomena which drive trends and determine acceptability and the likelihood and direction of policy change, despite attempts to quantify cultural variables (Janssen and Rotmans 1995). IAMs and sectoral models are dependent on reliable data from governments, politically constituted forecasts, and deal in moving targets and multiple uncertainties (Shackley and Wynne 1995). To take one example, there has been debate about the effect of removing fossil fuel subsidies on GHG emissions. Contrary to an IAM-based paper (Jewell et al. 2018) which argued that the effects were minimal, Erickson et al. (2020: 1) argue:

Although their approach uses common IAM techniques, it does not adequately capture investment dynamics in the supply of new fossil fuels, and therefore misses a major pathway for subsidy reform to affect CO_2 emissions. Specifically, their approach does not consider how the timing of producer subsidies (concentrated early in an investment lifetime) and the higher effective discount rates of investors (as compared with society) affect investment decisions to bring on new supplies of oil.

The argument is not for an abandonment of these models, but rather a call to make them more robust by including key political economy dynamics. Erickson et al.

(2020) suggest, for example, that fossil fuel supply in IAMs could be modelled using an investment approach and vintage capital structure, as is often applied to power plants that have upfront costs and default lifetimes. They suggest: 'The apparent small dollar values of producer subsidies in official, government-approved ledgers, and the limited emissions impact suggested by global models such as those used by Jewell et al., can be misleading. The actual impacts, particularly when one considers their social and political effects, are far greater' (Erickson et al. 2020: 2).

The important point is that methodological choices have political and institutional consequences through their determination of forecasting results that often legitimate societal planning and decision-making. Yet many such assumptions are protected from critical scrutiny and debate as professional networks and 'go-to' providers of modelling, from consultants to international agencies, hold on to their specialist power and role as knowledge brokers for incumbent actors, exercising a form of 'cognitive monopoly' (Midttun and Baumgartner 1986: 222). This inscrutability is further reinforced by the complex nature of the modelling which few are able to meaningfully challenge. The role of energy consultants is ripe for critical analytical scrutiny in this regard. Mason (2013), for example, looks at the culture of energy consulting firms engaged in projecting and realising industry futures. As Strauss et al. (2013: 25) note:

The formalization and commodification of energy knowledge by these information brokers has a significant influence on corporate and national policies, and on the assessment of risks associated with energy development. The meanings and values, both symbolic and material, that they assign to various sectors and institutions within the energy industry are packaged and reproduced across these elite communities, thus constituting new subjectivities.

Challenging these epistemic communities in the energy field and opening up their work to public scrutiny is a challenge, but one that is sometimes possible in moments of crisis. The example of the Windscale inquiry in the UK regarding a nuclear processing facility is sometimes taken as a case in point where pressure from a strengthened environmental movement (Hall 1986) and a more open-minded energy minister meant that fuller consideration was given to alternative energy forecasts (Midttun and Baumgartner 1986: 228). Likewise, in the wake of the oil crisis, Amory Lovins (1977) sought to bring in more societal dimensions to the models, as well as back casting from desirable futures so that a goal such as achieving energy independence is established and policies and pathways constructed that might achieve it. The scope for contesting the discursive hegemony of incumbents varies by country, the level of democratic space and policymaking styles. While conflicts in the UK were more open or compete in an open market (such as the USA), within many social democratic settings in Norway and

Denmark, for example, conflicts over forecasting are often kept internal to the state apparatus. Equally, in the face of strong opposition from industrial interests, more normatively oriented experiments get rejected in favour of traditional approaches to forecasting which predictably generate higher demand and supply forecasts. The state then is often at the centre of these battles over knowledge production around energy. As sources of finance and as key decision-makers, through infrastructures and ownership of major production systems, states both pursue their own interests and are the target of others seeking to secure support for their preferences.

3.5 Transitions within Business: The Business of Climate Change

The engagement of the energy sector with the threat of climate change and the need for energy transition have undergone a shift since the early 1990s when the efforts of many large users and producers of energy were heavily invested in discrediting the threat of climate change by questioning the science, highlighting the economic costs of mitigation action and using media and civil society channels, including the formation of 'astro-turf' (fake green) organisations to produce misinformation and seed confusion amongst publics (Levy and Newell 2005; Newell 2000; Newell and Paterson 1998).

With the conclusion of the Kyoto Protocol in 1997, which helped to establish global carbon markets, business attitudes, in some quarters at least, shifted (Kolk and Pinkse 2005; Pinkse and Kolk 2009; Okereke et al. 2012). Partnerships were formed with NGOs such as the Pew Centre and The Climate Group, climate change became a feature of companies' corporate social responsibility (CSR) strategies and voluntarism became the norm (Begg et al. 2005; Bumpus et al. 2015; Newell and Paterson 2010; Sullivan and Gouldson 2013). One strand of this strategy includes reporting and disclosure schemes such as the Carbon Disclosure Project, the Global Gas Flaring Initiative, as well as sector-specific initiatives of energy-intensive users such as the Cement Sustainability Initiative. Such efforts have been encouraged by governments and the scientific community, but there is a danger that voluntary standards and reporting provide a means by which corporate boards can shift responsibility for climate-related innovation to the accounting department, rather than taking a lead on it themselves. A broader risk, long emphasised in debates about CSR, is that while some corporates are drawn to voluntary initiatives, some of those incumbents that generate the most emissions stay away, suggesting the need for incentives for voluntary action ('carrots') alongside regulatory 'sticks'. For example, the majority of European firms, thought globally to be more progressive on climate change, have no CO_2 reduction targets (Neslen 2019) and only 5 per cent of companies indicate using scenario analysis to evaluate their climate-related risks and opportunities; further, amongst those companies that do disclose carrying out a scenario analysis, only half explicitly mention using a 2°C or more ambitious scenario (Vailles and Métivier 2019).

This challenge is particularly acute for many energy-intensive companies in sectors that are particularly 'sticky' and intractable in terms of the prospects of rapid decarbonisation. For example, while greenhouse gas emissions from the European power sector are on the decline, carbon pollution from heavy industry like steel, cement and chemicals has not decreased since 2012. To date, the EU's Emissions Trading Scheme (ETS) is the only tool to drive greenhouse gas emission reductions from heavy industry, but it has failed at this task according to most analysis (Stephan and Lane 2015). Due to its numerous exemptions and over-generous handout of free pollution permits, it pays companies windfall profits instead of making them pay for their pollution. This has been at the expense of other solutions including increasing energy savings and demand-side measures, scaling up renewable energy deployment and applying circular economy models.

Transport is certainly also very difficult to decarbonise. The transport sector is responsible for roughly one-quarter of emissions from the burning of fossil fuels, with road traffic being the largest culprit. Transport emissions in the G20 make up more than two-thirds of the global total, and G20 emission levels continue to grow. Transport represents 30 per cent of the total final energy demand globally, but only slightly more than 3 per cent of this energy is supplied by renewable energy, mainly biofuels (GIZ 2019). Regarding aviation, existing international climate policies for aviation will not deliver any major emission reductions according to recent studies (Larsson et al. 2019). The aviation industry in the form of ICAO (International Civil Aviation Organisation) has instead set up its own Carbon Offsetting and Reduction Scheme for International Aviation (CORSIA) in 2016 which relies heavily on controversial forestry sector offsets. The scheme was agreed by 192 countries through the UN's aviation agency. It is significant because of the aviation sector's large and rapidly increasing CO_2 emissions. If aviation were a country, it would be the sixth largest in the world, positioned between Japan and Germany. Yet the scheme can be expected to only modestly reduce the net climate impact of international aviation up to 2035 and, even then, only if high-quality offsets are used and those offsets are not 'double counted' by being sold to multiple buyers. Unless it is extended beyond 2035, CORSIA will cover only 6 per cent of projected CO_2 emissions from all international aviation between 2015 and 2050. NGOs have also raised concerns about lack of transparency in the CORSIA process and modelling of impacts and the inclusion of biofuels for aviation, leaving the door open for the use of destructive palm oil (Carbon Brief 2019). Instead, analysis of potential national aviation policy instruments shows that there are legally feasible options that could mitigate emissions in addition to the EU ETS and CORSIA. Distance-based air passenger taxes are common among EU Member States and through increased ticket prices these taxes can reduce demand for air travel and thus reduce emissions. A tax on jet fuel is also an option for domestic aviation and for international aviation if bilateral agreements are concluded (Larsson et al. 2019).

In Gramscian terms, there is a war of position underway, as incumbent actors seek to protect their political power and market access and accommodate threats to the business model through concessions to sub-altern actors, in this case environmental groups and concerned publics. Realising that attempts to discredit any action at all had failed, attempts from the mid-1990s onwards switched towards using their incumbent power to shape and then benefit from the market mechanisms that were formed in the wake of Kyoto (Stephan and Lane 2015). In Europe, the struggle was around the rules and conduct of the European Emissions Trading Scheme (ETS) which left loopholes for some actors (such as aviation) while allowing windfall profits for major energy companies such as Germany's RWE (Lohmann 2006).

Globally, moves were set in train to capture the benefits from new streams of revenue associated with the CDM created by the Kyoto Protocol in 1997. At national level, incumbent beneficiaries included 'Minerals Energy Complex' (MEC) actors such as energy majors and petro-chemical giants in South Africa, like Sasol and Eskom (Baker et al. 2014), and coal companies in India (Phillips and Newell 2013). South African industrial interests and the non-renewable electricity projects were well represented as recipients of carbon finance, including steel (Transalloys), brick (Corobrick), paper and pulp (Sappi Kraft), agribusiness (Tongaat, Omnia Fertiliser), oil (PetroSA) and mining (GFI South Africa). As Baker et al. (2014: 17) argue:

In this sense, both the number of projects developed and the lion's share of CERs [Certified Emissions Reductions] produced in South Africa have further entrenched the power of elite industrial actors central to the country's MEC, and whose main interests lie in the production and/or use of fossil fuels and in energy intensive industrial processes. These actors have the financial resources to afford the transaction costs associated with registering and managing a CDM project and high levels of institutional access to secure government support and approval for their projects.

Incumbent power can be used to secure privileged institutional access in rule-making, control market access to competitors through procurement (such as South Africa's renewable energy procurement programme which the power giant Eskom controls), while financial and material power can be deployed to manage the risks and play the system to their advantage where financial barriers exclude many smaller market actors.

Haas (2019), meanwhile, identifies five strategies used by transnational fossil fuel and nuclear energy corporations in an attempted 'passive revolution' that sought to slow Europe's energy transition and maintain dominance in Europe's electricity regime. The first of these strategies was to narrow environmental discourse in energy policy from sustainable development to energy decarbonisation. The second was to discredit and discourage the introduction of feed-in tariffs by national governments. The third strategy was to propagate the view that investment in expensive and non-competitive renewables hinders economic growth. The fourth was to effectively take over Europe's leading renewable energy industry associations. The final strategy was to restructure incumbent firms to protect traditional business models while positioning for new opportunities in renewables.

For many actors, the challenge is to show how they contribute to decarbonisation in the face of pressure to accelerate and deepen responses to climate change. The nuclear industry engaged in this opportunistic repositioning some decades ago, attending climate negotiations and presenting its industry as the most viable low carbon energy alternative. Meanwhile, with gas, a narrative has been constructed around its role as a 'transition fuel'. The French oil company Total used the hashtag #MakeThingsBetter in full-page glossy magazine adverts for its climate campaign and boasts of its investments in the 'cleanest fossil fuel', natural gas. Even ignoring the huge gap between rhetoric and reality about the bridge that natural gas is supposed to provide to a post fossil fuel future, this focus conveniently distracts from the brutal reality that Total is planning to spend around $192 billion on oil projects between 2014 and 2025 (Simms 2015). As the Oxford Institute for Energy Studies put it in a report on gas:

Significant threats and challenges to these narratives are already visible. These include short term geopolitical concerns stemming from dependence on Russian gas, 'hydrocarbon rejectionism', and an inability of companies to plan and invest for a post-2030 decarbonised future. The longer-term challenge will be to persuade governments to shift the current policy framework from competition to decarbonisation which will require a 'regulatory revolution'. But the gas community needs to be clear that, although government funding and regulatory support will be needed to achieve decarbonisation targets, very substantial corporate investment in projects for which there is currently no business case, needs to be part of its narrative. The next 5–10 years will be a crucial period for the gas community to put forward, and demonstrate how it will deliver, credible decarbonisation narratives. Failure to do so is likely to result in the adoption of electrification rather than gas decarbonisation options.[2]

Indeed, the rapid transition away from coal has placed renewed emphasis on gas. As German Chancellor Angela Merkel stated:

This conflict that you hear raging on our energy supply is also a bit exaggerated. We will continue to receive Russian gas and we will also receive liquefied gas from other sources. We're building up the infrastructure for LNG in all directions. We will also get supplies from the United States eventually. But if we leave coal, if we leave nuclear, then we will need more natural gas. Energy after all needs to be affordable   *(Mathiesen 2019).*

European gas consumption has, therefore, been on the rise in recent years, despite growing acknowledgement of the questionable climate benefits of natural gas due to methane leaks. Lobbying by this industry has been successful. The fact EU policies generally favour gas over renewables to replace coal-fired electricity has had the effect of stalling renewables development on the continent (Newell and Martin 2020).

The coal industry has not responded to this lying down. In the face of the accelerated decline of coal in some parts of the world and divestment by private financiers and sovereign wealth funds, the coal industry has faced a new threat to its legitimacy in the face of the climate crisis. For example, in January 2019, a stakeholder commission established by the German government agreed upon a schedule to decommission coal-fired power plants by 2038 at the latest and a framework for financial assistance to regions affected by the transition. Elsewhere, countries have joined a *Powering Past Coal Alliance* (Jewell et al. 2018). In the face of these drives for accelerated and managed decline, the industry has thus attempted to reinvent itself as clean, serving the needs of the energy poor. 'Coal has a fundamental role in providing access to base load electricity and is a critical building block for development', the World Coal Institute (WCI) claims. This includes '[a] pathway to zero emissions from coal'. Here the claim is that '[l]ow emission technologies exist which can make significant reductions in CO_2 emissions from coal use. High efficiency, low emission coal technologies and carbon capture and storage (CCS) are critical to meeting energy needs and our climate goals.'[3] Despite the claim of the IEA clean coal centre that it provides 'impartial information and analysis on how coal can become a much cleaner source of energy',[4] CCS is often not supported or market ready. Likewise, discursive claims about developmental benefits of ongoing fossil fuel use are at odds with large literatures on the resource curse which show that, while state and corporate elites can extract high rents from opening up new fossil fuel frontiers (Ross 2012; Watts 2009), most new energy goes to industry and not directly to meeting consumer needs, and many poorer people either a) are not connected to the grid as is the case for on average 80 per cent of people in Sub-Saharan Africa (Castellano et al. 2015) or b) cannot afford the electricity provided if they are.

Besides the question of fuel switching is the bigger question of what the role of business is in delivering what the IPCC SR15 describes as 'transformative, systemic change', at a speed and scale consistent with a 1.5°C pathway for which there are no historic precedents. To take one answer, in March 2019, Shell released a new report describing how the world might achieve the Paris goals. The report described a scenario called 'Sky', painting a picture of a possible future.[5] It is a future full of fossil fuels: in 2050, it has oil, gas and coal use at respectively 88 per cent, 93 per cent and 62 per cent of their current levels. Shell describes this as a 'rapid energy transition', albeit towards a world of climate chaos. Meanwhile, the big five oil companies have spent almost equal amounts ($200 million per year) both promoting their green credentials and lobbying to weaken climate action.[6]

There is certainly plenty of greenwash about. The American Petroleum Institute, long-term opponent of action on climate change (Newell 2000), launched a seven-figure ad campaign to confirm 'We're On It'. Even the Texas Oil and Gas Association, pushing full speed ahead on the world's largest oil expansion project, claims that it is 'absolutely committed to climate progress'. The CEO of the Climate Leadership Council recently wrote an op-ed insisting that oil and gas companies understand the scale of the challenge and 'want to be part of the solution'. We're essential 'partners' in the energy transition, the narrative goes. All the while, data from the International Energy Agency's (IEA) new report on *The Oil and Gas Industry in Energy Transitions* shows that oil and gas companies continue investing *against* a clean energy transition, directing 99.2 per cent of their capital expenditure towards fossil fuels in 2019.[7]

Yet a competitive dynamic has been set in train regarding the credibility of firms' climate commitments, with companies trying to outdo each other's claims about emissions reductions whilst also accusing one another of greenwash, as Swiss mining and trading giant Glencore did regarding BP's claims that it will achieve carbon neutrality by 2050, which it described as 'wishy-washy' (Hume 2020). The promise to halve the carbon intensity of products is potentially the most far-reaching part of BP's new strategy. It recognises that petroleum companies have a responsibility for how their products are used. Until now, they have tried to displace the blame for these so-called scope 3 emissions on to consumers. As Watts (2020) puts it, however, 'Looney, as CEO of Britain's biggest oil company, is trying to placate protesters and activist shareholders by promising to reduce the company's direct carbon emissions (those related to production, transport and other areas of operations) to zero over the next 30 years … But there is nothing in this statement to suggest BP will move away from previous plans to increase oil and gas production by 20% over the next 10 years.'

As the prospect of more meaningful and ambitious action increases, so the backlash intensifies. Contributions to political parties from fossil fuel companies have increased significantly in recent years as they feel the social pressure to address climate change. An Australian Conservation Foundation report showed that the fossil fuel industry in Australia has doubled its donations to the major parties in the past four years with the coal, oil and gas industry giving $1.9 million in 2018–19 (Knaus 2020). Meanwhile, in Brussels, Corporate Europe Observatory (CEO) et al. (2019) have exposed the level of corporate penetration of climate policymaking. Since 2010, just five oil and gas corporations and their fossil fuel lobby groups have spent at least a quarter of a billion euros buying influence at the heart of European decision-making. A key litmus test of the appetite for change of oil majors and other fossil fuel companies, then, is whether they continue to engage in and support lobbying organisations working to counter more ambitious climate action. There is a long history of this (Newell 2000; Newell and Paterson 1998), but it still goes on. For example, despite the moves described above, BP donated $500,000 to the inauguration of Donald Trump and then pushed the White House to cut environmental regulations. US government documents show that BP America lobbied in favour of Donald Trump's decision to dilute legislation, which could make it easier for new projects, such as oil pipelines and power plants, to move forward with far less federal review of their impact on the environment (Ambrose 2020). It is also a member of the American Petroleum Institute, a trade organisation that has actively campaigned against climate action and undermined climate science (Watts 2020). In Europe, meanwhile, ExxonMobil has been working hard to dilute more ambitious climate strategies. In meetings with the European Commission, lobbyists for ExxonMobil tried to stall an overhaul of the transportation sector, pushing for the EU Commission to remove the EU's strict CO_2 vehicle tailpipe standards in an effort to stall a push towards electric vehicles (EVs) (Davidson 2020).

Incumbent power is also visible at the international level. Though this might be thought to be a more acute issue at national level, there is increasing discussion about conflicts of interest at the international level. Attention has focused on delegates attending UNFCCC negotiations that are in the pay of oil companies and are able to stall progress of the negotiations by challenging the science and adopting delaying tactics in bad faith (Depledge 2008), observed most recently at the Madrid COP. For example, at COP25 more than forty Gulf state delegates were current or former employees of fossil fuel companies (Collett-White 2019). In other words, they have a clear material interest in slowing progress wherever possible and are using their veto power to block progress towards the stated aim of the negotiations, even rejecting the latest IPCC SR15 report (IPCC 2018) as a basis for action. And it is not just OPEC countries. One of Poland's leading coal companies was the first official sponsor of the UN climate talks held in Katowice. Jastrzębska Spółka Węglowa (JSW), a majority state-owned corporation and the EU's largest producer of high-quality coking coal, was an official partner for COP24. The Polish environment minister later announced that several other coal-sector companies had been chosen to sponsor the climate talks. JSW said the partnership would guarantee 'the company's active participation in the event and the possibility of promoting pro-ecological changes in the mining sector' (Farand 2018).

Amidst these efforts by incumbent actors to accommodate threats to their business models, others have shown themselves more willing to embrace fundamental changes to their business strategies. Unilever is committed to zero carbon by 2030, for example, while many leading European energy companies, notably E.On, Innogy and DONG, have changed or are changing their fundamental business models towards a stronger focus on renewable generation and grid development. Ørsted, the former Danish oil company known as DONG, plans to have reduced carbon by 97 per cent as soon as 2023 and has shifted entirely to renewable energy. An open letter from global CEOs to world leaders urged concrete climate action in the run-up to the Paris Agreement in 2015 and thereafter.[8] The coalition, convened by the World Economic Forum, comprising 43 CEOs from companies with operations in over 150 countries and territories which together generated over $1.2 trillion in revenue in 2014 stated:

[T]he private sector has a responsibility to actively engage in global efforts to reduce greenhouse gas (GHG) emissions, and to help lead the global transition to a low-carbon, climate-resilient economy. This coalition further seeks to catalyze and aggregate action and initiatives from companies from all industry sectors—towards delivering concrete climate solutions and innovations in their practices, operations and policies.[9]

The Corporate Leaders Group on Climate Change has likewise urged governments to deliver ambitious net-zero strategy and some companies have embarked on initiatives to align their corporate strategies with the goals of the Paris Agreement on climate change (Gockelen-Kozlowski 2020). Over 800 businesses are committed to meeting the 2-degree target according to the non-profit *Science Based Targets*.[10] More than 1,400 have agreed to take 'bold action' via the global coalition *We Mean Business*.[11] Climate risk assessments (CRAs) and science-based targets (SBTs) have been proposed as quantitative tools intended to mobilise action against climate change with SBTs used as a means to connect corporate carbon reduction goals to climate science and CRAs designed to help companies and investors document and mitigate climate change risks. Companies already experimenting with setting reduction targets based on climate science include British Telecom, which has a Climate Stabilization Intensity (CSI) target: a tool that links a company's financial and environmental performance to the necessary carbon reductions.

The mainstreaming of SBTs occurred through a collaboration between the WRI, the WBCSD and the CDP, culminating with the creation of the *Mind the Science, Mind the Gap* initiative in 2014 (Cummins and Aden 2014). More recently, the collaboration added the UN Global Compact and the *We Mean Business Coalition*. Combined, the organisation promotes a sector-level methodological approach towards target setting and provides guidance to private sector entities via its Science-Based Target Setting Manual (SBTi 2017). It also independently validates targets set by companies, certifying them as correctly following prescribed methodologies. To further entrench SBTs within private sector climate governance, in 2016 the CDP added SBT disclosures to its already vast climate disclosure questionnaire and scoring system (Walenta 2019). To date, according to SBTi, 850 companies are taking science-based climate action and 350 companies have approved science-based targets.[12] Such businesses include McDonald's, Wal-Mart and Unilever. SBTs have been criticised on the basis that participating firms might manipulate future financial projections to minimise targets (Trexler and Schendler 2015; Krabbe et al. 2015). In particular, they argue that the GEVA (greenhouse gas emissions per unit of value added) tool will not keep emissions within the budget and only a small number of firms can actually consider the aggressive targets needed. It is clear then that we need improved methods to derive consistent corporate target setting that keeps cumulative corporate GHG emissions within a specific carbon budget. Krabbe et al. (2015), for example, propose a method for corporate emissions target setting that derives carbon intensity pathways for companies based on sectoral pathways from existing mitigation scenarios: the Sectoral Decarbonization Approach (SDA).

Moreover, judging both by high levels of ongoing fossil fuel subsidies (Ericksen et al. 2020), which the IMF calculates to run at $10 million a minute (IMF 2015), and by the expansion in some areas of the world of coal, the very dirtiest energy source, and the opening up of new frontiers of extraction of oil, tar sands and fracking, it is clear that, while some battles are being won, the war is far from over. A report from the NGO Global Witness reveals that all of the $4.9 trillion in forecast investments in new oil and gas field production are incompatible with the IPCC's 1.5°C pathways (Global Witness 2019).

3.6 Labour

Questions of production and capital's ownership of the means of production cannot be divorced from questions of labour and livelihoods. It was argued earlier that the intimate connection between energy, land, labour and livelihoods provides a key rationale for understanding energy transitions in political economy terms.

Firstly, there is the question of the employment implications of different energy pathways. Large numbers of jobs are tied up with the fossil fuel industry, though there are big differences by region and fuel source. Even in Europe, where there has been some progress in moving beyond coal, there are forty-one regions in twelve EU Member States still mining coal. Further, 25 per cent of electricity comes from coal and across Europe the sector employs 185,000 workers directly and 400,000 indirectly.[13] Though coal extraction is not a large employer in aggregate, the employment effects are frequently used to justify opposition to mine closures or limit the transition away from coal. For example, in 2016 coal mining accounted for just under 66,000 jobs in the USA compared to a total employment of 153 million, but these jobs are concentrated in a small number of regions.[14] In India, coal mining accounted for around 358,500 direct jobs in 2012, out of a workforce in the order of 490 million. Australia has a pipeline of approved coal mines that stretches into the 2040s, but even if new coal mines were not approved, the impact on employment would be 0.04 per cent. That's because, despite exporting lots of coal, coal mining employs few people: 99 per cent of Australians do not work in coal mining and new mines threaten these existing jobs.[15]

Historical examples demonstrate, however, that significant transition in the coal extraction sector has been accompanied by large, persistent and painful social dislocation, such as occurred in the UK coal mining regions in the 1980s (Parker 1994; Hudson and Sadler 1987). But it is also the case that, as we have seen with the 'gilet jaunes' (yellow vest) protests in France, the role of climate abatement measures in displacing workers is often exaggerated and strategically motivated. As one report notes:

On the one hand, climate change solutions, like greenhouse gas regulation and carbon pricing, raise concerns about potential job displacement for workers in traditional energy sectors like oil and gas production and fossil-fuel generated electricity. Hence the calls for just transition. Our research, however, suggests that this blame may be at least partially misplaced. Energy workforce changes are currently affected by broader societal changes relating to fuel-cost differentials (i.e., natural gas cheaper than coal), automation, and the societal transition to non-unionized, unstable and lower-paying work. Greenhouse gas regulations and carbon pricing are certainly not the only driver of workforce change, and likely not, at least currently, the primary driver.

(Comeau and Luke 2018)

Given the painful experience of the rapid and forced decline of coal in the UK, it is unsurprising that the labour movement has taken up climate change issues following labour groups across Europe and in several countries around the world (Stevis and Felli 2015; Räthzel and Uzzell 2013). In 2013, the Trade Union Congress (TUC) in the UK unanimously passed a resolution for a moratorium against fracking, and unions have deployed innovative and traditional organising methods to oppose fracking (Metze and Dodge 2016). Representatives from major unions have campaigned alongside communities living near fracking sites to protest the development of the industry, called for disinvestment, lobbied the Labour Party, and worked with members and the public to promote their message. Meanwhile, unions representing energy workers are divided in their support for fracking. Unions like the Public Commercial and Service (PCS), representing 150,000 civil servants, and Labour coalitions like the 'Greener Jobs Alliance' are engaged in creating dialogue and actions with workers, including with miners and gas workers who have other perspectives, as well as with community activists to build a more united movement. Their efforts are part of a broader conversation that trade unionists in many countries are having around the future of work and energy and climate justice. Sam Mason (2019) argues:

> For too long, trade union debates on climate change have got stuck in a discourse that in calling for the end of the fossil-fuelled economy, is to call for workers to be made redundant. Rarely do we ground this in threats to the long-term impact on people's existence particularly in the global south, emergency responders, or other workers whose jobs may be destroyed as a consequence of a continued pursuit of greenhouse gas emitting jobs. In a movement built on solidarity, it's intriguing that a fossil fuel energy workers protectionism seems to be emerging that centres the energy transition and climate change responses to one exclusive group of workers. This is as opposed to confronting it politically and collectively by challenging the neo-liberal economic model that has sought to commoditise carbon and nature in the same way it has public goods and labour. The UN Intergovernmental Panel on Climate Change (IPCC) report in October 2018 set out in stark terms the 'rapid and far-reaching transitions in energy, land, urban and infrastructure (including transport and buildings), and industrial systems' which are needed to stabilise the climate. Confronting this task requires us to think and act beyond our sectoral interests, but can trade unions relinquish their fossil fuel industrial model and put themselves at the vanguard for a green and fair future? (Mason 2019).

These tensions are very real and surfaced in the USA in debates about a possible Green New Deal where some environmentalists argued that '[i]f we consider climate change an urgent existential threat that justifies the Paris climate targets, then at the very least phasing out fossil fuels and carbon pollution must be our top priority when crafting climate policy. Other concerns that undermine zero-carbon energy sources must be secondary, lest we sabotage our own climate-preserving efforts.'[16] These tensions are alive throughout the trade union movement. Despite the positive embrace of climate issues by some trade unions such as the PCS, as described by Sam Mason (2019) above, placing emphasis on creating jobs for energy workers in general (rather than just protecting jobs in fossil fuel sectors), there have been strong counter-moves by larger unions such as UNITE and GMB seeking to control the 'just transition' agenda, even challenging the viability and ambition of the UK Labour Party's timetable for a zero carbon commitment in its manifesto in the 2019 general election.

3.7 The Shifting Governance of Energy Production

The shifting terrain of global energy politics has not just affected capital and labour. There has been an evolution in approaches to governing energy production particularly with regard to the appropriate role of the state which, in turn, reflects deeper shifts in neo-liberalism. Electricity remains 'an essential feature of most post-Fordist accumulation regimes' (McDonald 2009: 7), but there has also been an important and discernible shift in ideologies of governance, which I describe further in Chapter 5. Neo-liberalism has brought with it a shift in ideas about the efficient and cost-effective provision of energy services centred on power sector reform and the unbundling of generation, transmission and distribution functions (Tellam 2000). Material power has been mobilised to enforce this ideological shift, primarily in the form of disciplinary neo-liberalism. Rewards are provided for following the line. This is visible in the giving and taking of aid. Kenya, for example, is often compared favourably with neighbours such as Tanzania, on the basis that, as a World Bank official puts it, 'Kenya has always been private sector focused and avoided the virulent forms of socialism of some of its neighbours' (Newell and Phillips 2016: 43). Aid is made conditional upon adopting the 'right' reforms. Power sector reform has been rewarded by support from bilateral and multilateral donors, opening up opportunities for foreign capital to meet the shortfall in energy supply (Tellam 2000) as part of what McDonald calls 'electric capitalism' (McDonald 2009).

This has been an uneven shift, however. In many contexts, states retain tight control over the nature and pace of energy transitions (Baker et al. 2014). There are varieties of energy sector privatisation and power sector reform, but many follow a common recipe. This includes the divestiture of state assets to private firms, the introduction of independent power producers and electricity distributors, the unbundling of generation, distribution and transmission and the contracting out of services and functions and the corresponding collection of user fees (McDonald 2009; Dubash et al. 2018). The outsourcing of services includes meter reading, infrastructure maintenance, fleet management and revenue collection. As noted in the Kenyan context (Newell and Phillips 2016) and pertains in the case of South Africa (Baker et al. 2014), 'privatisation is not an either/or situation' (McDonald 2009: 23) but, rather, reflects a reconfiguration of authority for the delivery of an accumulation strategy that benefits public and private actors and where the boundary between the two is clearly very blurred. It also extends into the introduction of private sector operating principles and forms of managerialism into the public sector around performance targets, surplus maximisation, cost recovery and competitive bidding through procurement programmes and the like. In the context of electricity in South Africa, McDonald (2009: 447) notes:

Publicly owned and operated though they may be, demands on electricity utilities by private firms and transnational elites for 'competitive' pricing, cost recovery, Taylorised management systems and macroeconomic planning that promotes outward-oriented trade regimes that compel these public entities to behave like private enterprises, forcing them to provide the kind of multi-tiered services needed to attract multinational capital while keeping a lid on subsidies for the poor.

What this means for energy transitions is that they are increasingly framed and enacted according to these neo-liberal proscriptions with a strong emphasis on private provision, unbundling and pricing mechanisms over regulation to achieve stated goals.

Sometimes this institutional work is called de-politicisation, but it actually requires immense political work on the part of actors like the World Bank: policing boundaries of what is at stake and preparing the ground for interventions which facilitate foreign investment. For example, when doing some work on energy transitions in Kenya, I was told how this process unfolds. Firstly, consultants prepare a study on the energy sector which inevitably highlights the need for power sector reform, unbundling and privatisation. Donors then help fund a strategy and process to implement this, which the government is expected to adopt because the donors are financing it. Then a series of investor events and trade fairs are hosted for businesses to assess investment opportunities facilitated by donor governments. Finally, the programmes of reform can commence (Newell and Phillips 2016). To attract foreign capital, for example, the Kenyan state has sought to provide an enabling environment to develop the country's geothermal sites, channelled through a government-owned special purpose vehicle, the Geothermal Development Company (GDC), which has been established to assume the risk of resource mapping and exploration that the private sector is unwilling to take. In other words, it distributes risk in favour of capital. Such interventions are employed to promote a private-led model of development (while allowing ample opportunity for the collection of rents by the state), which has significant export potential.

We also see the imprint of neo-liberal ideologies in governance for production. As I will also discuss in Chapter 5, a great deal of governance is aimed at securing and expanding production, locking in and protecting investor rights and interests, creating new openings and frontiers for production. Trade agreements help to secure this, as do bespoke energy agreements such as the Energy Charter Treaty (ECT). The ECT is the international community's most significant multilateral instrument for the promotion of cooperation in the energy sector and provides the legal basis for an open and 'non-discriminatory' energy market (Konoplyanik and Wälde 2006). It is also, together with the North American Free Trade Agreement (NAFTA), one of the most important multilateral treaties providing for the promotion and protection of investments (Dore and de Bauw 1995). The ECT was signed on 17 December 1994 and entered into force on 16 April 1998. It now binds forty-eight states as well as the European Communities. The ECT was adopted with a view to pursuing, on a legally binding basis, the objectives and principles of the European Energy Charter of 1991. The Treaty's Preamble defines these objectives as including, in particular, the creation of commitments on 'a secure and binding international legal basis' and of a 'structural framework required to implement the principles enunciated in the European Energy Charter' (ECT 1994: Preamble).

In the context of a global energy market, the creation of a single investment area has appeared as one of the means of achieving a unique playing field in the energy sector. One of the chief features of the ECT is indeed the promotion and protection of investments in the energy sector. Part III of the Treaty, entitled 'Investment promotion and protection', offers protection that is similar to that accorded by most bilateral investment treaties, including such rights as the fair and equitable treatment, the most constant protection and security of investments, the prohibition of discriminatory measures, the most-favoured-nation treatment, and the payment of prompt, adequate and effective compensation for any nationalisation, expropriation or measures having an effect equivalent to nationalisation or expropriation. The Treaty further provides for binding international dispute settlement, in particular with respect to investment disputes (Ribiero 2006).

Besides these forms of regional and global lock-in around the export of energy and the conduct of trade along (neo-)liberal lines, at the national level we have also seen efforts made to consciously and deliberately roll back environmental protections and safeguards to enable further forms of energy extractivism. Examples would include the tar sands in Canada and Arctic drilling in the USA. In political economy terms, the state plays a key role in managing cycles of crisis that are intrinsic to capitalism and its renewal. The state needs to adjudicate between the competing needs of different fractions of capital and to manage, assuage and contain opposition to energy production from activists and communities, in many parts of the world through violent means (Global Witness 2017). Energy producers seek from the state legally enforceable rules-based frameworks which protect their investments, even from the state itself, as we saw in the case of the ECT and from political interference and social conflict (Dore and de Bauw 1995). As noted later, even in countries that have gone through 'shock therapy' and largely privatised their energy sectors, private sector participation and regulation needs to be facilitated and enforced by the state. Many of the underlying risks associated with constructing and then maintaining and protecting infrastructures still fall to states.

The ideology and practices of the governance of energy production do not, however powerful they may seem, form part of an unquestioned, hegemonic project. Neo-liberalisation is best understood as a process – a non-linear one –

and not an end state. I have noted already the uneven nature of implementation and roll-out of neo-liberal programmes. They are full of tensions and contradictions rather than working as a uniform, imposed and uncontested project. Practices of neo-liberalism in the energy sector take different forms in distinct settings reflecting the varieties of capitalism into which they are inserted (Hall and Soskice 2001). This provides important entry points for change. Continual political work is involved in managing and obscuring structural contradictions that derive from the nature of energy in the economy and ecology and the competing goals of accumulation and legitimation that states seek to pursue simultaneously. Discursively, we can see how power is exercised in the accommodations and framing around the need to manage the tensions and contradictions between growth in energy use on the one hand, and environmental limits and resource constraints on the other, which find expression in appeals for 'green growth' where, whatever the problem, more growth is always the answer. The consequence of the processes I have described, nevertheless, is a failure to face up to the need for structural change and transformation and deal with the inherent unsustainability of conventional energy models.

3.8 Ecologies of Energy Production

As with other chapters in this book, ecology is invoked as a metaphor or approach to capturing interconnected dimensions of production, which is useful in capturing and explaining the functioning of energy assemblages, as well as in a literal sense of how energy systems are made of, are part of, impact upon and are subsumed within ecological systems.

In this vein, some scholars have used ideas about 'global production networks' to describe causal links between the organisational configurations of global production networks and uneven development (Coe and Yeung 2019). The concept has been applied to understanding the assemblages of energy systems, around solar PV, for example, to produce an 'analysis of the complex and multi-scalar relationships that exist between international and local institutions, as well as the embedded nature of renewable energy technology within a national and international political economy' (Baker and Sovacool 2017: 1). Others draw on the earlier literature on value chains (Gereffi et al. 2005) to understand the drivers of low carbon energy transitions (Shen and Power 2017; Schmitz 2017). An important dimension here is that 'as the complexity of production increases–including the distance between investors, producers, retailers, and consumers–the distribution of power in decision-making forums and production systems continues to shift, making it more difficult to identify and regulate actors across them' (Harnesk and Brogaard 2017:

158). This becomes important when seeking to apportion responsibility and liability for pollution and waste, for example, as well as identifying opportunities for environmental upgrading along value chains (Ponte 2019) or what other scholars refer to as 'global wealth chains' (Seabrooke and Wigan 2017). It raises the familiar problem of distancing that environmental justice scholars have drawn attention to, or what feminist scholars such as Plumwood (2002) describe as 'remoteness', whereby privileged classes remain spatially, temporarily, epistemologically and technologically remote from the ecological consequences of their decisions and choices in relation to production in ways that perpetuate ecological irrationality and environmental injustice.

In thinking ecologically about energy systems, there are several possible points of departure. Lifecycle analysis captures inputs of water (hydro, nuclear), demands on land (wind, solar, biofuels, biomass), impacts on biodiversity (wind) and use of chemicals (coal, oil, nuclear, solar PV), for example (Lund and Biswas 2008; Sørensen 2011). As Lund and Biswas (2008: 200) suggest: 'The lifecycle concept is a "cradle to grave" approach to thinking about products, processes, and services, recognizing that all stages have environmental and economic impacts. Any rigorous and meaningful comparison of energy supply options must be done using a lifecycle analysis approach.' This allows us to think more holistically in terms of inputs for manufacture, transportation and waste. Think, for example, of steel and cement for wind turbines, or cement for nuclear power plants. In other words, there is no such thing as 'clean' energy, only cleaner (and less polluting) forms of energy production. It is the case, however, that some systems of production, and their associated social relations, distribute those burdens more unevenly and unjustly than others within and across societies. This forms the starting point for some of the resistance strategies described in Chapter 5.

Nexus thinking also potentially enables an appreciation of the interrelated elements of water, energy and food (land) that need to be simultaneously addressed in any energy transition pathway (Kuzemko et al. 2018). It broadens the criteria for assessing energy pathways in relation to energy poverty, security and sustainability to include broader eco-systemic impacts and considerations. Acknowledging these connections does not of course do away with the conflicts and contestations that arise around attempts to govern multiple and interconnected policy goals, as demonstrated in relation to the governance of the 'nexus' around water, energy and food (Scott 2017; Weitz et al. 2017; Allouche et al. 2019; Zelli et al. 2020). The SDGs, agreed in 2015, explicitly recognised the 'integrated and indivisible' interconnections between sustainability goals, and are novel in the extent to which they attempt to move beyond traditional policy

siloes (United Nations 2015), but they provide few proscriptions for doing so. As
Weitz et al. (2017) argue, while the literature on the nexus around water, energy
and food identifies barriers to achieving coherence, it tends to do so without
exploring why such barriers are present, and what influences them, while ignoring the non-linearity and complexity of governance processes. Key barriers to
policy coherence include the unequal distribution of power, voice, access to
information, resources and capability among actors and institutions that inevitably derive from a political process of negotiation among unequal partners
(Allouche et al. 2019).

Concepts such as 'ecologically uneven exchange' are helpful for documenting
and understanding global ecological inequalities around energy extractivism, or
in relation to the import and export of energy through trade and the virtual carbon
embedded in these patterns of exchange which cloud and complicate processes of
allocating responsibility to address climate change (Foster and Holleman 2014).
As Roberts and Parks (2008: 169) show, forms of 'ecologically uneven exchange'
mean that the responsibility for pollution, as well as the pollution itself, is
redistributed globally such that: '(e)missions are increasing sharply in developing
countries as wealthy countries 'offshore' the energy and resource intensive stages
of production'.

Hornborg (2013) shows more broadly how energy/environment/food/water/
climate/financial crises are facets of a single problem: the fundamental and
incongruous relationship between modern social institutions and the law of
 entropy (the second law of thermodynamics). He suggests: 'As long as our
societal pursuit of economic growth is based on expanding combustion of finite
stocks of fossil fuels, our cultural understanding of growth and progress is thus
completely at odds with what natural law can tell us' (Hornborg 2013: 42).
Several writers raise the prospect that renewable forms of energy will struggle to
do the same work that fossil fuels have for capitalists, which suggests caution
about their future (Altvater 2006). Abramsky (2010: 11) suggests: 'It will take
many years before it is clear whether capital can harness new combinations of
energy that are capable of imposing and maintaining a certain stable (and
profitable) organization of work in the way that fossil fuels have allowed.' In
capitalism, it is also the case that there are always 'sacrifice zones' including for
energy (Abramsky 2010; McDonald 2009). The host communities of energy
projects are often not the beneficiaries as pointed to by the experience of the
DESERTEC project mentioned previously (Newell et al. 2011), but also observable in the new frontiers of renewable extractivism (Sovacool 2019).

Let us take the case of EVs as an example of how debates about the uneven
ecologies of different energy pathways play out in practice. I will quote anonymously

from an email exchange about EVs among scholars of energy transitions that went as follows:

Comment 1: 'German researchers have published research showing that an electric vehicle has greater life-cycle greenhouse gas emissions than a diesel vehicle. This analysis is based on the premise of an electricity mix like that of Germany, where coal still plays a big role (as it does many countries). However, if the energy mix is dominated by renewables, the EV comes out with lower emissions – but still far from zero. In my opinion, EVs are getting too much attention and resources, while public transport, pedestrians, cycling and various forms of electric micro-mobility are not getting enough attention.'

Comment 2: '[T]here are many studies out there that show different results. You are right that EVs is not a silver bullet and that mass production and use of EVs do not offer a sustainable solution. But if we agree that individual mobility is a value in some contexts and to some extent then, based on the facts I am aware of and considering the ongoing transitions towards renewable electricity, it makes sense to replace petrol and diesel cars with EVs for the sake of climate mitigation but also for air pollution & noise reduction and grid stability.'

Comment 3: 'Agreed, but what we're talking about here for me is less embodied energy concerns but the embodiment of concerns through the invisibilization of context. . . . The contexts within which issues such as biofuels and EVs are considered, however, is highly restricted – the systemic consideration of mass consumer capitalism is simply invisibilized as taken-for-granted, reduced to a doxa, Bourdieu's (1977) concept of something so generally accepted that it 'goes without saying because it comes without saying'. . . . surely the time for us to indulge in that particular luxury is long past and we need to be taking holistic systemic change into consideration every time we talk about embodied energy.' The discussion around EVs is similar to the one around biofuels; it's a piece-meal method of not looking at the 800lb gorilla in the room, mass consumption, and replacing some parts of it with renewable alternatives. We've already seen the massive destruction wrought by biofuels to sate the European hunger for replacing fossil fuels and pretending that makes a real difference; please don't let's go down the same path with EVs. The social may not always be technical, but the technical is always and endlessly social, and now geopolitical'.

Here we see the tension between 'incrementalism' and more radical proposals for reform and between transition and transformation around notions of substitutability and least worst scenarios, as opposed to moves to disrupt larger incumbent models of politics and economics that I discuss throughout the book.

A more global ecological account, as being advocated here, would need to trace and document the global flows and shadows of proposed alternative technologies and infrastructures. For example, in a letter to the UK Climate Change Committee by Professor Richard Herrington, it was suggested that the metal resource needed to make all cars and vans electric by 2050 and all sales to be purely battery electric by 2035 represents just under twice the total annual world cobalt production, nearly the entire world production of neodymium, three-quarters of the world's lithium production and at least half of the world's copper production during 2018. Moreover, extrapolating globally to the currently projected estimate of two billion cars worldwide, annual production would have to increase for neodymium and dysprosium by 70 per cent, copper output would need to more than double and cobalt output would need to increase at least three and a half times for the entire period from now until 2050 to satisfy the demand.[17]

This type of analysis points to the limits of what I have described in the book as 'plug and play' approaches to energy transition and suggests, picking up on the case above, for example, the need for a more frontal effort to address car culture and automobility as part of a shift towards more public and collective forms of transportation (Paterson 2006; Böhm et al. 2006). In other words, from a sustainability point of view, energy transitions cannot have as their primary aim servicing ever greater demands for more. As we've seen, electrification of everything exacts a heavy cost in terms of extracting natural resources.

Questions of reduced inputs through off-grid, micro and household generation bring us back to the political economy of *who* and *what* energy is for, which we introduced at the very start of the book. This underlines the critical importance of reducing demand and, from a more radical green point of view, a level of localisation to avoid transportation and waste as part of the deliberate shortening of circuits of production and consumption (Douthwaite 1996). A 'circular economy', for example, would turn goods that are at the end of their service life into resources for others, closing loops in industrial ecosystems and minimising waste (Raworth 2017). It would change economic logic because it replaces production with sufficiency: reuse what you can, recycle what cannot be reused, repair what is broken, remanufacture what cannot be repaired. A study of seven European nations found that a shift to a circular economy would reduce each nation's greenhouse-gas emissions by up to 70 per cent and grow its workforce by about 4 per cent (Stahel 2016). Circular-economy business models fall into two groups: those that foster reuse and extend service life through repair, remanufacture, upgrades and retrofits; and those that turn old goods into as new resources by recycling the materials. People are central to the model. Ownership gives way to stewardship; consumers become users and creators. In other words, control over production and shifts in power take place.

Placing ecology and sustainability front and centre means addressing limits and supply: using law and policy to enforce and recognise ecological limits (to production). In relation to energy, this means leaving large swathes of remaining fossil fuels in the ground and enforcing production limits (SEI et al. 2019). As noted already, there is growing momentum behind the idea of supply-side policy (Ericksen et al. 2018; Newell and Taylor 2020) including not only national policy measures such as moratoria and phase-outs, but sector-wide coalitions such as the *Powering Past Coal Alliance* and more general calls for a fossil fuel non-proliferation treaty (Newell and

Simms 2019). But there is also a need to address the social dimensions of enforcing limits. Managing decline in production in socially responsible ways presents a huge challenge (Kartha et al. 2018).

The example of Indonesia shows that phasing out oil and gas production can be done without major disruption to the government's budget and GDP (gross domestic product), even for a developing, lower-middle-income country. Oil and gas extraction decline in Indonesia happened due to a combination of geological maturation of fields and uncertainty over policies governing the sector rather than as a consequence of the government's direct intent, but the consequences of this development can be likened to those of a conscious managed decline. Since the beginning of the twenty-first century, Indonesia experienced a drop in government revenues from upstream oil and gas – from 35 per cent of the total revenues (7 per cent of GDP) in 2001 to just 6 per cent (less than 1 per cent of GDP) in 2016. Meanwhile, Indonesia's rates of GDP growth (at 3–4 per cent per year) and budget deficit (at 2–3 per cent) remained largely unchanged. In Indonesia between 2014 and 2016, oil and gas extraction contributed only 3.7 per cent of GDP, while coal mining contributed only 2.1 per cent of GDP.[18] This speaks to the tendency, noted already, of incumbents to exaggerate the importance of the fossil fuel sector in the economy.

Yet, both within and across societies, uneven social impacts have to be managed. Caney (2016) argues that an equitable approach to stranding assets should give priority to those who a) have a lower standard of living as measured by the Human Development Index, b) have extracted and benefitted least from past fossil fuel extraction and c) have the fewest alternative means of meeting their development needs. A complex set of factors is, nevertheless, involved in arriving at judgements about whether compensation is due and against which baseline when the determination of whether assets are stranded or not results as much from the falling costs of renewable alternatives such as solar or other drivers as the desire to keep fossil fuels in the ground (Lenferna 2018). In other words, is compensation owed only where climate protection is the explicit policy driver? If so, establishing that this is the case is still far from easy. And does this disincentivise state-led restrictions on production, which have been made without the carrot of compensation such as Costa Rica's 2011 moratorium on oil exploration?

3.9 Production as If the Planet Mattered

We come back, inevitably, to the question of the role of business at this juncture. Given that the IPCC SR15 made clear that we have twelve years to avoid catastrophic consequences associated with further global heating, structures of production will need to shift at historically unprecedented scales and speed. We also need reductions in demand, reduced consumption and not just shifts in production. This is clearly a far more difficult challenge of *business as unusual*. As writer Andrew Simms (2015) suggests: 'The acid test for business leadership on sustainability will be when they tell us to consume less of what they produce so we can live within our planetary means.'

Debates about energy transitions – their purpose, direction, speed and politics – cannot be divorced from these broader and critical debates about the sustainability of capitalism or industrialism more broadly (O'Connor 1991; Trainer 1996; Newell 2019). With a few exceptions (Feola 2019), they are often given scant attention in discussions about transitions, where they are often seen as tangential to the core concerns of transition scholars (Köhler et al. 2019; Newell 2019). Yet my argument here is that if we bracket the question 'transition to what?' and do not address the compatibility of the reconfiguration of sociotechnical systems with a more sustainable society, we fail to engage with one of the most pressing normative issues of our time. This means that besides being attentive to the co-evolution and constitution of technical and social systems, we need to ask and answer bigger questions about whether the broader economic system of which they are a part and which they sustain is viable on a finite planet. This means addressing larger questions of ownership, purpose and control of the means of production: who it serves, how and why, and whether we can envisage, engage with and support alternative ways of organising production in society that are compatible with realising social justice and sustainability and may involve conscious efforts to produce less, share more and consume less.

Besides conducting studies of particular sociotechnical reconfigurations in specific sectors, supply chains or regions, it means seeking to aggregate up and keep in mind the bigger picture of whether the patterns of production and consumption being built, expanded, rolled out and locked in are contributing to a more sustainable society. As Boyle (2019) puts it:

[T]here is a critical element of transition which is too often ignored. To make it work, we have to seriously reduce consumption, which means selling less stuff. It is all very well if you are an oil company putting in a few solar panels, but – are you prepared to shift out of fossil fuels entirely? And even if you are selling renewable energy, can you work out a business model that allows you to survive when you are able to sell a good deal less of it?

Wilhite (2013: 61) argues that the prospects for achieving this are 'grim': 'From the origins of the energy effort following on the oil shocks of the 1970s, governments have been reluctant to enact robust energy-reduction policies due to concerns about the consequences for employment, profits and economic growth. Policy efforts have been weak and fragmented.' Nevertheless, in order to re-launch a new cycle of accumulation, capital has to tackle this energy crisis. Without the forms of resistance described in Chapter 6 on mobilising, this could imply new adjustments, enclosures, dispossessions and forms of disciplining labour and social movements. As McDonald (2009: 6) puts it:

Electricity infrastructure is ... increasingly central to renewed capitalist production and accumulation. Electricity may not loom large in every accumulation crisis, but it often plays a critical role in rebuilding of the productive assets required for reconfigured accumulation regimes: new power plants for increased electricity demands; updated technologies for new production systems; expanded grid lines into new geographic areas of production and consumption.

Yet, these (spatial) fixes are necessarily temporary, unpredictable and unstable and can be unsettled by the shifting whims and formations of finance capital, the theme of the next chapter.

4

Financing Energy Transitions

Energy production needs to be financed. Traditionally it has been financed by governments, banks and corporations, but, increasingly, smaller business actors and even civil society organisations are also playing a role in funding alternative energy pathways. The energy sector is also subject to broader trends towards financialisation that have swept across other areas of the economy (Fine 2017). Energy futures are bought and sold on markets, and carbon credits get traded, while new asset classes are created from green bonds to finance climate mitigation, to new forms of insurance and derivatives for climate adaptation. Finance is the lubricant of the (energy) economy and can work to uphold and sustain the fossil fuel complex and incumbent actors or to accelerate their demise by switching investments into lower carbon forms of energy or, of course, to finance both pathways simultaneously.

The historical tension between creative construction and destruction of technologies and infrastructures brought about by finance capital is also apparent in the energy domain (Perez 2002). A central challenge in terms of the ecologies and sustainability of finance relates to the role of finance in an economy organised around sufficiency and producing and consuming less, not just differently, in which there are fewer outlets for profitable investment, as may be required by more radical visions of energy transformation. Finance has a powerful role to play in enabling and accelerating the transition to a lower carbon economy and we will always need money. But conventional finance is unlikely to play a key role in future energy systems organised along greener lines because of its expectations of high short-term returns and its near structural blindness to environmental considerations and negation of limits.

This chapter briefly explores the historical role of finance capital in fuelling energy booms and the growth of the fossil fuel economy, before looking at emerging shifts in strategy towards a more destabilising role in the face of concerns about un-burnable carbon and fears about the risk of stranded assets, as well as the potential returns to be made from expanding investments in renewable energy. In

Section 4.4 on the political economy of finance, however, I nuance this more optimistic reading of the role of finance, derived from an historical reading of its potential to drive waves of creative destruction, by looking at the practices of finance in the contemporary economy. Whether driving unbundling, power sector reform and the de-risking of energy assets and investment opportunities by governments and donors for international capital, or the creation of new financial instruments and asset classes for speculative profit, the power of finance is, to say the least, a mixed blessing when it comes to energy transitions, let alone deeper transformations.

Finally then, in Section 4.8 on ecologies of finance, not only do I look at the circulation and interconnectedness of different forms of finance, in which, despite the fetishisation of private finance, public finance still has a vital role to play in the form of aid, multilateral development bank (MDB) lending and procurement; I also explore the under-acknowledged challenge for finance of energy systems which will have to restrict supply and demand if they are to be compatible with a sustainable climate future. Here we encounter the structural limits of relying on the transformative potential of a financial system, however well realigned to the imperatives of sustainability in the short term, which, for the purposes of its own reproduction, has to seek out new sites of accumulation and fabricate new needs and demands and in so doing fuels unsustainable patterns of production and consumption. Following the money tells us a lot about which sorts of energy transitions different types of finance are willing and able to support, as well as those which they are not (Spratt 2015).

Which and *whose* energy transitions will be financed and *how* is a key topic of debate and often a stalling point in mobilising support for transitions. In the climate change negotiations, the lack of funding for lower carbon development pathways in poorer countries through 'new and additional finance' has been a frequent point of conflict between global South countries and richer industrialised nations amid concerns about double-counting: the re-labelling and the redirection of funds away from traditional areas of development spending such as health and education (Bulkeley and Newell 2010; Roberts and Park 2008). There have been calls for stability in climate finance to enable developing countries to plan for adaptation and restructure their economies towards low carbon energy pathways of development; for governance structures to be put in place to ensure the fair and effective dispersal of new forms of climate finance that are transparent and perceived as legitimate by key stakeholders; and for independent evaluation to be instituted from the start to ensure effectiveness and generate trust between donors and recipients. This means building on the lessons of past overseas development assistance (ODA) and creating independent monitoring organisations (Newell et al. 2009b). Across financing for both climate mitigation and adaptation, clear political economy themes of enclosure, exclusion, encroachment and entrenchment are apparent (Sovacool et al. 2017).

It is widely recognised that significant proportions of finance will have to come from the private sector, and that one of the key roles of governments is to create enabling environments that add value, fill gaps, steer, incentivise and de-risk those investments. The IEA estimates that 85 per cent of the required investments in non-fossil-fuel-based energy will need to come from private sources (IEA 2019). This would need to be longer-term finance, potentially therefore generating lower returns, implying a key role for 'patient capital'. A crop of new funds has emerged to fill this gap such as the Advanced Finance Mechanism and the Green Climate Fund brought into being by the Copenhagen Accord in 2009.

More recently, there have been calls and efforts to mobilise finance around a 'clean energy revolution', especially for Africa. A clean energy revolution for Africa was the promise being held out by donors, governments and investors at the critical Paris climate change summit in December 2015 amid claims of billions of dollars of investment being mobilised for renewable energy on the continent.[1] The Africa Renewable Energy Initiative (AREI), for example, aimed to build at least 100 GW of new and additional renewable energy generation capacity by 2020, and 300 GW by 2030. Participating in a side-event on this issue at the Paris climate change negotiations in 2015, I was struck by the calls from the UNDP (United Nations Development Programme), the World Bank and others to 'de-risk' private finance, while questions about what the finance was needed for, whose energy needs would be met, and even how we would know what those needs were, remained neglected. It was almost as if mobilising the finance was an end in itself. Lack of access to credit, inability to afford connection charges and distance from electricity infrastructures as barriers which inhibit poor people's access to electricity hardly featured at all in the rush to accommodate the preferences and needs of private capital to find new outlets for investment.

This framing around 'de-risking' and 'upscaling' finance sits easily with dominant narratives in the debate about financing energy transitions which focus on the enormous investment required. For example, the IPCC estimates that around US \$2.4 trillion or roughly 2.5 per cent of global GDP (gross domestic product) annually needs to be invested in the energy system between 2016 and 2035 (IPCC 2018). The IPCC suggests that to enable a transition to a 2°C pathway (let alone a 1.5°C one), the volume of climate investments would need to be transformed, along with changes in the pattern of general investment behaviour towards low emissions. Their report argued that, compared to 2012, annually up to a trillion dollars in additional investment in low-emission energy and energy efficiency measures may be required until 2050. The *New Climate Economy* report also published in 2018 found that about $90 trillion in investment was now likely over the next fifteen years, though the financing of 1.5°C would present an even greater challenge (Global Commission on the Economy and Climate 2018).[2] A 1.5° C-consistent pathway clearly, therefore, requires a transformation in both the *volume* of climate investments and the *direction* of finance towards a low emission and climate-resilient economy. Under the headline 'No more excuses', the *Environment Finance* magazine responded to the IPCC report by stating: 'The financial sector must play a critical enabling role to limit global warming to below 1.5 degrees. Investors need to quickly overhaul their strategies for climate change to be halted in just over a decade.'[3]

Shifts are occurring. We have seen the development of a Green Bond Market, for example. In 2013, the International Finance Corporation (IFC) packaged and issued a new financial instrument, a so called 'green bond', which was identical in price and returns to other IFC bonds, with the only difference being that the IFC promised to invest the money received for this bond in climate projects. The bond sold out in one and a half hours and was three times oversubscribed. A few days later, Korea's Export-Import Bank issued its first green bond for renewable energy, energy efficiency and water projects that the Korean government had planned. The day after the $500 million green bond sold out, an email was sent to the network of bankers working in capital markets around the world, with the header 'green is the new black' (a reference to earlier oil booms). Climate Bonds Initiative (CBI), a non-governmental organisation (NGO) which promotes and tracks the expansion of the green bonds market, believes that its growth potential is huge. Beyond the green bonds in the market that were labelled as such in 2017, CBI identified an additional $674 billion of 'climate aligned bonds' that have not been formally labelled and traded as green. This makes up a total universe of $895 billion climate aligned bonds in 2017, made up of 3,493 bonds from 1,128 issuers across 7 climate themes. Even with these staggering figures, demand for green bonds is currently outstripping supply – which allowed CBI to be confident that a target of $1 trillion market of bonds invested in climate solutions would be achieved by 2020.[4]

Viable future energy pathways will have to be climate resilient, able to deal with the impacts of climate change. In this regard, it is notable that we are also seeing the power of finance capital manifested in the increased financialisation of climate adaptation (Newell and Taylor 2020). From crop insurance to weather derivatives and catastrophe bonds, there are now a number of initiatives aimed at creating financial opportunities out of markets for adaptation and resilience (Isakson 2015). Indeed, insurance programmes have become a rare site of consensus in the contentious politics of climate finance as an avenue for delivering finance because of a preference for insurance-based approaches among G7 governments. The InsuResilience Global Partnership for Climate and Disaster Risk Finance and Insurance Solutions, launched in 2017 by the G7 countries to provide climate risk insurance for 400 million people in developing countries by 2020, is seen as a key avenue for scaling and delivering finance at all levels. Supporters contend that initiatives such as sovereign risk transfer can help countries to manage their risk to climate extremes and disasters by spreading risk over a long period of time and pooling risk within regions. Moreover, it is argued that the process of generating an insurance product can be useful in identifying areas of climate risk, while localised pricing structures can signal areas of unsustainable development, for example, where properties in risk areas become too expensive to insure (Jarzabkowski et al. 2019). In practice, though, there is very limited evidence that insurance schemes incentivise risk and vulnerability reduction in developing countries. There are a number of serious limitations to insurance-based approaches, in particular the costs of premiums in the face of escalating severity and frequency of extreme events. Insurance has always been an expensive climate risk management intervention, more so than either credit or savings schemes, while the level of pay-out is inherently constrained by the premiums that countries or donors can afford (Hillier 2018).

Around mitigation, there is evidence of both growing support among financial actors for a shift to a lower carbon economy, which is important and significant given the power that finance capital wields at this historical juncture, and continued near-term financing for fossil fuel infrastructures and technologies, often with the backing of governments and MDBs. For example, G20 governments more than doubled their support for coal power plants between 2014 and 2017, with their overall backing for coal power currently totalling $64 billion a year (Hill and Murray 2019). According to the *Production Gap* report by the UN Environment Programme and leading research institutions (SEI et al. 2019), governments are planning to produce 120 per cent more fossil fuels by 2030 than would be consistent with limiting warming to 1.5°C. That conclusion was backed up by the report *Oil, Gas, and Climate: An Analysis of Oil and Gas Industry Plans for Expansion and Compatibility with Global Emissions Limits*, also released at COP25, that showed how oil companies are planning to invest $1.4 trillion in new oil and gas extraction projects between 2020 and 2024. Further, 85 per cent of the expanded production is slated to come from the USA and Canada. This would lock in 148 gigatonnes of cumulative carbon dioxide emissions, equivalent to building over 1,200 new coal-fired power plants (GGON 2019).

At the same time, there does now seem to be an unstoppable trend towards disinvestment in fossil fuels among sovereign wealth funds and pension funds. If, as seems likely, finance *eventually* dries up for fossil fuels, we should see a radical shift which has the power to deliver the investment to the energy infrastructure we need. In fact, there appears now to be no shortage of investment money seeking a return in climate change-related shifts, maybe as much as $30 trillion (Whitley et al. 2018). Over the past five years, the investment world has seen its own rapid transition: we now also have the governors of thirty central banks concerned with the issue, and a new financial institution disinvesting in oil, coal and gas every week.[5]

In this chapter, I seek to nuance some of the more general claims about the role of finance as an enabler and disruptor of innovation, production and energy system change. The point of departure is that different types of finance are willing to support different types of transition and some types of transition are more compatible with certain types of finance than others. As Spratt (2015: 153) argues: 'Finance is not neutral: different forms influence the activities that they fund.' Most obviously, the return required on investment determines the minimum return that must be generated, a factor which enables some activities while precluding others. The key groups are equity (an ownership stake), debt (loans) and derivatives. Forwards, futures, options and swaps are all forms of derivatives. The higher the level of risk, the greater the return required, and different institutions are prepared to expose themselves to different levels of risk. While pension funds are quite risk averse, and have been targeted by fossil fuel divestment campaigns, equity, hedge funds and investment banks have higher thresholds for risk. There is also diversity within public finance too: from sovereign wealth funds to aid money and public procurement through things like South Africa's renewable energy procurement programme (REIPPP) (Baker et al. 2014), state development banks (Power et al. 2016) and public–private partnerships (PPPs) in the energy sector. Public finance includes national-level funds such as the emotively named 'Peoples' Survival Fund' in the Philippines to cover emergencies that insurance will not cover: the triage gaps (Jagers et al. 2005). Suggestive of the hybrid nature of many funding streams, several public financial actors seek to lever private capital, serving as 'multipliers' of private funding. This includes the Green Climate Fund (GCF) and the European Central Bank (ECB), for example, and the Scaling up Renewable Energy Programme (SREP) programme of the World Bank.

4.1 Historicising Energy Finance

It is important to recognise that the form that energy governance takes is a product of a particular historical moment. Right now, we very much see an energy system in motion: transitioning, albeit slowly, between one model of energy supply and demand and another in the face of the key global security and environmental challenges described in Chapter 1. Concerns with energy security, energy poverty and climate change have brought about changes in the discourse, practice and rationales of key institutions of energy governance in the public and private sectors. This is clear from the slow changes that have taken place at the World Bank, for example, regarding lending to fossil fuels or the launch of programmes such as SE4All to improve access to sustainable energy and given further impetus by the Sustainable Development Goals (SDGs). At a deeper level, however, there is continuity in dominant ideologies and governance regimes regarding the appropriate role of state and market, for example, across energy domains. How institutions govern energy finance reflects the historical moment in which they were created and the purpose they were set up to serve. But to retain relevance and credibility, they have to shift their strategies regarding how best to finance energy security, address energy poverty and steer finance towards the goal of tackling climate change while accommodating push-back from their critics.

Some initiatives are driven by the need to address a particular legitimacy crisis, rather than create a long-term and sustainable solution to a gap in the governance of energy finance. The Equator Principles on project finance, for example, might be seen as being driven by a concern to deflect criticism about the social and environmental damage being created by project financing, especially in the energy sector. In the case of the Carbon Disclosure Project (CDP), the driver was a need to be seen to address climate change amid fears of exposure on the part of investors for their complicity in financing carbon-intensive industries. The longevity of their contribution to the governance of energy finance depends, then, on a continued shared sense in which they perform a valuable function for those willing to engage with them.

The early history of energy finance was somewhat different. Capital for innovation was the key driver, as it is in many ways today, but concerns with regulation and governance to ensure social and environmental outcomes did not feature at that time. Historical accounts depict competition between oil barons trying to secure finance for their operations in the emerging oil rush (Yergin 1991). In the USA, early financiers of key energy entrepreneurs such as Thomas Edison included J. P. Morgan alongside other key actors of this era: the Vanderbilts, the Astors and, of course, the Rockefellers. With regard to the financing of the industrial revolution (Wrigley 2010), recent accounts have sought to emphasise the colonial origins of the industrial revolution in relation to the role of the global slave trade and the violence that underpinned the revolution (Satia 2018). The industrial revolution was funded by a few people who held the power to issue essentially infinite credit (Heaton 1937; Crouzet 1972). In many ways, there was a co-evolution of systems of banking and the early emergence of the fossil fuel economy.

As well as industry, therefore, banking developed during the industrial revolution from 1750 onwards as the demands of entrepreneurs in industries like steam led to a vast expansion of the financial system.

As the revolution grew and more opportunities presented themselves, there was a demand for more capital. While technology costs were coming down, the infrastructure demands of large factories or canals and railways were high, and most industrial businesses needed funds to start up and get started. Entrepreneurs had several sources of finance. The domestic system, when it was still in operation, allowed for capital to be raised as it had no infrastructure costs and you could reduce or expand your workforce rapidly. Merchants provided some circulated capital, as did aristocrats, who had money from land and estates and were keen to make more money by assisting others. They could provide land, capital, and infrastructure. Banks could provide short-term loans   *(Wilde 2019).*

The relationship was two-way, however, with the demand for the rapid development of productive systems necessitating new modes of financing. 'The growth in wealth and business opportunities increased the need for both somewhere for money to be deposited, and a source of loans for buildings, equipment and—most crucially—circulating capital for everyday running. Specialist banks with knowledge of certain industries and areas thus grew up to take full advantage of this situation' (Wilde 2019). There were notable regional differences in the financing of early waves of energy innovation, however.

In the US and Germany, industry used their banks heavily for long-term loans. Britons didn't do this, and the system has been accused of failing industry as a result. However, America and Germany started at a higher level, and needed much more money than Britain where banks weren't required for long-term loans, but instead for short-term ones to cover small shortfalls. British entrepreneurs were sceptical of banks and often preferred older methods of finance for start-up costs. Banks evolved along with British industry and were only a part of the funding, whereas America and Germany were diving into industrialization at a much more evolved level   *(Wilde 2019).*

The meta-story which forms the background and explanatory context for shifts in the provision and governance of energy finance during the contemporary period is the re-balancing of public and private power associated with neo-liberalism (Harvey 2005). There is a parallel and intimately interwoven story of the privatisation and commodification of energy as it has been gradually extracted from state hands (McDonald 2009), or actively shared with private actors, and the corresponding de-regulation of energy finance to invest in newly privatised assets. As explored elsewhere in this book, this has occurred through power sector reform programmes to unbundle and sell off profitable state assets during the 1990s and the repurposing of the state as an enabler of private capital accumulation in the energy sector. To draw on a political economy explanation, this is about the state becoming a 'competition state' (Cerny 1995) in a context of heightened globalisation: serving to assimilate and domesticate the preferences of transnational capital such that '[a] djustment to global competitiveness is the new categorical imperative' (Cox 1993: 260). Some of the shifts in energy governance described in Chapter 5 opened the door for investments in new infrastructures and service provision (such as GATS (the General Agreement on Trade in Services) or the work of the IFC in promoting and facilitating private participation in energy provisioning. More recent moves, meanwhile, have been about creating new asset classes and financial instruments in the energy sector as an end in themselves through swaps, derivatives and futures through key sites such as the New York Mercantile Exchange and the London's International Petroleum Exchange (Haigh et al. 2007).

4.2 Financing Energy Infrastructures and Technological Revolutions

Finance helps to build, sustain and then lock in infrastructures. We have already seen how finance is at the very 'epicentre' of fossil fuel economies. The effects are far from uniform, however. In South Africa, the 'minerals-energy-complex' (MEC) produces a finance-led system of accumulation strongly associated with mining and the energy industries (McDonald 2009: 9). The South African case shows how the history and sources of finance in the energy sector intersect closely with other exclusions and inequities. The lucrative contracts offered to mining companies, including incredibly cheap electricity, were aimed at securing energy independence during the apartheid era when international allies were harder to come by, to soften the effect of boycotts. Even today, opposition to market entry for renewable energy providers from Europe is sometimes framed in racialised terms around concerns that state finance is supporting European 'white capital' when it should be supporting the coal industries where there are many more jobs for black workers (Baker et al. 2014). Likewise, the nature of energy access in many countries in Africa (McDonald 2009) and elsewhere is racialised and ethnicity based (Newell 2020a).

State-led financing of new infrastructures is a global phenomenon though, and has many precedents. For example, in order to create a new industry, the French nuclear reactor programme entailed an upfront investment of US$50–100 billion (Grubler 2012: 15). Post-war, from 1956 the US Interstate Highway System managed to build 47,000 miles of highway in just over three decades, 'changing commerce and society' (Jacobson and Delucchi 2009: 59). Britain had, of course, in earlier periods of engineering endeavour, demonstrated a thirst for rapid infrastructure development. Between 1845 and 1852, 4, 400 miles of railway track were laid in Britain. On a single weekend in 1892, by contemporary standards, engineers began a project of breathtaking ambition on the morning of Saturday 21 May, and finished it by 4 a.m. on the following Monday morning, 23 May. In just two days a small, perfectly co-ordinated army of 4,200 workers laid a total of 177 miles of track along the Great Western route to the South West, converting the old broad-gauge lines to the new standard, or narrow, gauge (Simms 2013). Historical examples such as these suggest that the roll-out of alternative infrastructures can clearly happen apace when the political will and finance are mobilised.

As well as the historic role of finance in literally fuelling the industries and underwriting the infrastructures that have given rise to our current planetary predicament, finance is also increasingly central to debates about divestment from fossil fuels, disclosure and repositioning investments in fossil fuels as liabilities rather than assets (Newell and Paterson 2010). This raises the question of whether the transformative power of finance also affords an opportunity for disruptive change. Carlota Perez's (2013: 10) work reminds us of the key role of finance in supporting previous historical transitions: the 'grand experiments' she refers to 'when unrestrained finance can override the power of the old production giants and fund the new entrepreneurs in testing the vast new potential'. Though current debates about transitions and transformation place technology centrally in their vision of how to move towards a lower carbon model of development, Perez shows that finance capital is crucial to the Schumpetarian 'waves of creative destruction' that challenge and dislodge the power of incumbents. Examples include the technological revolutions produced in the industrial revolution, what she refers to as the 'age of steam and railways', and around 'oil, automobile and mass production' in the Fordist era, for example (Perez 2002). Indeed, as Arrighi (2010: xi–xii) notes: 'Throughout the capitalist era financial expansions have signalled the transition from one regime of accumulation on a world scale to another. They are integral aspects of the recurrent destruction of "old" regimes and the simultaneous creation of new ones.' This is the basis of a more optimistic reading of the finance-led 'regime of accumulation': moves towards divestment by companies, foundations, sovereign wealth funds and universities can potentially radically shift the pathway we are on. Added to this are trends towards disclosure from diverse sources such as the private-led Carbon Disclosure Project, the US government's Securities and Exchange Commission (SEC) and shareholder activism targeted at companies such as BP and Exxon (Newell 2008), the engagement and mobilisation of the insurance industry and interest in green bonds, noted earlier. If finance, as the lubricant of the global economy, dries up for fossil fuels, we will see a radical shift which has the power to unsettle the incumbent regime (Leggett 2014).

Contemporary manifestations of this include discussions about 'un-burnable carbon' and the 'stranded assets'[6] that many investors may be left with if states get more serious about climate change and force companies to leave the 'oil in the soil' and the 'coal in the hole' so that ambitions to keep warming below 1.5 or 2 degrees can be achieved. This relates to the point, raised in Chapter 1, that future transitions may be driven by scarcity and limits, as much as by discovery of new resource frontiers, as has often been the case in the past. By some calculations, between 60 per cent and 80 per cent of coal, oil and gas reserves of publicly listed companies are 'un-burnable' if the world is to have even just a 50 per cent chance of not exceeding global warming of 2°C let alone achieving the 1.5°C aspirational goal in the Paris Agreement (McGlade and Ekins 2015). This may be a conservative assessment, however, as these estimates rely on large-scale and, as yet, unproven negative emissions technologies for carbon capture (Anderson and Bows 2011). If undelivered, an even larger percentage of known reserves would need to be left in the ground.

In the words of Carbon Tracker, which is advancing this approach, 'the two worlds of capital markets and climate change policy are colliding' because major institutional investors are starting to think about these issues such that 'there will be increasing pressure from stakeholders for explanations about how capital is being allocated' (Carbon Tracker Initiative 2013). Even ExxonMobil, traditionally a recalcitrant in the climate debate, has faced a large investor inquiry issued to the forty-five top fossil fuel companies, co-ordinated by Ceres and Carbon Tracker, and representing $3 trillion (£1.8 trillion) in assets asking Exxon to report on how it was preparing for a carbon-constrained world where greenhouse gas (GHG) regulation and market forces strand uneconomic assets, and whether money spent finding more reserves is in shareholder interests. In exchange for withdrawal of the proposal, Exxon committed to publish a report on how it assesses carbon asset risk (Lamb and Fugere 2014). In terms of where that finance is being reinvested, from 2000 to 2010, global annual investment in solar PV increased by a factor of sixteen, investment in wind grew fourfold and investment in solar heating threefold (Sovacool 2016).

In the face of this pressure, some trading and financial houses are reallocating capital. Glencore has vowed to cap its coal production in the face of pressure from big investors who are pushing natural resource companies to take firmer action on climate change. The mining and trading group said it would cap its production of thermal and coking coal at about 150 million tonnes per year, close to its planned output level in 2019, with further expansion of its coal business largely ruled out (Hume et al. 2019). Meanwhile, BlackRock, the world's largest asset manager, said that one of its fast-growing green-oriented funds would stop investing in companies that get revenue from the Alberta oil sands (Flavelle 2020). There are also some interesting things going on around aligning the financial system with the imperatives of sustainability. A recent UNEP report finds evidence of a 'quiet revolution' taking place in the actions of key financial actors in banking, insurance, capital markets and investment and across a range of policy areas including laws in Sweden and Netherlands requiring financial players to show how their activities contribute to these goals (UNEP 2015). This reinforces the point about the role of the state and highlights the need to create 'long, loud, legal' signals about direction of change to bring about reallocations of capital towards lower carbon and more sustainable technologies and pathways (Hamilton 2009).

Fossil fuel incumbents will fight hard to resist this reallocation of capital. According to Lenferna (2018: 218), adhering to the 2°C target could result in $28 trillion in lost revenue in the next two decades with the oil industry accounting for $19.3 trillion, gas $4 trillion and coal $4.9 trillion. Incredibly, the vast majority of fossil fuel reserves are not held by publicly traded companies, with 74 per cent of reserves either state-owned or owned by private companies not registered on the stock market. Wright and Nyberg (2015: 28) point to what they call 'creative self-destruction' at play here to encapsulate the bizarre notion that 'the only available response to a problem caused by the market's ever-expanding reach is to expand that reach further still'. It finds expression also in the idea of the 'green paradox': that efforts to limit supply intensify competition to extract remaining reserves that might become 'stranded' (that is, unusable), driving up fossil fuel production in the short term (Sinn 2012). Here we encounter the limits of the destabilising potential of finance capital, which we return to in Section 4.8 on ecologies of finance; namely, that shifts in allocations of finance are motivated by the prospect of more and greater returns. This is the idea that only more consumption can remedy the devastating consequences of over-consumption (Wright and Nyberg 2015: 28).

4.3 Financialisation and Commodification of Energy and Climate

Besides the longer pre-history of the marketisation of the energy sector and energy governance as explored in Chapter 5, in terms of the history of energy finance, the growing trend towards financialisation is a key contemporary phenomenon with important implications for the future form of energy transitions. The longer pre-history of the rise of finance can be told in relation to the gradual dis-embedding of finance from public control (Helleiner 1994) and the growth of offshore (Palan 2003). This has formed the basis of what Regulation theorists refer to as today's finance-led regime of accumulation. This describes a new 'regime of accumulation' and 'mode of regulation' (Aglietta 2000). The concept of a regime of accumulation explains the way in which production, circulation, consumption and distribution organise and expand capital in a way that stabilises the economy over time. The modes of regulation required to stabilise these regimes include the law, state policy, corporate governance and cultures of consumption which are increasingly trans-national in nature. In this regard, the alignment of responses to climate change and the imperative of energy transition with the needs of finance capital can be understood as a function of a particular historical conjuncture and the presence of a finance-led regime of accumulation in particular that has been embedded since the 1970s (Aglietta 2000; Koch 2012).

What is of particular concern here, though, is the more recent creation of new asset classes and the repurposing of the state with regard to energy financing as an enabler and multiplier of private capital in the energy sector. While ostensibly performing a night watchman role, this belies a reality of significant state financing and underwriting of innovation and research and infrastructures for production and distribution. The drivers of financialisation in the energy sector include crises of over-accumulation, whereby an over-investment in capital stock combined with the adoption of more labour-saving technologies means that it is no longer possible to bring all goods to market profitably. As profit rates in the productive sector fall, capital begins to move out of reinvestment in plants, infrastructure and labour and into financial assets of one sort or another (McDonald 2009). This sets in train a process whereby financial capital becomes dominant in decision-making about public and private investments in infrastructure, as described later in relation to PPPs and de-risking investment. Such strategies in Harvey's (1981) terms offer a 'spatial fix' for this crisis of over-accumulation. Such crises are commonplace under capitalism where profitable outlets for finance have to be identified and expanded as a way of dealing with crises of surplus production and under-consumption. There always have to be winners under new accumulation regimes, and in relation to 'climate capitalism' – the generation of opportunities for investments in low carbon economies – it is finance capital (Newell and Paterson 2010).

The pursuit of the expansion of finance as an end in itself has been enabled by innovations such as automated trading that alter some of the ways in which finance capital interacts with energy transitions. It is less about picking and backing winners and particular energy futures, and more about tracking share values. As MacKenzie et al. (2012) show, some 60 per cent of trading on stock exchanges is high frequency trading where automated systems are used to track price changes and follow them. As Buck (2006: 63) suggests: 'Capital, as value in motion, does not care about what it makes, the machinery used or the motive source. It cares only about its self-expansion and valorization.'

The way finance engages with processes of energy transition is often problematic from a more critical political economy, and certainly an ecological, perspective, as we will explore later on. It raises a series of problems characteristic of financialisa-tion in general in terms of exacerbating inequalities and deepening economic insecurity (Fine 2017; Thomson and Dutta 2018). Such problems manifest themselves in calls to de-risk finance to open up profitable investment opportunities in Africa's energy systems, for example, to generate 'bankable' projects, or to engage in carbon trading for speculation and profit: a financial strategy that was given a new boost by the Paris Agreement and net zero targets where there is wide latitude for offsets and what are referred to in the agreement as 'internationally transferable mitigation outcomes'.

One way in which we see these dynamics play out is in relation to de-risking. A key role is imagined for and demanded of public institutions and financiers to lever private finance for energy through de-risking, largely by the 'de-risking state' (Carruthers and Stinchcombe 1999). The verb to 'de-risk' was one of a flurry of new words entering the lexicon of the financial sector in the aftermath of the credit crisis, referring to the process of removing or minimising risk in financial operations and de-risking new asset classes through subsidies, guarantees and securitising bank energy loans. Steckel and Jakob (2018), for example, suggest that financing costs can be lowered by either addressing the underlying sources of investment risk (policy de-risking) or shifting risk away from private sector investors (financial de-risking) on the domestic and the international level. O'Boyle (2018) further specifies three types of risk: technology risk, development risk and pricing risk. Addressing each of these risk profiles helps investors such as utilities, banks or other institutions find the necessary will to invest in renewable projects. Renewable energy is especially capital sensitive because while renewable energy technologies have high initial costs, they then cost very little to operate because they do not require fuel. One consequence of this capital-intensive nature is that renewable energy is very sensitive to the cost of capital: to the interest rates or return rates demanded by those who lend or pay for renewable energy technology up front. So, for example, high interest rates can significantly increase the overall cost of a wind farm. If public policy can drive down risk, it can drive down cost. And the difference can be dramatic, cutting overall costs by close to 50 per cent in some cases (O'Boyle 2018).

What de-risking can also do, however, is shift risk back to cash-strapped governments that are expected to set up corporations to undertake surveys, secure land rights, mobilise financial guarantees and deposits and put in place 'enabling regulation' to make the extraction of profit as risk-free and painless as possible. The example provided previously of the Geothermal Development Corporation in Kenya provides a case in point. Key risks for finance include interest rates, grid integration issues, political risk insurance, as well as protection against revenue shortfalls. Prevented losses from climate change are even discussed as 'resilience returns'.[7] But risk is also shifted onto the victims of climate change such as farmers in drought-stricken areas that are encouraged to purchase crop insurance or invest in weather derivatives (Isakson 2015). In this scenario, the financialisation of energy strategy connects a crisis of accumulation in the global North with the climate crisis in the global South.

4.4 Political Economy of Energy Finance

4.4.1 Financing Incumbents

We have already seen how finance is crucial to the strategies of both incumbents and niche actors: at once reinforcing and disrupting incumbent power (Skovgaard and van Asselt 2018; Erickson et al. 2020). The case of fossil fuel subsidies is revealing of the political economy of finance and the power of incumbent actors to capture benefits and slow the pace of transition (Newell and Johnstone 2018). The International Monetary Fund (IMF) reported that in 2015, fossil fuel subsidies (including the non-pricing of externalities) amounted to US$5.3 trillion. This equates to US$145 billion per day, US$600 million per hour, US$10 million per minute and US$168,000 per second (IMF 2015). Beyond the vast scale of the subsidies, what is also notable is the systematic bias in favour of fossil fuels compared to other forms of energy production. A 2017 report from several NGOs found that the Group of 20 (G20) countries provided four times as much public finance to fossil fuels as they did to clean energy (OCI 2017).

The state clearly plays a key role in sustaining incumbents through the forms of financial support it provides, with the effect of delaying shifts away from dominant fossil fuel regimes. Fossil fuel subsidies and energy subsidies more broadly provide a useful lens for understanding incumbency enacted through the state. For example, both kinds of subsidies can be understood as state aid granted to the private sector to help deliver explicit policy goals. This can be done benignly in the creation of safety nets for the poor, in de-risking investments in lower carbon forms of energy, or through tax breaks for improving access to key technologies that improve the energy security of the poor, in line with the SDGs. But it also serves less explicit state strategies of clientelism and securing and buying support from key political constituencies by using subsidies for particular groups of the poor and the rich. Examples from the literature include the provision of kerosene subsidies for farmers in India, where the subsidies create a political constituency dependent on their provision and resistant to their reform (Shenoy 2010), or tax breaks for large investors to induce them to invest in particular regions, sectors or infrastructures. Hence, a combination of poor and wealthy political 'clients' benefit from fossil fuel subsidies, which makes it harder to bring about their reform in the face of broad-based resistance. The dual use of subsidies, both to keep fossil fuel businesses solvent and to keep the wider public tied into fossil fuel systems of production, is revealing of the dynamics of incumbent power. Likewise, as Sovacool (2017: 157) notes, 'subsidies become self-replicating because, once enacted, they continue to shape energy choices through the long-lived infrastructure and capital stock they create. This justifies further expenditures to operate, maintain, and improve existing technologies. Coal and nuclear plants built 40 years ago, for example, still receive subsidies for coal mining and uranium enrichment.' Koplow (2014) refers to this as the energy subsidy 'trap', whereby once a government begins subsidising, such efforts become protected and defended by beneficiaries.

The material and political properties of fossil fuels also make them attractive to state elites and entrench reluctance to reduce state subsidies to them. Work on the 'resource curse' emphasises the shared interests of (neo-) extractivist elites, such as in Nigeria and Venezuela, in using rents from oil to insulate themselves from popular pressure (Ross 2012). The 'lootability' (Bridge and Le Billon 2013) of oil makes it an attractive 'political resource' because it provides a steady flow of lucrative revenue for state and corporate actors. It also generates sufficient surplus rent to buy off local opposition or dissipate pressure for reform through populist distributional measures, including subsidies for energy consumption. The ability to extract rents and maintain high degrees of control over the production and consumption of fossil fuels is often preferable to state and corporate elites than pathways organised around off-grid, decentralised and renewable energy systems, where the same degree of rent-seeking might not be possible. In Kenya, for example, Newell and Phillips (2016) show how fossil fuel extraction and geothermal exploration enjoy fuller state support compared to off-grid renewable energy provision because they enable political control over key resources and the negotiation of contracts remains in the hands of national elites.

Fossil fuel subsidies are not just a subsidy to private actors, however. Given the ongoing dominance of state-owned enterprises, especially in many of the world's 'rising powers', they essentially serve as a subsidy by the state for the state (Victor et al. 2012). Governments own 50 per cent of the world's production of fossil fuels, and 70 per cent of oil and gas production occurs through companies that are wholly or partly state-owned. McDonald (2009: 440) notes in relation to South Africa's wind sector, echoing the point made earlier, that much of the development of wind power is being generated by private firms in South Africa, 'often with state subsidies contributing to de facto privatisation of this subsector'. It is unsurprising, therefore, that there are often high levels of policy support for, and fewer regulatory demands made of, state-owned enterprises, even in the face of citizen protests (Newell 2005a). This poses challenges both for subjecting state-owned enterprises to state climate regulation and for discontinuing financial support in the form of subsidies when there may be few incentives to reduce the activities of enterprises whose revenues flow directly to state coffers.

The imbalance in financial support to fossil fuel incumbents, as opposed to renewable energy niches, is also apparent in MDB funding. While MDBs such as the World Bank have sought to position themselves as key funders of climate action and low carbon energy through funds such as the Climate Investment Funds and the Scaling up Renewable Energy Programme (SREP), they still provided over $9 billion in public finance for fossil fuel projects in 2016, with the vast majority of transactions approved after the Paris Agreement was reached. Indeed, the total MDB finance for oil and gas exploration more than doubled from 2015 to 2016, from $1.05 billion to $2.15 billion. The World Bank Group, the European Investment Bank and the Asian Development Bank were the largest financiers of fossil fuels in 2016. At the same time, renewable energy still made up less than a third of MDB energy finance (OCI 2017).

4.4.2 Creating New Sites of Accumulation

Besides the more general financialisation of the energy sector which I have described briefly, and the potential for financial capital to accelerate transitions to a lower carbon economy by redeploying capital away from fossil fuels and into renewable energy, here I focus on another aspect of financing transitions: carbon trading. This has a contentious and difficult history (Newell and Paterson 2010; Ervine 2018; Meckling 2011), but it provides an illustrative example of the role of finance in shaping responses to climate change through creating markets for the buying and selling of carbon: making money from responses to the crisis. It also demonstrates the need to historicise debates about energy transitions because by the time the Kyoto Protocol was being negotiated in the late 1990s at the height of neo-liberal environmentalism, market mechanisms were clearly the preferred way of responding to the crisis for leading state and business elites. Low carbon transitions were essentially about pricing carbon and creating new market opportunities around its exchange.

In late 2014, the World Bank Group, the World Economic Forum (WEF) and the We Mean Business Coalition announced that they would be convening a carbon pricing leadership coalition with business and government leaders. The coalition included 1,000+ companies and investors with more than $24 trillion in assets, along with 74 countries and 23 states, provinces and cities representing 54 per cent of global greenhouse gas (GHG) emissions, 52 per cent of global GDP, and almost half the global population (World Bank 2014). At the UN level, ongoing negotiations around the international community's attempt to manage and govern climate change are focused on the construction of new market mechanisms, most recently in the form of Article 6 of the Paris Agreement. Outside of the UN system, at a regional and national level, a swathe of new carbon markets and emission trading schemes are coming online in places like China, South Korea, Vietnam, Thailand, California, Kazakhstan, Mexico and Quebec. In total, twenty-seven jurisdictions are now implementing twenty Emissions Trading Schemes (ETSs) across scales covering 8 per cent of global GHG emissions. Another six jurisdictions are putting in place their systems that could be operating in the next few years, including China and Mexico. Twelve jurisdictions are also considering the role that an ETS can play in their climate change policy mix, including Chile, Thailand and Vietnam (ICAP 2019). Yet, at the same time, carbon markets are in crisis. Repeated and well-publicised scandals have engulfed the UN's Clean Development Mechanism (CDM) (Schneider and Kollmuss 2015) as well as the flagship EU Emissions Trading Scheme (ETS). Australia's carbon trading scheme, inaugurated in 2012, was promptly discontinued in 2014 with the arrival of Tony Abbott's conservative administration (Hudson 2018) and, globally, carbon prices continue to be too low to incentivise investment in low carbon technologies.

One way of making sense of the ongoing development of the carbon markets, in spite of their failings, is to view them as representing part of a finance-led regime of accumulation that has come to dominate the global economy (Paterson 2012). The modes of regulation required to stabilise these regimes include the law, state policy, corporate governance and cultures of consumption (Aglietta 2000), where the power of financial capital is used to discipline social and political forces through the imposition of neo-liberal governance practices. In particular, Paterson (2009: 107) notes: 'The interests of finance in both deregulated "solutions" to problems like environmental ones, and the fetishisation of "markets" as solutions to all sorts of problems which is associated with the rise of finance, produce the ideological context within which environmental governance has developed since the late 1980s.'

Consistent with this interpretation, the idea of emissions trading became so popular so rapidly from its 1996 introduction to climate mitigation discussions in the UNFCCC, precisely because of the creation of markets and accumulation possibilities: 'Emissions trading as a project has been and continues to be propelled by the realisation by powerful financial actors that here was a new commodity to be sold, new profits to be made' (Paterson 2009: 112). It is in this context that it has been argued that the development of climate governance mechanisms, and specifically carbon trading, represents an attempt to stabilise the contemporary, post-Fordist, financially-led regime of accumulation resulting in an emergent form of 'climate capitalism' (Newell and Paterson 2010). Patrick Bond (2015) has taken a different approach in interpreting carbon market development as part of a series of interconnected projects to manage multiple capitalist crises. He sees it as an effort 'to subsidize the bankers' solution to climate crisis:

> The attraction of carbon trading in the new markets, no matter its failure in the old, is logical when seen within a triple context: a longer-term capitalist crisis which has raised financial sector power within an ever-more frenetic and geographically ambitious system; the financial markets' sophistication in establishing new routes for capital across space, through time, and into non-market spheres; and the mainstream ideological orientation to solving every market-related problem with a market solution.   *(Bond 2015)*

Felli (2015) locates the development of market-based instruments, meanwhile, as a means to depoliticise the implementation of environmental limits to growth in response to their politicisation during the 1960s and 1970s. For Felli (2015), this depoliticisation sees emissions trading markets as neo-liberal, not in the sense that they commodify or privatise nature, but in the sense that they entrench the power of financial capital. For many powerful actors, carbon markets constitute a preferable solution to either regulation or taxation. Taxation, albeit offering a market-based solution aimed at 'internalising' externalities by making the 'polluter pay', has often lost out to carbon trading because it offers less flexibility in compliance and allows potentially greater scope for free-riding by firms not subject to the tax, raising the twin spectres of carbon leakage and capital flight, threats frequently invoked by organised capital to resist carbon taxes (Newell and Paterson 1998).

The commodification of carbon in offset markets provides a spatial fix (and a temporal one by discounting the future) by displacing carbon reduction efforts to areas of the world where it can be achieved more cost-effectively. But there is certainly also an ideological element at play here. The ongoing development of the carbon markets is justified and ultimately legitimated on a twofold basis: that they are simply the most effective *and* the most efficient means of reducing GHG emissions. The World Bank Group squarely states that carbon pricing is 'considered one of the most effective ways to bring down greenhouse gas emissions' (World Bank 2014). Connie Hedegaard (then the EU's Climate Commissioner) made the overriding importance of this clear in 2011 when she stated that European climate policies need to work 'in a way that will not hamper economic growth in Europe but which leaves companies maximum flexibility to cut emissions at least cost' (Hedegaard 2011). In addition, there is a cross-fertilisation of practices and actors between markets. For example, in assembling carbon markets, 'carbon market actors borrow from existing financial practices to make the emerging market readily intelligible, to enable it to operate as a matter of financial routine' (Descheneau and Paterson 2011). As well as mobilising capital and investor interest, there are also the intermediaries, brokers and 'market-makers' that actually facilitate the operation of the markets and ensure that rents are created (Newell 2009; Lovell and MacKenzie 2011).

A reflection of the ongoing power of finance and the resilience of the ideology around the benefits of market-based approaches is the fact that, despite their poor performance in the past, significant effort is now being placed in reviving them and scaling them up, in part under the umbrella of the Paris Agreement. This has been referred to as the 'zombie' phenomenon: the apparent contradiction between the seeming failure of carbon markets to date and ongoing support for them among state and corporate elites (Newell and Lane 2016). Carbon markets until recently appeared effectively dead, yet still politically unstoppable (Reyes 2011; Lipow 2014), staggering ever onwards from crisis to crisis. Carbon markets have repeatedly failed to adequately price carbon either effectively or efficiently. In spite of bailouts through back-stopping and voluntary cancellation schemes, the EU ETS remains Europe's 'flagship tool to fight climate change' (European Commission 2015). Similarly, collapsing prices, wild market fluctuations and widely reported corruption have not prevented continued faith being placed in the ability of the markets to deliver meaningful reductions in GHG emissions. This is what Newell and Taylor (2020) refer to as the 'strange non-death' of carbon markets, invoking the title of Colin Crouch's (2011) book about neo-liberalism.

This drive to revive carbon markets as the preferred way of addressing climate change was given a key boost by Article 6 of the Paris Agreement, which opened the way for a new wave of carbon market activity. A new Sustainable Development Mechanism will allow emission reduction credits to be traded on an open carbon market across countries, cities and businesses, in contrast to the current CDM which operates more as an inter-state credit transfer mechanism between countries in the global North and South. Some countries, including Australia, Brazil and India, want to be able to use old, unspent CDM credits in the new system and hence have a strong material stake in preserving carbon trading. Negotiations have largely focused on two concerns: avoiding double counting through the application of adjustments and strong accounting rules and disallowing the carry-over of Kyoto Protocol credits to countries' commitments under the Paris Agreement (Newell and Taylor 2020).

4.5 Governance of Energy Finance

The political economy of energy finance invites questions about governance and the procedural and distributional politics of *who* invests in *what* and *how*. Strong and effective systems of governance are required to steer energy finance towards the fulfilment of policy goals around energy security, energy poverty and sustainability. The governance of finance refers to the ensembles of actors, policymaking processes and institutional arrangements set up to steer energy finance towards the achievement of these goals (Florini and Sovacool 2009). It describes collective acts of steering and management aimed at raising and screening, allocating and distributing finance in the form of aid and investment from the public and private sectors. I have analysed elsewhere the different governance dimensions associated with (i) the public governance of public finance, (ii) the public governance of private finance and (iii) the private governance of private finance, arguing that there remains a substantial imbalance towards governance *for* energy finance over governance *of* energy finance, which has important implications for constructing effective solutions to the multiple challenges that energy policy currently faces (Newell 2011).

In relation to the spectrum of global governance institutions operating in this area, there are issues, already noted, of key institutions such as the World Bank mainstreaming and integrating their lending practices with their professed climate change commitments. But these bodies also play a key role in policy transfer and diffusion of governance norms vis-à-vis the energy sector. Through seemingly neutral policy advice and technical assistance, ideas are transferred and embedded that change the way in which energy is governed. MDBs have played a significant role in propagating new 'wisdoms' about the institutions and instruments that should govern the energy sector (Nakhooda 2011). Moments of crisis provide opportunities to press for far-reaching reforms, as was seen with the promotion of electricity privatisation in the wake of the East Asian financial crisis, as part of broader packages of macroeconomic reform. Preferences and power are revealed in the way that power sector reform was required of borrowers, whereas addressing issues of sustainability and clean energy was largely optional (Tellam 2000).

Private financial flows in the energy sector increasingly outstrip those in the public sector and many governments, through processes of power sector and energy reform, have relinquished at least some control over the provision of energy services. Yet, while private finance and investment are to some extent governed by trade and investment rules, they often lie beyond the reach of systems of energy and environmental governance at the international level, such as they exist. As Sir Nicolas Stern put it in a blog for the World Bank:

Public resources can bridge viability gaps and cover risks that private actors are unable or unwilling to bear, while the private sector can bring the financial flows and innovation required to sustain progress. For this partnership to reach its full potential, investors need to be provided with the necessary signals, enabling environments, and incentives to confidently invest in emerging economies.   *(Stern 2015)*

MDBs have a key role to play in mobilising climate finance. Through offering concessional resources, the Climate Investment Funds (CIF) of the World Bank, for example, seek to lower high capital costs, absorb risks that other financiers would not bear, and extend repayment rates to better match project cash flows. This in turn enables the unlocking of additional finance from MDBs' own balance sheets and the private sector. For example, the CIF's portfolio of US$8.1 billion is expected to leverage an additional US$55 billion in finance for low carbon development, adaptation and forestry. There have also been a number of regional initiatives aimed at using public governance to steer private finance towards the achievement of environmental goals. These include the €3 billion *Energy Sustainability and Security of Supply Facility*, authorised in June 2007 by the governors of the European Investment Bank or the EU Global Energy Efficiency and Renewable Energy Fund (GEEREF) which was designed in 2006 to support small and medium-sized energy projects by offering loans to mobilise private investments in energy technologies in order to support sustainable development in developing economies.[8]

There are also forms of private governance aimed at the governance of risk around energy finance. These can take a number of forms but include networks such as the 'Investor Network on Climate Risk' formed by a group of institutional investors to examine opportunities and strategies for investment in clean energy and climate technologies. Its 'Clean Energy Investment Working Group' involves collaboration between the Coalition for Environmentally Responsible Economies (CERES) investor network on climate risk and the Clean Energy Group. It aims to 'develop an ongoing framework within which participants can explore the risks and rewards in making investments and allocating capital to the clean energy sector and other climate-related opportunities'.[9] These may result in co-ordinated action by institutional investors, including the adoption of new investment policies and the creation of investment fund vehicles and partnerships with state-owned clean energy funds.

A further element of private governance is governance through disclosure. The most relevant example to energy finance is the Carbon Disclosure Project (CDP 2020). The CDP, by systematising information about companies' emissions, creates the means to pressure firms to invest in renewable rather than fossil fuel energy solutions. The CDP now covers over 525 investors with US$96 trillion in assets in 8,400 companies (CDP 2020). The scope of private regulation is, therefore, impressive and reaches key actors not subject to other forms of governance. The CDP questionnaire and reports are public and can be accessed via the internet; responses from companies are available without restriction. The CDP operates on an essentially self-select basis, however, and firms are able to choose which of their operations they include in their emissions disclosure. Indeed, most companies signed up to the CDP place a disclaimer that the information they enclose does not include their activities in some developing countries. Moreover, there is no institutional control mechanism in place to monitor and verify company responses.

Another aspect of the private governance of private finance concerns the role of private flows in the fields of philanthropy and private donations that are subject to little more than individual discretion in terms of priority setting and governance. Nisbet (2019) suggests: 'Current laws allow foundations as non-profit charities to operate without transparency, making decisions at closed-door meetings, under the cover of opaque announcements and press releases.' The only legal obligation for US foundations is that they spend 5 per cent of their net assets annually, file a financial statement with the Internal Revenue Service, and conduct an annual audit. Indeed, they use this lack of scrutiny as an advantage allowing them to take bold risks that are beyond the scope of governments or corporations. The Rockefeller Brothers' Fund, the Children's Investment Fund, the Climate Works Foundation and the Gates foundation are examples of these actors.

The funds they bring to the table are not insubstantial. At the 2018 Climate Action Summit, twenty-nine of the world's largest foundations pledged $4 billion in grant funding over the next five years to accelerate efforts to limit GHG emissions and to transition to clean energy. Interventions include the following. Since the 1990s, major foundations have distributed several billion dollars in grants intended to influence US federal, state and international policy. The most notable priorities have been the failed effort in 2010 to pass federal cap and trade legislation, and the years of negotiations that eventually led to the 2015 UN Paris Agreement. They have also spent heavily on influencing the direction of specific geographic regions and industry sectors, including backing efforts to pass renewable energy mandates in dozens of states and promoting the adoption of renewables and efficiency practices among utilities, municipalities and companies. As Nisbet (2019) puts it: 'By framing the challenges and defining the priorities, funders have promoted a specific way of thinking about climate change, focusing otherwise disconnected advocates and experts on shared approaches to the problem.'

The effects are hard to judge, but, in the words of an influential 2007 report from a group of major philanthropies, entitled *Design to Win*, they will 'prompt a sea change that washes over the entire global economy', accelerating the transition towards solar and wind power, energy efficiency practices, sustainable agriculture and clean transportation (Nisbet 2019). Many of the market and social forces propelling renewable energy today are a result of the decades-long road map pursued by major climate funders. Indeed, they have achieved some successes already. Examples cited include the 99 per cent decline since the early 1990s in the cost of solar panels, which would not have happened without the types of market-stimulating policies long favoured by philanthropies. At the same time, despite the billions spent by philanthropy on climate change, this funding still only accounts for 1 per cent of all foundation giving (Nisbet 2019).

Beyond just de-risking, there is clearly a key role for proactive steering and regulation on the part of the state of these diverse forms of private capital. Firstly, governments can use policy tools at their disposal to create the enabling conditions to lever and improve flows of private finance. Tax, regulation and use of subsidies, as noted, are among the suite of measures available. Areas covered might include supply chain requirements (e.g. content and other rules: feed-in, Non-Fossil Fuel Obligations) and rules around inwards investment and utility sector structure and regulation (e.g. power purchase agreements and planning rules). Sending clear signals that are 'loud, long and legal' is key to unlocking private finance (Hamilton 2009). 'Loud' refers to incentives that are strong enough to make a difference to bottom-line investment decisions. 'Long' means of a duration that reflects the financing horizons of projects. 'Legal' implies targets and regulatory frameworks that show that policy goals are stable and provide the basis for long-term capital-intensive investments.

Another source of public governance and financing for private investment is export credit agencies (ECAs). These are used to provide support to private investors wanting to invest overseas (Wright 2011). They allow for an important, though often under-used, opportunity to screen investments in the energy sector for their social and environmental impacts. In the UK, for example, no project has ever been denied support from the Export Credit Guarantee Department (ECGD) on environmental grounds. Yet it was revealed by an audit committee report that UK Export Finance (UKEF), which provides lines of credit and insurance to help companies win business overseas, spent £2.6 billion in recent years to support the UK's global energy exports, of which £2.5 billion was handed to fossil fuel projects. Only 4 per cent of its funding, or £104 million, was used to support renewable energy projects (Ambrose 2019a). Groups such as Bank Watch and ECA Watch have launched several campaigns exposing the use of public funds to support large projects with damaging social and environmental impacts. UKEF's latest annual report, published two months after parliament declared a 'climate emergency' in 2019, for example, shows an eleven-fold increase in support for fossil fuel projects compared with the previous year, when £175 million was provided (DeSmog 2019).

The need to mobilise and reallocate public and private finance to drive change in industry, infrastructures and technology is almost a given in debates about transition. As well as the need to realign the financial system with the imperatives of sustainable development (UNEP 2015), issues are often raised about whether sufficient sources and scales of finance can be mobilised in time to accelerate necessary transitions. For example, an estimate of the investment needed to set the UK on a low carbon transition pathway commensurate with the necessary action demanded by climate science suggested a programme of around £50 billion per year (Green New Deal Group 2008).

This clearly also requires us to withdraw support from fossil fuel incumbents, as we saw with reference to fossil fuel subsidies. Levering private finance to address energy poverty, energy security and climate change needs to be balanced with significant disincentives for business as usual investments in energy that undermine the achievement of these policy objectives. Globally, this implies a substantial shift of subsidies and support away from the fossil fuel economy to a low carbon economy, even if energy poverty imperatives may mean that transition is more sequenced in some least developed country settings. There is a huge gap between the expectations of what private energy finance should deliver in terms of tackling energy poverty and climate change in particular, and the weak governance systems currently in place to mobilise, channel and distribute that finance to where it is most needed. Hence, though the private sector is expected to provide the lion's share of finance for energy and climate mitigation, public financial flows also have an important role to play. These can be directed to 'correcting market imperfections' and targeting areas overlooked by the market, as the World Bank suggests (World Bank 2010: 258), but governance mechanisms can be used to raise, steer and distribute many types of energy and climate finance.

Indeed, there is some evidence of the resurgence of a state capitalism model of steering in the energy sector, especially in those countries that are set to increasingly dominate energy production and consumption such as China and India. From research to extraction to distribution and consumption, states and public institutions are heavily involved in governing public energy finance. The public sector provides capital for large infrastructure projects. Hence, although governments account for less than 15 per cent of global economy-wide investment, they largely control the underlying infrastructure investments that affect opportunities in the energy sector (World Bank 2010: 261). Recent interest in a Green New Deal demonstrates the return of the state in steering finance.

The case of BNP Paribas in France makes clear the key role for state regulation of finance. The French Energy Transition Law of 2015, mandating listed companies to disclose how climate risks are managed, has provided a legislative environment that has accelerated the transition of French banks including BNP Paribas away from fossil fuels. BNP Paribas's climate strategy purposely aims to align financial flows with the Paris Agreement's objective of limiting global average temperature rises to below 2°C (BNP Paribas 2015). This strategy explicitly focuses on the twin goals of reducing financing to high carbon sectors and mobilising capital for the low carbon transition. In practice, this means, firstly, reducing activities within carbon-intensive sectors that are not compatible with the Paris Agreement; and, secondly, increasing financing and support to new sectors, companies and projects that will build the infrastructure for a low carbon world. BNP Paribas has already begun to reduce exposure to fossil fuel industries, starting with the most carbon-intensive including tar sands, shale gas, arctic exploration and production, and thermal coal-related infrastructure; and has also strictly limited its support of companies who are predominantly active in these industries (BNP Paribas 2017a, 2017b). As well as moving out of fossil fuels, BNP Paribas is also mobilising capital to accelerate the transition to a low carbon society. By the end of 2017, total renewable energy sector financing had reached EUR 12.3 billion which enabled the construction of 6 gigawatts (GW) of new renewable energy capacity (BNP Paribas 2018).

Ultimately, *for whom* (for other governments, businesses) and *for what* finance is intended (e.g. as aid or investment) makes a big difference to *how* it is governed and *who* benefits. The way in which the different institutions and organisations surveyed here govern energy finance clearly reflects their mandates and whom they consider to be their main clients or constituencies. Grants and concessional finance often come with donor conditions and the need for guarantees about how money will be spent since public money has to be accounted for. With market-based mechanisms, governance systems reflect the fact that the aim is to facilitate the market and ensure environmental integrity, whereas the governance of sustainable development benefits is much weaker (Newell 2011).

4.6 Ecologies of Energy Finance

Though it circulates on exchanges and often seems to have virtual properties, money also lands in particular places (and not others), in particular industries, regions and communities (and not others) and does so in socially uneven ways and always with consequences for particular ecologies. Following and tracking energy finance flows is difficult. Not all transactions are properly and publicly recorded, there is plentiful corruption around energy financing, despite the efforts of initiatives such as the Extractive Industries Transparency Initiative (EITI), and different definitions are applied to different types of climate and energy finance. It is also often blended, meaning that accurately calculating proportions of public and private finance is complicated. Finance is also in flux. As Marx noted, capital is 'value in motion' (Marx 1974). Indeed, the talk at the intersessional meeting of the climate negotiations in Bonn (SB50) was of 'ecosystems of finance' across debt and equity financing, credit, insurance and loans. These are the circuits of capital that fund and disrupt energy systems.

There are also social constructions of scarcity and gaps in financing which are invoked to justify new expenditure. Projections of demand, supply and financing gaps afford power to those conferred with the authority to build those forecasts and scenarios that underpin policy. A lot is at stake as new rounds of investment and expenditure are opened up or closed down. And there are questions about the coherence of the overall direction of finance. The findings of the World Energy Investment 2019 report signal a growing mismatch between current trends and the paths to meeting the Paris Agreement and other SDGs. The report noted that global energy investment stabilised in 2018, ending three consecutive years of decline, as capital spending on oil, gas and coal supply bounced back, while investment stalled for energy efficiency and renewables, according to the International Energy Agency's latest annual review (IEA 2019a). The impact of the coronavirus may well require a revision of these figures. At the same time, there are few signs of the substantial reallocation of capital towards energy efficiency and cleaner supply sources that is needed to bring investments in line with the Paris Agreement and other SDGs.

Finance is constantly realigning to fill perceived gaps in supply. The world is witnessing a shift in investments towards energy supply projects that have shorter lead times. In power generation and the upstream oil and gas sector, the industry is bringing capacity to market more than 20 per cent faster than at the beginning of the decade. This reflects industry and investors seeking to better manage risks in a changing energy system, and also improved project management and lower costs for shorter-cycle assets such as solar PV, onshore wind and US shale. Even though decisions to invest in coal-fired power plants declined to their lowest level this century and retirements rose, the global coal power fleet continued to expand, particularly in developing Asian countries. The continuing investments in coal plants, which have a long life cycle, appear to be aimed at filling a growing gap between soaring demand for power and a levelling off of expected generation from low carbon investments (renewables and nuclear). Public spending on energy research, development and demonstration (RD&D) is far short of what is needed (IEA 2019). In short, finance from the green entrepreneurial state is not yet in place.

There are also uneven geographies of energy finance. The poorest regions of the world, such as Sub-Saharan Africa, face persistent financing risks. They received only around 15 per cent of investment in 2018 even though they account for 40 per cent of the global population (IEA 2019). The experience of the CDM reflected a similar pattern where larger economies in Asia, such as India and

China, attracted by far the greatest share of the projects and proceeds while Sub-African Africa captured less than 2 per cent of the market. This will be a challenge that confronts the new Sustainable Development Mechanism under the Paris Agreement. Far more capital needs to flow to the least developed countries in order to meet the SDGs. There are shifting geographies of finance on the investor side, too. China, India, Brazil and South Africa are all in the top ten global rankings for clean energy investment (Gallagher 2018). China is the top country by far in terms of the sums invested in renewables capacity during the decade up to 2020. It committed $758 billion between 2010 and the first half of 2019, with the USA second on $356 billion and Japan third on $202 billion (UNEP BNEF 2019).

The flows of finance are also gauged and governed by metrics which generate their own logics. As with monitoring, reporting and verification (MRV) requirements attached to climate finance, what counts is what can be counted (Lovell and MacKenzie 2011). This has produced distortions in CDM markets, for example, because only emissions reductions are counted and rewarded, and not the second goal of the CDM, which is to bring sustainable development benefits; these are not quantified and, therefore, fall off the radar of investors. Finance also has its own metabolism. Rhythms and imperatives of finance such as internal rate of return, return on investment and bankability shape the nature and direction of circuits of capital. These are often misaligned with notions of limits, carrying capacity and tipping points. There are tensions here between the need for patient capital and longer-term investments in rewiring the economy and using finance for resilience, planning and minimising rather than exacerbating disruption, on the one hand, and, on the other, the prevalence of short-term volatility and the drive for high returns. Despite the more hopeful and optimistic rendition of the role of finance in disrupting and accelerating the creative destruction of fossil fuel industries sketched here, it remains the case that finance has to have something to invest in and that the fate of productive capital is not divorced from that of financial capital through shares, shared directorships and the like.

4.7 Contesting Finance

These processes of financialisation of the energy sector and responses to climate change have not gone uncontested. There have been social demands for 'de-financialisation' (Knuth 2018) and the return of key energy assets to the state. And there is, of course, a long history of contestations of energy infrastructures from resistance to dams (McCully 1996) to nuclear power plants and pipeline projects such as the XL and Dakota pipelines in the USA (see Chapter 6). There has also been significant lobbying around the uses and abuses of climate aid and climate finance led by groups such as Bretton Woods Project, Oil Change International (OCI), Global Witness and BankWatch. Opaque and inequitable governance and decision-making structures of key funding institutions have often inhibited campaign effectiveness, however. When the World Bank's CIFs were first proposed, governance issues featured highly among the concerns of civil society groups and Southern governments including limited consultation of developing countries (Nakhooda 2011), lack of clarity over whether money going into the funds would be additional to previously agreed overseas development aid and whether it would be in the form of grants or loans, the extent to which the funds would undermine already existing processes under the UNFCCC, and an apparent disregard for the Paris Declaration on Aid Effectiveness (Newell et al. 2009a).

As well as resisting infrastructures and contesting public institutions, as we will see in Chapter 6 on mobilising transitions, significant effort has been vested in challenging flows of finance to incumbent economies. The divestment movement that is centred on groups such as 350.org (discussed further in Chapter 6) is particularly notable here, but so too are groups such as OCI and IISD's Global Subsidies Initiative targeting fossil fuel subsidy reform. Broader campaigns around fossil fuel finance clearly affect the ecologies of finance: where and to what it flows. The challenge is to burst the balloon of fossil fuel finance, rather than squeeze it out of one location only for it to reappear elsewhere.

4.8 Ecologies of Governance of Energy Finance

The multiplicity of forms of governance of energy finance is suggestive of fragmentation and nested hierarchies, but with clear centres of political gravity. Amid the landscape of fragmentation and differentiation of institutional mandates and purposes described thus far, there is also a notable degree of convergence around the necessity of levering private sector finance if ambitious goals around energy poverty and sustainability, in particular, are to be realised. In earlier phases of global energy governance, this was primarily driven by an ideological commitment to, and material interest in, opening up markets to private sector investment (Tellam 2000; Dubash and Chella Rajan 2001). Power sector reform programmes of one part of the World Bank (International Development Association) opened the way for its private sector arm, the IFC, to set up lucrative investments with private capital. More recently, it reflects the reality that the levels of carbon and energy finance needed to ensure that future growth in demand for energy is fuelled by low carbon sources simply cannot be achieved by governments alone. Hence, above and beyond the issues of duplication of initiatives (as with initiatives and institutions supporting renewable energy), failures of co-ordination among institutions (such as donors), and conflicting mandates (climate versus energy security based on fossil fuels), there is evidence of a systematic bias towards market-enabling forms of governance, albeit pursued by different means (e.g. financing and partnerships).

At the national level, the embedding and adoption of market-enabling forms of governance through un-bundling, deregulation and competition in the energy sector have brought with them extra sets of governance challenges where governments have either relinquished control or agreed to share power with private actors over areas of energy policy. This is what makes proactive, deliberate, large-scale transitions towards different energy futures so difficult, as governments are deprived (or have been deprived) of many of the tools necessary to drive and shape those transitions in a context of neo-liberalism. What emerges by default is precisely the forms of steering complex interdependencies and managing networks of networks that constitute the predominant mode of global governance of energy finance. The growing power of countries such as India and China that have a stronger commitment to a state-capitalist model of development, reflected in strong state support for financing 'clean energy' sectors (such as India's Solar Mission), may yet set positive precedents for state-led low carbon energy transitions.

It is notable overall, however, that stronger and more robust systems of governance are in place *for* energy finance than *of* energy finance (Newell 2011). Many trade and investment treaties seek to liberalise energy sectors and protect investor rights, even over those of other governments. Sweeping reform of the energy sector has been overseen by international financial institutions in many parts of the world with a view to opening up markets. States have made considerable use of their powers to mobilise and attract private investment in the energy sector. They have notably not gone so far to date in using such powers to steer energy finance towards tackling energy poverty (Sanchez 2010) or climate change. Many of the initiatives are aimed at facilitating private investment and creating the right enabling environments (through policy and use of aid) rather than regulating existing flows. This is in spite of calls for a stronger role for UN-Energy to drive an integrated and co-ordinated energy agenda internationally and across the UN system (Karlsson-Vinkhuyzen 2010). Levering positive and new investments in clean energy is one thing, but who will regulate existing energy financing which contributes neither to tackling energy poverty and energy security nor to improving environmental sustainability? A transition to a more effective system of global energy governance surely requires us to do both. We currently have a situation in which institutions bequeathed formal roles and mandates in relation to energy are not necessarily those that wield the most direct power over energy finance, the lack of governance of private energy investment being a case in point.

There also appears to be an important geopolitics to the governance of energy finance. The location of an institution is important politically in terms of how energy finance is governed and by whom. The World Bank's location in the USA and close relationship with (and dependence upon) the US Treasury create openings and opportunities for those seeking to challenge or change the mandate of the institution. The identity of REEEP and REN21 as European initiatives may reflect the desire by the countries that drove their creation and help to fund them (the UK, France, Germany, Austria, Denmark and Spain) to project global leadership on efforts to tackle climate change as well as consolidate their reputation as leaders in renewables and as desirable investment locations for energy finance.

The global governance of energy finance can be characterised as highly pluralised (involving many actors); fragmented (with compartmentalised policymaking in discrete areas of energy policy) and ad hoc; dispersed (in terms of decision-making authority and across governance scales); uneven (some areas are subject to far more governance than others); and unequal (in terms of who sets the rules, who participates and who, by definition, does not). Governing, steering and managing something as complex, dispersed and deeply political as energy finance perhaps means that this is inevitably the case.

Inequities among actors, institutions and policy objectives in global energy governance reflect prevailing geometries of power and deliberate choices. The imbalances between the World Bank and regional development banks, backed as they are by powerful states wishing to promote financing for particular technologies on the one hand and PPPs such as REEEP and REN21 on the other, are vast, and their impact on global energy governance incomparable. Even within the G7, a body whose members could transform the existing landscape of energy governance, little has been done to successfully promote clean energy when compared with its other mandates (Boyce 2009; Lesage et al. 2009). That this is the case is perhaps no accident in a world which continues to be heavily dependent on the use of fossil fuels. But it does require us to be cautious in feting the undoubted boom in global governance initiatives in the area of energy, without a serious analysis of power and answers to questions about whom they serve and how. This is an issue we will return to in Chapter 5.

4.9 Conclusions

Debates about financing energy transition often start (and frequently end) with a discussion about the staggering volumes of capital that need to be mobilised to decarbonise the global economy and effectively address the climate crisis. This deficit model and the promise of new infrastructures, financial products and services, technologies and projects that will serve as key outlets for finance, combined with powerful and strategically important win-win discourses, often obscure the equally important need to divest, redirect and withdrawal capital from climate change inducing fossil fuel infrastructures and patterns of growth.

At root, whether or not the world transitions away from fossil fuels in time to avert catastrophic climate change will likely *not* be a function of whether we have enough money available. It may have a lot to do with how much capital continues to be directed to investments that drive us past any chance of achieving a 1.5°C trajectory. But, in the end, it has more still to do with confronting political power, institutional inertia and social and cultural lock-in, all of which are closely related to the everyday functioning of a highly industrialised, resource-intensive growth-oriented capitalist political economy. Finance provides entry points and wields important disruptive power, but it is just one part of the picture despite the degree of attention it receives in policy debates.

Hence, finance is clearly critical as a lubricant of political, social and economic and technological change. But at the same time, we also need to avoid the festishi-sation of the increasingly important role of private finance in order to challenge dominant narratives around what private finance is capable of and willing to do in relation to transitions to sustainability. For all the talk of a 'clean energy revolution in Africa' (AREI 2015) at the Paris COP and new initiatives in this area promising billions and trillions of investment, these are likely to bypass the poor, could create another bubble, and will likely be targeted at financing energy for industry and not sustainable energy for all. Many problems lie in the real economy where finance continues to invest in the reproduction of an unsustainable economy. We also need to desegregate different forms of finance: patient (pension funds) and speculative (venture or vulture capital) in terms of what return they expect and over what time frame. As Mazzucato and Semieniuk (2018: 8) suggest: 'Financial actors vary considerably in the composition of their investment portfolio, creating directions towards particular technologies.' There is clearly a key role for public money (state development banks, aid and MDBs) as well as private finance (Spratt 2015), but the investment models need to change. While finance can be mobilised and divested quickly in support of environmental goals, private capital has few incentives to ensure that rapid transitions are also socially just ones. Here the role of the state will remain key.

In sum, we are not facing the situation we confront today for lack of finance. The world is awash with capital and technology, albeit often directed towards destructive and unsustainable, yet hugely profitable, ends. Indeed, the drive of restless capital to find new outlets and sites of accumulation, however short-lived and socially and environmentally destructive, signals the need to regain public and social control of finance through stronger regulation. This implies a far bigger transformation in the relationship between finance and society, to be reorganised around different ideas of prosperity and sustainability than we have witnessed to date, or are considering seriously now. The role of governance in enabling such a shift is the focus of Chapter 5.

5

Governing Energy Transitions

Energy is and has always been governed by a variety of means and a plurality of actors. The nature of those means, their underlying goals and the types of actor involved have shifted over time. But all energy transitions are governed. Even if they are not. What I mean by this seemingly contradictory statement is that non-regulation, and an absence of governance of aspects of energy policy, is also a political choice: albeit not always one over which governments have full control. What I refer to as 'un-governance' and deliberate neglect – pathways not taken and policy options not adopted – are also exercises of power (Phillips and Newell 2013; Scarse and Smith 2009). They reflect political choices not to intervene in the market: for example, to allow other actors to provide and profit from the generation and transmission of electricity; for example, to allow for laissez-faire regulation of incumbent interests, or to enact more ambitious action to combat climate change. They embody power, ideology and political preferences. And they bear uneven social and economic consequences, even if these cannot always be deliberately and consciously foreseen.

This goes to the heart of tensions around the role of energy regulation and governance in relation to the role of the state, cast simultaneously as promoter and regulator of industries, with all the tensions and contradictions that flow from this (Newell 2008). As Levi-Faur (2005: 14) puts it, regulation is, or rather has become, 'both a constitutive element of capitalism (as the framework that enables markets) and the tool that moderates and socializes it'. The functions of *production* and *protection* are overseen by the same actors, often with close ties to those they are charged with regulating and often even with common material interests at stake, as with state-owned companies, for example, or where politicians have shares or hold directorships with private entities they are meant to regulate.

With energy, as many other domains of policy, there is a big difference between *governance in theory*, which describes separation of functions and clear lines of authority, independence from private actors, checks and balances and the existence of mechanisms of accountability and oversight, and *governance in practice*, more often than not characterised by blurred and shifting lines of authority as priorities shift, leadership changes and opportunities and threats alter the operating environment, and often underpinned by social networks of power which span across the state and broader political society which wields uneven political power in shaping policy outcomes. As I noted in a study on the governance of carbon markets in Argentina, but in terms which apply to many scenarios of energy governance,

governance is characterised by tight networks of specialists from government and the private sector whose roles elide and overlap in ways that challenge and give lie to the conventional wisdom about the separation of project developers from national regulatory agencies and verification bodies. This is not just about low levels of capacity and expertise, although that is part of the story, but also the social and political networks which govern and constitute policy-making in a real sense.   *(Newell 2014: 12–13)*

This power is concentrated in a small and tightly-knit community of state officials and 'market makers' (project developers, financiers and auditors) who encounter one another on a frequent basis, problematizing assumptions about the separation between their roles and responsibilities in ensuring fair play in carbon markets.   *(Newell 2014: 15)*

The distinction between governance in theory and governance in practice underscores the importance of researching 'every day' and informal decision-making through networks and practices of power that run through energy politics.

As Gore (2017: 157) suggests, at its most basic level,

[t]he notion of governance draws attention to the relationship between actors in a particular process, the knowledge that is included and excluded from a process, the spaces or opportunities for deliberation or engagement provided, and the institutions or rules that condition and structure interactions. A focus on 'energy governance' ... offers a lens through which we can view the multilevel power relations in a given process, how certain ideas and approaches come to dominate at the exclusion of others, and how different actors shape energy transitions and transformations.

In Section 5.1 on the histories of energy governance, I show how ideologies and strategies of governance have been shaped by broader shifts in capitalism, particularly during its neo-liberal phase, regarding the role of the state and the re-scaling of the global economy through processes of globalisation. In the former case, critiques of the role of the state as a provider of energy services have driven a wave of power sector reform in large parts of the majority world enforced by actors such as the World Bank and the IMF (International Monetary Fund). From this perspective, energy transitions are, therefore, part of broader attempts to deepen and extend neo-liberal discipline and market society: opening up new investment opportunities for capital through access to investments in energy infrastructures. In the latter case, this has served to regionalise and globalise energy markets and led to new forms of co-ordination and governance at those levels which energy producers and investors have sought to shape and influence. I argue below, building on the argument in Chapter 4, that overall this has taken the form of governance *for* energy investors and the energy industry, rather than governance *of* those actors, especially as we will see in Section 5.6 on the ecologies of energy governance, with regard to the environmental impacts of energy pathways.

In Section 5.2 on the political economy of energy governance, I show how at every level – from local, city, national, regional and global governance – political systems reflect and are imbued with the structural and material power of incumbent energy providers and interests, reinforced by institutional power through high levels of access and representation in the key centres of decision-making and further entrenched by discursive power to frame their needs as congruent with those of the state, and their preferred energy pathways as the most viable and attractive ones to deal with the energy trilemma of simultaneously tackling energy poverty, security and sustainability. This power derives, in part, from the peculiar relationship between energy and growth whose expansion provides the *raison d'être* of capitalist economies and the competition this generates between political authorities at all levels to attract mobile capital. Conceptually, the exercise of power in these ways has been described in a diversity of ways (Stirling 2014b) from the community power debates of the 1960s (Bachrach and Baratz 1962), which drew attention to the power to keep threatening issues off public and political agendas, to discussions about the 'captive state' (Monbiot 2000) and the capture of political systems (democratic and undemocratic) by fossil fuel interests and indeed the fragility of the division between the interests of state and capital (Holloway and Picciotto 1978). Globally, such power finds expression in what some scholars have referred to as 'oil hegemony' in the international system (Bromley 1991) or 'private empires' (Coll 2012). Taken together, this clearly points to the necessity of a political economy account of energy governance. I show too, though, how incumbent power is maintained and reinforced by a spectrum of social and cultural, as well as political, economic and military arenas of power.

In Section 5.6 on the ecologies of energy governance, I describe an energy governance complex: a web of distributed (but unevenly concentrated) power and agency over different parts of the energy system and its multi-functionality. Ecologising governance draws attention not only to the interconnections and interdependencies that characterise this governance complex, but also to its ecological blindness. This is observable in the ways, as we saw in Chapter 3 on production, in which certain supply- and demand-side reduction options are systematically marginalised in mainstream policy debates, the environmental impacts of everyday and routine energy planning and investment decisions overlooked or normalised and, at a more fundamental level, discussions of the incompatibility between energy-led industrial growth and sustainability obscured, denied and marginalised. This underlines the need once again for shifts in power relations within and beyond those institutions if more sustainable and progressive energy pathways are to be imagined and enacted.

5.1 Historicising Energy Governance

Forms of energy governance bear the hallmark of the historical period in which they are conceived, the national and regional context in which they were developed and for which they were designed, and of the actors, institutions, social forces and ideologies that shaped their emergence. This implies attention to disparate and uneven energy statecrafts, contests between national and global capitals, the fluctuating power of labour and the role of civil society and social movements.

We can observe a shifting balance of power between public and private control over the governance of energy (as we saw in Chapter 3) from state control to privatisation and the neo-liberalisation of energy governance, which I described as a process rather than an end state. In the early 1970s, for example, there was a trend towards states asserting control over supply. This came in the form of the expropriations of assets (Libya, Algeria), unilateral decisions to fix maximum rates of production (Kuwait) or the unwillingness to accept production expansions which had been scheduled by the companies (Saudi Arabia) (Odell 1981). Energy nationalism was then challenged with neo-liberal reform programmes for the power sector throughout the 1980s and 1990s, though in many contexts the state retained a key role (Baker et al. 2014). In Africa, though arguably elsewhere, McDonald (2009) suggests that this political shift took the form of 'electric capitalism'. As he suggests, 'electricity is not necessary for capitalism' (McDonald 2009: 3) per se, since capitalism began before the advent of electricity and it continues to operate in many part of the world without it (where in Africa, for example, less than 20 per cent of the population has access to electricity and as little as 2 per cent in many rural areas), though largely one could argue in areas and among populations that have yet to be fully integrated into market society. Electricity is clearly also not the only input that sustains capitalism, though energy, perhaps particularly in the form of oil, plays a critical role in fuelling the globalisation of capitalism. The importance of electricity is also not restricted to neo-liberal capitalist modes of production as the experience of contemporary China or the former USSR and Eastern bloc countries, where electrification and state-led industrialism have evolved hand in hand, clearly shows.

Yet, as McDonald (2009), Altvater (2006) and others have argued, there is something 'remarkably synergistic about electricity and capitalism' (McDonald

2009: 4). As it has evolved historically, electricity has become more and more intrinsic to the functioning and expansion of markets. Most forms of industry, manufacturing and service provision require large inputs of electricity to success-fully operate. Around IT, big data, automation, electrification and artificial intelli-gence (AI), the demands for greater electricity generation and distribution are set to greatly intensify, even as we seek to decarbonise the grid. Search engines and mega-servers are huge consumers of electricity. As McDonald (2009: 5) puts it:

Electricity may not be an innate feature of the capitalist mode of production but it has become an essential one, providing a stable, yet dynamic platform upon which to build new production systems and products that lend themselves to the rapid pace of change in contemporary global markets. And as the capitalist centre of gravity shifts towards the service sector (particularly finance), electricity becomes an even more indispensable input, heightening pressures for cheap and reliable supplies of electric power from the 'command-ing heights' of this new global economy and the transnational elite that runs it.

Some of this is not peculiar to neo-liberalism per se, but rather forms part of a deeper and historically constituted relationship between capitalism and electri-city. McDonald (2009: 5) argues: 'The electricity sector is not solely responsible for this kind of ideological imperialism, but the expansion of electricity is illustrative of the kinds of micro and macro-mechanisms of neo-liberal control being imposed around the world . . . from the disciplinary powers of pre-paid electricity meters to the private sector conditionalities of international financial institutions in infra-structure development.'

He further suggests that 'electricity has become an integral part of all capitalist activity and that we can best understand the inequities of its availability and affordability by looking at the (neo-liberal) market dynamics within which it operates' (McDonald 2009: xv). Questions of access to and the distribution of electricity are often subject to capitalist accumulation dynamics whereby the needs of industry and richer consumers are systematically privileged over those of poorer and labouring classes. The poor often pay more for their electricity in real terms, as opposed to merely as a percentage of their incomes (Sanchez 2010). McDonald (2009: 25) notes, for example, in the South African context, that '[c]ommerce and industry make up 60% of electricity consumption in Cape Town but they pay much less on average than domestic consumers'. In extreme cases, such as South Africa, we can see this in the disproportionate weighting of the demands of the mining and energy industries, part of the Minerals-Energy-Complex (Fine and Rustomjee 1997), but also in the extraordinary levels of state support given to nuclear power in the UK (Cox et al. 2016), for example, at a time of austerity and fuel poverty for many in the population at large. Efforts to extend energy services to the poor are often also undermined by aggressively pursued cost recovery programmes (McDonald 2009).

These modes of energy governance are not fixed, however, but do reflect different political economies and models of organising state–market relations. Sometimes dramatic recalibrations of energy governance occur in the wake of crises which call upon the state to intervene. In relation to rapid transitions in the energy sector, a Revolución Energética in Cuba moved the country to a more efficient, decentralised system with smaller generator stations and shorter distances to transmit energy. For example, old, inefficient incandescent light bulbs were removed almost entirely, by mandate, in just six months. Fidel Castro's comment at the time was: 'We are not waiting for fuel to fall from the sky, because we have discovered, fortunately, something much more important: energy conservation, which is like finding a great oil deposit' (Simms 2013: 209).

More proactively, the Chinese state has driven a series of energy transitions reflecting its new-found power as a global energy leader (Ockwell et al. 2017). It has also pursued them at pace. For example, pilot cook stove programmes were set up by the government in hundreds of rural provinces. From the start of the programme in 1982 until 1998, 185 million improved cook stoves were installed, facilitating the penetration of improved stoves from less than 1 per cent of the Chinese market in 1982 to more than 80 per cent by 1998 – reaching half a billion people (Sovacool 2016: 207). More recently, China's capacity around wind and solar not only grew fast, it grew much faster than in any other countries in the world. By 2010, it had surpassed the two largest wind power countries, Germany and the United States, and by 2016 China had installed more than twice the capacity of the United States, making up 36 per cent of the capacity installed globally. A similar phenomenon occurred in the field of solar energy, but in an even more compressed time frame. In the space of three years, from 2013 to 2016, China installed 50 GW of solar power. It overtook Germany in 2015 to make 26 per cent of the global solar power capacity in 2016 (Goron 2017). In Indonesia, meanwhile, the government both lowered kerosene subsidies and constructed new refrigerated LPG terminals to act as national distribution hubs. Within just three years – from 2007 to 2009 – the number of LPG stoves nationwide jumped from a mere 3 million to 43.3 million, meaning that they served almost two-thirds of Indonesia's 65 million households (or about 216 million people). The programme reached all of its targets including six entire provinces and Jakarta, the capital, and all kerosene subsidies were withdrawn. In the case of Brazil's Proálcool programme, introduced in November 1975 to increase ethanol production and substitute ethanol for petroleum in conventional vehicles, by 1981, six years later, 90 per cent of all new vehicles sold in Brazil could run on ethanol (Sovacool 2016). State-led programmes, visions (such as India's solar mission) and programmes of technology innovation and development clearly, then, can and do flourish within a neo-liberal global political economy which questions the efficiency, desirability and effectiveness of such interventions in the energy sector.

5.2 Political Economy of Energy Governance

5.2.1 States of Transition

The state, by its presence or absence, and either despite or because of historical shifts in governance, remains the central actor in energy governance. This is true even in relation to more liberalised and privatised sectors, and of global institutions where states remain the key actors and jealously guard their authority. Even with regard to the tremendous growth of transnational energy governance, state authority is still often called upon for institutional backing and enforcement. Likewise, as we saw in Chapter 4 in relation to governing private finance or shaping social norms and cultural preferences (as we will see in Chapter 6), the state performs critical roles.

Understanding the role of the state in energy transformations requires an appreciation of context: what is possible given enormous differences in capacity and resources, autonomy and uneven access to different energy sources and technologies. Which technologies and energy systems receive support, whose energy needs get prioritised, and which actors are charged with the responsibility for meeting energy needs are functions of very different decision-making processes, political systems and political economies. Key political economy dynamics include (i) the organisation of the state; (ii) the political nature of the state; and (iii) the role of the state in the global political economy (Ockwell et al. 2017). We noted in Chapter 2 that specific concerns have been raised about the extent to which 'the state' is properly understood and accounted for within transitions scholarship (Johnstone and Newell 2018). This includes thinking about the state's role in transitions and transformations (Meadowcroft 2005, Kuzemko et al. 2016; Lockwood et al. 2016) explored through transition management approaches (Loorbach et al. 2015), work on the governance of energy transitions (Verbong and Loorbach 2012) and around specific state functions in relation to transitions, such as the entrepreneurial state (Mazzucato 2011) or the use of industrial policy (Pegels 2014). But there continues to be a neglect of more systematic and comparative thinking about the relationship between different forms of state and statehood and different approaches to transition and transformation. This constitutes a broad canvas: from an exploration of how types and depth of democracy produce different types of (energy) pathways, for example (Johnstone and Stirling 2020); to the role of electoral and party systems and specific policy processes and styles of decision-making (Kern and Rogge 2018), to different political economies constituted by an array of state–society complexes captured in part by the notion of varieties of capitalism (Hall and Soskice 2001; Ćetković and Buzogány 2016) and the politics of which states are best able to accelerate transitions (Roberts et al. 2018).

This raises questions about the viability and desirability of generic prescriptions for 'managed transitions' in light of such diversity in state forms and functions, the different ways in which they interact with energy systems and the evident limits of the sorts of transitions and transformations that states alone can steer, manage or impose. This speaks directly to critiques of prescriptions for 'managed transitions' (Stirling 2011, 2014a), with their implicit assumption that a monolithic state-like entity can prescribe actions necessary for transitions in order to effect some form of 'seemingly amorphous, singular, depoliticized "way forward"' (Stirling 2014a: 5). Ockwell et al.'s (2017) analysis challenges explicit and implicit assumptions about how transitions might be managed or controlled, demonstrating how, even in highly centralised states such as China, assumptions of complete state control are often illusory. Assumptions about state capacity are built into international treaties like the Paris Agreement, as well many national transition plans, visions and strategies which envisage a top-down process of state-led energy transformation, one which sits awkwardly with the historical experience to date of the practice of energy transitions which imply key roles for a diversity of actors.

A key issue is whether transformations can be engineered or planned from above, as is implied or imagined in national transition plans, or rather can also emerge more organically from below. After all, there was no blueprint for the industrial revolution, suggesting a disconnect between current assumptions and practices about how to organise and govern transformations and historical evidence of how they have occurred in practice (Newell 2015). Nevertheless, there are many examples of the proactive use of state power to bring about rapid transitions which speak to the increasing recognition that the role of the state will be key to accelerating transitions to sustainability (Johnstone and Newell 2018). The role of the state in accelerating transitions can range from supporting research, development and innovation in its entrepreneurial form (Mazzucato 2011), employing a plethora of policy tools and economic instruments to tax, support, protect and regulate industries, and using the machinery of democratic government to promote and safeguard spaces of deliberation over competing energy futures (Eckersley 2004).

There are many examples of proactive state-led transitions in today's world, including those noted in Section 5.1. More ambitious strategies for embracing renewable energy have been adopted in countries ranging from China and Kenya to Uruguay, Germany and Denmark for a variety of different reasons including seeking to secure first mover advantages (Germany, Denmark, India and China) for state-owned and private firms, reducing dependence on imported energy (India, Uruguay) and reducing vulnerability to the effects of climate change on energy generation capacity (such as hydropower) (Kenya). Uruguay, for example, has adopted bold emissions reduction targets and plans to derive 94.5 per cent of the country's electricity from renewable energy (Watts 2015). More recently still in Norway, France and the UK, targets have been set for the phase-out of petrol and diesel-only vehicles within eight years in the most ambitious case of Norway. Many government announcements followed declarations by car producers such as Volvo that they would only make fully electric or hybrid cars from 2019 onwards. The importance of economy-wide state visions for green transitions is most recently manifested in interest in the Green New Deal which, in Europe, takes the form of a region wide, sector by sector carbon descent and investment plan.

States can also set limits on production. Encouragingly, there have been recent bold moves by governments to leave fossil fuels in the ground. A combination of divestment of finance from fossil fuels by major investors and laws and regulations that many governments have recently shown themselves willing to adopt to cap production (such as recent moratoria on new oil exploration and production announced in 2017 and 2018 by a number of countries including New Zealand, France, Costa Rica and Belize), or which set clear near-term timetables for their phase-out as is happening in China, show what is possible. Costa Rica, for example, has a moratorium on oil exploration in place that was recently extended to 2021, the year by which Costa Rica also intends to be carbon neutral. There are also moratoria on fracking in a number of jurisdictions globally such as France, Germany, Ireland, Wales, Scotland and Uruguay. In February 2020, Mayor Bill de Blasio announced New York City's intention to stop all new fossil fuel projects within and serving the city. This is the largest municipal ban announcement of its kind globally.[1] Most recently, the Spanish Climate Change and Energy Transition Bill, currently in development, is likely to include a ban on new oil and gas exploration and exploitation activities.

Internationally, there are precedents such as the moratorium in place for mining projects in Antarctica (Article 7 of the Environmental Protocol of the Antarctic Treaty). The International Council on Mining and Metals has committed its members (including the World Coal Association) to not explore or mine in World Heritage Sites and 'respect legally designated protected areas'. Likewise, there are calls for banning oil drilling in the Arctic Sea and to halt exploitation in protected areas and on indigenous lands (LINGO 2018). The *Lofoten Declaration for a Managed Decline of Fossil Fuel Production Around the World* developed in 2017 by a group of activists, academics and analysts meanwhile, signed by over 500 organisations, highlights the need to put an end to fossil fuel development and manage the decline of existing production (Lofoten Declaration 2017). In this regard, a number of governments have signed up to the 'Powering Past Coal Alliance', launched in November 2017, including more than twenty-five nations that have pledged to phase out coal-fired power generation. Membership of the Alliance requires states to make (non-binding) public declarations that they will refrain from building new, unabated coal-fired power stations and will phase out existing ones (Jewell et al. 2019). This led to calls for a global coal mining moratorium (Blondeel and Van de Graaf 2018). Bolder still have been calls made at the United Nations Security Council for a *Fossil Fuel Non-Proliferation Treaty* (Newell and Simms 2019).

What these initiatives point to is the obvious need not to leave the pace and nature of energy transitions to the 'historical cycles' or 'invisible' hand of the market to take their course through 'natural decline' and adjustments to supply and demand, but rather to proactively force disruptive change by setting some energy pathways off limits and thereby facilitating the rapid switching of investment, innovation, technology and policy towards climate-compatible alternatives (Wilson and Tyfield 2018; Wilson 2018). Though the power of incumbent industries and lock-in to particular production models is often stated as a reason for the impossibility of rapid transitions, historically states have played a key role in managing adaptations to external shocks or rewiring their economies in line with shifting domestic needs and global demands within short periods of time. This includes large-scale industrial conversion, often in war time. But current responses to the coronavirus also illustrate the willingness and ability of the state to support the rapid re-purposing and conversion of industries: in this case to produce ventilators and other essential medical equipment.[2]

The issue is not just the type of state in a generic sense: whether it is more liberal or co-ordinated, or the extent to which it is democratic. We also need to be attentive to politics *within* the state. Different states are characterised by uneven power and resources that they can mobilise behind low carbon transitions, reflected in the ways in which they organise and are able to implement responses to energy policy challenges. It is possible to discern two broad types of organisational integration that characterise governance by different states. The first is the level of *vertical governance* integration. This refers to degrees of centralisation/de-centralisation, which have consequences for the form of energy politics, the types of transition that are possible and whether they can be 'steered' from above. It can, for example, take the form of centre–province relations, such as in China, or result from constitutional changes bringing about the devolution and delegation of authority and access to resources for counties, as has happened in Kenya.

The second type of organisational characteristic is the level of *horizontal governance* integration. This refers to the organisation of bureaucracies and imbalances of power across government, which have implications for interventions in the energy sector (e.g. the balance of power, authority and resources between ministries of energy and planning, as opposed to those dealing with environment and rural development) and how trade-offs around energy poverty, security and low carbon imperatives are resolved or not as a result. Some ministries have more power than others. To take an example, in India, the Ministries of Power and Coal command much greater financial resources and political power within government than either the MNRE (Ministry of New and Renewable Energy) or the MoEF (Ministry of Environment and Forests). Phillips and Newell (2013: 660) use the term 'ungovernance' to refer to

areas of deliberate and active neglect, where power is exercised to ensure action is not taken and prevailing material and bureaucratic interests protected. In this context it entails recognition that the actors and institutions with primary responsibility for clean energy development are rarely those actors which yield most power over the course of energy policy development. It manifests itself in the way the incumbent regime, largely centred around the continued use of fossil fuels, accommodates niche initiatives on clean energy without reducing its position of power within India's energy regime.

Moreover, 'whilst the MNRE may provide avenues of stakeholder engagement (however imperfect) for promoting low carbon, pro-poor energy technologies, there is no evidence to suggest that the Ministry of Power is obliged to include MNRE within its decision making on policies that affect the power sector' (Phillips and Newell 2013: 660).

Because of the centrality of energy to growth, ministries of energy and planning often wield more power and authority than departments and ministries responsible for the environmental, health, labour or other aspects of energy policy decision-making. These are often reinforced by close and often revolving-door relationships with energy utilities and providers with whom they have to negotiate to secure their buy-in and support for key state strategies. As Newell and Phillips (2016) show in the case of Kenya, for example, failure to ensure the buy-in of the energy ministry in early consultations led to the stalling of attempts to get a national climate action plan adopted for the country. For energy policy to be effectively implemented, there is a need for buy-in across all levels of governance, both horizontally and vertically. Likewise, policy alliances among central regulators without effective participation from key local, financial and market stakeholders will face challenges at the implementation stages of these top-down initiatives, as these non-state actors' financial and technological resources are indispensable at project level.

This is especially the case given the importance for energy policy of 'non-energy energy policy' by which I mean trade, transport, housing and agriculture policies which generate energy demands and reproduce energy regimes through their preference for particular policies, pricing regimes and infrastructures. It is not just states that generate energy demand or shape pathways in these ways. As Royston et al. (2018: 129) put it:

They are formulated not only by nation-states but also, at one end of the scale, by international organisations, multinational corporations and trans-national policy networks, and at the other, by regional and local authorities, and institutions like prisons, schools and hospitals. All such institutions, whether national, trans-national or local, have policies, priorities and agendas which shape energy demand ... all such institutions have some degree of power and autonomy in the steering of demand.

But key actors use material and institutional power to make their voices heard to the state. Companies are generally reluctant to disclose such lobbying expenditure of course, but a report from InfluenceMap used a methodology focusing on the best available records along with intensive research of corporate messaging to gauge their level of influence on initiatives to halt climate change (McCarthy 2019). To take one example, fossil fuel political giving outdoes renewables thirteen to one. During the latest mid-term election cycle in the USA, the fossil fuel industry paid at least $359 million for federal campaign donations and lobbying (Kirk 2020). As of December 2019, 134 members of Congress and their spouses own as much as $92.7 million worth of stock in fossil fuel companies and mutual funds (Kotch 2020). This has global implications given the weight and profile of the USA in global climate politics. Globally, every year, the world's five largest publicly owned oil and gas companies spend approximately $200 million on lobbying designed to control, delay or block binding climate-motivated policy (McCarthy 2019).

Moving to the international level, the importance of which part of the state engages in policy becomes alarmingly clear in the climate change negotiations where delegates from OPEC states such as Saudi Arabia, paid for by the oil company Aramco, come predominantly from the Ministry of Petroleum which has no mandate whatsoever for environmental protection. A key issue, then, is how to prevent the more active and explicit sabotage of the process by a small group of oil-exporting countries willing and able to hold the world hostage to their desire to protect the profit flows of oil majors such as Saudi's Aramco. Attention has focused on these delegates attending UNFCCC negotiations that are in the pay of oil companies and able to stall progress of the negotiations by challenging the science and adopting delaying tactics (Depledge 2008). For example, at COP25 more than forty Gulf state delegates were current or former employees of fossil fuel companies (Collett-White 2019). In other words, they are using veto power to block progress towards the stated aim of the negotiations and have a clear material interest in slowing progress wherever possible. Quite the contrary: their mandate is to expand the supply and export of more climate-changing oil, a fact which has led to calls for their exclusion from the negotiations on the basis that they are acting in bad faith and subject to clear conflicts of interest.

An appreciation of the tensions and power imbalances within and across the state underscores the need to get inside the state and not view it as a monolithic and unitary actor. Power balances shift over time as personnel and their interests and expertise change. In the UK, as a result of an ideological shift on the part of an incoming government, for example, the Department for Energy and Climate Change was dissolved and merged into the department for Business, Energy and Industrial Strategy, affording less priority to climate change. The implementation of high-level energy policy goals can also meet barriers in the form of variegated interests, stratified, often simultaneously, across both vertical and horizontal levels of governance. Networks, alliances and coalitions are required to carry policies and overcome incumbent resistance and barriers to action (Meckling et al. 2015). Sometimes bureaucrats feeling isolated on an issue will seek alliances with external actors from civil society or business in order to bolster their position, a dynamic that has been observed in the European Commission around energy and climate policy, for example (Grant et al. 2000). This means adopting framings or developing issue-based coalitions that can carry a policy and enjoy the broad support of a policy network (Hess 2018).

Beyond questions of the organisation of the state in bureaucratic terms along vertical and horizontal lines and the ways in which this affects energy pathways, the nature of the political system that operates within a state is also vitally important in shaping procedural and distributional effects of energy interventions. This refers to different degrees of democracy and the scope for democratisation of decision-making, for example, around identification of energy needs and priorities (Lehtonen and Kern 2009; Johnstone and Stirling 2020). This might be extended to decision-making about technology choices and R&D (research and development) priorities and in relation to energy planning, electrification and pricing. Who participates, on whose terms and what difference does it make? Who gets consulted or not, and perceptions of energy needs, concretely affect energy policy decisions. The politics of energy in specific contexts are revealing of which social and economic interests the state seeks to serve. Newell et al. (2014) demonstrate how Kenyan central government interest in low carbon energy is strongly focused on large, grid-connected infrastructure (e.g. geothermal) and the needs of large, powerful industrial interests, a phenomenon that others have noticed elsewhere in South Africa (McDonald 2009) and India (Phillips and Newell 2013). At the same time, in some settings at least, we have seen moves to open up low carbon development strategies to broader forms of citizen engagement (Newell and Martin 2020).

5.3 Regulation

The desire for growth, and implicitly increased energy consumption, has historically been coupled with an expanding state role (Caldwell and Woolley 1976). States are not neutral arbiters in energy policymaking and can best be thought of as the locus and epicentre of broader social conflicts between competing social forces (Poulantzas 2014). Although broadly seeking to serve particular class interests, states enjoy a sufficient degree of autonomy that energy industries need to compete to align their preferred technology and energy source with (shifting) perceptions of the national interest, and some policies adopted in the general interest will run counter to the preferences of a specific fractional interest (Holloway and Piccottio 1978). Newell and Paterson (1998) discuss this in terms of competing 'fractions of capital'. For transition scholars, this is understood more narrowly in terms of contests between 'niche' and 'regime' actors (as discussed in Chapter 2). This is not the same as a pluralist argument that all such interests are equal and that systematic biases do not exist. With energy this is demonstrably not the case because of the particular relationship between energy and growth.

It remains the case, nevertheless, that states use their power to serve these general interests in order to maintain the profitability of private production through financing and tax breaks, provision of infrastructures and disproportionate representation in policy processes and, where required, through using coercion and violence to discipline dissent in relation to energy projects (Brock and Dunlap 2018). We often see this most clearly in relation to energy sources of high political and strategic importance such as oil, over which wars have been fought and military interventions made (Kaldor et al. 2007; Colgan 2013) as well as significant intrastate violence enacted (Okonta and Douglas 2001). But more routinely and mundanely, state and police violence are mobilised for protests around anything from fracking to wind farms to pipeline projects, as we will see in Chapter 6. As Polanyi (1957 [1944]: 250) reminds us, 'the market has been the outcome of a conscious and often violent intervention on the part of government which imposed the market organisation of society for non-economic ends'. And yet, as Caldwell and Woolley (1976: 118) suggest, 'although the state has been forced to underwrite more and more of the costs of production and capital accumulation, profits continue to be privately appropriated'. The state does this through bailouts, compensation (of the coal industry, for example), subsidies (predominantly to fossil fuels as we saw in the last chapter), financing riskier investments (such as nuclear power) and decreasing taxes when profits fall to cushion the effects of cycles in the capitalist economy.

We will see in Section 5.6.1 on global energy governance how powerful states use their influence within multilateral institutions and banks to lever open new markets for energy investments by their companies through trade agreements, as a condition of structural adjustment, or through power sector reform programmes (Tellam 2000), extending and consolidating their power globally. This is an additional way in which states use and project their influence to the benefit of domestic capital to create new outlets for surplus production and new sites for accumulation overseas; whether it is the Brazilian state using commercial diplomacy to build a global production model for biofuels (Power et al. 2016), the British state promoting geothermal in Kenya (Newell and Phillips 2016), the Danish state promoting wind energy in South Africa (Baker et al. 2014) or the Chinese state creating new sites of accumulation for Chinese solar PV firms in the face of diminishing returns in domestic markets (Shen and Power 2017). For Hammarlund (1976: 168), 'the state's principal mission is to promote favourable conditions for growth by reducing vulnerabilities and lowering the costs of national adaptation to the changing global energy situation'. Indeed, as we saw in Chapter 4, states have often faced criticism for using state aid money or export credits to support their energy industries overseas, even in ways which contradict their own climate change ambitions. The UK's decision to ban fracking at home while supporting the 'vaca muerta' fracking project in Argentina is a case in point (Ambrose 2019b).

What these patterns of influence highlight is the hybrid nature of policy and commercial networks where business groups have uneven access to different parts of the state, and state and commercial interests coalesce around particular energy technologies and pathways, often in competition with one another. The reality of hybrid forms of power and the meshing of public and private actors, networks and finance calls into question the respective discursive constructions of the failures, inefficiencies and comparative advantages of states and markets alike in enabling energy transitions, when the two are intimately bound together. It also further exposes the limits of assumptions about governance in theory regarding independence, autonomy and accountability. Nevertheless, we have seen throughout the book the role of powerful narratives on the part of investors and donors towards the state which embody claims about what form a desirable 'business climate' would take in terms of security of investments, predictability and certainty around policies and time frames (Besant-Jones 2006).

Despite their critiques of the state, there is also intense competition among business actors to represent themselves as best able to deliver state energy goals, and there are fierce battles over state regulation and support to protect or undermine incumbent actors and nurture or squeeze niche actors. This includes the use of the state by private actors to close down competition from other niches, as the gas and nuclear industries are accused of doing to renewable energy in the UK. The Kenyan

PV case also provides an example of such efforts to close down competition within the emerging new PV niche. In the late 1990s and early 2000s, the Kenyan Bureau of Standards was persuaded by actors in the PV industry that something needed to be done to introduce formal standards around the quality of solar home systems. A committee of existing Kenyan PV actors was convened to advise on this and agreed on the introduction of PV regulations. These introduced strict, legally enforceable rules around PV in Kenya and were seen by some as an attempt by the established actors to shut out new entrants and consolidate what they have already gained (Ockwell et al. 2017). Balances of business power are in flux across actors and sectors, however, and, as Rennkamp et al. (2017: 214) show, powerful coalitions of political actors can get renewable energy programmes implemented even in fossil rich middle-income countries such as Mexico, South Africa and Thailand, where they currently make up a small percentage of the energy mix.

Different energy policymaking styles in many ways reflect varieties of capitalism (Benney 2019) which create uneven political opportunity structures for energy industries to shape policy. Many accounts describe the privileged role of energy industries in policy (Steen 1994), in part due to their structural power acquired because of the critical importance of energy for growth (Newell and Paterson 1998), but also as a function of particular political systems. Often well-resourced and well represented, some political systems through committee structures and party donations are more open to such influence. Caldwell and Woolley wrote in 1976 that 'the US energy industry has a unique ability to influence the political process due to its own resources and the highly fragmented nature of the policy-making system' (p. 114). In South Africa, a powerful minerals-energy-complex (Fine and Rustomjee 1997) operates to manage energy transitions away from coal at a pace and in a direction that is non-threatening to incumbent interests by conferring control over the speed and nature of reform and the scope for niche competitors to enter the market upon an incumbent actor, Eskom, and stacking key committees addressing climate change with fossil fuel interests (Baker et al. 2014). Likewise, around responses to acid rain, Boehmer-Christiansen and Skea (1991) describe differences between the UK and Germany in terms of coal industry access to key ministries and the counter-veiling power of environmental movements.

There are also clear differences among states in terms of resource endowments, autonomy and capacity to chart their own energy pathways (Power et al. 2016; Newell 2018). As well as looking at the organisation and political nature of the state and its particular relationship to energy, it is important to locate the role of the state in energy transitions in a global context which takes account of the power that a range of public and private transnational actors bring to bear on seemingly state-based energy pathways. As with the organisation and political nature of the state, such global political economy dynamics are material to shaping the procedural and distributional effects of energy interventions. Issues of policy autonomy and 'developmental space' are important here: the ways in which the scope governments have to independently chart and follow their own energy pathways is affected by levels of aid dependence, trade ties, their status as energy importers or exporters and how much scope they have to impose conditions on investors around employment, local content requirements and so on (Power et al. 2016; Newell 2018).

There are different ways of conceptualising this. Newell and Phillips (2016) draw on Gill's (1995) notion of 'disciplinary neoliberalism', to understand how key development agencies and multilateral development banks (MDBs) constrain the policy autonomy and 'developmental space' of poorer countries over whom they exercise control through their lending practices (Gallagher 2005). They suggest that this has occurred through first wave power sector reforms and then a second wave of interventions aimed at trying to address energy poverty (produced in part by the first wave of reforms) and the challenge of decarbonisation simultaneously, a dynamic usefully understood through the lens of 'governance states' (Harrison 2004). Harrison (2004: v) uses this term to describe the World Bank's attempts at 'reconciling a global political economy with its own designs and a specific set of challenges posed by the African region'. McDonald (2009), meanwhile, illustrates two key moments in neo-liberal reform processes. One that dismantles the ideological and institutional vestiges of the previous Fordist-Keynesian regimes of accumulation and a second that creates new and revised modes of neo-liberalism that respond to the failures and contradictions of the first wave of reforms. What follows is what we have seen in the energy sector: a belated recognition by the World Bank and other actors of the importance of the state and the limits of market-based approaches alone in the face of resistance and failed initiatives (World Bank 2010). The popularity of public–private partnerships, state-led development corporations and efforts to de-risk finance are examples of this partial recognition of the need to combine public and private power and resources. The projects remain the same, however. As Brenner and Theodore (2002: 362) put it, it is 'the creation of new infrastructure for market-oriented economic growth, commodification and the rule of capital'. Ironically, this roll-out phase often implies a strengthening rather than a weakening of the state (Peck and Tickell 2002).

In states characterised by high levels of aid dependence and a high level of external influence, whereby the World Bank is intimately involved in policy-making, any clear distinction between the Bank and an autonomous state become difficult to discern. Energy pathways are narrowed or opened up by the presence and interests of global actors and their interactions with state elites (Sovacool and Brisbois 2019). This raises key questions about what instruments states have available to them to address the challenges of decarbonising their economies in a socially just manner, when many have ceded direct control over the energy sector. The disciplinary role of international finance institutions in shaping energy sector liberalisation in these contexts, therefore, suggests the need for accounts that are also transnational in nature, with due attention to how capital and domestic political economies are intertwined (Newell and Phillips 2016). As Newell and Bulkeley (2016: 655) note based on their work in Southern and Eastern Africa:

[I]n many settings it is clear the state is not in a position to perform key roles in relation to innovation, lacks convening power and resources to deliver targets and goals and often also has only limited autonomy to assert policy preferences that diverge from those of transnational businesses, donors and other powerful states. Especially where they are heavily aid-dependent (such as Mozambique) or through processes of power sector reform have relinquished a degree of control over the energy system to private providers, many states find it hard to set the terms of energy sector reforms aimed at decarbonization – even if they have the political will to undertake them.

Where energy enterprises are state-owned, the lines between regulator and promoter of energy industries become further blurred, often resulting in poor levels of protection for host communities of potentially hazardous production (Newell 2005a). States are often willing to override opposition to local planning decisions on behalf of energy companies, such as with fracking in the UK when Lancashire council's decision to reject a fracking application was overturned by the central government. Conversely, the experience of the shift in Swedish energy policy in 1970s where grassroots study groups were set up to discuss and input into energy policy, resulting in policies to reduce energy demand and increase taxes on energy, suggests that more radical change in policy is more likely to come about when open to a plurality of actors and voices (Caldwell and Woolley 1976). This is the exception to a general tendency in energy policy towards small technocracies and tightly knit networks of experts, industry representatives and sympathetic policy officials. We return to this point in the discussion of energy forecasting and the politics of knowledge production about energy which is closely allied to the need to legitimate positive forward projections for preferred technologies. Caldwell and Woolley (1976: 124) write:

[G]iven a short-term view, a reactive orientation, an acceptance of the primacy of the integrity of production, and a highly restrictive decision-making process dominated by technocrats and energy producers, there is, as part of the structure of the situation, a propensity to adopt policies that are sympathetic to the problems of producers and designed to encourage and underwrite their efforts to guarantee supplies.

'Seeing like a state', to borrow Scott's (1998) phrase in relation to energy, means getting to grips with that technocracy: of energy planning, central control, targets and narrow notions of applicable expertise. For example, the domination of engineers and planners in energy ministries was offered to me as a key explanation for the slow uptake of renewables in Argentina, despite the enormous potential of wind and solar energy (Newell 2014). The argument was that technicians and energy bureaucrats and the consultants that advise them were trained to think in terms of centralised grid provision, meeting (not reducing) energy demand and in terms of models of constant (rather than variable and 'smart' supply). There is also an element of rent-seeking here, as Newell and Phillips (2016) show based on their work in Kenya, where central planners and regulators are reluctant to cede power and authority over energy policy to regional and local governments because they do not want to lose control of contracting and procurement with major energy providers, which often bring lucrative side-payments. These actors' desire to concentrate control and access to wealth shapes which energy pathways are adopted and whose interests are served by them.

The effect of these forms and practices of statecraft in the energy domain is to narrow the frame and control the terrain around which the relevant questions can be posed (Gramsci 1971) where, because of a set of assumptions that go largely unchallenged, conventional and dominant pathways are naturalised and alternative ones ridiculed or ignored altogether. An example of this would be dismissal of demands from the group Extinction Rebellion for net zero by 2025 or challenges to Centre for Alternative Technology (CAT) models on the basis of technical and political feasibility. Dominant and incumbent actors exercise significant power in shaping the discourse about what is 'viable' and 'acceptable', eliding questions about whether their preferred approaches to incremental change and minor modifications to business as usual, implying climate chaos for large swathes of the world's population, count as 'viable', or for whom they would be considered 'acceptable'. An important part of the story here is state legitimation: being seen, on the one hand, to serve capital well in order to protect its power and, on the other hand, to increase overall welfare and maintain social harmony, two functions that, as others have pointed out in relation to climate change, are often in tension with one another (Paterson 2010; O'Connor 1973; Miliband 1969). This relates to the discussion earlier in this chapter about the contradictions that arise from the relationship between production and protection.

Regarding the notion of what political economists refer to as a fiscal crisis of the state, it is the case that efforts to socialise the costs of production to underwrite private profits could cause a structural gap between expenditures and revenues as the costs of health impacts, extreme weather events and climate adaptation take a rising toll. Thus far, as Clark (1990: 368) points out, '[c]heap energy has attracted a stronger political constituency than has social welfare'. In this regard, regulation seeks to occupy the terrain between these (potentially) competing goals such that regulation is a critical function for ensuring the continued accumulation of capital. Understandings of the form and prospects of state intervention and regulation in the energy sphere need to be cognisant of this broader structural context within which the state operates in a capitalist society (Miliband 1969; Jessop 2002).

Discursively, it has been relatively straightforward for key energy providers to claim that they serve the needs of capital in general because of their centrality to the pursuit of growth (Newell and Paterson 1998). But political work needs to be undertaken and policy and discursive tools employed to manage the contradictions among energy, growth and sustainability. As Lane (2015) shows, though often the dominating international preoccupation with economic growth is simply assumed, this preoccupation is in fact a mid-twentieth-century development (Arndt 1978: 13; Dale 2012), and one that coincides with the 'great acceleration', the sudden post-war speeding up of economic growth, oil consumption and environmental despoliation (Steffen et al. 2015).

5.4 Governing Technology and Innovation

The role of the state in facilitating and frustrating technological innovation has received significant attention, not least because of the roots of a lot of transition studies in technology and innovation studies. As Kuzemko et al. (2016: 101) emphasise, however, there is a need to bring political perspectives to bear:

> By understanding governing for sustainable innovations as part of a more complex political whole this allows us to question which interactions between governance actors and actors in energy systems are delivering sustainable practice change and which constrain such change. Just as this is true for scholarly research so should this also be true for policymaking analysis . . . . [I]t is also necessary to understand the historical energy landscape: who the important actor groups are, what interests they represent and their relationship to governance.

This addresses classic concerns with which technological options should be supported through strategic niche management and what incentives should be provided to speed up development and deployment from R&D to prototyping and demonstration through to commercialisation and deployment. Traditionally, this implied a key role for the state in 'picking winners' from competing options (Watson 2009), but this view came under attack in the late 1990s and early 2000s from bodies such as the IEA. The military has also played an important role as an incubator and innovator of new approaches. For example, a key reason for accelerating the shift from coal to oil was because of military preoccupations with naval supremacy at the time of the First World War (Ediger and Bowlus 2018). More recently, Watson (2009: 128) notes the key role of governments in supporting solar PV and gas turbine technologies which 'transformed many electricity industries in the 1990s' and 'simply would not exist without indirect state support through military budgets'.

Governments can shape both 'technology push' and 'demand pull', but increasingly there is recognition of the networked nature of innovation and the role of a multiplicity of actors in enabling it – documented through innovation histories (Becker et al. 2013). This methodology helps to challenge accounts of heroic private entrepreneurs and overly simplified accounts of entrepreneurial states. In the case of the success of Solar Home Systems in Kenya, for example, such accounts overlooked years of donor support to networks of innovation which preceded the market entry of private business actors who feature highly in the histories constructed by actors such as the World Bank (Ockwell and Byrne 2017). At the same time, governments can steer and herd, but '[e]xpecting governments to single-handedly enable the green transformation would be unrealistic, given the complexity of this undertaking, its effects on the economy and society at large, and the political dynamics that such a process unleashes' (Pegels et al. 2018: 30). Innovations can be both more incremental and radical and bottom-up or grassroots (Smith et al. 2016a; Seyfang and Haxeltine 2012) as opposed to top-down. The latter are often explicitly aimed at taking control back from the state (and sometimes the market) over the purpose and direction of innovation. Informal spaces of repurposing, reusing and recycling, such as repair cafes, perform an important and subversive role in the context of the relentless drive for consumerism, in prolonging the life of goods, sharing skills and saving energy involved in producing and transporting new products.

As argued previously, the allocation and direction of support for particular technology and innovation pathways are sharply determined by both the availability and nature of finance and the scale of anticipated profits. As well as offsetting, sharing or de-risking the upfront costs of investment, states have a key role to play in giving 'long, loud, legal' signals about the direction of change and its permanency (Hamilton 2009). State investment banks (SIBS) such as the Clean Energy Finance Corporation (CEFC) in Australia, the Kreditanstalt für Wiederaufbau (KfW) in Germany and the Green Investment Bank (GIB) in the UK, for example, have also played a critical role in this regard. SIBs can take a broader approach to mobilising finance than capital provision and de-risking, as well as signal trust and 'crowd-in' private finance (Geddes et al. 2018). Some forms of state support are about addressing market failures produced by the under-pricing of pollution or seeing technology developers through the 'valley of death' as they move from demonstration stage to commercial deployment. State-based bodies such as the Carbon Trust in the UK have a mandate to support firms through this challenging stage of the business cycle (Foxon 2003). With energy, there are added issues because of the long-lived nature of the capital assets and the high potential for lock-in (Unruh 2000).

The balance of agency and leadership in the energy domain may be expected to shift once again in the face of the climate crisis. As Pegels et al. (2018: 29) note,

[w]hile innovation has been supported, technology diffusion has been left to the market. Supply and demand have largely been taken as given, and market dynamics have led to the selection of certain technologies. In contrast, environmental pressures are now making it necessary to deliberately disrupt established pathways and replace them with new, sustainable ones. This will require support not only for low-carbon technology innovation but also for diffusion—through, say, the creation of markets.

It will also require deliberate disruption, managed decline of incumbent industries and supply-side policies as we saw in Chapter 3.

The same environmental pressures have led to renewed interest in the return of state-led industrial policy and a shift away from a predominantly laissez-faire model of industrial development towards various versions of a Green New Deal (Chomsky and Pollin 2020; Pettifor 2019; Klein 2019). For Pegels et al. (2018), the available instruments of what they call 'green energy policy' can be grouped into mandating, incentivising, and nudging instruments. Moreover, they need to be designed under conditions of technological uncertainty, to be more selective and directional by narrowing technological development corridors, and to cover long periods to support long-term transformation processes. Conditions for the success of such policies include efficiency, effectiveness and legitimacy. Capacity to produce such conditions varies hugely, of course, across societies. As Rodrik (2007) has argued, effective policy first and foremost needs an institutional setting that balances embeddedness and autonomy of governments vis-à-vis the private sector.

We can see the importance of this in relation to competition and contestation over subsidies to renewables and around the Non-Fossil Fuel obligation that was introduced in the UK, or in relation to the vast subsidies for nuclear energy where in the UK the Hinkley Point nuclear power plant is now the most expensive piece of infrastructure on record and is negotiating a model whereby costs can be recovered up front (Watt 2017). Political and institutional lock-in around industrial policy can also be observed in the contracts to provide tariff-free electricity to mining companies in South Africa that were negotiated in the apartheid era when the government was desperate to attract investors amid international ostracisation for its racist regime (Baker et al. 2014). Returning to themes of policy autonomy and development space, it is also important to emphasise the scope for states to adopt industrial policies such as infant industry measures and procurement policies that are some-times circumscribed by WTO rules (Lewis 2014). Recent controversial cases that have come before that organisation concerning the use of policy measures by the government in Ontario or the Chinese government's use of subsidies for solar provide cases in point (ICTSD 2011).

5.5 Political Economy of Distribution

The state clearly has a key role to play in distributing and managing the gains and losses from energy transitions. Lenferna (2018) poses the question 'Can we equitably manage the end of the fossil fuel era?'. It is a good question and a very difficult one to answer. More specifically, given historical inequities in contribu-tion to the problem and use of fossil fuel reserves and contemporary inequities in access and responsibility, how do we fairly decide who gets to extract the last fossil fuels in a carbon constrained world (Kartha et al. 2018)? Lenferna (2018: 217) argues that 'equitably managing the end of the fossil fuel era is complicated by how economic efficiency or the interests of frontline communities might at times diverge from global distributive justice'. Initial steps towards trying to reconcile these criteria point to the need to identify areas where they converge. For example, this might include more capital and resource-intensive Norwegian oil and gas production, Canada's oil tar sands or the development of coal fields in the USA, Australia or Germany. Collier and Venables (2015) make a strong argument for targeting coal in the first instance because of the array of costs its burning imposes on society, the relatively low numbers of workers and commu-nities directly affected and their concentrated nature, which makes targeted regional redevelopment, compensation and retraining packages easier to effect-ively target. It is also possible to extend the boundaries of responsibility for harm committed by fossil fuels to those exported to other countries (Moss 2018; Healy et al. 2019); the virtual and embedded carbon phenomena which are often disguised by production-based emissions metrics that currently underpin the climate change negotiations. This comes down to discussions of fair shares of remaining carbon budgets, as well as the ability of countries and communities to diversify. Addressing equity issues is further complicated by the fact that impoverished communities in fossil fuel-rich areas may be in favour of their exploitation, including on occasion groups such as the Native American Crow Tribe (Lenferna 2018). Establishing who speaks for whom in representing the interests of particular groups in different energy futures itself presents a huge challenge for procedural justice. For communities, rich and poor, North and South, these are real and live issues that they have to confront as the required speed and scale of the decline in fossil fuel use is so sharp and steep that few very nations will be protected from its effects.

One high-profile initiative to address the issue of international compensation for leaving fossil fuels in the ground was Ecuador's Yasuní-ITT initiative. This proposal from the Ecuadorian state asked the international community for compensation for a percentage of the revenues the country could earn from exploiting the Ishpingo Tambococha Tiputini oilfields, but which it was willing to forgo if an adequate price was paid. The government asked for $3.6 billion, roughly half the value of the oil fields, in order to prevent more than 400 million tonnes of potential carbon dioxide being released into the atmosphere, as well as protecting a biodiverse area of particular importance to indigenous communities. The funds, had they been received, would have been used for social and environmental programmes aimed at supporting Ecuador's transition to a post-oil future. In the end, the project collected only $13 million of the requested $3.6 billion and so was called off in 2013 (Lenferna 2018), but the battle for the protection of Yasuní continues. Yet as Sovacool and Scarpaci (2016: 169) put it, 'the proposal essentially asked the world: Who wants to pay for stranded assets? The deafening answer [appeared] to be nobody.'

The role of the state in managing distributional costs is perhaps especially pertinent in the case of rapid transitions in the energy sector. The Dutch government decided in December 1965 to abandon all coal mining in the Limburg province within a decade, doing away with some 75,000 mining-related jobs, impacting more than 200,000 people. What made the transition successful was that the government strategically steered it, implementing countermeasures such as subsidies for new businesses, the relocation of government industries from the capital to regions of the country hardest hit by the mine closures, retraining programs for miners, and offering shares in Groningen to Staatsmijnen (the state mining company) (Sovacool 2016). This illustrates the potential for the managed decline of some sectors and to actively discontinue some pathways. In 2003, the government of Ontario committed to retiring all coal-fired electricity generation by 2007, something it did accomplish, albeit a few years behind schedule. To achieve this transition, Ontario invested more than $21 billion in cleaner sources of energy including wind, hydroelectricity, solar, and nuclear power, as well as $11 billion in transmission and distribution upgrades and other investments in energy efficiency (Sovacool 2016: 210). Critically, beyond the climate change benefits, the 'coal switch' was estimated to save $4.4 billion per year in health, environmental and financial damages along with $95 million in displaced operating and maintenance costs, suggesting a series of social co-benefits of such a move. Recent studies of coal transitions around the world also demonstrate the central role of the state in managing social dislocation that can be produced by rapid shifts away from particular energy regimes (Caldecott et al. 2017). For example, in the 1990s in Gelsenkirchen, Germany, a city that was a renowned industrial hub for coal, steel and glass industries until the relocation of heavy industry, local officials decided to regenerate land abandoned by the industry and set up an energy technology park. Supported by the European Union, the federal government and the utility RWE, solar technology became the new focus of development. In 2001 the city took on a voluntary carbon reduction target aimed at transforming it from a city of a thousand furnaces to 'a city of a thousand suns' (Newell et al. 2011).

Policies can generate both co-benefits and adverse side-effects and can compound or lessen inequalities depending on contextual factors, policy design and policy implementation. The risk of negative outcomes is greater in contexts characterised by high levels of poverty, corruption and economic and social inequalities, and where limited action is taken to identify and mitigate potentially adverse side-effects. Negative inequality impacts of climate policies can be mitigated (and possibly even prevented), but this requires conscious effort, careful planning and multi-stakeholder engagement. Seemingly, the best results can be achieved when potential inequality impacts are taken into consideration in all stages of policy-making, including policy planning, development and implementation (Markkanen and Anger-Kraavi 2019).

5.6 Ecologies of Energy Governance

5.6.1 Political Economy of Global Energy Governance: Coping with Complexity

Though work on sociotechnical transitions lists 'institutions' as one among many 'landscape' factors that can shape conditions for disruptive change, critical thinking about the role of global governance institutions in enabling and constraining transitions remains under-developed (van Asselt 2014). There is, nevertheless, a growing body of work on global energy governance (Goldthau and Witte 2010; Lesage et al. 2010) which looks at key institutions such as the International Energy Agency (IEA), OPEC (the Organization of the Petroleum Exporting Countries) (Colgan 2014) and co-ordinating mechanisms such as UN-Energy (van de Graaf 2013; Karlsson-Vinkhuyzen 2010). This has focused mainly on classic international relations (IR) questions of how much autonomy such institutions enjoy from states, the power they exercise over their members and how successfully they are able to co-ordinate co-operation. The climate implications of the lack of institutional integration of energy and climate policy have received comparably less attention (Heubaum and Biermann 2015; Falkner 2018).

The extent to which and the ways in which global governance institutions shape, enable or inhibit particular transition pathways has also been less explored. This includes the reverse ways in which emergent and diverse energy pathways connect to, and might be supported by, the climate regime, for example, through finance and technology transfer (Newell and Bulkeley 2016). Some emerging work is looking at how decarbonisation strategies impact on other areas of the global political economy, such as trade and finance, in important geopolitical ways. For example, how oil exporters might lose global influence, whereas importers will be empowered. And how new relationships and allegiances, such as the Global Energy Interconnection Development and Cooperation Organization (a platform for companies and enterprises) might replace state-led clubs of old such as OPEC (Bazilian et al. 2019). Hence, a global political economy of transitions requires an account of the ways in which institutions of global energy and climate change governance, as well as a broader set of multilateral economic institutions, and their unequal interrelationships enable and constrain particular energy pathways (Newell 2018).

The multiple and overlapping dimensions of energy transitions, particularly the need to address energy security, energy poverty and climate change issues simultaneously, create a huge challenge for the current global order centred on an energy regime complex where different institutions are charged with addressing each of these issues separately. None has the mandate or capacity to orchestrate the restructuring of the global energy order, as opposed to supporting discrete national or sociotechnical transitions. Indeed, scholarship on global energy governance demonstrates that it has traditionally been very weak (Florini and Sovacool 2009; Karlsson-Vinkhuyzen 2010). It is possible to overstate the influence even of those actors in global energy governance considered to wield the most power, including 'producer clubs' such as OPEC (Colgan 2014), 'consumer clubs' such as the IEA, or groupings dominated by wealthier countries such as the G7 and OECD.

Despite greater attention to energy issues in international relations from the Gleneagles summit in 2005 onward, and the proliferation of public–private partnerships (PPPs) and transnational governance in the energy domain (Bulkeley et al. 2012), overall global energy governance remains weak, fragmented and incoherent from the point of view of delivering low carbon transitions. For example, the World Bank, one of the most powerful actors in this arena as interim trustee of the Green Climate Fund and with its own extensive portfolio of Climate Investment Funds, and despite its ambition to lead the world on climate change, continues to provide high levels of finance to fossil fuels. MDBs provided over $9 billion in public finance for fossil fuel projects in 2016 with the vast majority of transactions approved after the Paris Agreement was reached. Clean energy still made up less than a third of MDB energy finance in 2016. Total MDB finance for oil and gas exploration more than doubled from 2015 to 2016, from $1.05 billion to $2.15 billion. Overall, the World Bank Group, the European Investment Bank and the Asian Development Bank were the largest financiers of fossil fuels in 2016 (OCI 2017).

One, often neglected, aspect of this broader landscape of global energy governance are the private energy clubs or informal regimes such as the International Energy Forum convened in the wake of the 1991 Gulf War which bring together top producers and consumers of oil and gas with executives from those sectors and related industries to build dialogue around critical issues affecting their industries (Harks 2010). It also includes organisations like the Oil Policy Group, which seeks to bring order to the world oil market (Odell 1981: 229), as well as regimes for compensation for oil industry marine spills which function as civil liability regimes (Faure and Hui 2003) whereby companies pay into them to cover losses from individual spills, a way of sharing collective responsibility. It is possible to speculate whether future clubs will also function to share the costs of damages claimed for their contribution to climate change.

Operating transnationally, there is also a critical role for urban energy governance given that cities consume 75 per cent of natural resources globally (materials, energy, water), produce 50 per cent of global waste and generate 60–80 per cent of greenhouse gas (GHG) emissions (Rutherford and Jaglin 2015). New governance tools to enable these actions include the ecoCity Footprint Tool (EFT) which allows cities to map flows of energy and materials (urban metabolisms), understand their ecological footprints and measure their consumption-based and territorial carbon emissions as prerequisites to more ambitious action (Moore 2015a). Also operating across scales are more than forty-six dedicated transnational multi-stakeholder partnerships on sustainable energy. These seek to enable knowledge dissemination and technology transfer, building of institutional capacity and training, and technical implementation and innovation with a few seeking to create new energy infrastructures on the ground (Szulecki et al. 2011).

Nevertheless, the observed under-development of global energy governance to date would not surprise most IR scholars. The proximity of energy to core state strategy, given its centrality to security and growth, makes it a highly political issue. Energy chapters in trade agreements are often the most contested (Newell 2011). Indeed, the problem is the extensive un-governance of energy (areas of deliberate non-intervention) where lock-in means that investor interests are well protected by trade rules and investment arbitration procedures observed in cases brought against governments by energy companies claiming to have been subject to trade discrimination (Newell 2007; Tienhaara and Downie 2018). This is not to rule out an important future role for institutions of global governance in setting new rules, levering new finance and creating new infrastructures, or playing more proactive co-ordinating functions, as occurs in regional contexts such as the Energy Charter. Indeed, there are frequent calls to strengthen existing institutions or to create new initiatives such as pleas for a global Marshall Fund or Apollo programme (King et al. 2015) or to scale up support for renewable energy development and deployment as proposed at the Paris COP21 by the 'Breakthrough Energy Coalition' of twenty-five leading investors (Milman 2015) or even to negotiate a Fossil Fuel Non-Proliferation Treaty (Newell and Simms 2019).

Yet, looked at together and more critically, it is clear that the purpose of existing global bodies with a direct mandate to address energy issues is more 'market-enabling' than 'market-restricting': providing regulation 'for' energy corporations rather than 'of' them and showing a strong commitment to energy market liberalisation. Bodies such as the IEA, the World Bank and OECD are unsurprisingly committed to a 'market liberal' view of the role of the state and the means by which decarbonisation, in so far as it is considered at all, is to be achieved: through pricing, innovation and technology development and transfer, to the exclusion of other pathways to transition or transformation. Within this ecosystem of global governance there are also key power imbalances in the interrelationships among and between institutions of global energy governance where trade bodies exercise increasing power and where bodies associated with particular energy sources wield uneven power. Comparing OPEC and IRENA, for example, it is not hard to see that the former wields far more direct and structural power in the international system through control of pricing and market access, as opposed to the more general support provided by the latter.

The unevenly shared power to shape transition pathways is especially relevant when considering the relationship between MDBs and poorer states in the global South. I noted previously the practice of 'disciplinary neoliberalism' (Gill 1995): a set of strategies pursued by key international institutions and MDBs that constrain the policy autonomy and developmental space of poorer countries over which they exercise control through their lending practices, conferring financial support upon policies they approve of, or withdrawing it from those they do not (Gallagher 2005). This raises key questions about which instruments states have available to address the challenges of decarbonising their economies when many have ceded direct control over their energy sectors and when forms of policy intervention historically used to support new energy regimes in the past (e.g. subsidies, infant industry protection and looser forms of intellectual property protection) are increasingly circumscribed by trade rules.

The increasingly obvious need for regulation and steering of economies onto a lower carbon energy trajectory has become apparent at a time when many states have relinquished, or been forced to relinquish, control over key parts of their energy sectors (such as generation, distribution, transmission) as a result of energy and power sector reform programmes promoted by the World Bank in particular (Tellam 2000). For example, Kenya's adoption of neo-liberal energy sector reforms has been rewarded by support from bilateral and multilateral donors, opening up opportunities for foreign capital to meet the shortfall in energy supply. In this sense, it is unsurprising that Kenya has been described as an obvious choice of pilot country for climate finance mechanisms such as the World Bank's Scaling up Renewable Energy Programme (SREP). Kenya has been described as 'the pilot for everything' and is often compared favourably with neighbours, such as Tanzania that are perceived to be more hostile to private investors (Newell and Phillips 2016).

In a more critical vein, and going beyond a focus on questions of institutional emergence, evolution and effectiveness, critical international political economy (IPE) might also offer useful insights into the question of the role of energy in the maintenance of world order. Following the neo-Gramscian work of Robert Cox (1987) implies a focus on the relationships among power, production and world order: the ideas, institutions and material capabilities that produce a particular energy order. Di Muzio (2015) refers to 'carbon capitalism' as a way of understanding the interconnections among energy, social reproduction and world order which reproduce a particular type of 'petro-market civilization'. Here the emphasis is on how particular ideas and institutions reflect and seek to protect particular structures of power and production. This is sustained by a particular material base, enforced by military means to secure supplies, and expressed institutionally in the forms of global governance described here. This takes us into the realms of the geopolitics of energy. Beyond detailing and accounting for power and resistance to change, this work also has an explicit focus on transformation: how one order declines and another rises (as with the transition from the Pax Britannica to the Pax Americana) over decades and centuries (Bromley 1991). Major reorganisations of production, such as those associated with Fordism, which peaked in the post Second World War decades of American dominance and mass consumerism, are intimately connected to projections of US global power (Rupert 1995), just as the expansion of the industrial revolution was to Pax Britannica. Oil was central to the Fordist vision and securing access to it has become a key geopolitical goal in its own right as part of the project of the 'new imperialism' pursued under the guise of creating a 'new world order' (Harvey 2003; Kaldor et al. 2007; Rees 2001).

The securitisation of energy at once fuels and reinforces the power of the military industrial complex consolidating the material capacity to secure and extract more energy. In this sense, as Huber (2008: 105) notes, 'the ecological politics of climate change and the anti-war politics of Iraq both converge on a similar object of disdain – oil'. Moving beyond carbon means unsettling a politico-military order that both consumes and secures vast amounts of fossil fuels. The US military alone uses more oil than any other institution in the world (Belcher et al. 2019). Indeed, the US military consumes more liquid fuels and emits more GHGs than most medium-sized countries: if it were a country, its fuel usage alone would make it the 47th largest emitter of GHGs in the world, sitting between Peru and Portugal (Crawford 2019).

This world ecology of power is not a static one, however. It is a world order in flux characterised by ongoing redistributions of power among states. Hence discussions about transitions should engage with a shifting landscape of power (in a general sense and in the sense in which transition theories use the term). Shifting geometries of power and geopolitics would include the enhanced power and resource demands of so-called 'rising powers' such as India and China. This refers not just to the strategies for acquiring new sources of energy, especially oil (Taylor 2006), to meet their energy and growth demands in ways likened (problematically) to a new wave of colonialism (Ayers 2013; Carmody 2011); nor does it refer merely to the enhanced bargaining leverage that these powers now exercise in global institutions such as the WTO; it also refers to whether and how their rising growth ambitions can be squared with climate constraints. There is growing attention to how to make the trade system work for the climate (Das et al. 2018). But beyond multilateral arenas, powers in the global North and South are routinely making key decisions with huge and long-lasting lock-in effects for other richer and poorer countries, pursued both through energy statecraft and via the investment strategies pursued by state owned enterprises and private TNCs. The global inter-dependencies that result from globaliszing strategies for securing energy security further challenge conventional ideas about state control over energy resources whether in relation to fossil fuels or through investments in 'clean energy', or as leading exporters of renewable energy technologies.

The emerging energy order is, therefore, increasingly multi-polar and more fragmented, but not necessarily more inclusive or sustainable. There has been a re-balancing of power in the energy sector as with other domains away from the West and towards China and India in particular, and a greater accent on resource nationalism which potentially challenges neo-liberal orthodoxies. At the same time, and despite growing interest in capitalizing on the low carbon economy and the export and first mover advantages it confers upon rising powers, the enrichment of state and corporate elites in all parts of the world has meant that energy security and growth continue to trump efforts to seriously reverse either energy poverty or climate change. While inter-state balances of power have shifted, intra- and trans-state power imbalances between competing social forces persist with the result that market liberal transitions prevail over broader social and economic transformations of energy politics (IRENA 2019).

The answer to why this is the case lies in the transition to what Bernstein (2000) calls 'liberal environmentalism' between the 1972 Limits to Growth Report released during the Stockholm Conference on the Human Environment that same year, and the 1992 United Nations Conference on Environment and Development (UNCED) in Rio. As Bernstein (2000: 7) notes, the 'norm-complex' governing global environmental practices shifted from one focused on environmental protection at the beginning of the 1970s, to the acceptance of 'the liberalization of trade and finance as consistent with, and even necessary for, international environmental protection' by the early 1990s. This 'liberal environmentalism' promoted market and other economic mechanisms (such as tradeable pollution permit schemes or the privatisation of commons) over 'command-and-control' methods (standards, bans, quotas and so on) as the preferred method of environmental management. Yet global governance for energy transformation would have to look very different, making greater use of precisely these types of supply-side measure (Erickson et al. 2018).

5.7 Conclusion

We can see from the discussion above that energy systems are governed in a variety of formal and informal ways by public and private institutions alike and across levels and through networks, representing a classic challenge of multi-level governance. Amid this dispersion of authority and multiplicity of sites of decision-making, there are concentrations of political power in particular institutions, geopolitical centres and classes. This has an important bearing on the direction and form of energy pathways and who benefits from them.

I noted how the state, in particular, plays and performs a range of, often simultaneously, supportive and disabling roles with respect to energy transitions and transformations. This reflects differences within and between states across a number of dimensions. I have noted throughout that what we expect of states with regard to energy transitions needs to be cognisant of the variety in state capacity, autonomy, resources and power to deliver on intended outcomes. Each of these are shared and contested by a multitude of public and private actors within and beyond the state. I explored both horizontal governance challenges across the state and between different ministries and bureaucracies competing for authority and resources associated with energy programmes and interventions, as well as vertical governance challenges that the state faces shaped by processes such as devolution and contests between the central government and provinces respectively. We also saw how the political nature of the state, how much democratic space exists to participate in energy politics, to define policy priorities and contest projects and interventions, strongly affects distributional outcomes and which actors are able to capture the benefits of different energy pathways. Finally, we saw how the degree of autonomy and independence that states have from 'landscape' actors such as donors and transnational corporations that play such a key role in financing energy technologies and infrastructures impacts upon their ability to project and realise their preferred vision of energy transformation.

In this sense, we need to place the state in context. A relational focus invites exploration of state–society complexes and the relations of power which underpin them, which are not confined within bounded territories and are often transnationally constituted (Johnstone and Newell 2018). It means not treating the state as an independent, atomised rational actor. Rather, it requires an appreciation that the state is not neutral with respect to the actors and processes it is charged with regulating (Saurin 2001). This is perhaps especially true with regard to energy because of the nature of its relationship to growth, development ambitions and militarism and the potential for state elites to secure rents from energy resources in the ways described by work on resource curses (Ross 2012). Moreover, lack of access to energy and revenues from energy has the potential to generate popular social unrest. Popular resistance to changes to fossil fuel subsidy regimes in many parts of the world (Lockwood 2015) illustrates clearly why state elites tread carefully when considering changes to the energy regime.

We have seen how hybrid networks bring businesses and state actors together around particular visions of how the energy system should be organised, inviting a more nuanced understanding of where agency lies and how far it can be attributed unproblematically to a sprawling entity such as 'the state'. Notwithstanding evidence of positive state leadership with respect to innovation, investment and regulation, this does point to the need to be wary of the illusions of control regarding state-led transitions that permeate a lot of academic writing and policy work on energy transitions. It points to the difference in Stirling's terms between attempting to manage 'the Transition' and cultivating 'plural radical progress' (Stirling 2014a). It invites further reflection on how different ways of organising states, their diverse political complexions and levels of democracy, types of political economy and relationship to the energy base produce, facilitate and frustrate different types of energy pathway and, more challenging still, to establish which ones are most likely to simultaneously achieve the goals of tackling poverty and decarbonisation of the energy system.

We can clearly observe a diversification and multiplication, some might say fragmentation, of sites of energy governance across regions, scales and functions. There is an increased blurring and interplay of public and private governance. The dominant drivers and logics of energy governance remain those of opening up new markets, mobilising finance and constructing new infrastructures in order to meet the energy needs of states, investors and high-end consumers. Environmental and energy poverty considerations struggle to gain attention despite the creation of new initiatives, funds and institutions and the shifts towards renewable energies, in particular, that we are witnessing. The majority of governance, in its purpose and design, is aimed at providing governance *for* rather than *of* the energy sector. For deeper shifts in energy governance to occur, including a reorientation around different goals and purposes, a shift of power relations would need to occur to challenge and reverse the power of incumbents and give greater access, voice, representation and power to groups and issues that are currently more marginal. On this basis, it is to the role of resistance and mobilisation that we now turn our attention.

6

Mobilising Energy Transitions

Given the level of lock-in around production, finance and the governance of energy for the benefit of the fossil fuel complex and, relatedly, the industrial provision of energy described in the preceding chapters, the prospects of achieving the forms of 'transformative systemic change' that the IPCC (2018) suggests are required appear on one level somewhat dim. As well as more state-led or elite financial-driven transformations, however, many transformations emerge from 'below' in civil society and from the actions of movements fighting for progressive change around health, poverty and environment in the places where we 'live, work and play', to coin a phrase from the environmental justice movement. Momentous disruptions and interventions from state and corporate actors around policy, financing or the development of new technologies are often prefigured by years of campaigning, resistance and building alternatives from below which create pressure and prepare the ground for interventions by elite actors. Incumbent regimes are actively unsettled not just by restless capital or shifting state priorities, as explored in previous chapters, but also by social pressure for purposive and equitable transitions and deliberate destabilisation (Turnheim and Geels 2012).

In this regard, there is growing attention to the role of civil society in energy transitions (Princen et al. 2015; Cheon and Urpelainen 2017). This has taken a number of forms including research around resistance (Brock and Dunlap 2018; Abramsky 2010), questions of social acceptance and ownership of energy technologies and infrastructures (Barry et al. 2008), attempts to build alternatives such as community energy (Seyfang et al. 2012; Smith 2008; Mundaca et al. 2017; Dütschke and Wesche 2018), as well as more formal engagements with policy processes through lobbying and advocacy including around the climate-related aspects of energy policy and legal activism (Newell 2008, 2014). Yet there is clearly further work to do in understanding the ecologies, political economies, geographies and histories of civil society engagement and resistance to energy regimes as the question of social transformation comes to the fore as being critical to the success of projects of technological revolution (HM Government 2008) and broader transformative, systemic change (IPCC 2018). Indeed, the rise of movements such as Extinction Rebellion is in many ways grounded in anger and frustration that governments and corporations have failed to act on climate change, a critique of the limited effectiveness of the strategies of mainstream environmental groups and a strong belief that civil disobedience constitutes the most effective way of demanding urgent and widespread change.

In this chapter then, I explore the role of social mobilisation and cultural shifts in creating ruptures and destabilising effects, in generating demands for alternative energy systems, as well as actually doing the work of transition and building the basis of wider transformative change by constructing alternative pathways: differently organised, produced and financed, making use of alternative technologies and often developed through more open, participatory and inclusive processes. In this sense, the argument advanced is that some social movements are seeding, culturing and practising transformation in the present. They are not lobbying others to enact transitions, or even broader forms of systemic change; rather, they are challenging power relations and creating alternatives in the here and now. Whether it is food and energy cooperatives, transport sharing or repair workshops, solidarity economies and experiments in communal living, 'nowtopians' are not waiting for others to deliver structural change, nor willing to assume that it will take a form consistent with their values; they are doing it for themselves, building concrete utopias in the present. Carlsson (2015: 182) suggests: 'When people take their time and technological know-how out of the market and decide for themselves how to dedicate their efforts, they are short-circuiting the logic of the market society that depends on incessant growth.' These are the 'revolutions where you live' that van Gelder (2017) describes.

In transition terms, these forces can widen cracks and fissures in existing systems, lending support to niche actors (as well as becoming niche actors themselves as we see in the case of community energy, discussed in Section 6.7.1) all the while heightening the influence and amplifying the impact of landscape pressures for regime change. For example, movements such as Extinction Rebellion in the UK have successfully pushed local councils to declare 'climate emergencies' in the light of the IPCC SR15 report published in October 2018. Beyond engagement with existing regimes, therefore, they can also articulate and actively construct alternative visions of energy systems, economies and societies, organised according to different principles and value systems, for example around cooperation, solidarity and sufficiency. In other words, they enact, nurture and enable micro-transitions in practices, values and behaviours that are a precursor, or even a prerequisite, for bolder socially progressive transformations. This resonates with the distinction that

Polanyi draws between embryonic 'moves' and more fully-fledged 'counter-movements' to prevailing systems in market society (Polanyi 1957 [1944]; Mittelman 1998). This may be the case even where they appear to be under the radar. Living, working and sharing to form communities of practice, to cultivate and enact (post-materialist) values of cooperation, solidarity, non-monetarised exchange, compassion and non-capitalist relations, which in reality constitute the majority of social interactions even in a deeply marketised society, *is* transition.

This can be empowering in terms of encouraging people to be the change they want to see in society following Gandhi's ethos. Do-It-Yourself (DIY) politics can be very liberating and provide forms of self-defence in the face of lack of leadership and responsibility from state and corporate actors. Think of the (now global) transition network, discussed in Section 6.5, which has as one of its aims preparing for a world after oil to build local resilience to the effects of environmental change, as well as reducing negative contributions to it in the here and now. This implies, to use an over-used phrase 'taking back control', acquiring power to determine their own future based on their own imagination of it, rather than relying on elite action and shifts in incumbent behaviour (Hopkins 2019). This is the case even if such experiments, mobilisations and alternative communities have to co-exist and in many ways depend on the acquiescence to, or at least grudging acceptance of, more powerful forces which can and do use means at their disposal to close down and undermine projects perceived to be threatening to incumbent interests, as the case of community power makes very clear.

In Section 6.1, I briefly trace early struggles over energy systems from smogs and the Factories Act in the heartland of the industrial revolution in the UK, as well as long histories of indigenous activism against extractivism, through to contemporary battles for energy and climate justice and resistance to new infrastructures, projects and policies which further embed rather than disrupt the fossil fuel economy (Bond 2012). Section 6.2, meanwhile, points to the ways in which mobilisations have sought to challenge existing political economies and distributions of power, as well as construct alternative ones. This includes community energy, re-powering initiatives,[1] as well as campaigns for feed-in tariffs, and advocacy around climate change and fuel poverty. Individually and collectively, these 'moves' and movements raise questions about and contest the unjust distribution of the externalities of contemporary energy economies such as air pollution and land degradation along the lines of race, class and gender (Newell 2005).

There is a rich ecology of resistance which I then describe, from lobbying and litigation to direct action and resistance, pressuring all parts of systems of production, finance and governance, as well as seeding alternatives which present challenges for incumbent actors to crush or ignore them, co-opt or replicate and learn

from them, even at times supporting and scaling them up. These different reper-
toires of protest reflect the ideological positions of groups, their diverse theories of
change, the level of resources they have access to and the nature of their membership, as well as the context in which they operate: both the nature of political
opportunity structures that exist, as well as the degree of democratic space available
to safely and legitimately question incumbent power. In many parts of the world, it
continues to be the case that to do so is to put your own life at risk (Global Witness
2017; Butt et al. 2019). But what is also significant is that these different strategies
gain traction from one another: they rely and depend on other strategies to create
openings, raise awareness, lever spaces and mobilise people in ways that benefit
strategies of change. I develop this idea of the interrelationship between strategies
in Section 6.10.

These different strategies reflect a sense of where power lies, and embody
and enact diverse theories of change. But they also create new relations of
power by involving excluded actors in debates and decision-making about
energy pathways, bringing about a democratising effect, even if in a limited
way at first, countering the idea that decision-making about energy systems is
the exclusive preserve of planners, economists, lawyers, businesses and experts
in technology. As well as bringing in new voices and creating new spaces of
engagement and deliberation, they also democratise in another sense. They
bring about improved accountability and widen the range of issues at stake,
offering up alternative framings around energy or climate justice and asking
difficult questions about who the energy system should serve and how, and so
draw attention to the possibility of alternative pathways. They do this, for
example, by exposing the ecological impacts of different energy systems from
campaigns on fossil fuel subsidy reform which highlight the maldistribution of
public resources towards incumbents by organisations such as Oil Change
International (OCI) and the IISD Global Subsidies Initiative, and which expose
corporate lobbying to prevent more ambitious climate action (such as
Greenpeace UK energy desk exposés about BP's lobbying regarding methane
emissions), to campaigns targeted at multilateral development banks (MDBs)
(from the World Resources Institute, the Policy Studies Institute and OCI) to
fossil fuel divestment (led by 350.org amongst others). They can also support
and socialise new ideas for alternative frameworks as is the case with a new
non-governmental organisation (NGO) coalition that is building support for the
idea of a Fossil Fuel Non-Proliferation Treaty.[2]

There are many ways in which energy transitions are cultured, can be shaped 'from
below' by actors other than those that wield direct control over production, finance or
technology, or that are charged with the formal business of governing. Indeed, for

many, history suggests that more progressive transitions and transformations are generally those which originate and bubble up from below by groups challenging incumbent institutions and power relations or dominant social values (Leach and Scoones 2015). The story of this chapter, then, is less of civil society as one more stakeholder in the global political economy of energy transitions or a passive recipient of the decisions of others. Nor is it one of 'compliant communities' (Smith 2008: 180) implementing the decisions of elites in energy policy. It is more of civil society as an active shaper of energy transition pathways: enabling, resisting, building and imagining energy futures. As Abramsky (2010: 7, emphasis added) notes: 'The process of building a new energy system, based around a greatly expanded use of renewable energies, has the *potential* to make an important contribution to the construction of new relations of production, exchange and livelihood that are based on solidarity, diversity and autonomy and are substantially more democratic and egalitarian than the current relations.' That potential has yet to be realised and, as we will see, without shifts in relations of power or even modes of production, we may just end up with exploitative forms of renewable extractivism and not a more progressive energy pathway.

6.1 Historicising Mobilisation

Social mobilisation around energy is clearly not a recent phenomenon, even if the intimate connection between energy systems and climate change has served, in recent years, to significantly escalate the attention that the environmental movement pays to energy systems and industries. There is indeed a long and rich history of activists seeking to construct alternative energy pathways, as well as contest dominant ones (Smith 2008), from opposition to transmission lines (Furby et al. 1988) or nuclear energy to the advocacy of 'soft energy' paths (Lovins 1977). Podobnik (2010: 73) makes a strong case for the fact that social struggles have played a decisive role in previous energy transformations, suggesting that the historical evolution of the global energy system 'has been strongly impacted by mass movements of people who have struggled to change the energy trajectories of their communities and nations'. He continues (Podobnik 2010: 73–4):

Growth patterns in energy sectors are not dictated by the kinds of resources that are found in the ground. Instead, their evolution is driven by decisions made by government officials and corporate executives and by resistance movements created by workers and citizens … [S]ocieties have been set on fundamentally new energy paths because of complex interactions between these different types of social conflict. We can learn from these earlier struggles and increase our ability to create an effective mass movement on behalf of a clean revolution in the coming decades.

The point is well taken, even if we might caution against invoking direct historical parallels because of the urgency required of contemporary energy transformations and the distinct alignments of social forces apparent at this historical conjuncture.

Though it is undoubtedly correct that the 'dynamics of social mobilisation have had far-reaching impacts on the evolution of global energy systems during the last two centuries' (Podobnik 2010: 74), they operate not in isolation but rather as part of a configuration of other factors and forces in a specific historical moment alongside dynamics of geopolitical rivalry and inter- and intra-capital competition. But their significance should not be underestimated.

The historical record clearly demonstrates that social struggles of various kinds have had broad impacts on the evolution of global energy systems. Miners employed in the most dangerous, exploitative kinds of occupations organized themselves into unions and transformed coal industries across the world. Citizens and political leaders in oil-exporting nations mobilised against the wealthiest multinational corporations in the world, and succeeded in nationalising huge oil reserves. And environmentalists across the world created mass movements that restricted the expansion of nuclear power. In each case, mobilisation strategies emphasised the creation of broad coalitions that drew people in from all walks of life, and from all political backgrounds. Similarly, moderate and radical activists each played important roles in coal unions, nationalist struggles and environmental campaigns. These earlier campaigns can inform and inspire those who are now beginning a new, mass-based effort dedicated to refashioning the energy foundations of our world

(Podobnik 2010: 76).

Examples of social mobilisations around energy abound. They include interest in 'soft energy paths' (Lovins 1977) involving a drive towards energy efficiency, conservation and renewable energy which gained pace in light of the OPEC oil shocks in the 1970s and which remain popular today. But earlier, air quality was a key concern. Indeed, the Factories Act in the UK was forged on the back of public outcry over 'pea soupers'. The 'Great Smog' of 1952 in London which caused over 4,000 deaths, prompting widespread public outrage, 'damaged coal's legitimacy' and the 'anti-smoke' movement used the incident to increase pressure on politicians to introduce the Clean Air Act (Turnheim and Geels 2012: 40). Air quality, the 'silent killer', is the driver now for congestion charges and the phase-out of diesel in the UK and beyond. Early conservation and wilderness movements also often decried the despoliation of countryside associated with rapid industrial development and urbanisation. The 1970s anti-nuclear movement, opposed to both nuclear power and nuclear weapons, in many ways gave rise to green politics in Europe (Kelly 1994). It also changed the trajectory of civilian nuclear power. In this instance, a series of nuclear accidents served as the catalyst for an anti-nuclear movement which involved a mix of mass demonstrations, political advocacy and civil disobedience. Podobnik (2010: 75) suggests: 'The ability of mass movements to contain nuclear power in many countries again demonstrates the capacity of grassroots mobilisations to alter the evolution of energy industries on a wide scale.'

Transport and mining industries, central to energy systems, have also often been at the forefront of labour struggles. Mitchell (2011) tells the story of how the materiality of specific energy sources such as coal and oil played a large part in shaping democratic politics as some forms of extraction and exchange could be blocked and disrupted more easily, leading to concessions to labour demands for welfare, for example. Labour militancy from the 1880s to the beginning of the First World War, and then again during the Second World War and its aftermath, disrupted the operations of the coal mines and helped accelerate the shift towards oil. Though successful in improving wages and working conditions, 'this militancy had the unintended effect of pushing government authorities and private investors towards greater reliance on emerging oil industries' (Podobnik 2010: 74). Unions linked to energy and energy-intensive industries have traditionally been very powerful. Think of unions representing car workers involved in defining struggles over the gender pay, for example, focusing on the Ford car company and documented in the film *Dagenham Girls*. More recent debates about 'just transitions', discussed in Section 6.7, have raised awkward questions for unions about which workers they represent, where some have sought to promote jobs for 'energy workers' as a whole, a move which allows for retraining and redeployment of workers into lower carbon sectors, while others seek to defend jobs associated with particular industries such as car manufacturing, nuclear or fracking.

Strikes by oil workers, when combined with popular demonstrations in parts of the Middle East and Latin America, also spurred on waves of energy sector nationalisations which caused significant disruption to global energy systems. This posed a threat to the control of the energy system by the major oil companies (the seven sisters) as well as giving a temporary boost to energy efficiency and efforts to develop renewable energy in the global North, whereby wind and solar went through a first phase of development and commercialisation in the wake of turmoil in the international oil system. Populism also played a part in the re-nationalisations of oil companies such as Repsol-YPF in Argentina in 2012 under the government of Christina Kirchner. I have already noted the disruptive power of *un*civil society in the form of al Qaeda and other terrorist organisations damaging energy infrastructures but also funding their activities through energy rents (Haynes 2009). As a result, Podobnik (2010: 75) suggests that 'growing social conflict in the Middle East could have the unintended effect of speeding a transition toward new energy technologies in the twentieth century'. The drive towards fracking in the USA was at least partly driven by this desire to reduce dependence on energy supplies from the Middle East.

There is also a long history of resistance by poorer and marginalised communities to the imposition and environmental effects of polluting energy infrastructures (Garvey and Newell 2004). Such activism is often concentrated in 'sacrifice zones' and 'energy boomtowns' in poorer areas of countries at the frontiers of energy extractivism. Early social impact studies (Rosa et al. 1988) and later environmental and energy justice work (Walker and Bulkeley 2006; Bickerstaff et al. 2013; Sovacool and Dworkin 2014) has looked at the way in which social inequalities intersect with energy politics around planning and citing decisions, distributions of risks, benefits and waste, and access to remedies to contest the concentration of controversial and hazardous energy investments in poorer neighbourhoods. Being out of sight is an important criterion for location decisions and so is an abundance of cheap land. Rural areas are often home to a preponderance of energy resources and are often also targeted as disposal sites for toxic energy products (Rosa et al 1988). In this regard, indigenous and native American communities have often been particularly exposed to toxic energy waste storage and disposal, especially nuclear waste, as well as being in the frontline of extractivism around mining for energy and oil drilling (Strauss et al. 2013). Perhaps unsurprisingly, they are also at the forefront of land struggles over the siting of wind energy parks in places like Mexico (Dunlap 2018).

The expansion and the modification of energy systems are inextricably linked to justice concerns and climate change which an embryonic 'energy justice' literature seeks to account for (Sovacool and Dworkin 2014; Walker and Bulkeley 2006). Energy issues, then, including questions of transition, need to be understood in relation to systemic marginalisation, the uneven socioecological impacts of different modes of production, and disparities in the recognition of diverse voices and livelihoods.

6.2 Political Economy of Mobilisation

It is not merely the case, as we saw in Section 6.1, that there is a long and rich history of social mobilisation around energy. It is also the case that the targets and strategies adopted have shown an evolution, reflecting and adapting to shifts in the centres of power in energy systems and the broader global political economy of which they are part. This includes, for example, shifts towards targeting corporate actors directly as those actors assume a greater role in the production and distribution of energy. They do this through forms of liberal and critical civil regulation (Newell 2001) that aim to work with and against the market to generate new forms of 'soft' regulation: norms, private standards, codes and partnerships, and increased mobilisations and advocacy targeted at multilateral, regional and bilateral development banks that in recent decades have come to play a critical role in reconfiguring energy systems and rebalancing power towards private actors in particular. These shifts are in many ways a manifestation of deeper shifts in capitalism towards a more globalised and neo-liberal form, as explored in earlier chapters.

'Civil society' should not serve as a shorthand for referring to the progressive potential of social mobilisation for energy system transformation, however. It is the case that mobilisation can bring about shifts in both the political economy of energy production and finance. Yet as Gramsci (1971) noted, civil society also often serves as the outer trenches of the state: civil and political society. Churches, schools and the media are also part of civil society and are often very conservative and system-preserving in nature. It is no mistake that they have formed key battlegrounds in struggles around climate change with climate-sceptic organisations targeting churches in the USA and schools being mobilised by climate protestors as part of the international 'School Strike 4 Climate' movement. Another way in which civil society can embed and reinforce incumbent state and corporate power is through the phenomena of corporate funded 'astro-turf' (fake green) organisations with benign and innocuous-sounding names such as the 'Public Information Council on the Environment', which seek to discredit the consensus on climate change, for example, by producing videos and brochures for schools and other public audiences, casting doubt on the science of climate change (Beder 1997; Rowell 1996).

Each of these areas of civil society forms a key battleground for competing social forces, as we will see in Section 6.3 in relation to divestment, but is also apparent in media advertising by the energy industries and the 'School Strike 4 Climate' movement discussed further in Section 6.6. Different elements, at the same time, can serve conservative and emancipatory functions. Indeed, the very conceptualisation of social movements identifies them as a form of collective action for the dual purpose of challenging, as well as at times defending, institutional or cultural authority (Benford and Snow 2000).

6.3 Redirecting Finance

As we saw in Chapter 4, activists are keen to lever the power of finance to accelerate a transition away from fossil fuels and towards lower carbon energy. There is a long history of doing this going back to Greenpeace's engagements with the insurance industry in the mid-1990s (Paterson 2001) and it continues today with broad-based civil society campaigns targeted at bank lending for fossil fuels, insurers underwriting them and investors, including asset managers, pension funds and endowments. The demand is for the finance sector to end all support for new fossil projects, and drop any coal, oil, gas or petrochemical company that does not immediately stop expansion and wind down existing operations.[3]

Campaigns targeting financial actors have also found more recent expression in relation to the fossil fuel divestment movement (Ayling and Gunningham 2017). This is a global social movement that emerged in the early 2010s, though with antecedents in the anti-apartheid struggle in South Africa, and it has grown and spread rapidly, gaining significant public attention in a short space of time. The divestment movement began in the summer of 2011, when student activists launched campaigns in six universities in the USA to divest their endowments from coal. More than fifty US universities had divestment movements by spring 2012, which broadened to a call to divest from all fossil fuels and invest in clean energy. The movement grew considerably in 2012 due largely to the climate advocacy group 350.org, founded in 2008, which joined forces with the student activists and launched its divestment campaign in 2012, with co-founder Bill McKibben successfully amplifying claims about 'unburnable carbon' in his popular article 'Global Warming's Terrifying New Math' (McKibben 2012).

Regarding the first divestment campaign in 2011, Lenferna (2018: 218) notes that 'it became the fastest growing divestment movement in history'. To date, 688 institutions and 58,399 individuals across 76 countries have committed to divest from fossil fuel companies. By 2018 the fossil fuel divestment movement marked the 1,000th divestment in what has become by far the largest anti-corporate campaign of its kind, bringing the total size of portfolios and endowments in the campaign to just under $8 trillion (£6.4 trillion) (McKibben 2018). There are signs that early adopters have begun a substantial asset movement worth $2.6 trillion. While oil and gas might not feel the direct impact of divestment, coal is already suffering from divestment and perceived financial risk as insurance companies have pulled out equities and bonds worth $20 billion from coal investments and a growing number are refusing to underwrite new coal projects, making them uninsurable (Bergman 2018). Pension funds and insurance companies now represent the largest sectors committing to divestment, reflecting increased financial and fiduciary risks of holding fossil fuels in a world committed to staying below 2°Celsius warming.

Many of the groups involved are student organisations, although religious organisations, local and regional governments and other public bodies have also divested or have been targeted by divestment campaigners. The movement has successfully forced actors as diverse as the G20, the world's major financial establishments, universities and pension funds into acting on the issue. Some of the world's major cities have also moved on the issue. Over the past few years, many cities, from Berlin to Berkeley and Melbourne, have announced their intention to divest, a move now followed by New York City (NYC). When NYC Mayor Bill de Blasio, Comptroller Scott Stringer and several trustees of the city's pension funds announced that the city would divest from fossil fuel reserve owners by 2022, the move positioned NYC at the centre of the divestment movement. NYC's retirement system is the largest municipal pension system in the United States, controlling a total of US$194 billion in investments (ICLEI 2019).

At the heart of the divestment movement is 350.org, an international network of local groups and activists. The movement has a corresponding positive demand which is reinvestment in lower carbon alternatives such as renewable energy, energy efficiency, low carbon infrastructure and demand reduction. For example, Power Shift (a US-based youth and university student movement) calls for universities to reinvest 5 per cent of their endowment in 'climate solutions' as part of their divestment campaign.[4] Elsewhere, a number of major investors, including pension funds and insurance companies, are already starting to shift their investments. For example, over 400 investors with US$25 trillion in assets have joined the Investor Platform for Climate Actions (see Figure 6.1), committed to increasing low-carbon and climate-resilient investments, including by working with policymakers to ensure financing at scale.[5]

When I was one of the organisers of the Sussex University fossil fuel divestment campaign, we had to deploy a range of tactics to persuade the university's administration to use an endowment fund that does not invest in fossil fuels. This included the formation of an alliance between university staff and students, a petition, awareness-raising events on campus and screenings of the 350.org video 'Do the Math', marches and a critical mass bike ride involving the local member of parliament and which attracted local media, the production of our own video,[6] the generation of a carefully researched document outlining the case for divestment which was shared with university decision-makers, as well as open letters from academics calling on the university to make this move. This was combined with quieter lobbying of members of the university's senate and private correspondence with finance personnel: a mix of insider and outsider strategies. In relation to local councils, involvement with the Divest East Sussex campaign group afforded me the opportunity to address the local council on behalf of the group that was targeting the pension committee. Since one of the council's objections to divestment was the lack of precedents for such a move, the divestment group would submit, in advance of each meeting, an ever-growing list of organisations that had pledged to divest from fossil fuels. One by one the group has sought to challenge the reasons given for refusing to divest.

Divestment has been criticised, nevertheless, for its naivety and hard-line stance and dismissed as having little impact on fossil fuel finance since funds divested to

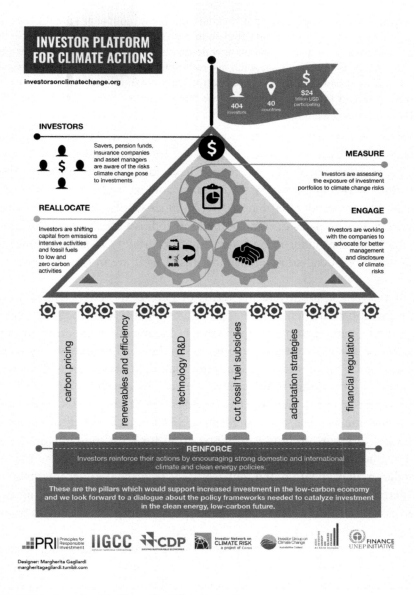

Figure 6.1 Investor Platform for Climate Actions

date have been far too small to financially challenge the global fossil fuel industry and its financiers. Yet as Bergman (2018: 1) suggests:

While the direct impacts of divestment are small, the indirect impacts, in terms of public discourse shift, are significant. Divestment has put questions of finance and climate change on the agenda and played a part in changing the discourse around the legitimacy, reputation and viability of the fossil fuel industry. This cultural impact contributed to changes in the finance industry through new demands by shareholders and investors and to changes in political discourse, such as rethinking the notion of 'fiduciary duty.' Finally, divestment had significant impact on its participants in terms of empowerment and played a part in the revitalisation of the environmental movement in the UK and elsewhere.

The distinction, in many ways, is between direct or material impacts, for example the impact of money already divested from the fossil fuel and finance industries; and indirect or contextual impacts, which have long-term significance, through shaping the socio-economic and institutional context and norms, even if their immediate effect is small (Bergman 2018). In other words, the direct effect of the divestment campaign pales in comparison to its indirect effect through stigmatisation of the fossil fuel industry and increasing uncertainty around its longer-term financial viability: socialising the idea that fossil fuels are in the end game (Helm 2017).[7]

Part of this is about shifting the terms of debate and engagement, even for powerful incumbent actors. For example, divestment has touched the fossil fuel industry, with some companies publishing documents countering arguments about stranded assets. Exxon, for example, felt the need to justify why its assets are not at risk of being stranded, claiming that all its reserves will be needed. Traditionally a recalcitrant in the climate debate, ExxonMobil has faced a large investor inquiry issued to the forty-five top fossil fuel companies, co-ordinated by Ceres and Carbon Tracker, and representing $3 trillion (£1.8 trillion) in assets. It asked Exxon to report on how it was preparing for a carbon-constrained world where greenhouse gas regulation and market forces strand uneconomic assets, and whether money spent finding more reserves is in shareholder interests (Lamb and Fugere 2014). Exxon defending its viability and using the language of stranded assets was evidence that the industry had to respond to activist framings. The oil giant, in a report on *Energy and Carbon – Managing the Risk*, ironically released the same day as an UN IPCC report warned of the catastrophic effect that climate change will have on world populations, stated: 'We are confident that none of our hydrocarbon reserves are now or will become "stranded"', predicting that there was no danger that shareholders would lose value in a carbon-constrained world (O'Meara 2014).

Other means of hitting incumbents financially include the organisation of consumer boycotts and attempts to close down petrol stations and to shut the branches of banks heavily involved in lending to fossil fuels, as happened recently to Barclays bank in the UK in a campaign orchestrated by Greenpeace. In the past, such campaigns have been targeted at Shell over its alleged involvement in human rights violations in Nigeria, Exxon over its funding of climate-sceptic organisations and Texaco regarding allegations of oil spills in Ecuador (Newell 2001). In other cases, campaigns by groups such as Friends of the Earth have sought to get supporters to switch away from the 'big 6' energy providers in the UK, thereby penalising incumbents and rewarding niche actors such as Good Energy and Ecotricity that generate electricity from renewable energy.

The struggle is also, however, about the social licence to operate, questioning social and cultural legitimacy and challenging power. Returning to the example of divestment, Bergman (2018: 14) suggests: 'Divestment has stigmatised the fossil fuel industry and challenged its legitimacy, putting it on the defensive.' In a very real way, the setting and policing of boundaries around the 'conduct of conduct' has real material implications. As one investor put it: 'Ensuring that pension funds and other asset stewards recognise that they are being actively watched—and could be at risk of legal challenge on the issue—is, to be realistic, part of the change process' (quoted in Bergman 2018: 15). In turn, these pressures empower shareholders within companies to raise awkward questions about corporate strategy and exposure to risk, or to engage in forms of shareholder activism (Newell 2008). This comes on the back of warnings from then head of the climate negotiations Christiana Figueres, who urged investors to move away from high carbon assets: 'Institutional investors who ignore the [climate change] risk face being increasingly seen as blatantly in breach of their fiduciary duty to their beneficial owners' (quoted in Bergman 2018: 11).

Contestations over this licence to operate, building on the Gramscian understanding of civil society introduced earlier, have been extended to cultural and public arenas. They are observable in campaigns by groups such as Art Not Oil Coalition, and Platform, with a series of recent victories having seen key cultural institutions such as the British Museum and the Royal Shakespeare Company sever their sponsorship deals with oil companies. There is also growing pressure on media outlets to refuse to accept advertising revenues from fossil fuel companies in the wake of the UK-based newspaper *The Guardian*'s move along those lines (Waterson 2020). This broader sense of stigmatisation felt by the fossil fuel industry is also evidenced by the way it handles its opponents. For example, even when Greenpeace violated several injunctions that the oil major BP had secured to prevent protestors from mounting one of its rigs in the North Sea, the company chose not to take further action, which people inside Greenpeace suspected was a strategic move on the part of BP to avoid a direct confrontation with Greenpeace in which it anticipated that it might lose public legitimacy. Indeed, when legal action was ultimately taken, it was initiated by Transocean, the owner of the rig, and not BP itself (Mackay 2020).

6.4 Participation in Policy

Governments and private providers of energy and electricity have often been reluctant to share decision-making power with their citizens. Yet limited opportunities for public engagement can contribute to the persistence of energy vulnerabilities, energy injustices and social exclusion as the concerns of poorer groups get overlooked (McDonald 2009). Conversely, social involvement and civic participation in energy system planning and operation can help sensitise policy to the needs and experiences of poorer energy users, enabling new energy-related businesses and jobs, helping citizens and industries to flourish while respecting climate and sustainability constraints (IRENA 2017).

Where once citizens would have been seen as passive consumers with little role in broader energy systems, they have now come (in some quarters at least) to be seen as playing an important role in building more sustainable futures. Firstly, this is often expressed as a concern over potential public resistance and the need to gain societal 'acceptance' of urgent yet difficult energy policy decisions and technological changes (Roddis et al. 2018). Fear of public backlash is often a key driver for testing energy policy interventions with stakeholders and representatives of different publics. Secondly, the concern with citizen engagement can centre on the desire to change the energy behaviours of citizens, shifting or 'nudging' them into more sustainable patterns of use (Dubois et al. 2019). But, thirdly, there are also arguments being increasingly deployed that citizens themselves should drive sustainable energy transitions in more distributed and 'bottom-up' ways, through community energy, grassroots innovations and so on, as part of a broader democratisation of energy systems (Smith et al. 2016a).

The argument for participatory governance emphasises that hierarchical steering characterised by a government-led, expert-centred approach is not always adequate for policymaking or problem-solving (Stirling 2005). In many least developed country settings, this is exacerbated by limited regulatory capacity, reflecting human-resource and financial constraints. It has been argued that governments, therefore, need to involve non-state stakeholders in the business sector and civil society to plug gaps in capacity, implementation and expertise (Wesselink et al. 2011). Participatory processes offer the potential for a more comprehensive and inclusive evidence base by including local knowledge, which may improve decision-making by acknowledging the potential social and environmental impacts of infrastructure development. Social acceptance literature also suggests that public participation has contributed to public acceptance of renewable energy in countries including Germany, Denmark and Canada (Jarbandhan et al. 2018; Renn et al. 2014). Involvement of local citizens and actors in the funding and governance of sustainable energy transitions has been seen to provide benefits such as increasing the economic spin-offs and transforming the role of citizens from that of consumers to more active proponents for transition (Rüdinger 2019). However, the depth and the progressive nature of this move towards participatory governance have been questioned amid claims about the incompatibility of neo-liberalising programmes and participatory governance (Abram 2007, 2008). These highlight how participatory or inclusive governance may be hijacked in neo-liberalising processes, deflecting local resistance through 'talking shops' rather than offering effective democratic and inclusive governance.

It is certainly the case that public participation does not guarantee equitable outcomes. Engaging the public is time-consuming and costly and may not result in consensual outcomes. Involving the public may give rise to scepticism rather than enhancing trust when the public express doubts or challenge the equity of the participatory processes and outcomes in terms of policy impacts. In particular, frustration can arise when participants perceive that participatory approaches are used as a means of deflecting protest, inhibiting actions or 'rubber-stamping' a predetermined decision. Around citizens' assemblies, for example, which I have been involved in developing in my own local area of Brighton and Hove in the UK, issues arise around: the choice of experts to inform the process, the selection of facilitators, making sure that this process is seen as crossing party political lines and not driven by particular movements or interest groups (despite it being a core demand of Extinction Rebellion) and how decisions are arrived at to focus on some rather than other areas of policy. For example, a decision was made that what in my area is being called a 'climate assembly' should focus on transport policy since this is an area where the local council exercises more direct control over policy, which makes some sense. But this narrowing of inputs around the zero-carbon strategy of the city to one area was not taken with public input and so raised concerns amongst some activists.

Channels of engagement are, nevertheless, key for groups to exercise and demand their rights. Social movements have an important role to play in demanding and then protecting rights of access to energy and electricity. This is not just about protection from the ill effects of energy production, which have been a characteristic of energy justice struggles for decades (Sovacool and Dworkin 2014); it is also about the expression of positive and proactive demands on the state to meet the energy needs of its citizens. In South Africa, for example, McDonald (2009) describes the importance of campaigns for 'free basic electricity' by groups such as the Soweto Electricity Crisis Committee (SECC), despite (unlike water, for example) there being no explicitly defined constitutional rights to electricity. The SECC contested controversial cut-offs where in the early 2000s tens of thousands of poorer consumers were having their supplies cut off because of non-payment.

Access to energy is not just conferred from above, therefore. Poorer people often mobilise around fuel prices, subsidies and demands over the right to energy, sometimes with successful results. For example, in Nepal people are exercising their right to energy, granted through a programme in which communities pay certain charges for grid connectivity and take over the management (including billing). This is reshaping the ways in which electricity is distributed and managed across rural Nepal, all the way from a mothers' group in North Pokhra to a forest users' group in Bangesal to a Thame Bijli Company that has trained eleven Sherpas as linesmen and meter readers (Yadav 2010). Meanwhile in Brazil, local farmers have been driven by limited electricity supply, poor reliability and high prices to take control of the previously dysfunctional and undemocratic CRERAL (Cooperativa Regional de Eletrificação Rural do Alto Uruguai Ltda) electricity cooperative. Taking advantage of low local capital costs, an existing distribution network and the availability of commercial loans and carbon credits, CRERAL has been able to finance and manage two mini hydro plants that now supply around a quarter of local electricity needs to its membership of around 6,000 families. Local meetings on decisions are held in all of the cooperative's municipalities, giving all members the opportunity to express local priorities and suggest appropriate uses for CRERAL annual income at the General Assembly. In this case, more localised decision-making allows for greater adaptability in dealing with local issues, such as the allocation of electricity or individual families that face financial difficulties (Newell et al. 2011).

As well as exercising voice directly, some civil society actors mobilise on behalf of niche actors to seek to tip the balance in their favour. When the UK government announced plans to end payments for surplus power for new solar homes, thousands of people joined the campaign to stop the 'daylight robbery', as activists labelled it. After more than 7,000 people wrote to their MP as part of a campaign by the 10:10 group (now called Possible) demanding fair treatment for solar, the government was forced to publish a policy that would replace the export tariff. It is now consulting the public on this idea and proposals to bring in a 'Smart Export Guarantee' (SEG) (BIES 2019). Possible also played a key part in reversing the freeze on support for onshore wind farms in the UK announced in 2020, which it had campaigned for since 2016 (Langford 2020). In understanding the role that civil society groups play in this regard, Seyfang and Haxeltine (2012: 381) draw on ideas about strategic niche management theory to understand how movements develop beyond a niche 'to foster deeper engagement with resourceful regime actors; to manage expectations more realistically by delivering tangible opportunities for action and participation; and to embrace a community-based, action-oriented model of social change'.

As well as participating in policy and contesting it, some actors also seek more profound governance innovations. As discussed, some movements, such as Extinction Rebellion, have called for the establishment of citizens' assemblies as an important governance innovation to help chart new ways forward, less subject to corporate lobbying and other special interest group politics and more representative of the societies they come from and are accountable to (Willis 2020). NGOs such as the Foundation for Democracy and Sustainable Development and the World Future Council, meanwhile, have called for a more explicit representation of the interests of future generations in decision-making, including around energy pathways. Such representatives already exist in the Welsh assembly and the parliaments of Israel and Hungary, for example, where they can exercise a power of veto over decisions that fail to properly consider the interests of future generations (World Future Council 2012). Further such innovations in governance and representation could have profound implications for the viability and pursuit of different energy futures.

6.5 Co-producing Energy Governance

Civil society actors have also been co-producers of governance in the energy sector, filling gaps left by the absence of action by governments and international institutions. Often uneven in global representation and sectoral coverage, such civil, private or hybrid governance nevertheless makes an important contribution to the architectures of governance shaping energy transitions. A lot of this has emerged through transnational climate change governance (Bulkeley et al. 2014), but includes energy focused initiatives such as REEEP (Renewable Energy and Energy Efficiency Partnership), REN21 (Renewable Energy Network), the Global Methane Initiative, the Green Power Market Development Group and the Johannesburg Renewable Energy Coalition (Bulkeley et al. 2014; Newell 2011; Szulecki et al. 2011).

REEEP, for example, is an international public–private partnership funded by governments, businesses and development banks, aimed at identifying barriers to and opportunities for the uptake of renewable energy and energy efficiency opportunities (Parthan et al. 2010). Often described as a 'hybrid' organisation (Florini and Sovacool 2009), REEEP is focused on the development of market conditions that foster sustainable energy and energy efficiency and works to structure policy and regulatory initiatives for clean energy. Hence, it seeks both to improve the existing legal and political frameworks that govern clean energy and to finance projects that can attract investors and financiers who can develop and deploy clean energy technologies in other markets. It has supported around 180 clean energy projects in developing countries to date.[8] Yet it relies on voluntary funding from several governments (mainly the UK and Norway) the instability and unpredictability of which may reduce the organisation's effectiveness compared with other actors in the governance of energy finance, particularly in terms of planning of future activities. REN21, meanwhile, describes itself as 'a global policy network that provides a forum for international leadership on renewable energy'.[9] Its goal is to bolster policy development for the rapid expansion of renewable energies in developing and industrialised economies, but it does not fund projects in the way that REEEP does. Open to a wide variety of dedicated stakeholders, REN21 connects governments, international institutions, NGOs, industry associations and other partnerships and initiatives. Both REEEP and REN21, therefore, are small organisations with limited capacity in terms of staff and resources, heavily reliant on collaboration and partnership with other organisations and not yet able to shape energy finance on anything like the scale of other institutions, as we saw in Chapter 4.

There is also a great deal of city-based urban climate change governance involving civil society actors such as C40, Cities for Climate Protection, the Global Covenant of Mayors for Climate and Energy as well as civil society-led initiatives such as Transition towns and carbon rationing groups (Bulkeley and Newell 2015). Transition towns and carbon rationing groups and 'low carbon communities' groups sprang up in towns across the UK from about 2005, in response to increasing concerns about climate change. But the transition network now has a significant global presence. By May 2010 there were over 400 community initiatives recognised as official Transition towns, and by September 2013 there were 1,130 initiatives registered in 43 countries from Chile to New Zealand, to Italy, Canada and the UK (Transitions Network 2017). There is an element of DIY (Do-It-Yourself) politics and 'big society' in some of these approaches: being entrepreneurial and stealing a lead, but also mobilising to fill gaps left by the retreat of the state.[10] They perform a range of functions from creating markets, mobilising finance and setting standards (in particular those in which business actors are prominent), to promoting particular technologies, lesson learning and information sharing (often involving international organisations), to, at the civil society end, enabling mobilisation, building communities of practice, future proofing through resilience and reducing energy consumption.

Regarding city-based initiatives, in 2004, conversations amongst the mayors of London, Stockholm, Toronto and San Francisco resulted in the formation of what became the Cities Climate Leadership Group (C40). Its aim was that every city should have developed and begun implementing a climate action plan with a deadline of 2020, to deliver action consistent with the objectives of the Paris Agreement. Owing to impatience with the lack of policy or planning from national governments and recognition of the huge contribution of cities to global emissions, the idea was to harness the power newly invested in mayors to accelerate climate action. A series of EU and UN city-led groupings eventually morphed into the Global Covenant of Mayors for Climate and Energy, an alliance of cities and local governments with similar aims. Deadline 2020 was the first significant route map for achieving the Paris Agreement, outlining the pace, scale and prioritisation of action needed by C40 member cities over the next five years and beyond. As part of Deadline 2020, seventy-two global cities are committed to delivering on the objectives of the Paris Agreement of 'holding the increase in the global average temperature to well below 2 degrees [Celsius] above pre-industrial levels, and to pursue efforts to limit the temperature increase to 1.5 degrees [Celsius] above pre-industrial levels'.[11] Like C40, the Global Covenant of Mayors for Climate and Energy is a global city-led network committed to climate leadership. It builds on the commitment of over 9,000 cities and local governments from 6 continents and 127 countries representing more than 770 million residents.[12] They must commit to targets at least as ambitious, or more so, than their own country's targets under the Paris Agreement.

Though not assuming a new form of governance in and of itself, other forms of activism have sought to provide a new mandate to local councils to accelerate change in the energy system in response to the climate crisis. Recently, there have been popular drives to get councils to declare 'climate emergencies' with potentially direct implications for local energy pathways and trajectories. From almost nowhere, local authorities in the UK, for example, have started declaring 'climate emergencies' and committing to plans genuinely in line with meeting climate targets. When the small Welsh market town of Machynlleth became the first council in the UK to declare a 'climate emergency' in late 2018, it was viewed as laudable but not altogether surprising. It is after all the home of the Centre for Alternative Technology (CAT), a green energy research centre dating back to 1973, and a pioneer of zero carbon strategies. But following swiftly after Machynlleth came Bradford, Bristol, Milton Keynes, Norwich and London. It was obvious that something new, different and rapid was happening. Within just three months, forty had signed the pledge – representing over 17 million people between them in the UK and more than 34 million in the USA, Australia, Canada and Switzerland. Signatories committed to a climate emergency pledge to reduce CO_2 emissions by at least 40 per cent by 2030. Populations covered by governments that have declared a 'climate emergency' now exceed 31 million citizens in four English-speaking countries and Switzerland, with 17 million of these living in the UK. A growing wave of local action is emerging from the inertia of national governments.[13]

The 'climate emergency' movement uses local democracy directly in a new way, being bottom-up rather than top-down. Organisations such as Extinction Rebellion,

Climate Mobilization, and Council Action in the Climate Emergency (CACE) are using fleet-of-foot methods of grassroots organisation to stimulate direct action and activism on a local, national and international level. For a council to have called a 'climate emergency', commonly advanced guidelines say that it must have used these specific words in a motion or executive decision; have set a target date to reduce its local climate impacts consistent with the IPCC Report; have set up a working group to report within a short timescale; and engaged with a cross-section of the community.[14]

So far, councils' pledges and aims have varied enormously. For example, Scarborough council in the UK has committed to a target of zero carbon emissions by 2030 and will seek up to £80,000 in funding over two years for a sustainability officer to help achieve its goals. Meanwhile, Liverpool City Council deleted all references to declaring a 'climate emergency' and many of the suggested actions to be taken. Its plan has no stated target, no timeline and no budget. In Lancaster, a citizens' assembly is being set up as a deliberative process in which a representative group of citizens, selected at random from the population, learn about, discuss and make recommendations. When in 'emergency mode', councils must allocate discretionary funds towards climate action. That includes things such as educating the community, advocating for action from higher-level governments, mitigating and building resilience against the impacts of climate change, and funding or undertaking the planning and research needed to implement full state and national emergency mobilisation.

Interestingly, some of these forms of activism are taking root in contexts of active hostility to climate action by their own state leaders. Yet, the organisation Climate Mobilisation used the Trump administration's outspoken denial of man-made climate change as a rallying call. Montgomery County in Maryland had already voted to reduce greenhouse gas emissions by 80 per cent by 2027 and 100 per cent by 2035. Other jurisdictions joined in, setting their own targets, but focused largely on the Paris Agreement. California, for example, recognising its vulnerability to climate change in the form of drought, wildfires and flooding, aims to reduce its carbon emissions by 40 per cent below 1990 levels by 2030. To reach this, it will be setting benchmarks for developing green enterprise zones, renewable energy, cultivating food locally, restoring biodiversity, planting more trees and supporting low-carbon transportation and zero waste.[15]

Greenpeace, in a message to its supporters, produced its own list of elements of a climate emergency taken from its broader strategy (Greenpeace 2019). These included a ban on all new oil and gas production in the UK, including fracking, a tripling of renewable energy by 2030, planting of 700 million trees, introducing a Frequent Flyer Tax, ending the sale of all new petrol and diesel cars by 2030, rolling out free bus travel for young people and those on lower incomes, ending carbon emissions from heavy industry such as steel and cement, creating millions of jobs in a new green economy, retrofitting homes to go zero carbon and radically changing the farming and food system to encourage a less meat-based diet. As I have argued elsewhere, declarations of emergency create an opportunity (i) to involve citizens through citizens' assemblies and other processes of participation and consultation in setting priorities for ambitious carbon reduction and understanding and engaging with the difficult choices that implies; (ii) to create healthier, more resilient and sustainable local communities powered by locally generated low carbon energy, served by affordable and sustainable transport, higher-quality and more efficient housing stock and fed by sustainable food and land systems; and (iii) to undo business as usual. In a time of cutbacks, this means reversing costly policies and investments in carbon-intensive infrastructures such as roads and airports and divesting council pension funds from fossil fuels.[16]

As part of applied and activist research for this book and in my role on the advisory board of the local council sustainability group ADEPT (Association of Directors of Environment, Economy, Planning and Transport),[17] I had meetings with local councils and local government associations in which it became clear that they are struggling with how to realise the broad aims and ambitions of a climate emergency. Due to the neo-liberal pressures towards outsourcing transport, catering, waste and other services, they feel that they have very little direct control over large areas of service provision. Having been part of community mobilisations towards a citizens' assembly in my own area of Brighton and Hove, and the youth strikes that preceded it, I have been fortunate enough to see the process unfold firsthand. A key issue is incentivising people to engage and participate in such an assembly when they are unclear or unsure whether any recommendations will be accepted or acted upon by local government officials. Likewise, local councillors cannot agree in advance to accept proposals which they have neither the resources nor the authority to enact. These are not new dilemmas, and local action around sustainability transitions has a long history. Local Agenda 21, which grew out of the original 1992 Earth Summit, led to a range of important initiatives and capacity building at local level, only to now be largely forgotten, much to the frustration of local government officials.

6.6 Restricting Production through Resistance

As well as working with and through public institutions and seeking to co-produce new forms of governance involving a range of stakeholders, for many community activists and radical environmentalists, resistance in the form of direct action and civil disobedience forms a key plank of the activist repertoire. Whether it is the more spectacular occupations of oil rigs, as Greenpeace managed to do to BP in the North Sea, or shutdowns of company headquarters, or ongoing wars of attrition over infrastructural projects and new sites of extraction in places as diverse as Alberta in Canada, Colombia and Nigeria, there is a long history of resistance to energy production. Given the manifest unwillingness of governments and corporations to accept the need to leave large swathes of remaining fossil fuels in the ground, this form of protest is likely to escalate.

Such forms of resistance threaten to disrupt the circuits of energy capital, whether fossil or renewable based, if key social and environmental concerns are not addressed. Resistance puts down limits to production, as has occurred with fracking activism, where the UK has now introduced a ban. In Europe in 2019, both the MidCat pipeline between Spain and France and the Gothenburg terminal in Sweden were cancelled. Meanwhile, indigenous leaders and allies held a March–May 2019 training tour for 1,160 people in 9 US cities answering the call to stop the Keystone XL pipeline and protect water and ancestral lands, a project whose licence was revoked in April 2020 (Lakhani 2020). Earlier precedents for these forms of direct action include roads protests (Seel 1997) and airport activism by groups such as Plane Stupid.

As well as restricting opportunities for capital accumulation, through contestation, media coverage and public debate, such protests also raise questions about the desirability and sustainability of these projects. Maintaining camps and a constant protest presence creates the need for constant policing to guard against disruption and sabotage at the site of extraction, something I learned first-hand through involvements in the road protests in the UK in the mid-1990s. Legal cases provide activists with the opportunity to question the licence to operate. Kingsnorth power station in Kent owned by E. On was occupied by six Greenpeace activists in 2008. In their defence, the activists argued that they were trying to prevent the greater damage to property caused by climate change, a point highlighted by leading climate scientist James Hansen whom they enrolled as a witness, and they were subsequently acquitted (Vidal 2008). Similar defences have been invoked to justify actions that stopped a train delivering coal to the Drax power station in York in the UK, and large-scale mobilisations in defence of the Hambach forest in Germany against RWE's open pit mine (Brock 2018). Criminalisation of dissent and counterinsurgency is one of the ways in which the state intervenes to protect incumbents and existing accumulation strategies (Brock and Dunlap 2018). It does so because such protests disrupt circuits of energy capital by posing a direct affront to property rights regimes such as is the case with the Treaty Alliance Against Tar Expansion signed by more than 122 first nations and tribes.

Beyond seeking to disrupt, delay and cancel specific carbon-intensive infrastructures, groups such as Rise up!, Enough and Extinction Rebellion also provide a fundamental critique of the unsustainability of capitalism or even industrialism more broadly (Porritt 1989). Here the focus is less NIMBY (not in my back yard) and more NOPE (not on Planet Earth). As noted already in relation to the divestment movement, a key concern for incumbents is squaring accumulation with legitimation; a central tension and dynamic in capitalism (Paterson 2010). In this regard, mass protests, especially by young people and those most affected by climate change, constitute a public relations disaster for companies when it is harder to dismiss children and teenagers as extremists or professional activists as troublemakers. In a radio interview for Talk Radio in London, I was attacked by the presenter for having signed a letter in support of the school strikes and thus encouraging what she was choosing to call 'truancy'. I pointed out that, at least when I was younger, truancy didn't normally involve teach-ins on the science of climate change, poster and banner making and mobilising others to attend demonstrations and petition politicians to take action. The success of the 'School Strike 4 Climate' movement has meant that in the UK alone it amounted to a full-time job for activist (and former student of mine) Jake Woodier.

The movement of which he is a part, inspired by the schoolgirl Greta Thunberg, has grown exponentially. On her first day of protest in her native Sweden outside the parliament in September 2018, she sat alone; the second day, others joined in; after a few weeks, her quiet protest had captured the imagination of the media. By October, eight girls in Victoria, Australia, decided to organise a demonstration on the other side of the world and, by November, participants numbered in their thousands. A global youth movement to force government action on climate change has now brought 1.4 million children and young people out on strike.[18] On Friday 15 March 2019, children walked out of schools in 2, 233 cities and towns in 128 countries, from Australia to India, the United Kingdom and the United States, according to the 'Fridays for the Future' initiative. This is not to say that the protests have not produced negative reaction in some quarters. For example, in my interview mentioned above, the interviewer tried to belittle and dismiss the significance of the protests by insisting that they were not driven by genuine concern for climate (but rather an excuse to take time out of school), that the issue of climate change was already on the national agenda, and that in any case the threat of climate change was exaggerated![19] This movement is part of a broader wave of youth-based activism, however. The summer of 2018 was a catalyst for change in other places where in the USA, for example, the Sunrise Movement launched 'Sunrise Semester', employing seventy-five full-time youth organisers across five key states to build their power and mobilise their communities. They aim to hold fossil fuel executives and politicians accountable, and only elect politicians who commit to action on climate change.[20]

Legal actions also open up other avenues of resistance and accountability. The landmark youth climate lawsuit against the US government (*Juliana* v. *the United States*) is a constitutional climate change case against the US federal government, filed by twenty-one young individuals in 2015. At the time, the youngest was eight and the oldest nineteen. This case looked at the actions of the federal government for the past several decades of helping to perpetuate the climate crisis by continuing to fund the fossil fuel economy, endangering the lives of all citizens, but disproportionately harming the lives of younger citizens and future generations. In the end, the court found that the Juliana plaintiffs lacked standing to press constitutional climate claims against the federal government, but the case attracted welcome publicity to the government's role in perpetuating the climate crisis.[21] In terms of using the law to challenge infrastructures, the case of the proposed expansion of London's Heathrow airport offers another case in point. Plans for a third runway at Heathrow airport have been ruled illegal by the court of appeal because ministers did not adequately take into account the government's commitments to tackle the climate crisis (Carrington 2020). The case sets a potentially critical precedent that new infrastructural projects will have to demonstrate compatibility with the goals and ambitions of the Paris Agreement, to which the UK government is a signatory. Elsewhere, after years of resistance, in June 2019 a Kenyan tribunal cancelled a developer's licence to build a new coal plant at Lamu, a stunning coastal UNESCO world heritage site. And in a historic victory, after years of campaigning, the state of Paraná in Brazil passed a law in July to permanently ban fracking and Santa Catarina state followed weeks later, meaning that Latin America's largest shale reserves will go untapped. So, despite the challenges of making effective use of the law as a strategy for securing environmental justice (Newell 2001), victories can be won.

6.7 Building Just Transitions

As discussed elsewhere in this book, measures to accelerate the decline of particular energy industries or to impose new taxes on fuels, for example, are always controversial, having an impact, as they often do, on poorer members of society. They can generate popular backlashes, protests and even direct action. Examples include protests about fuel taxes in the UK in 2000 which brought the country to a standstill as oil tanker drivers blockaded depots, or protests about the withdrawal of fossil fuel subsidies in Nigeria and Indonesia. In contexts of fragile states, restrictions on access to fuel and proposed price rises often inflame existing antigovernment sentiments around taxation and corruption, while outages are interpreted as a violation of citizens' social contract with the state, and access to subsidies is sometimes seen as a right.[22] The strength of protest can provoke policy reversals. Lockwood (2015: 475) cites the example of Nigeria's attempt to remove subsidies on petrol and diesel; after little more than two weeks of violent protests, 'the government reduced prices again by 60%, reversing a large part of the reform. Over a year later, subsidies for road transport fuels in Nigeria remain in place'. More recently, the yellow vest movement in France started as a protest against a fuel tax rise and spiralled into a broader, and at times violent, mobilisation against the government of Emmanuel Macron.

At the other end of the class spectrum, there has been a wave of middle-class activism, sometimes called NIMBYISM, around the sighting of wind turbines in rural areas. Behind localised protests in the UK, there are often organised lobbies with strong media support from right-wing press and vocal commentators willing to denounce the projects (such as the late former TV conservation celebrity David Bellamy). Such campaigns have been backed by Country Guardian, the Council for the Protection of Rural England (CPRE) and the National Trust, bodies that have traditionally represented landed aristocrats, with such projects concentrated in Conservative voting areas, enabling them to gain leverage. There is a danger in both cases of resistance being seen as a barrier and an obstacle that needs to be overcome rather than engaged with. This tension is likely to intensify as the urgency of scaling up near-term responses translates into pressure for immediate and bold interventions.

For this reason, it is important that new and progressive alliances and coalitions are also emerging to accelerate more inclusive and just transitions in order to pre-empt crises such as those described. The Just Transition Alliance (JTA) in California, for example, is a coalition of environmental justice and labour organisations. Together with frontline workers and community members who live alongside polluting industries, it seeks to create healthy workplaces and communities. It focuses on contaminated sites that should be cleaned up, and on the transition to clean production and sustainable economies. For example, on issues such as 'clean coal', the JTA voices objections based on local as well as global impacts, including local air pollution, working conditions and detrimental environmental impacts of mining on local landscapes and water use. 'City Retrofit' Los Angeles, meanwhile, is a grassroots coalition of community-based organisations, trades unions and environmental groups that campaigned to ensure that programmes by the city council to improve energy efficiency and the use of renewable energy also brought economic benefits to disadvantaged people living in the city. This included retrofit of public buildings in low-income communities, jobs for poorer people and supporting businesses owned by local minorities and women. There are similar historical cases where the purposes for which production is organised can change rapidly such as the Lucas Plan to re-employ workers in armaments factories in socially useful alternatives (Smith 2014). Likewise, in Australia's Hunter Valley, communities mobilised to take hold of their own transition. Community distress about the cumulative local ecological and human health impacts of mines and power stations and alarm about global climate change have given rise to a vocal, growing and globally linked social movement that is challenging the primacy of coal and demanding a transition from coal dependency to a clean energy economy. Key aspects of a just transition to an ecological economy that protects vulnerable communities include boosting resilience and adaptive capacity, public investment in the industries of the future, and alliances amongst the climate justice, environment and labour movements (Bird and Lawton 2009; Evans 2010; JTA 2011).

There is important advocacy work for such alliances to do around the state's role in managing just transitions. The German government advisory body WBGU has proposed what it refers to as 'a just and in-time transformation' that takes into account all people affected, empowers them, holds those responsible for climate change accountable, and creates both global and national prospects for the future. In this regard, it calls on the German federal government to promote four exemplary initiatives of a just and in-time climate policy targeting (1) the people affected by the structural change towards climate compatibility (e.g. in coal-mining regions), (2) the legal rights of people harmed by climate change, (3) the dignified migration of people who lose their native countries due to climate change, and (4) the creation of financing instruments for just and in-time transformation processes (WBGU 2018).

6.7.1 Building Alternative Systems of Energy Production: Community Energy

Innovation is clearly a key aspect of energy transitions, and transition scholars have increasingly turned their attention towards grassroots and social innovation (Smith et al. 2016b) and the ways in which civil society actors can offer up new paradigms and ways of thinking, construct alternatives and often provide more experiential and participatory forms of knowledge, as well as build support and prepare the way for alternative pathways, serving as transmission belts for the articulation of societal preferences in everyday policy. Smith (2008: 201) notes: 'Clusters of activities can be conceived as contributing towards unsettling and delegitimising regimes (and thereby opening windows of opportunity for sustainable alternatives), nurturing alternatives in niche settings and helping solutions translate from marginal to mainstream settings.'

Civil society spaces are often more conducive to innovation and experimentation because of the ability and willingness to take risks, low expectations or pressures to deliver short-term returns to investors, acceptance of intrinsic uncertainties, and an embrace (or at least acceptance) of failure because not everything is hanging on the success of one isolated initiative. With regard to local experimentation, high levels of trust and social capital and an embedded understanding of a local culture and how things work in a particular place further enhance the prospects of success of transition initiatives.[23] Motivations often include wider objectives such as supporting the local economy, promoting energy security, cutting carbon and building more sustainable communities (Walker et al. 2007). Corresponding challenges and limitations of course include lack of, or unpredictability of, flows of funds, a reliance on voluntarism and the goodwill of people, and lack of interest in partnering with profit-driven or larger entities, as well as a reliance on state support for the devolution of power over energy infrastructures (Smith 2008).

In relation to energy, community energy has attracted particular attention and is seen by some as a route to energy democracy (Burke and Stephens 2017; Seyfang et al. 2014). As Chapman (2018: 5) makes clear: 'This transition is at the same time a great opportunity to achieve the goal of energy democracy. We should remember that when the green movement protested against nuclear power in the seventies, it was not only because of the ecological risks of nuclear energy. It was also a rejection of a – by conception – very centralised top-down energy system.' To put it simply: nuclear plants have to be managed like military bases, while wind turbines can be community owned. Technological developments are now providing many more opportunities for a decentralised energy system that can be organised in a democratic manner. In this, energy system citizens' cooperatives and local authorities can play a crucial role, developing public–civil partnerships. Momentum often comes from below and ownership matters (Overy 2018). The activist origins and aims of such transition experiments clearly have a bearing on how they are conceived of, owned and managed and what the purposes and who the intended beneficiaries of the project are imagined to be (Brummer 2018). In the case of Sweden's first co-operatively owned wind farm on Gotland, it was a group of anti-nuclear campaigners who were pioneering local community ownership of wind energy by setting up a company, Vindkompaniet (Chapman 2018).

Beyond the desire to combat climate change, the rationale is often community regeneration. Studies show that by 2050, around 45 per cent of all EU households could be producing their own renewable energy, and more than a third of our energy could come through renewable energy co-operatives. This constitutes a huge opportunity for regional economic development, as locally owned renewable energy projects deliver eight times the value of projects owned by private companies that are not from the area (Chapman 2018). There is also an interesting transnational diffusion effect, giving lie to the assumption that community energy constitutes and is restricted to a parochial notion of energy transition. For example, Community Energy in the UK started with Baywind co-operative, founded in 1996 by a Swedish company that had developed community-owned wind farms in Sweden and in 1996 built a wind farm in Cumbria, north-west England. In turn, 2002 Baywind set up Energy4All to help other communities develop and own renewable energy systems. Energy4All[24] has subsequently worked with many communities, helping them to develop, own and operate renewable energy projects.

In one study on the factors that determine the size of financial investments made by community renewable energy members, it was found that the return on investment is the most important determinant for members of large communities of interest, while environmental, social and other non-economic drivers tend to dominate financial motives for members of smaller communities of place. The presence of other co-operative members in close social networks plays a particularly important role in the latter kind of communities, highlighting the strength of social interactions as a driver for investments (Bauwens et al. 2019). Many companies are majority owned by the community energy organisations they serve (Hasanov and Zuidema 2018). For example, Mongoose Energy is a company that is majority owned by the community energy organisations that it provides services for, bringing together local people and commercial developers to identify, develop, finance, build and manage community-owned, renewable energy projects, which it has primarily done for large-scale solar photovoltaic (PV) projects in the South-West of England.[25] Echoing the point above about the clear normative values that often drive community energy, the previous director of Mongoose Energy was the former CEO of The Climate Group, a corporate-facing climate change NGO.

In the case of Denmark between 1998 and 2007, Samsø became the world's first 100 per cent renewable energy-powered island, having been entirely dependent on fossil fuels, and has been cited as one of the most inspiring examples of a sustainable energy community (Sperling 2017). Supported by market-based policy instruments (e.g. subsidies for wind energy), it is estimated that investments in the island totalled €57 million, resulting in approximately twenty person-years of employment each year over the period 1998–2007. Five of the ten offshore wind turbines are owned by the municipality, three are privately owned and two are cooperatively owned by many small shareholders. Of the onshore wind turbines, nine are owned privately by local farmers and two are owned by local co-operatives. From a baseline of approximately 11 tonnes of CO_2, Samsø residents now have an average annual carbon footprint of negative 12 tonnes per person, compared with the Danish average of 6.2 tonnes and 10 tonnes per capita in the UK.[26]

The history of this transition is revealing of some of the key dynamics of local energy transitions. In 1997 the Danish government launched a competition to develop a model renewable energy community, in order to prove that the country's Kyoto climate target to reduce carbon emissions by 21 per cent was doable. The 4,000-inhabitant island applied and won with a proposal based on strong community engagement and a co-operative ownership strategy. By the year 2000, eleven wind turbines covered the island's electricity needs. A further ten offshore turbines were erected in 2002, generating sufficient energy to offset emissions from the island's cars, buses, tractors and the ferry that connects it to the mainland. Three-quarters of the island's heating and hot water is fuelled by biomass boilers fuelled with locally grown straw.

Ownership is key (Mey and Diesendorf 2018). On Samsø, oft-cited concerns about the visually unappealing nature of onshore wind turbines were addressed by the proactive inclusion of the community in the ownership structure of the turbines. The principle that was put into practice was that if you could see a turbine from your window, you could sign on as a co-investor. The fact that so much of the island's community has a direct stake in the wind turbines helped to build the near unanimous consensus that the transition to self-generated renewable energy was a positive development. The shared ownership structure is consistent with the Danish co-operative tradition: of the eleven onshore wind turbines, nine are owned privately by local farmers and two are owned by local co-operatives. Of the offshore turbines, five out of ten are owned by the municipality, three are privately owned and two are co-operatively owned by many small shareholders.[27]

Social networks are often critical in guaranteeing demand for such ventures. An important component of local assemblages, infused with social capital, is networks of financial and legal professionals who offer pro bono advice to community-led low carbon projects. They often rely on community share models too, whereby societies can raise capital by issuing shares. Shareholders become members and the society is owned jointly by its members. Shareholders are paid interest on their shares. It is a highly regulated financial model in many ways because shares can only be sold back to a society and the society has control over who becomes its members. Many community share offers, for example, give priority to those who are local to the project for which funding is being sought. As Chapman (2018: 28) suggests, '[a]n important factor in the growth of community energy in the UK has been its co-operative ethos and in particular the willingness of people involved to share information and help each other'.

Other community energy projects have helped communities reduce their emissions in very direct ways, installing solar PV systems on leased roofs, for example. There have also been cases of community-owned hydro projects. Early community ventures in wind in the UK were also reliant on the Non-Fossil Fuel Obligation (NFFO), initially introduced in 1990 as a means of supporting nuclear energy. This was supplemented in many cases by finance from ethical banks such as Triodos in the UK, as well as grants from government units such as the Department of Trade and Industry's Energy Technology Support Unit (ETSU); in Scotland, more extensive support was available from the Community and Renewable Energy Scheme (CARES). In the UK, community energy grew and by 2015 there were thought to be 150–200 community energy organisations, owning solar, wind, hydro and biomass boilers. However, the growth in community energy was brought to a halt in 2015 when the newly elected Conservative government announced drastic cuts to its support for small-scale renewable energy. Thereafter, the number of new community energy groups fell from about thirty a year to just one in 2017. The feed-in tariff (FIT) export tariff ceased from March 2019, meaning that small-scale generators have no guarantee that they will be paid a fair price, or any price at all, for electricity that they export to the grid, and the government has no plans for new public support for renewable energy until 2025 at the earliest (Chapman 2018).

What this highlights is the problem of being reliant on unpredictable state support. The Solar Trade Association, for example, said that 32 per cent of jobs in that industry were lost by the summer of 2016 and the Renewable Energy Association has said that the changes to FITs in 2015/16 resulted in 9,000 jobs being lost (Macalister 2016). The shifting policy uncertainty has had a detrimental effect on community energy groups. As Howard Johns (2015: 247) from the Ouse Valley Energy Services Cooperative in Lewes UK put it: 'The changes took us and the whole solar industry by surprise and meant that we suddenly had a rather scary deadline to work to. We had to raise £350,000 and then build what was at the time a sizeable project in a matter of weeks.' Given this, and in order to represent and defend their interests, community groups have sought to mobilise a political presence nationally. Within the UK context, organisations to represent and lobby for the community energy sector now exist in England, Scotland and Wales.

Community energy does continue to grow, though primarily through the acquisition of existing generating capacity (particularly large solar farms but also large-scale wind), with some new installations by existing, established organisations. But the lesson of community energy in the UK is that, for it to flourish, a series of key conditions need to be met. These include the financial viability of small-scale renewable energy systems; the availability of motivated and committed people to set up community energy organisations that have control of buildings or land suitable for renewable energy; sources of help and expertise for those people; legal structures that enable co-operative ownership of assets; and the stability of financial incentives and policies on renewable energy. Having all of these things aligned at the same time is no easy task.

The issue is not just mobilising finance, therefore, but redesigning and building alternative infrastructures such as micro or smart grids. For example, as Chapman (2018) points out, the electricity grid in the UK was built to take electricity from predominantly centrally located large coal-fired power stations to businesses and homes across the country. The high-voltage transmission network is owned and operated by National Grid plc. The low voltage distribution network, which takes power into homes and businesses, is owned by regional distribution network operators. These are private companies who are monopolies within their region, regulated by Ofgem, whereas an electricity system supplied by renewable energy will consist of smaller, more dispersed generators. Renewable energy requires land, which is more abundant in rural areas. But many rural areas have a weak distribution network that needs upgrading to be able to accommodate the energy from renewable generation.

The normative nature of many community energy projects is underscored by the fact that in the UK context, for example, many were linked to or founded by members of the Transition town network described in Section 6.5. They were also linked to other local carbon and climate change action groups, and people with links to the Green Party were amongst the most active. They set about doing energy audits of people's homes and community buildings, calculating carbon footprints and providing advice on how to reduce energy use. Groups often got funding and other support from their local authorities, local strategic partnerships or the sustainability funds. The Energy Saving Trust ran a programme called Community Action for Energy (CAfE) where a Low Carbon Communities Network was set up in 2008 to be a voice for all these groups and enable them to learn from each other.

Process is also key to the acceptance and embrace of community energy. In the case, described earlier in this section, of Samsø island in Denmark, the transparent and consultative bottom-up process of implementation was vital to its success. From the very beginning, there was full disclosure of information. The masterplan was made public in the local library, and information on the process was shared through the local newspaper and discussed in great detail at regular community meetings. The consultation process built on the island's long tradition of agricultural co-operatives, which ensured strong local engagement. Generous time frames were provided for discussions and decision-making, which allowed for confidence in the project and a strong sense of collective ownership of the decisions taken. The transition was also made possible by local and deeply committed leadership of key individuals. Responsiveness to community concerns was an important part of this. For example, there was considerable debate around where the onshore wind turbines would be located. Although the proposed locations of the turbines were determined by techno-economic feasibility studies of where they could be most easily installed and where the wind generation capacity was greatest, those implementing the project ultimately agreed to adjust their plans in order to meet the community's wishes. This meant that the community felt genuine ownership over the siting of the wind turbines, which helped to dispel any negative feelings about them.

Studies on social acceptance of wind power projects typically evaluate wind power in isolation, or as a choice between wind and no wind. However, as Firestone and Kirk (2019) show, at a societal level, the choice is limited not to whether, how or where wind turbines should be sited, but to whether society should generate electricity by wind or from some other source. Consequently, it is important to understand whether those living near local wind projects prefer them relative to other local power projects. Firestone and Kirk (2019) show that approximately 90 per cent of individuals in the USA who live within 8 km of a wind turbine prefer their local wind project to a centralised power plant sited at a similar distance.

There are always questions about scale, impact and market share, of course. In the UK, the total electricity-generation capacity in 2017 was 168 MW, comprising 157 projects and producing 202 GWH of electricity (Chapman 2018). But it is also clear that, in a more supportive environment, greater ambition could be achieved. At a smaller scale, other community energy experiments include solar water heating clubs, insulation clubs, Carbon Net networks as well as co-operatively owned renewable energy systems (Walker et al. 2007; Bulkeley and Newell 2015). Sometimes these are externally supported and funded, such as in the case of the UK Labour government's 'Low Carbon Community Challenge'. As Smith (2008: 197) suggests, though, there is 'a tendency to treat community projects as marginal to energy regimes, rather than exploring how mutual adaptations may contribute to new sustainable energy system hybrids'.

6.8 Culturing Change

Besides mobilising, 'culturing' is clearly a key part of the story of transformation past and present (Stirling 2014a), including around energy. As Strauss et al. (2013: 10) put it, '[o]ur beliefs about energy shape how we use it; our uses of energy simultaneously shape our cultural concepts of and beliefs about energy'. Human use of energy is understood through diverse and competing cultural frameworks, even as it assumes a taken for granted and unspoken status as a given aspect of quotidian social life: the background to modernity. Cultural conceptions of energy, for example as invisible, omnipotent or dangerous, are imagined, developed, utilised and contested in everyday contexts around the world (Sovacool and Griffiths 2020). Talk of energy transformation hints not only at possibilities of social change, but also at collapse and reinvention. As noted, the collective ability to imagine and harness the disruptive power of energy shapes human destinies in profound ways and has given rise to powerful cultural narratives such as the American dream or the industrial revolution, and now counter-culturally around ideas of energy democracy (van Veelen and van der Horst 2018). These have been, and continue to be, important mobilising devices for states, capital and social movements to rally societies behind diverse projects of reinvention, nationalism and aggrandisement, independence and de-colonisation, as well as new waves of accumulation.

Norms, values, belief systems towards institutions, behaviour and ideologies of politics play an important role in pathways to sustainability and unsustainability alongside everyday practices and habits which eschew or reinforce dominant ways of producing and consuming resources (Shove et al. 2012). Precisely because they are so deeply held, entrenched and 'given', they are often resistant to rapid change. This is why economists often focus on 'nudge' theory: making it easier for people to make the 'right' choices from the point of view of sustainability (Thaler and Sunstein 2009). There is often a preference for the use of pricing mechanisms to trigger behavioural change, such as making consumers in the UK pay for the use of disposable plastic bags as a way of deterring their use. Yet cultural understandings of energy, central to the politics and possibilities of transition, give lie to the assumptions and logics of neoclassical economic efficiency and the rational actions of utility-maximising individuals devoid of social setting and cultural context.

The blurring and close association of the mass production and consumption of cheap energy with central cultural givens in modern society around growth and progress point to the scale of the task of re-culturing different ideas about comfort, well-being and needs. Energy befits its description as the 'master resource' (Strauss et al. 2013:11) for its ability to empower and transform the world. Yet 'energyscapes' (Appadurai 1990) look different at local, national and international levels. Rather like capital, energy is always in motion through currents and flows and along powerlines, shifting value as it changes state and function. New futures have to be imagined for energy to excite and mobilise finance capital, justify state support and finance for new infrastructures and cultivate and propel new societal and consumer behaviours required to bring new energy futures into being. We have seen this around claims that nuclear power would be too cheap to meter, that electric vehicle (EV) cars represent the future and that renewable energy can meet 100 per cent of our energy needs by the middle of the century. This claim-making, complete with models, advocates, marketing and public relations, requires political work to engage and convince decision-makers. Paths are made by walking, but people need to be persuaded to take the first steps in a new direction. Contradictions and tensions need to be managed away through appeals to the possibility of 'green growth' and a 'third industrial revolution' or 'triple-win scenarios', where development, mitigation and adaptation needs can be met seamlessly and simultaneously (Mitchell and Maxwell 2010). Imagined futures help to justify new investments in science and technology research and development; in turn, such advances reaffirm the state's capacity to act as a responsible steward of the public good. Sociotechnical imaginaries serve in this respect both as the ends of policy and as instruments of legitimation.

6.9 The Turn Towards Behaviour

Discussions of individual behaviour change form an increasingly important part of facilitating cultural shifts that underpin and sustain energy transitions. Initiatives targeted at individuals and households have included the use by local, state and national governments of traditional regulatory measures, market mechanisms and behavioural interventions. The complex influences on individual behaviour and the challenges of designing and implementing effective large-scale interventions have resulted in large gaps in existing knowledge. The possible contribution and position of households in climate policies is not well understood, nor do households receive sufficiently high priority in current climate policy strategies such that sustainable behaviour is a critical, yet often overlooked, aspect of climate mitigation, and how to address it has become deeply contested (Dubois et al. 2019). Such efforts assume increasing importance in light of attempts to scale behaviour change that is compatible with a 1.5-degree pathway. In terms of the scale of the challenge, recent research has suggested that we need to aim for hugely ambitious per-person carbon footprint targets of 2.5 (tCO_2e) in 2030, 1.4 by 2040 and 0.7 by 2050 (Lettenmeier et al. 2019).

A recent renewed focus on individual behaviour has emerged from the growing recognition that additional emissions reductions from large industrial sources would be expensive and inadequate to achieve many environmental goals. This reflects a sense that shifting behaviours may be easier, in the short term at least, than changing structures, even if the ultimate goal may be to transform both.[28] This has been compounded by a belated recognition that individuals, if viewed as a discrete source category, often contribute more emissions than the industrial sector. Contributions to understanding by political scientists, sociologists and psychologists of the influence of norms on environmentally significant behaviour and the conditions under which informal social control can address collective action problems have lent further support to increasing attention to behaviour change (Kasser 2016). These bodies of work have strengthened challenges to standard accounts of economic rationality and assumptions about atomised utility-maximising individuals.

The result is that the issue of behaviour change is now gaining the increasing attention of policymakers. As the IPCC noted with 'high confidence' recently in its 1.5°C report, 'pathways that include low energy demand ..., low material consumption, and low GHG-intensive food consumption have the most pronounced synergies and the lowest number of trade-offs with respect to sustainable development' (IPCC 2018). Indeed, there have been a number of initiatives in this space from governments, businesses, local councils and civil society actors. These have attempted to reduce household emissions through informational and norm campaigns addressing car use and household electricity use, for example. A series of issues arise here, however. First, household living situations, such as size of home, greatly influence the household potential to reduce its footprint (Dubois et al. 2019). Second, household decisions shift over time through different phases such as childhood, adulthood and illness, as well as in relation to key life course events and pivotal moments such as retiring or becoming a parent (Burningham and Venn 2017). Third, as Dubois et al. (2019: 144) show, 'voluntary efforts will not be sufficient by themselves to reach the drastic reductions needed to achieve the 1.5°C goal. Instead, households need a regulatory framework supporting their behavioural changes'. Fourth, there is what they describe as 'a mismatch between the roles and responsibilities conveyed by current climate policies and household perceptions of responsibility' (Dubois et al. 2019: 144).

The role of behavioural and value change also provokes mixed reactions in environmental debates. On one side of the debate, environmentalist Mary Heglar puts it bluntly:

> The belief that this enormous, existential problem could have been fixed if all of us had just tweaked our consumptive habits is not only preposterous; it's dangerous. It turns environmentalism into an individual choice defined as sin or virtue, convicting those who don't or can't uphold these ethics ... While we're busy testing each other's purity, we let the government and industries – the authors of said devastation – off the hook completely. This overemphasis on individual action shames people for their everyday activities, things they can barely avoid doing because of the fossil fuel-dependent system they were born into
> *(Heglar 2019).*

'Fight the oil and gas industry instead', she argues (Heglar 2019).

Indeed, despite the prevalence of shaming strategies, where in Sweden there is a word for flight shame, evidence suggests that whilst they make those doing the shaming feel better about their own conduct, they do not induce positive behaviour change in the targets of the shaming. Hence, it becomes a form of virtue signalling rather than generating positive social change. The focus on behaviour change is sometimes seen as a diversionary strategy to deflect attention away from the need for action by states and corporations in relation to changing structures and infrastructures, fetishizing the actions of individual consumers (Shove 2010; Newell et al. 2015). The widespread fire that the oil company BP drew for asking people on Twitter what personal changes they were making to address the climate crisis, all while planning to extract vast swathes of oil that blow the Paris Agreement budget, seemed to underline the point.

Focusing too much on individual behaviours fails, in this view, to account for social and cultural as well as economic 'lock-in' (Unruh 2000) and what Shove (2003) calls the 'social organization of normality' where social and infrastructural factors lead to and reproduce certain patterns of demand. This refers to the normalisation of habits, routines and everyday practices of consumption around washing, showering and laundry, as well as travel and heating, for example. The argument then is that ever-closer focus on the determinants of individual behaviour is distracting researchers and policymakers alike from addressing difficult and important challenges concerning the social and economic circumstances that give rise to unsustainable practices. This relates in turn to an 'Energy Cultures' framework, described by Stephenson et al. (2010) as a 'culture-based approach to behaviour'. From this perspective, the responsibility for societal transformations cannot be put on the sum of all individual shoulders. Such transformations can only be achieved when embedded in sustainable systems change integrating shifts from individual values and community behaviour to societal changes in institutions and governance.

Despite this, many policy approaches have been built around so-called 'ABC' models of behaviour change, in which attitudes (A) drive behaviour (B) and hence choices (C) (Shove 2010). Typically, individuals do not consciously decide to emit carbon. Rather, emissions are associated with the practices and routines of everyday life, from cooking to travelling. In this case, should you live somewhere with poor public transport, or where available energy sources are predominantly fossil fuels or biomass, people will not simply be able to choose alternatives. Similarly, the routines of daily life are often embedded in the use of technologies, materials and systems which individuals have little power to alter. As such:

Interpretations of comfort and of the 'need' to heat and cool buildings to a steady 22 degrees C whatever the weather outside are not facts of nature, nor are they simply expressions of individual preference and choice. These issues require opening up discussions regarding the definition of taken for granted needs and the different means by which warmth and welfare, freedom and mobility, and economic and energy security might be achieved in different settings   *(Newell et al. 2015: 537).*

For others, however, larger transitions will not be possible until citizens have demonstrated 'demand' for them, as politicians fear adopting unpopular measures

(Willis 2020). Though frequently invoked to justify inaction, since most people are not asked about the level and pace of change they would like to see, or which of the costs associated with doing nothing they would be willing to bear, such claims need to be treated with extreme caution. Yet it is true that efforts to change behaviours have avoided the toughest challenges of changes to diet (meat consumption), mobility (especially air travel and car use) and heating, instead focusing on lower-hanging-fruit options such as home insulation and switching off lights (Moberg et al. 2019). Nevertheless, there has been growing interest within the social sciences in managing carbon reductions through techniques that influence environmentally significant behaviours and lifestyles at the individual and household level. As noted, it has been suggested that dangerous climate change cannot be avoided without behavioural change by individuals and communities. Adopting 1.5° C-consistent pathways assumes substantial changes in behaviour (Lettenmeier et al. 2019). As Dubois et al. (2019) found, up to 50 per cent reductions in lifestyle emissions can be generated from voluntary action alone. This is not an insignificant sum.

For example, through their consumption behaviour, households are responsible for 72 per cent of global greenhouse gas emissions, making them key actors in reaching the 1.5°C goal under the Paris Agreement (Dubois et al. 2019). Similar degrees of impact apply to the whole range of sustainable development goals (SDGs) when we consider impacts on land, forests and marine environments, for example, of everyday patterns of consumption, by wealthier citizens in particular. Individual behaviour undoubtedly drives both energy-intensive lifestyles and a large share of global carbon emissions, yet it is also a potential source of large, low-cost emissions reductions. Moll et al. (2005) estimate that 70 to 80 per cent of national energy use in the UK is related to household activities. Research suggests that the opportunity for household carbon reductions could be substantial. An interdisciplinary study of sixteen action types concluded that the implementation of the most successful behavioural programmes could reduce US household carbon emissions by 20 per cent by 2020, an amount equal to all of the emissions from France (Dietz et al. 2009). According to Cafaro (2011), individuals can save immense amounts of carbon in a so-called 'behavioural mitigation wedge', as much as 15 billion tons (gigatons) by 2060, simply by changing their diet to avoid meat or by forgoing air travel. Other data also underscores the sheer magnitude of emissions reductions that behavioural change can accomplish (McLoughlin et al. 2019).

Psychologists tend to focus on the role of individuals as a way of understanding how to shape behaviour change. As Gifford (2008) puts it, 'amelioration of that part of . . . climate change over which we have some potential control occurs at the individual level' (Gifford cited in Capstick et al. 2015: 2). This requires us to understand 'carbon capability': the situated and contextualised meanings of carbon and energy in everyday life and decisions that relate to individuals' abilities and motivations to reduce emissions (Whitmarsh et al. 2011). The focus then becomes enabling 'pro-environmental' or climate behaviours through information, monitoring and metering, as well as rewards systems (a mix of 'antecedent' and 'consequent' interventions). Behavioural economists refer to this as 'nudge' theory, that is, making it easier to do the 'right' thing, while critics refer to it as 'neoliberal soft paternalism' (Capstick et al. 2015: 5). What makes it neo-liberal is the emphasis on the individualisation of responsibility. In other words, the propensity to ascribe responsibility for addressing climate change primarily to individuals (rather than to governments or institutions) is itself a manifestation of dominant political assumptions that emphasise the centrality of consumers as rational and autonomous actors in effecting change via preferences expressed through the market. In this model of change, if enough consumers change behaviours, businesses will adapt to their preferences, scaling up shifts in production and consumption.

Even leaving aside concerns about whether this is the appropriate focus of action, evidence about impact is limited where reviews of interventions have found that, while there is some evidence that targeted campaigns can bring about change among those who are already motivated, for the most part, interventions have not been very effective (Capstick et al. 2015). This is compounded by the fact that the interventions considered have almost without exception focused upon direct emissions (within the home or from personal transportation) or domestic recycling, with very little attention paid to indirect emissions arising from consumption activities, through carbon embedded in products and services, such as food, consumer electronics, clothing and recreation. It also tends to encourage the mistaken and problematic view that minor incremental tweaks to lifestyles are sufficient by way of social response. Minor behavioural changes may even lead to increased emissions in other areas via rebound effects (Sorrell et al. 2020). Many such approaches are also under-specific about who and which communities bear the most responsibility. For some psychologists, this highlights the need to target 'the middle': those people that might be open to changes in lifestyle rather than those that have already embraced change or those that are actively hostile to doing so.[29]

The international climate policy debate has thus far been fixated on technology and economic incentives and has often relegated behavioural change to an afterthought. The implication is that we must become much more focused on changing consumption, or demand side options (Moberg et al. 2019), in addition to emphasising mitigation via technology or policy on the supply side. We must also consider lifestyles as targets of policies, rather than a voluntary add-on by individuals. Policy can enable and strengthen motivation to act on climate change via a suite of top-down or bottom-up approaches, through informational campaigns, regulatory measures, financial (dis)incentives, and infrastructural and technological changes. As well as seeking to shape production pathways, governments need to pay much more attention to demand management and reducing consumption through behaviour change across a range of sectors from energy, industry and transport to food and agriculture. For example, given that livestock are responsible for more GHG emissions than all other food sources and that, globally, savings of CO_2 equivalent to between 29 per cent and 70 per cent are possible by shifting to a plant-based diet, overall emissions from food systems could be reduced by targeting the demand for meat and other livestock products, particularly where consumption is higher than suggested by human health guidelines (Newell and Phylipsen 2018).

Nevertheless, there remains a need to understand the barriers to and motivations for consumption changes at the individual level of consumers, especially when connected to the urgency of global decarbonisation pathways (Dubois et al. 2019). Both bottom-up and top-down initiatives show that there is huge potential for reducing emissions through mainstreaming low-impact living via policy tools, innovative communications, changing cultural norms and shifting choice architectures to facilitate the normalisation of sustainable behaviours.

This suggests the need for understanding pathways to change which combine top-down and bottom-up, state, market and civil society-led transformations (Scoones et al. 2015). Understanding the role of enabling environments which go beyond 'nudge' approaches and the individualisation of responsibility is critical. Institutional disincentives are also an important barrier. For example, public and private utilities are the principal interface between households and many sources of information, resources and technologies that could increase energy efficiency and reduce carbon emissions. With limited exceptions, the rate structure provided by public utility commissions creates incentives to sell more electricity, gas and water each year. These utility gatekeepers thus may have incentives to meet specific demand-reduction goals and to maintain a positive public reputation, but they have strong disincentives to implement programmes that would achieve substantial reductions in the sale of their products (Vandenbergh and Sovacool 2016). Intermediaries that shape consumer choices around the purchase of a house or car or heating system, for example, have an important role to play given the longevity of lock-in along lower or higher carbon lines of those choices (Sovacool et al. 2020). There is also growing emphasis on what private organisations can do to drive household emissions reductions, including how private governance initiatives can reduce emissions directly through behavioural interventions.

It is important, however, to contextualise, nuance and globalise this discussion across cultures and regions and to look at the interface with different social cleavages and dynamics such as race, class and gender. The focus to date has been on behaviour change in richer societies for obvious reasons to do with higher carbon footprints and historical responsibility (Kenner 2019). Yet, as others note, the developing world is projected to contribute almost all of the growth in carbon emissions, and increases in household consumption are driving much of that increase. The desire to increase standards of living in developing countries is strong, but it will be impossible to achieve widely adopted climate targets if the emissions from the burgeoning middle class in China and India reach the per capita levels of the USA and the EU (Vandenbergh and Sovacool 2016). For this reason, there is increasing attention in the UNEP Emissions Gap report (2020) to issues of lifestyle and behaviour change in major emitters such as China, India and Brazil. Though without change in historical high emitters in North America and Europe, for example, calls for elites in 'rising powers' to limit the emissions associated with their lifestyles will likely invite cries of hypocrisy.

There is also increasing attention to the role of the richest 1 per cent in driving climate change in a way that cuts across some of these national and regional differences. Dario Kenner's (2019) work illustrates the disproportionate role of what he refers to as 'the polluter elite': the 1 per cent of wealthiest contributors to the problem of climate change through their luxury consumption, investments they have in fossil fuel companies and the political influence they exercise over decision-making on climate change. This relates to Brand and Boardman's (2008) claim that reducing national carbon emissions principally requires the 'taming of the few'. Carbon emissions increase sharply with income. With respect to personal travel, for example, the top 10 per cent of emitters are responsible for close to half of all emissions, while the share of the bottom 10 per cent of emitters is closer to 1 per cent (cited in Capstick et al. 2015: 7). Capstick et al. (2015) show how prevailing social scientific, economic and political orthodoxies have precluded the possibility of non-marginal change. They suggest that a truly radical approach to reducing personal emissions would need to challenge dominant norms and givens in (capitalist) society. For example, 'to deliberately promote reduced consumption as a means of lowering people's embedded carbon emissions … immediately collides with powerful and deep-rooted political and economic assumptions about the importance of consumer spending as a means of driving economic growth. Indeed, the paradigm of economic growth is itself used as a proxy for societal well-being' (Capstick et al. 2015: 7).

This represents a deeper and more profound challenge to prevailing policy orthodoxies and cultural norms. Cultures of consumption (Dauvergne 2008) are critical here alongside the dominant focus in transitions debates on productionist drivers of technology, innovation and finance and their role in meeting rising demand. Managing demand and addressing consumption, rather than just varying supply, are key (Bengtsson et al. 2018). For example, how far should we invest in new carbon supply as opposed to reducing supply? Retrofitting existing buildings is essential as 90 per cent of buildings today will still be operational in 2050. Retrofitting and demand reduction are much more cost-effective, but the debate is all about expanding supply (Boardman 2012). Discussions around food and energy futures tend to forecast and then presume ever-increasing demand and consumption such that the only remaining choices are over which technologies and policies can enable that growth (rather than whether that growth is sustainable, or whether demand can be reduced or efficiency and conservation measures adopted to reduce waste).

There is an important role for activism as well as interventions by public authorities in managing and regulating the content of advertising, as well as its location (outside or inside schools and hospitals, for example) and timing (such as restrictions on advertising after certain time thresholds to avoid exposure to children, as exist in some countries). Rolling back the onslaught of appeals to us to consume more products and services, which often has a determinantal effect on our well-being as well as eliciting significant environmental damage, is a critical complement to efforts to support sustainable consumption and, at the very least, to not undermine them. On the activist front, groups such as Adbusters[30] have led the way in creating spoof adverts while several cities around the world have taken bold moves to either restrict or ban advertising in more public spaces. In 2007, Brazil's biggest city, São Paulo, introduced the Clean City Law. The result was a near-total ban affecting billboards, digital signs and advertising on buses. In Paris, rules were introduced to reduce advertising on the city's streets by 30 per cent and cap the size of hoardings. Moreover, no adverts are allowed within 50 metres of school gates. The Indian city of Chennai banned billboard advertising completely, and Grenoble in France recently banned commercial advertising in public places in the city's streets, to enhance opportunities for non-commercial expression.[31] Even within a capitalist economy, there is scope to place some limits on consumerism.

When they choose to do so, national governments can also play a proactive role in dramatically and rapidly shifting cultural practices around consumption. During the Second World War, resource conservation was the greatest challenge and rationing was centrally planned. In the UK, household waste reduction was large-scale and rapidly achieved. Every week 31,000 tonnes of kitchen waste were saved. Land was converted from livestock to cereals, rabbit and pig clubs developed, and there were 1.7 million allotments by 1943, producing a garden army (Simms 2009: Longmate 1971). As a result, dependence on food imports halved over the course of the war. 'Fair shares' was a slogan from the UK Board of Trade's 1941 campaign to popularise clothes rationing. Hugh Dalton, head of the Board of Trade, famously put it in 1943: 'There can be no equality of sacrifice in this war. Some must lose their lives and limbs, others only the turn-ups on their trousers' (Simms 2013: 201). Behind all the schemes to manage demand, the objective was to '[s]ecure the fairest possible distribution of whatever supplies are available and to ensure ... as far as possible that the things that everybody needs shall be within the reach of all' (Simms 2013: 201). For systems of resource rationing to succeed, though, government, needed to convince the public that rationing levels were fair; that the system was administered transparently and fairly; and that evaders were few in number, likely to be detected and liable to penalties if found guilty (Roodhouse 2007). This has important implications for debates about carbon rationing and individual carbon budgets.

Amazingly, from today's standpoint of rampant mass consumerism, efforts were invested by the state in the 1940s in de-legitimising wasteful consumption. Railway companies advertised that needless travel is a crime. The Railway Executive Committee produced a poster that read 'Is your journey really necessary?'. 'War gardens' were promoted 'for victory', while the UK Ministry of Fuel and Power appealed to people not to 'squander electricity' and to 'save fuel', 'mend, sew, repair'. In the USA, the Food Administration urged citizens not to 'waste food' and issued a list of instructions about how to comply which included: '[B]uy it with thought, cook it with care, use less wheat and meat, buy local foods, serve just enough, use what is left.' In the UK, between 1938 and 1944, a complete revolution in consumption patterns was devised and implemented and the broad-based engagement of the population was secured. Behaviour towards food, fuel, transport and civic engagement altered rapidly. Apart from some well-known privations, an outcome of the rapid changes was not just a successful reduction of consumption and equalisation of access to resources among the population, it was also a dramatic improvement in general health, life expectancy and infant and maternal mortality (Simms 2013).

A challenge in terms of drawing too many parallels from the experience of rationing is that, while publics may have been willing to make temporary sacrifices for a war effort, societies may be less willing to accept the changes as a new norm of reduced consumption that would be required to tackle climate change. That said, during the 2007–8 financial crisis, people looked at radical measures to reduce public spending. This involved working less, with the benefit of reducing stress. The state of Utah in the USA introduced a four-day week for public sector workers and studied what happened. There was a 14 per cent drop in CO_2 by closing public buildings for the extra day, well-being rose, and absenteeism dropped as workers were happier (Simms 2013: 393). Although they changed the time period for accessing public services, a third of the public thought that services had improved and many workers wanted to continue working four days a week. Parallels being drawn as I write between involuntary but dramatic reductions in consumption because of quarantine restrictions being imposed to tackle the coronavirus and the potential to lock in lower carbon behaviours point to similar problems about the extent to which imposed constraints, rather than cultured self-restraint, offer the more viable and desirable way forward.[32]

Shifts in wider social norms are critical here too. Recent environmental campaigns around fracking and fossil fuel extraction have invoked arguments about companies not having the 'social license to operate', echoing the stigmatisation strategies adopted by the divestment movement. Green (2018) describes the emergence and growing acceptance of what he calls 'anti-fossil fuel norms'. Practices of de-legitimation and declining social acceptability, as well as shifts in norms, are important here, including regarding individual behaviours. Historical examples of shifts in attitudes towards capital punishment, slavery, smacking children, seat belts and smoking show what is possible. Smoking is interesting because it is a personal choice (albeit with consequences for others) and therefore it is easy to dismiss health interventions as those of a 'nanny state'. It is also a highly addictive habit, raises lots of money for treasuries from powerful tobacco companies and hence comes with few incentives for governments to do much. Yet litigation battles, growing scientific consensus and obvious health benefits meant that the battle was won space by space (trains, planes, pubs and public spaces). Shifts such as these in social norms about acceptable conduct take time and often involve fraught and complex legal cases, but transformations can be brought about and produce rapid cultural change before they become embedded in policy and law (Simms 2018).

6.10 Ecologies of Mobilisation

The interconnected, mutually dependent, contingent nature of mobilisation strategies is what seems to make them effective. Despite the binaries of inside/outside, reformist/revolutionary or reform/transformation that run through so much academic analysis, strategies often build upon and depend on one another, amplifying effects. In practice and in reality, citizens and activists move in and out of different spaces and moments of engagement and opposition, collaboration and contention. This is certainly the case with energy and climate activism. I am reminded of one colleague who told me he joined a roadblock in central London, an act of civil disobedience led by the collective Extinction Rebellion. This was en route to a meeting with oil company BP to discuss its climate strategy! There are many routes to change, and most of us carry within us multiple theories of change and a shifting sense of how and when change can best be brought about, making use of spaces and opportunities to engage as and when they present themselves.

With regard to energy transitions, reformist strategies are said to include reform of the electricity sector, better demand management, greater investment in renewable energy and the democratisation of electricity institutions through better consultation and participation perhaps through 'electricity committees', greater levels of transparency and accountability, and, on the social side, fairer pricing and cost recovery schemes. These strategies hit their limits, however, because, as McDonald (2009: 445) suggests, 'any effort to democratise electricity institutions and involve the broader public in decision-making will be compromised by private sector ownership/management'. This is not to 'fetishize' the public sector or public ownership, where channels of meaningful citizen engagement are often weak or entirely lacking, but rather to acknowledge the circumscribed nature of engagement about different pathways when profit maximisation is already fixed as the objective which will trump all others.

More radical strategies, following this line of argument, include ruptures of social relations and productive systems. This could include de-commodification and re-commoning of the energy sector (such as the Re-powering initiative mentioned previously) or some visions on the Left of a Green New Deal, or for green energy plans bringing electricity utilities back under state control, as previously proposed by the Labour Party in the UK.[33] The fate of such moves cannot be predicted given that '[a]ny anti-capitalism path will have to be organic, arising out of the historical possibilities at the time and the material and ideological forces at play' (McDonald 2009: 450). This more counter-hegemonic project would have energy transformation as just one battleground in a broader social transformation. Consistent with the ecological analysis in this book, it is critical to make sure that any such shift in the mode of production, and the social relations which accompany it, does not pursue a similarly productivist approach to energy, albeit in public hands.

In many ways, the global networks of civil society actors and social movements working on energy issues mirror in their globally dispersed network configuration the globally organised production networks of energy companies whom they are campaigning against. Think of the multi-sited nature of resistance to mining and oil using all leverage through use of the law, media, NGO networks, shareholder activism: a range of strategies of liberal and civil regulation working through and against the market (Garvey and Newell 2004; Newell 2001). Possibilities are very much shaped by the availability of democratic space, political opportunity structures and the nature of the legal system. Key challenges include confronting and overcoming potential lines of division between rural and urban communities and workers, between workers in sectors described as 'dirty' and 'clean', and the relation between communities and workers in energy-producing as opposed to energy-consuming regions of the world (Abramsky 2010). Building globally 'just transitions' means resisting displacement of toxic projects elsewhere, from NIMBY (not in my back yard) to NOPE (not on Planet Earth), and keeping in check the use of spatial and temporal fixes for crises facing elites in the global North and increasingly the global South. For Abramsky (2010: 20), this means mobilising 'the kind of mass social and political force that is necessary for an accelerated transition to a decentralized, equitable and ecologically-sensitive energy system, which contributes to a wider process of building emancipatory relations'.

There are precedents for broad-based movements that reflect ideological diversity. Podobnik (2010: 77) notes: 'In the case of coal, anarchists, socialists and apolitical miners were pulled together into broad-based unions that drew strength from their ideological diversity.' Likewise, in the case of anti-nuclear struggles, 'a remarkably diverse movement emerged that included housewives, green activists and scientists and many other groups' (Podobnik 2010: 77). Such breadth and diversity were key to the expansion and success of these movements. Hence concerns around climate change do not need to be the main driver of mobilisations for energy transitions for religious or community groups, for example, more concerned about generating their own energy in ways that guarantee access and affordability.

Thinking ecologically about mobilisation means reflecting on the interrelationship and mutually reinforcing (at times) effect of the diversity of strategies and tactics employed. These range from negotiations, partnerships, legal activism, media work and marches through to strikes, occupations, boycotts, civil disobedience and direct action and damage to property (such as attacks to infrastructures of extraction). As noted elsewhere in this chapter, there is a geography to these patterns of mobilisation. Podobnik (2010: 78) suggests:

In the countries of the global north, the emphasis has been on mounting media campaigns, trying to change consumer behaviour, marshalling voter pressure and developing legislative and legal mechanisms for enforcing energy reform. In the global south, meanwhile, conflicts have tended to emerge around hydro-electric dam projects, oil industries and mining projects and they have often escalated from non-violent disobedience to violent confrontations between local residents and officials.

There is also an element of political opportunism that activists need to take advantage of. This refers to the role of rupture, disruption, zeitgeist and when political tipping points and turning points represent opportunities to disturb the political equilibrium. The key is to mobilise and be prepared for openings: to use moments when incumbents are disoriented, uncertain and facing legitimacy crises to push for concessions and reforms and demands that would normally be rejected outright. This means having well-developed ideas and alliances built that can be mobilised when opportunities present themselves. This might be thought of as the positive side of 'shock doctrine' (Klein 2007) following the maxim that activists should never waste a crisis to advance their goals. As Milton Friedman (2009 [1962]: 14) argued: 'Only a crisis – actual or perceived – produces real change. When that crisis occurs, the actions that are taken depend on the ideas that are lying around. That, I believe, is our basic function: to develop alternatives to existing policies, to keep them alive and available until the politically impossible becomes the politically inevitable.' Making a similar point but in a more positive fashion, E. F. Schumacher (1974: 31) said: 'Perhaps we cannot raise the winds. But each of us can put up the sail, so that when the wind comes we can catch it.' These moments of change might come in surprising forms as we are seeing at the moment in the midst of the global coronavirus pandemic, allowing governments to make bold moves towards car-free spaces in cities, for example, or to use 'doughnut economics' (Raworth 2017) to rethink urban planning, as is happening in Amsterdam. There are also often unintended consequences. Gore (2017: 9) shows, for example, how electricity reforms introduced by actors such as the World Bank, in its attempt to embed its preferred vision of a neo-liberal energy sector, nonetheless 'enlivened the capacity and advocacy of domestic state and non-state organizations' by opening up space to challenge government control through new channels of accountability and to appeal directly to international institutions.

Tackling energy incumbents and accelerating transitions away from fossil fuels can also be done by mobilising around bans or the replacement of products which contain large amounts of fossil fuels in their manufacture (Piggot 2017). Plastics are interesting in this regard. There has been a huge consumer backlash against single use plastics, in part triggered by the popular David Attenborough documentary *Blue Planet*. The response by governments and supermarkets has been phenomenal and not just in the UK, with restrictions imposed by China on importing plastic waste. The growth in plastics is seen as a key future source of demand by the oil industry. Spencer Dale, BP's chief economist, predicted that such measures around the world could mean 2 million barrels per day lower oil demand growth by 2040 (Vaughan 2018). Activism around plastics has a knock-on impact on the fossil fuel economy, therefore.

This points, once again, to the ecologies of change: how different pathways to transition interrelate and reinforce or undermine one another. The challenge is to recognise that instances of decisive change and leadership by powerful actors often come on the back of years, if not decades, of cultural change and shifts in values and norms, protest and agitation when explaining and attributing agency. In this regard, Sovacool (2016: 204) quotes O'Connor as stating: 'Big transitions are the sum of many small ones. Looking at overall energy consumption will miss the small-scale changes that are the foundation of the transitions and the cumulative effects of changes in practice.' Looking for primary drivers of major disruptions inevitably reveals a partial and incomplete picture. As Hopf (2018: 19–20) suggests:

[P]ractical agency, is both ubiquitous and invisible. It is ubiquitous in the sense that every actor going on in the social world has to apply rules and perform her identities in ways that necessarily have an effect on the prevailing social structures. However, these practices are largely invisible because most social scientists and historians ... do not pay attention to these daily "micro-disruptions," focusing instead on the big bang of reflective agency. Indeed ... even in retrospect, scholars are likely to reconstruct events as if there were a key reflective moment, robbing the masses of their due credit for years or decades of practical agency, the daily practice of change.

It is indeed the case that 'major transitions' are only easily identifiable because of a series of 'minor transitions' that have occurred in a concerted manner. We have seen in this chapter how civil society is a key space for experimentation, contestation, democratisation and the seeding and nurturing of alternatives.

A confluence of practices of governance, finance, mobilisation and culture will be key to enabling the likelihood and probability that transitions can be accelerated. Actors and their agency need to be looked at in relation to one another rather than in isolation. As Scoones et al. (2015) show, while green transformations can be more state-led, market-led, technology-led or citizen-led, in reality they converge, compete and reinforce one another in different combinations across diverse contexts. This is not a search for a mono-casual big-bang theory of change, therefore. The changes are always multidimensional. As Sovacool (2016: 205) shows: 'In order to counteract path dependence, inertia, and lock-in, scholars looking at transitions theory have argued that truly trans-formative change must be the result of alterations at every level of the system simultaneously', from technology niches to regimes and the broader landscape which shapes them.

What is clear is that civil society's role in energy transitions is far from cohesive or monolithic. It is rather an expression of different geographies and cultures of protest, competing ideologies and relationships to different political economies, and ultimately has very different sociotechnical imaginaries (Jasanoff 2018) and theories of change. While many of those actors most directly engaged with transitions focus their attention on making the business case for a low carbon economy, including lobbying for particular policies and technologies, working with business actors to redirect and upscale finance, others are seeking an energy system that is democratically owned, organised along the lines of what is sustainable and the associated need to deliver drastic cuts in production and consumption in the rich world. This is what divides groups such as E3G, The Climate Group, Forum for the Future who work with and for business, from the Transition Network and more activist elements of civil society that work to develop their own alternatives that are controlled neither by the state or nor by capital. While others adopt a more transformational perspective, as Smith (2008: 181) puts it, some areas of civil society 'remain indifferent to sustainable energy aspirations, and are effectively conserving incumbent practices and perpetuating existing energy systems. These civil associations contribute to the re-production of social norms, values and practices that rely upon (and are part of) incumbent energy systems.'

We have also seen, however, how lines blur, and categories and identities become redundant and meaningless. Smith (2008: 185) notes the case of a principal engineer at Ecotricity, the renewable energy provider, who was previously part of an autonomous ecological community in the North of England. I also noted the many cases of activists that move in and out of movement spaces and more formal 'invited spaces', depending on the opportunities available for change and the prevailing political context. In doing the research for this book, I have had conversations with people who worked for oil major Shell before leaving to work for an organisation dedicated to challenging materialism among younger people. People's agency is constrained, and we all hold and act on multiple, and sometimes conflicting, identities. Strategic choices are not one-off fixed decisions; rather, if they are to be effective, they reflect ongoing reinterpretations of where traction can be gained, new avenues explored, and change brought about and accelerated. They reflect a recognition that agency lies in the surprising places, that organisations are not homogenous and fixed entities, even if they do respond to structural imperatives.

Likewise, organisations – their profile, membership, mandate and strategy – necessarily and inevitably evolve over time. The Centre for Alternative Technology (CAT) evolved from an ecological commune to a research, teaching and advocacy organisation and visitor centre and many grassroots innovations and political experiments (such as wind energy in Denmark) get appropriated into mainstream commercial and public settings. As Smith (2008: 187) suggests, 'many sustainable energy niches in civil society can trace their historical roots back to radical routes for societal change'. Rapidly shifting political and economic landscapes have implications for alliances, campaigning priorities, resourcing and the scale and nature of change that can be achieved. Academic analysis of the role of civil society in energy transitions, as in many other areas of politics, would do well to try to capture and recognise this.

It is also a mistake – one frequently made – to suggest that civil society should provide blueprints for change and singular visions of alternatives. The call to articulate them often comes from incumbent actors, throwing the challenge back to those contesting their strategies: what's your solution? What is your alternative? This can serve as a way of diverting struggles into a process of protracted navel-gazing and negotiation over priorities and demands, only for what results to be dismissed as unrealistic and not politically plausible if it goes against the grain, or considered too broad since it incorporates a diversity of perspectives. This is different from helping to construct narratives or imaginaries of alternative futures, underpinned by different values and modes of political engagement, of what the good life might look like, thus repositioning what counts as viable and realistic, and who gets to determine this in practice. Challenging the failure of imagination through posing 'what if' questions (Hopkins 2019) about what alternative energy systems might look like if structured, owned and organised along different lines, and guided by different values, represents a valuable first step in bringing all alternative energy future into being.

6.11 Conclusion

[T]he historical record shows very clearly that deep, enduring changes in energy industries require the mobilization of mass social movements. We cannot simply wait for visionary politicians to forge the way, though they will be an important part of the solution. We cannot rely on new energy entrepreneurs to resolve the crisis, though again they will be crucial allies . . . Instead, history shows that we must draw large numbers of people, from all across the world, into a broad social movement that fights for fundamental change in the energy system
(Podobnik 2010: 77).

We have seen in this chapter how tentative and embryonic alliances among environmental movements, trade unions, community groups and indigenous groups are emerging, either around resistance to particular projects or around support for more democratic, community-owned and renewable energy alternatives. But fragile alliances disguise important differences over vision and strategy and what is possible and likely to gain traction varies hugely depending on context. We have also seen how poorer groups desperate for employment and income are rarely the owners of land or assets, and are vulnerable to being used by incumbent actors to resist change to the energy system status quo. Their interests can be invoked to lobby for privileged and ongoing support for coal and nuclear, for example, or for the expansion of fracking, as well as against support for renewables on the basis that they are able to employ fewer people. This underlines the importance of questions of power and politics in any such analysis. If the model of energy generation and distribution is extractivist and unlikely to deliver benefits to poorer communities expected to host energy projects and infrastructures, socially at least, it makes little difference whether it is coal or wind if the same patterns of exclusion and exploitation persist. Indeed, many mining giants such as Rio Tinto and Glencore are involved in both coal mining and mining for cobalt and copper. As the title of this book suggests, we clearly need a power shift.

7

Conclusions

How do we move from narrower visions of transition to the transformation of energy systems and their politics? How do we move beyond approaches which substitute and replace technologies and sources but not systems – 'plug-and-play' strategies that merely re-fuel capitalism – towards longer-term solutions to ecological crisis in which the need for an overhaul of energy systems is viewed as part of this wider predicament? What does a global political economy (GPE) analysis suggest about ways forward? Each chapter in the book has sought to shed light on distinct, but strongly interrelated, aspects of the global political economy of energy transitions. It has sought to do so through a more political, material and global as well as historical and ecological account, the like of which has been missing to date.

In relation to production, it was argued that we need to rethink how we produce energy and how much we produce, including putting down limits on production and supply and revisiting ideas about *who* produces energy and for *what* purposes. Using less energy and using energy differently are potentially transformative: of work, health, the distribution of power and even global geopolitics. Shorter circuits of energy production and consumption and greater local control over the supply and distribution of energy, alongside radical reductions in demand through more rational planning and shifts in lifestyles and cultural attitudes towards consumption, imply severing dependencies on fossil fuel incumbents and reconfiguring the global geopolitics of dependence on fossil fuel-producing areas of the world. This implies a power shift, therefore, not only among global, national and local, public and private, state and capital, state and citizens, capital and labour, East–West and North–South, but also among social groups.

To use a slightly hackneyed phrase, 'giving power to the people' could help to decolonise energy and energy transitions. It would make it harder to pass on the costs of energy transitions to poorer parts of the world and the poorest communities within them through distancing via lengthy supply chains and sites of extraction in areas of conflict and weak governance. It would enable local control over priorities for energy production and consumption, not subject to price rigging by monopolies or virtual monopolies of a smaller number of utilities (such as the big six providers in the UK). Such shifts, it has been suggested, if they are to be sustainable and viable, need to come as part of embedding sustainability and 'green' thinking across all policy areas (Newell 2019). Accompanied by shifts towards political de-centralisation, attempts at re-commoning resources, and repurposing the economy around goals of well-being and prosperity, rather than narrower ideas of growth, these more transformative shifts in energy systems will be easier to achieve than if they are proposed in isolation. Such shifts may imply a new social contract between states and citizens around energy. This might entail, for example, a shared respon-sibility for provision and distribution, or a dislocation of relations of dependence on particular infrastructures and allocations of subsidies, in ways which key actors, including the state, can be expected to fiercely contest given the high levels of rent-seeking and corruption currently associated with the contracting and management of energy services delivery. The intimate relationship between energy and growth, emphasised throughout the book, means that capital will be looking for guarantees from the state about the provision of 'cheap' energy, by which I mean not just low cost but 'cheap' in the sense in which Patel and Moore (2017) use the term to highlight how costs of production are socialised, particularly to poorer groups in racialised and gendered ways, as has historically been the case. Proposals to disrupt the systematic privileging of the needs of capital for particular energy systems will not be welcome by elites.

With production, as with other areas of the economy, climate change in particular represents a legitimation crisis for global capitalism in which incumbent actors need to demonstrate that the expanded extraction, production and use of their energy sources is beneficial for all, despite overwhelming evidence to the contrary. The need to manage contradictions between growth and sustainability runs through attempts to accommodate and incorporate pressures for system change. Discourses around the 'just transition' have been mobilised effectively in some cases to align organised labour with fossil capital in managing transitions on the terms of incum-bents, placing pressure on advocates of ambitious action to resolve historical inequalities and exclusions as a prerequisite for accelerated decarbonisation. Likewise, in the context of the current coronavirus, bailouts for fledgling airlines and oil companies are being justified under the guise of protecting workers' jobs rather than industry profits (Topham 2020).

Regarding finance, it was suggested that we need a different model of financing energy with a greater role for patient capital, different ownership structures and much stronger and more effective governance of finance for the common good at national, regional and global levels. We also need massive divestment from incumbent industries, projects and infrastructures. Key sites of contention discussed include battles over fossil fuel subsidy reform, campaigns to shift the lending strategies of bilateral, regional and multilateral donors, and legal struggles over the climate compatibility of carbon-intensive infrastructures such as airports and pipelines. We can expect these contestations to ratchet up in scale and intensity with time as the climate crisis deepens. We need to harness the creative destruction that finance capital is able to unleash to disrupt incumbent power and the infrastructures and technologies over which it prevails, as it has done so many times before in the past (Perez 2002).

We need a proactive state and more effective global governance to address blind spots and current areas of neglect (Newell 2011). With energy, as many other areas of life, we need to recall that the accumulation of finance is not an end in itself. For it to be socially and environmental usefully, it needs to be redirected and steered towards socially productive ends. We need a reallocation and repurposing of finance and the spectacular levels of wealth that run through the veins of the global economy along the lines proposed by the United Nations Environment Programme (UNEP 2017) report including new thresholds of risk and return (to finance). Regulation and greater community control over finance and budgeting decisions make it more likely that this will happen. I argued, however, that though a 'finance gap' is frequently highlighted in transition debates around the need to mobilise ever greater sums of private capital to decarbonise the economy, the real issue is the misallocation of capital. It is fossil fuel subsidies and tax breaks for fossil fuel industries, the funding of carbon-intensive infrastructures by public and private banks and the endless search for new outlets for investment unguided by social need or environmental limits. Re-balancing the economy and strengthening levels of social and environmental control over finance will not be easily achieved, especially against the backdrop of a finance-led regime of accumulation. As a dominant fraction of capital, we can expect the interests of finance to continue to play a significant role in shaping future energy pathways, but it is a role that must be circumscribed by social pressure.

In relation to governing energy transitions, I argued that we need bold and interventionist regulation, including greater use of supply-side measures, and we need stronger global and regional energy governance. But we also need democratisation – downwards control of energy and stronger participation in deliberation around energy policy – underpinned by principles of precaution and respectful of limits. Principles of subsidiarity might be usefully invoked to determine the appropriate levels and arenas for decision-making with a positive preference for the local where possible and practicable. The growing interest in citizen assemblies suggests just one small way in which the design of energy futures can involve broader publics. To guard against top-down impositions of radical decarbonisation pathways which enforce the preferences of incumbent technology owners and providers, these social checks and balances and accountability mechanisms have an important role to play.

Going further, this broader social engagement might imply a new social contract within and across societies about energy pathways that prioritise needs within limits, guided perhaps by the overarching principles of doughnut economics aimed at preserving a 'safe space' between the fulfilment of the core social needs of all and respect for outer planetary boundaries (Raworth 2017). Especially where energy inequities have such deep and pervasive social and historical roots, the servicing of energy needs within the context of limited and finite global carbon budgets needs to prioritise the needs of the poorest within and across societies. The institutions and policymaking procedures we currently have fall well short of what would be required to deliberate upon and act upon such priorities, but we need to demand that they do. Institutions of energy governance need to reverse the ideological and institutional lock-in they currently provide *for* energy investors and incumbent interests, rather than *of* those interests. Expanding the policy autonomy and developmental space of countries to pursue energy pathways and policy tools of their choosing, as long as they are compatible with the achievement of climate goals, should be a key aim and strategy for moving beyond 'disciplinary neoliberalism' in the energy sector (Gill 1995). Such a repurposing of the mandates and objectives of key institutions implies shifts in power within and between states, as well among social forces contesting energy pathways including capital, labour and the environmental movement.

In Chapter 6 on mobilisation, I sought to demonstrate how mobilisation is vital to shaping energy pathways. We have seen repeatedly how shifts in the lending policies of multilateral and regional development banks, such as the European Investment Bank and the World Bank, or the corporate strategies of key investors and oil majors and mining companies have been circumscribed by activism. Resistance has caused disruption, added to costs, and brought unwanted media attention and public scrutiny. As I write, Transocean, the oil rig company responsible for BP's North Sea operations, is taking Greenpeace to court for disrupting its operations over a series of days in 2019. The court has heard that the activists took the action to avoid the greater damage of the oil being drilled and fuelling climate change, a problem the severity of which BP's own directors have publicly acknowledged (Carrell 2020).

Elsewhere, resistance by indigenous and environmental groups has successfully reversed decisions around oil pipeline projects, new coal mines, hydroelectric dams and fracking sites. As well as putting down limits, therefore, resistance also 'makes markets' (Paterson 2009). What this means is that corporate actors wanting to invest in particular projects or to engage in carbon trading or any commercial venture in this contentious domain have to anticipate backlash: protests, disruption, shareholder campaigns and doubts being raised about the social and environmental impacts of projects, as well as, increasingly, the economic risks associated with projects. For example, voluntary private governance around project financing such as the Equator Principles or the Extractive Industries Transparency Initiative, or standards aimed at pacifying critiques of carbon market projects such as the Offset Quality Initiative, Voluntary Carbon Standard or Gold Standard certification scheme, seek to accommodate and manage criticism of investments to enable them to continue (Newell and Paterson 2010). Activism, therefore, shapes market conduct in very direct and material ways: changing the nature and location and type of investments that are made. This speaks to a theme touched on throughout this book, namely, the tension that capitalist states have to navigate between accumulation and legitimation (Paterson 2010). A challenge for activists is to contest and push the boundaries of what counts as legitimate forms of wealth creation in the energy sector and beyond in a carbon-constrained world. To be effective in shifting this debate, new and broader alliances will be necessary with labour, indigenous groups, gender, health and human rights activists to amplify their voices and influence and to challenge dominant energy systems on a range of fronts.

In Chapter 6 on mobilisation, I also showed how many advocacy strategies are aimed at claiming spaces from incumbents for representing other actors and interests: opening up policy processes to a greater diversity of actors and interests. Strategies have to be adapted to key contexts and degrees of democratic space, and transnational mobilisation is critical to filling some of these gaps where there is limited scope for domestic contestation. Beyond traditional forms of mobilisation aimed at the state and corporate actors around specific policy spaces or investment sites, we have also seen efforts coalescing in recent years around challenging the social licence to operate more broadly. This has involved efforts to challenge media spaces of advertising from fossil companies and to challenge the ethics of sponsorship deals for arts and cultural institutions.

But culturing transition, as well as broader transformations, is also key. Shifting values, norms and behaviours is a crucial part of the story of transition and deeper transformations of energy systems. Challenging givens and expectations about energy needs around things like heating, cooling, mobility, powerful orthodoxies about energy supply, big infrastructures, the normalisation of over-consumption and, at a deeper level, the ideology of growth is an immensely difficult thing to do. Insights from practice theory show how cultures of energy use around showering, washing and heating, for example, play a key part in embedding and normalising unsustainable behaviours over time (Shove 2003). These point to the interactions among things, people, knowledge and social contexts which have important implications for efforts to change energy consumption (Butler et al. 2016). Wilhite (2013: 67) suggests that this 'displaces the starting point for a policy framework from individuals and individual choices to clusters of energy practices such as those associated with heating, lighting, cooling, preparing food and so on'. Newell et al. (2015) similarly argue for the need to start with needs and practices rather than individual behaviour change in a way which distributes responsibility for change more widely. There is important political work to be done drawing on insights from anthropologists about how to 'defamiliarize lifestyles and social arrangements that have come to appear natural and desirable' (Hornborg 2013: 41).

Clearly, each of these areas is interrelated. Which forms of production are economically viable, socially acceptable and legally permissible reflects the risk appetite of finance, the level of social resistance to proposed production and what the regulatory framework allows for. Finance itself is also governed and is exposed to mobilisation and protest, as the case of the divestment movement plainly shows. Finance underpins and enables production, but it does not take a singular form, despite commonalities in global structural conditions. There are different cultures of finance, shaped by diverse political economies and regulatory arrangements. Mobilisation is disciplined, enabled and constrained by different governance arrangements. What is permissible in the UK or Denmark is often not so in Kenya or China. Degrees of democratic space shape the scope for engagement with energy regimes across the spectrum of strategies from policy lobbying, legal activism and protest politics. As we saw in the discussion on materialities, certain modes of production and circuits of finance enable and constrain particular forms of protest and leverage points for the articulation of social and environmental demands (Mitchell 2011). Cultures of mobilisation reflect this, as well as embodying deeper, but diverse, cultural frames about the relationship between energy and society – both its production and its consumption – and intimate links to identity, freedom and social status given its deep imbrication in household consumption, travel and food.

Cultures of energy transition are shaped by histories of production: their abundance and scarcity, for example, which produce notions of the 'normal' – what is given and expected to be defended. This is a function of combinations of culture (ideas about convenience and expectations of wealth and consumption), geography (distribution and allocations of resources and the size of countries and their associated energy demands) and ideology (notions of freedom and entitlement and the nature of the social contract between state and citizen regarding taxation, for example). At state level, this was evident in the statement by President George Bush Snr that '[t]he US lifestyle is not up for negotiation' (Chatterjee and Finger 1994). Whether energy resources are seen and experienced as a 'curse' is closely related to class, racial and gender dimensions about access, entitlement and responsibility, which have deep cultural, historical and often colonial roots around expectations that the import of 'cheap energy' from former colonies to richer countries can and should continue indefinitely, despite poor levels of energy access in the exporting country. Who gets access to energy and on what terms is also, of course, a function of available finance in the form of credit and access to the banking system. Attempts to democratise this have had implications for access to energy, as the remarkable rise of M-Pesa in Eastern Africa shows clearly. The politics of access and distribution are also deeply political. We see this around extension of the grid to areas supporting incumbent actors and the importance of energy provision to understandings of statecraft and state power (Gore 2017).

Energy is a key part of the social contract between states and citizens where the latter expect the state to provide the basic infrastructure and often financing for the provision of domestic and industrial needs. This suggests that moves from low carbon transition to broader social and ecological transformations require and imply realignments of power and purpose across each of the areas covered in this book: production, finance, governance and mobilisation. Shifts in one area will be unlikely, in isolation, to trigger the sorts of changes across society and energy systems that are required without corresponding shifts in all other areas because of the interwoven nature of each of these systems. In many ways, the challenge is to set in train mutually reinforcing dynamics of change where, for example, protests might bring about shifts in regulation which have the effect of redirecting finance and then enable changes in production. There are ecosystems of transformation within which there are numerous entry points, levers and moments to try to accelerate disruptive change that can reverberate beyond the original place of intervention because of connections and interdependencies across assemblages of production, finance, technology, the state and civil society. Ecosystem here refers to interdependencies between pathways to transformation: how finance, state, production and civil society interrelate and overlap. This points to more sites of vulnerability and scope for change. Shifts in one area of the ecosystem can trigger change elsewhere: spreading and reverberating outwards, even if agency is unevenly distributed with the state playing a key role in orchestrating these ecosystems of transformation.

Governments are particularly well-placed to orchestrate other ecosystems of transformation using a variety of levers and tools at their disposal. Supply-side policies (which restrict access to remaining reserves of fossil fuels) can redirect finance in new directions, bringing about shifts in business practice away from fossil fuels when combined with new rules on disclosure and corporate governance. Enhancing the representation of the beneficiaries of climate action in policy processes can tilt the balance of power towards more ambitious action when combined with measures to withdraw state support to fossil fuel industries. Tax and fiscal measures to support local businesses and cities in raising their level of ambition can trigger change from below, setting off waves of change among transnational city networks. But civil society can also enable mutually supportive forms of interaction (or virtuous cycles) between the production, financing, governance of and mobilisation around transitions. Shifts in finance stemming from social pressure, such as divestment, policy or large public procurement programmes, can trigger changes in global value chains, accelerating the move away from 'stranded assets'. Civil society must also play an increasingly important role in strengthening corporate accountability to ensure that shifts in production and finance yield the desired justice-oriented outcomes.

In the first instance, the momentum for these deeper transformations will have to come from coalitions, as well as looser alliances and broader constituencies of the 'willing' and the 'winning' (Meckling et al. 2015), not necessarily bound together by consensus on strategy or a common clearly articulated alternative vision but, rather, by a sense that, for a range of different reasons and motivations, an alternative energy system is both possible and desirable as well as achievable. This means carving out the political space for a redefinition of energy politics around *how* energy is generated (whether it is decentralised, off-grid, off-shore, low versus high-tech and through what sort of process: extractivist or solidaristic economies), *by whom* (states, communities, corporations, cooperatives), *where* (on land, sea, overseas, within households or communities), *for what* (energy poverty, security, industry, infinite growth, reduced demand), *for whom* (capital, the wealthiest 1 per cent in society, the energy poor or future generations). The sorts of shift in power implied by energy transformations are captured in Table 7.1.

7.1 Pathways to Change

As well as there being ecosystems of transformation and multiple entry points for catalysing change, there are also, of course, multiple theories of change. There is no one pathway. More often than not, there are combinations of state-led, market-led, citizen and technology-led trajectories of change (Scoones et al. 2015) depending on the nature of the energy sector and the political and economic system in which the transition is taking place and the transformation sought. Consistent with the emphasis throughout the book on justice within and across societies, there are also

Table 7.1 *Power shift: Competing energy pathways*

Scenario	Who produces energy?	How?	For whom?	For what?
Today	States Corporations	Global extraction of fossil fuels Nuclear Hydro Renewable energy (components sourced globally)	Industry Consumers State (including military)	Conventional growth
Low carbon/climate capitalism	States Corporations	Renewable energy Carbon pricing Smart grids	Industry Consumers State	Low carbon growth
Green/eco-socialist alternatives	Communities Households Small businesses State	Greater decentralisation Small-scale renewable energy Local sourcing of materials Mini-grids Reduced demand	Communities Smaller locally facing businesses	Needs Prosperity rather than growth

near-term strategic questions about how to square urgency and equity. Is it possible to accelerate transitions in inclusive ways? Can rapidity be squared with attending to questions of equity and social justice? The question here, then, is less whether transitions can be just and more whether rapid transitions can also be just transitions.

As we have seen throughout the book, the need to increase the speed and depth of transitions to sustainability is every day more apparent. From the IPCC special report on 1.5°C to concerns about mass biodiversity loss and the passing of planetary boundaries, the signs that the current system as a whole and the energy sub-systems within it are not sustainable are clear for all to see. Yet there is debate about whether, by emphasising urgency and the need for radical and rapid interventions, we make it more likely that top-down and potentially regressive transitions are likely to be imposed from above. From nuclear energy, to fracking and geo-engineering, the severity of the threat of climate change in particular has been invoked to justify the adoption of these controversial technologies.

The fear and the danger are that this creates ripe conditions for what has been called 'post-politics' and the bypassing of the normal politics of deliberation and contestation by diverse publics (Swyngedouw 2010). Crisis induces states of exception, as we know from processes of securitisation in other areas of politics and in responses to the coronavirus. Instances of this in the energy sector include moves by the UK government to override the decision of Lancashire Council to reject fracking on the basis that it is a necessary part of the transition to a low carbon economy, or efforts to speed up the approval process for new nuclear power plants under a similar guise. The corresponding assumption is that more progressive social transformations and just transitions are those which come 'from below' through mobilization by social movements aimed at building new norms, challenging prevailing values and confronting existing distributions of power, the contours of which I explored in Chapter 6. Movements combating patriarchy, slavery and colonialism might be examples of where this has happened in the past. Arguably, there is something potentially unique about contemporary energy transformations in that they have to be made against the clock. To avoid runaway climate change, we need 'transformative' and 'systemic' change within the next ten to twenty years. This is in the language of UN scientists and bureaucrats, not that of revolutionaries, but its implications are no less staggering.

There is a dilemma here. Short-term action may mean going with the grain of where power lies and facing up to the reality of where control of production, finance and technology is currently concentrated. On the one hand, it is precisely the reluctance of incumbent actors to address challenges of sustainability through denial, greenwashing, false solutions and foot-dragging that has led to our current predicament. And despite acknowledgement of the power of restless capital to drive waves of creative destruction, as described in Chapter 4 on financing transitions, in the end investors are looking for a new and more profitable round of accumulation which would be unlikely to take the form of a 'just transition'. Rapid but ill-conceived transitions, imposed from above and without social acceptance, also have their costs. Most technological waves of innovation rise on the tide of optimism about their ability to deal with all problems that have troubled their predecessors, while bringing unprecedented levels of wealth. Think of the rapid expansion of hydro- or nuclear power fuelled by promises of electricity 'too cheap to meter'. The belief in the transformative power of carbon pricing and trading, which continues to grip the imagination of the World Bank, with numerous governments setting up emission trading schemes (ETSs), has, critics suggest, served as a decade-long distraction for efforts to effectively confront climate change (Lohmann 2006).

As Stevis argues: 'It is important that we demand that green transitions serve the common good because they are not inherently socially just and, in fact, are frequently less just than other transitions, such as gender or racial emancipation. Nor are they necessarily ecologically just. Decarbonized industrial policy can be as ecologically unjust as the current, carbon-based, industrial policy by externalizing harms across space, time and ecosystems.'[1] Mertins-Kirkwood, meanwhile, argues that deciding who is included in the just transition conversation is a more complicated question than it first appears. If a productive, equitable outcome for all workers is the goal of a just transition, then we must look beyond the immediate impacts on fossil fuel workers and consider who else may be vulnerable. Failing to put equity considerations first can result in just transition policies that ignore the people most in need of support.[2] The 'gilets jaunes' protests over fuel tax rises in France, earlier such protests in the UK, and fears about regional decline in parts of Central and Eastern Europe highlight the danger of forcing through transition policies from above where buy-in and alternatives are limited. As one newspaper put it: 'Energy transitions are about people. The protests happening in France send that signal loud and clear. If green policies are seen to be unjust or to be worsening inequality they will not be accepted, regardless of a government's good intentions. The government of President Emmanuel Macron violated two important principles of what is known as a "just energy transition": they failed to engage in social dialogue and they failed to formulate concrete benefits of the reform for those who are less privileged' (Gerasimchuk and Roth 2018).

Since power plants and coal mining in most of the affected EU countries are located in economically weak regions, the planned phase-out of lignite-fired power generation puts the economic development of these regions on the political agenda.

The increasing political populism in many of these regions adds weight to this issue. Structural change in particular, if it is politically enforced (rather than market induced), meets resistance as job and income losses loom. This is especially difficult to overcome politically in many regions in Eastern Europe that suffered a massive structural break in the 1990s that is still very present in people's memories and increases the (political) pressure for socially-embedded transition policies. An exemplar for such a region is the Lusatian coal district in Eastern Germany that is now confronted with the phasing-out of lignite-based electricity production in Germany. While local populations in the vicinity of where coal is burnt would secure large gains from the closure of coal, populations in the vicinity of where coal is extracted would suffer large losses. Coal mining is distinctive in requiring a large, specialised workforce, which is spatially highly concentrated and often remote from large centres of employment. These features imply both that coal miners would suffer substantial economic and social costs from closure, and that they would find organised political opposition to closure relatively easy. Hence, while closing coal is economically attractive, it is politically difficult, and this obstacle has to be addressed by some combination of financial incentives and moral pressure. Engaging with and anticipating the inevitable need for transition pro-actively through managed decline is preferable to socially divisive and marginalising disruptions imposed externally (Johnstone and Hielscher 2017). For example, the economics of coal mine closure can move quickly, often leading actors to try to catch up to the unfolding reality, rather than piloting their own future. When this occurs, the results are often much more severe for companies, workers and regional communities. Getting ahead of economic realities is crucial since, as Caldecott et al. (2017: 4) suggest, '"structural breaks" in the market environment often occur faster and can be more disruptive than key actors think is possible until they actually occur'.

On the other hand, the window of opportunity to avoid more catastrophic forms of climate change is closing, and so insisting on addressing all social inequalities and challenging power relations as a precondition to transition can also be a recipe for intransigence. After all, although capitalism is prone to crisis and instability, it has demonstrated a remarkable capacity for resilience over 400 years and is unlikely to come to an end any time soon. Rejecting all state-led and market pathways to change also comes with a price. Interestingly, though arguments about the need to attend to all social inequalities and exclusions as part of a transition often come from the political Left, incumbent industry actors often make similar arguments under the guise of advocating for a 'just transition'. Calls for retraining and compensation for poorer workers in sectors that will lose out from the restructuring and managed decline that form an inevitable and necessary part of transitions and processes of 'creative destruction' make sense and appeal to an intrinsic sense of fairness. But they can also be employed as a political device by fossil fuel industries, for example to undermine calls for more ambitious action. Whereas, under capitalism, businesses routinely uproot their operations and relocate to other jurisdictions with job losses and devastation for communities left in their wake, there are rarely calls for special treatment to cope with the social effects of adjustment. Somehow fossil fuel industries, because of their structural power, are afforded special privileges. Hence, in an ironic twist, powerful fractions of capital invoke a previously undetectable concern for workers' welfare when faced with profit losses due to enhanced action on climate change. To be clear, the concern for the welfare of workers in incumbent industries is something we need to address. But we need to be wary of industry managers' new-found concern for the 'just transition'.

Poland opened the COP in 2018 calling for a pathway of 'just transition' allowing those still dependent on fossil fuels a period of time in which they can convert to other energy sources and industries. The declaration has been seen by some as a tactic to win yet further subsidy for an already heavily subsidised energy sector, more likely to slow the process of change. The sense of doubt was underlined when the first sponsor of the climate talks was revealed to be one of Poland's biggest coal companies, Jastrzębska Spółka Węglowa (JSW) (Simms 2018). Likewise, when attending a workshop on just transitions at SB50 in Bonn in June 2019, involving representatives from government, trade unions and coal bodies, I was struck by the emphasis on process considerations and the need to have all stakeholders on board as part of a seemingly open-ended process around managing decline. The elephant in the room was the lack of critical discussion of limits and the need to keep some options off the table if the goals of the Paris Agreement, to which all the parties in the room had signed up, are to be achieved: starting with the fact that most remaining coal needs to stay in the ground, whereafter the discussion can focus on building economic alternatives. When I asked the panel about how to square inclusivity of process with these obvious limits, the question was met with silence.

So, where does this leave progressive action for just transitions and broader transformations?

Firstly, it is worth recalling that delaying action also has a justice implication. As temperatures rise, vulnerable populations of the poor the world over are the first in line to suffer the effects of climate change, a problem to which they have contributed very little. The human and social costs of climate change increase markedly every time action of the required scale is delayed into the future. In this instance, perfection may be the enemy of progress. Muddling through, engaging in the messy politics of negotiation and compromise, learning by doing: these are the incremental, inevitable and necessary day-to-day politics of transition. Not from a preferred starting point, but in a world not of 'our' choosing with all its attendant injustices and problems. Trying to reframe key questions, from meeting ever-expanding demand to demand reduction, for example, and posing 'what if' questions about energy systems (Hopkins 2019) are critical alongside questioning of underlying logics and assumptions. Merely saying that we wouldn't start from here is not useful. Lenferna (2018: 222) captures the dilemma nicely where she states: 'It may be an injustice to not end the fossil fuel era entirely equitably, but much graver injustice and harm will come from not reducing fossil fuel production and acting on climate change, particularly for least developed and developing nations. On the other hand, if we put in place measures to ensure an equitable end to the fossil fuel era, we may also reduce resistance to it coming to an end.'

Secondly, the conversation about justice has to be opened up to its global and even intergenerational dimensions in ways that go beyond the national focus of most discussions and dialogues on energy transitions. One country's energy choices cannot be seen in isolation from their global effects in terms of shifts in demand for land (for biofuels, for example) (Harnesk and Brogaard 2017), for minerals (for car batteries or PV panels, for example), or the waste they generate (nuclear, for example). Church and Crawford (2018), in their study on 'green conflict minerals', show how the search for minerals for low carbon technologies can fuel conflict (Zehner 2012; Sovacool 2019). The issue then is systemic (social and environmental) justice and not just the justice implications of adopting one technology over another. Abramsky (2010: 9) notes: 'The idea that a massive introduction of "clean energy" or "renewable energy" on its own is enough to solve the problems at hand maintains the illusion that it will be possible to sustain current levels of energy consumption, levels that continue to expand unstoppably.' He implores us to recall that '[c]apitalist relations arose during the era of renewable energies and their associated technologies. Wind-powered sailboats conquered the world, windmills ground sugar cane on slave plantations and land was drained by wind and water-powered pumps. This was the energy basis of Italian city states; British, French, Spanish and Portuguese naval empires and Dutch hegemony' (Abramsky 2010: 11). The point is not to downplay the manifest and evident expansion of capitalism which fossil fuels enabled, but rather to suggest that strategies of imperialism, exploitation of the periphery of the global economy and environmental degradation are unlikely to disappear, even if fossil fuels do, as the energy basis of global capitalism. As Abramksy (2010: 13) continues, 'the experience of capitalist renewable energy regimes of the past stands as a reminder that social relations of production based on enclosures and exploitation, are not exclusively associated with fossil fuels and nuclear energy. There is nothing automatically emancipatory about renewable energies.'

Justice is oftentimes relative then and not absolute in most cases, so it is often a case of minimising injustices and maximising justice for the majority of the world's citizens in handling complex trade-offs. The principles by which this should proceed are deeply contested and we do not yet have democratic institutions for adequately dealing with issues of representation and participation across regions and time. Civil society advocacy in global fora fills some of the void, but we also know its limitations. Alternative mechanisms of representation have been proposed for climate change (Stevenson and Dryzek 2014), but for the moment these remain in the ambit of political philosophers' useful, but presently utopian, visions.

Thirdly, we need to challenge the idea that top-down rapid change is necessarily regressive. A combination of divestment of finance from fossil fuels by major investors and laws and regulations that many governments have recently shown themselves willing to adopt to keep fossil fuels in the ground (such as recent moratoria on new oil exploration and production announced between 2017 and 2019 by a number of countries including New Zealand, France, Costa Rica, Spain and Belize), or which set clear near-term timetables for their phase out, show what is possible. Deeper shifts in culture and values are surely key to embedding change in practices and behaviours of all social actors, as well as challenging power. But they can also change quite rapidly in ways which force responses from corporations and states alike.

Fourthly, justice has procedural as well as distributional elements so opening up spaces for deeper and more meaningful engagements with different pathways for transitioning to a lower carbon economy, for example, could usefully subject to more rounded and critical scrutiny the pros and cons of different options, as discussed in Chapter 6. This could ensure that advocates of more rapid transitions are more attentive to near and longer-term social justice implications, but also that those resisting such claims are obliged to spell out proposals for rapid reductions in emissions compatible with pathways of 1.5 or 2 degrees warming, for example. This might help widen the circle of engaged actors from business, labour and environmental groups to others that have entirely different visions for near-term, but deeper, change that might include serious efforts at demand reduction, big changes to planning regulations, agreements to leave fossil fuels in the ground or to reallocate fossil fuel subsidies. All proposals would have to be compatible with a pathway that keeps warming below 1.5 degrees if they are not to further immiserate many of the world's poorest people.

This would shift the debate away from the narrower discussion of which combinations of big technologies and infrastructures can meet rising energy demand in a warming world without first attending to the possibility of reducing demand and questioning patterns of consumption and production through changes to work (a shorter working week), different models of mobility, localising economies and shifts to the tax regime, for example. This allows us to pose (and engage with) the more difficult questions of who and what transitions are for and who sets their terms, as well as the overall direction of change. This suggests at least one way that 'rapid' and 'just' can be squared in a way that goes against the grain without bypassing the necessity and inevitability of the messy politics of compromise and negotiation.

This is where debates about precedents that can be derived from historical transitions hit their limits. It is certainly the case that, left to their own devices, market-driven energy transitions take decades at minimum and potentially evolve over more than a century (Smil 2016). But we have not yet experienced a situation of the like we now encounter where there is a need for urgent reordering and reconfiguration of energy systems, not dictated by tastes and comfort alone, or by the exhaustion of the worth of existing assets, or even the potential returns from a new wave of investment and innovation: though each of these remains important. Rather, the reality of climate change and its potential to profoundly disrupt the viability of life on the planet for the majority of its citizens demands unprecedented actions and interventions. This is not to erase, overlook or diminish the lessons of the past about energy systems. Quite the contrary. I have argued that lessons about where state action can be forthcoming remarkably quickly, finance mobilised in new directions over a short space of time, industries repurposed, and mobilisations take hold, provide the basis for 'evidence-based hope'. They provide indications, nothing more, but illustrations of the possibility of rapid change, the sort which is now required to preserve our existence on this planet. None has taken place in a co-ordinated or global fashion or on the scale, across regions and sectors and within time frames, that is now demanded as the IPCC SR15 made clear. The challenge we now all face is to ensure that we make this happen in today's world.

This represents a challenge for political economy analysis of transitions. Political economy analysis is often strongest and best at explaining why radical change does not come about. With reference to the structural power of key state, corporate and institutional actors and their control over the means of production, their hold over finance and technology in the contemporary global economy and the power of elites to project and maintain the status quo as normal and given, it is strongest when explaining why business as usual prevails and radical alternatives are accommodated and diluted, crushed, delegitimized or ignored (Gill 2008; Levy and Newell 2002). More challenging is to look back historically and infer lessons for the present about when radical, disruptive and socially progressive change has been possible before, and could be again, in the face of sustainability challenges. As Sovacool and Geels (2016: 236) put it in relation to transition studies: 'We wonder if the very hesitancy from us to validate the notion of expedient transitions, and the continued dominance of techno-economic analyses rooted in modelling, contributes in part to the very "lock-in" or "path dependency" we critique'. Smil's (2016: 196) depressing projections that 'even the fastest conceivable adoption of non-carbon energies will fall far short from eliminating fossil fuel combustion by the middle of the 21st century' should not cast doubt on the possibility of rapid transition. It merely highlights the need not to leave this transition to the 'natural' forces of the market and the normal cycles of technological innovations within it, but rather to demand of governments that large swathes of remaining reserves of fossil fuels are put off limits so that investors, innovators and companies are steered in a different direction. As Kern and Rogge (2016) argue, history is useful, but it affords only a partial guide to the future.

I have noted many of the challenges and limitations associated with trying to project into the future based on a (necessarily selective) reading of previous periods of rapid transition. Historical experience is largely instructive rather than predictive (Sovacool and Geels 2016). The dynamics may be different going forward and questions of sustainability bring with them particular challenges around urgency and the need for a fundamentally different model of economic development that goes beyond replacing one mode of accumulation and regulation for growth, with its associated technologies, flows of finance and models of production, with another. For this reason, as Fouquet and Pearson (2012: 3) put it, 'past energy transitions may not be the best analogies for a future low carbon energy transition'. Sovacool (2016: 210) further suggests: 'Future transitions may also become a social or political priority in ways that previous transitions have not been—that is, previous transitions may have been accidental or circumstantial, whereas future transitions could become more planned and coordinated, or backed by aggressive social movements or progressive government targets.'

For example, returning to the discussion in Chapter 2, unlike earlier transitions driven primarily by price or an abundance of resources, future ones may be driven by scarcity and the unaffordability of resources or stranded assets and un-burnable carbon. In terms of the knowledge base, scientific consensus and broad policy toolkits needed to address these issues that are now available – production tax credits, feed-in tariffs and renewable portfolio standards that can hasten the adoption of preferred technologies – a positive enabling environment may be said to exist. Despite this, transitions may well be incremental, cumulative, messy and multidirectional for the most part. As Sovacool (2016: 211) suggests, 'most energy transitions have been, and will likely continue to be, path dependent rather than revolutionary, cumulative rather than fully substitutive'. But, as I have shown here, this does not exclude the possibility and imperative of rapid disruptive change over shorter time frames where shifts in governance, financing, mobilisation and culture of the sort I describe here coincide, overlap and drive one another through ecosystems of transformation. I concur with Grubler (2012: 8): 'History does not preordain the future, but it is the only observational space available from which to draw lessons . . . and to inform policy models and makers of what it takes to initiate and sustain a much-needed next transition towards sustainability.' It provides an invaluable starting point but needs to be checked against emergent social trends and reconfigurations of social forces that could precipitate departures from historical precedents.

Any rapid transition that does occur will do so in circumstances of uncertainty around timing, process and outcome that, on one level, are unique to a particular context and configuration of circumstances. Nevertheless, like it or not, our current collective predicament, and best available knowledge, posits an imperative of rapid transition if we are to avert the irreversible passing of key planetary boundaries (Rockström et al. 2009; Rogelj et al. 2015). It is critical, therefore, to ask what we can learn from precedents about creating the most positive, and most socially just, conditions in which such transitions can occur. In this book, I have looked at examples and ways of thinking about governing, producing and financing transitions, as well as mobilising and culturing broader transformations, in search of pertinent and proactive examples of change which speak to possibilities of change relevant to contemporary struggles for transformation of the energy system and a more sustainable society.

In many ways we have two options facing us. We either hope we can decarbonise the economy much more rapidly than in the past, given the actors now aligned behind such a project, and hope that historical precedents and examples are only partially useful (Kern and Rogge 2016). This implies the continuation of the conventional framing of the challenge of energy transitions in the face of climate change as about the need for more. More finance, technology, infrastructure, property rights, pricing and markets. Or, we can seek to go beyond business as usual to a scenario in which the climate regime is not just focused on regulating emissions into the atmosphere, or creating markets to enable trading and commodification. Rather, we can accept that future responses cannot be based on having to make the business case. We have tried voluntarism, market-based solutions and most have not worked in delivering the scale or pace of change we need. There is a need for regulation *of* rather than just regulation *for* capital. This implies rewiring the global economy so that trade and investment and their governance reflect in treaties and competition rules, the imperatives of sustainability. It would mean managing the decline of one energy order and supporting the establishment of another through, for example, limits on production and the proactive design and financing of equitable alternatives. In this scenario, business does not dictate the terms and pace of change. Rather, limits are put down in a variety of forms, especially supply-side policies (Erickson et al. 2018). This might include a Fossil Fuel Non-Proliferation Treaty (Simms and Newell 2018).

But more than this, it raises bigger questions about growth and about means and ends. It forces us to think about who and what business is for, rather than being an end in itself. The structure of markets relying on the shareholder model also demands that companies must grow. But the best analysis available suggests that growth in OECD countries cannot be squared with halting warming at 2°C, 3°C or even 4°C (Simms 2013). This means recognising the *limits of liberalism* rather than being *liberal with limits*, as with the current trajectory, passing planetary boundaries at will. This is not necessarily about more state, less market. It is about a different type of state and a different type of market and the move from an extractive to a regenerative economy. It implies the creation and expansion of space for democratic engagement with alternative pathways and control over the means of producing energy and other critically important resources such as food and water. Businesses operate, and have always done so, within a social framework of rules and regulations and in most cases need a social licence to operate. We need business for the common good, including a re-commoning of energy, and we need to articulate the limits to capital. This is important to avoid the scenario that Abramsky (2010: 8) paints:

Energy generation and distribution plays a key role in shaping human relations. Every form of energy implies a particular organisation of work and division of labor (both in general and in the energy sector in particular). The most significant social, economic, cultural, political and technological transformations in history were associated with shifts in energy generation: from hunting and gathering to agriculture, from human and animal power for transport and production to wind and the steam engine, from coal and oil and nuclear fission as drivers of industry and war. All these transformations have led to increased concentration of power and wealth. And a very real possibility exists that the coming transformation in the world's energy system will result in similar shifts in power relations.

As the title of this book suggests, we need a power shift. Without greater social and democratic control over the ownership, direction, regulation, production and consumption and financing of energy, it is likely that the power to determine energy pathways will remain in incumbent hands. Technologies may change, systems of transmission and distribution may be altered, or even revolutionised, and modes of service delivery overhauled. But if the purposes of energy policy and assumptions about whose energy needs take priority and who pays the social and environmental price of conventional energy pathways are not up for discussion and contestation, the prospects of a meaningful just transition, let alone broader transformations, appear remote indeed. This does not do away, of course, with the need for advocacy aimed at shifting debates, contesting assumptions, resisting individual projects and investments that may look like incrementalism, but which can lead to deeper and longer-term change, and which in any case reflects the fact that we do not begin this battle in conditions of our own choosing, or with the power to determine the terrain of struggle. Messy compromise, coalition-building, learning by doing are inevitable and important. The speed, direction and form that transitions take are not singular, fixed or linear, but rather emergent from collective choices and struggles with uncertain outcomes. But we must also keep in mind a bolder notion of the sort of relationship between energy and society that we would like to see, which we believe is possible to construct and which we see in the making in 'moves' all around the world and with reference to what has been achieved in the past by a range of actors and movements.

Future battles will be around the terms on which these deeper transformations are fought. After all, actors as diverse as the IEA, Greenpeace and The Climate Group have called for an 'energy revolution'. The question is revolution in *which* parts of the system and *whose* revolution is it? Is this confined to major reorganisations of technology, finance and infrastructure, or also institutions, societies and relations of political power? This goes to the very heart of fundamental questions about how societies determine what and for whom energy is for. It relates to its potentially contradictory functions: on the one hand as a highly profitable commodity for production and exchange in the world market, and on the other as something that sustains human life and well-being, without which no basic needs could be met. We have seen throughout the book how states, corporations, international institutions and civil society organisations struggle to reconcile these competing dimensions, a tension magnified and exacerbated by the ecological contradictions that energy industrialism (and therefore not just capitalist economies) now faces.

Notes

1 Introduction

1. www.rapidtransition.org.
2. www.rapidtransition.org/commentaries/the-business-of-rapid-transition/.

2 Theorising Energy Transitions

1. https://steps-centre.org/

3 Producing Energy Transitions

1. Personal correspondence with staff at Oil Change International (OCI).
2. www.oxfordenergy.org/wpcms/wp-content/uploads/2019/02/Narratives-for-Natural-Gas-in
   -a-Decarbonisinf-European-Energy-Market-NG141.pdf. The gas community needs to 'develop
   decarbonisation narratives' or risk being supplanted by electrification.
3. www.worldcoal.org/reducing-co2-emissions.
4. www.iea-coal.org/about/.
5. www.shell.com/energy-and-innovation/the-energy-future/scenarios/shell-scenario-sky.html.
6. InfluenceMap, 2019, Big Oil's Real Agenda on Climate Change. https://influencemap.org/report/
   How-Big-Oil-Continues-to-Oppose-the-Paris-Agreement
   -38212275958aa21196dae3b76220bddc.
7. http://priceofoil.org/2019/11/13/iea-weo-response/.
8. www.weforum.org/agenda/2018/11/alliance-ceos-open-letter-climate-change-action/.
9. www.weforum.org/projects/alliance-of-ceo-climate-leaders.
10. https://sciencebasedtargets.org/.
11. www.wemeanbusinesscoalition.org/.
12. https://sciencebasedtargets.org/companies-taking-action/.
13. Public event on the Just transition at the Bonn SB50 climate negotiations, June 2019.
14. www.rapidtransition.org/stories/dethroning-king-coal-how-a-once-dominant-fuel-source-is-falling
    -rapidly-from-favour/.
15. http://tai.org.au/content/palaszczuk-and-turnbull-governments-are-adani-mines-lonely-fans.
16. https://thebulletin.org/2019/01/a-green-new-deal-must-not-sabotage-climate-goals/?utm_source
    =Outlook&utm_medium=Outreach%20Email&utm_campaign=GreenNewDeal.
17. www.nhm.ac.uk/press-office/press-releases/leading-scientists-set-out-resource-challenge-of-meeting-
    net-zer.html.
18. www.iisd.org/library/beyond-fossil-fuels-indonesias-fiscal-transition.

4 Financing Energy Transitions

1. Africa Renewable Energy Initiative (AREI) http://newsroom.unfccc.int/lpaa/renewable-energy/africa-renewable-energy-initiative-increasing-renewable-energy-capacity-on-the-african-continent/.
2. Global Commission on the Economy and Climate (2018) *The New Climate Economy.* https://newcli mateeconomy.report/2016/.
3. www.environmental-finance.com/content/market-insight/no-more-excuses-financing-1.5c.html.
4. www.rapidtransition.org/stories/the-rise-and-rise-of-green-bonds/.
5. See, for example, www.newyorker.com/news/dispatch/the-divestment-movement-to-combat-climate-change-is-all-grown-up.
6. Stranded assets are thought to be 'assets that have suffered from unanticipated or premature write-downs, devaluations or conversion to liabilities' (Ansar et al. 2013).
7. Attendance at 'Climate Risk and Financing' session hosted by Munich Re at the Bonn SB50 negotiations (Bonn, 24 June 2019).
8. GEEREF invested in fifteen funds across Africa, Asia, Latin America and the Caribbean before its investment period closed at the end of May 2019.
9. www.ceres.org/networks/ceres-investor-network.

5 Governing Energy Transitions

1. https://350.org/press-release/nyc-fossil-fuel-project-ban-2020/.
2. www.rapidtransition.org/stories/converting-industry-how-rapid-transition-happens-in-crises-and-upheavals/.

6 Mobilising Energy Transitions

1. www.repowering.org.uk/our-story/.
2. www.fossilfueltreaty.org/.
3. www.financeclimatechallenge.com/.
4. www.powershift.org/.
5. https://theinvestoragenda.org/.
6. www.youtube.com/watch?v=B5aVCPCJ0rY.
7. https://carbontracker.org/was-2019-the-peak-of-the-fossil-fuel-era/.
8. www.reeep.org/9th-funding-cycle.
9. www.ren21.net/.
10. Interview with Rob Hopkins, founder of Transition towns, 18 May 2020.
11. www.c40.org/other/deadline_2020.
12. www.globalcovenantofmayors.org/.
13. www.rapidtransition.org/stories/local-civic-action-is-growing-a-climate-revolution-from-below/.
14. www.rapidtransition.org/commentaries/what-would-a-climate-emergency-plan-look-like/.
15. Ibid.
16. www.rapidtransition.org/commentaries/what-would-a-climate-emergency-plan-look-like/.
17. www.adeptnet.org.uk/about-adept.
18. www.rapidtransition.org/stories/the-simple-strike-goes-global-led-by-young-people/.
19. https://talkradio.co.uk/radio/listen-again/1550212200#.
20. www.sunrisemovement.org/.
21. http://climatecasechart.com/case/juliana-v-united-states/.
22. www.ids.ac.uk/projects/demanding-power-struggles-over-energy-access-in-fragile-settings-a4ea/.
23. Interview with Rob Hopkins, founder of Transition towns, 18 May 2020.
24. Energy4All has set up twenty-four member co-operatives who are themselves members of Energy4All, which together have around 14,000 individual members, own 30 MW of renewable

energy generation and have raised around £70 million in funds for renewable energy installations (Chapman 2018).

25. Conversation with the director of Mongoose Energy, Sussex 2018.
26. www.rapidtransition.org/stories/the-worlds-first-renewable-island-when-a-community-embraces-wind-power/.
27. www.rapidtransition.org/stories/the-worlds-first-renewable-island-when-a-community-embraces-wind-power/.
28. Interview with Tim Kasser, 28 April 2020.
29. Interview with Tim Kasser, 28 April 2020.
30. https://www.adbusters.org/.
31. https://www.rapidtransition.org/stories/adblocking-the-global-cities-clearing-streets-of-advertising-to-promote-human-and-environmental-health/.
32. www.sussex.ac.uk/ssrp/resources/forum/peter-newell.
33. http://theconversation.com/labours-low-carbon-plan-is-a-good-start-but-a-green-transformation-must-go-further-104052.

7 Conclusions

1. https://medium.com/just-transitions/stevis-e147a9ec189a.
2. https://medium.com/just-transitions/mertins-kirkwood-778748c14a6a.

Bibliography

Abram, S. (2007) 'Participatory Depoliticisation: The Bleeding Heart of Neoliberalism'. In C. Neveu (ed.) *Cultures et pratiques participatives: perspectives comparatives*. Paris: l'Harmattan, 113–33.

(2008) 'Public Participation and the Problem of Exclusion'. In C. Garston and M. Lindh de Montoya (eds.) *Transparency in a New Global Order*. Cheltenham: Edward Elgar, 201–22.

Abramsky, K. (2010) *Sparking a Worldwide Energy Revolution: Social Struggles in the Transition to a Post-Petrol World*. Edinburgh: AK Press.

Aglietta, M. (2000) *A Theory of Capitalist Regulation: The US Experience*. London: Verso.

Allen, R. (2012) 'Backward into the Future: The Shift from Coal and Implications for the Next Energy Transition'. *Energy Policy* 50: 17–23.

Allouche, J., C. Middleton and D. Gyawali (2019) *The Water-Food-Energy Nexus: Power, Politics and Justice*. Pathways to Sustainability Series. London: Routledge; Earthscan Publications.

Altvater, E. (2006) 'The Social and Natural Environment of Fossil Capitalism'. In L. Panitch and C. Leys (eds.) *Coming to Terms with Nature*. Published in 2007 edition of *Socialist Register*, Vol. 43. London: Merlin Press, 37–60.

Ambrose, J. (2019a) 'Government "Funding Fossil Fuel-Burning Plants Abroad"'. *The Guardian*, 10 June. www.theguardian.com/environment/2019/jun/10/government-funding-fossil-fuel-burning-plants-abroad?CMP=share_btn_link.

(2019b) 'UK to Use Finance Meant for Green Energy to Support Fracking in Argentina'. *The Guardian*, 22 October. www.theguardian.com/environment/2019/oct/22/uk-to-use-1bn-meant-for-green-energy-to-support-fracking-in-argentina.

(2020) 'Trump Weakened Environmental Laws after BP Lobbying'. *The Guardian*, 23 January. www.theguardian.com/business/2020/jan/23/trump-weakened-environmental-laws-after-bp-lobbying.

Anderson, K., and A. Bows (2011). 'Beyond "Dangerous" Climate Change: Emission Scenarios for a New World'. *Philosophical Transactions of the Royal Society A: Mathematical, Physical and Engineering Sciences* 369(1934): 20–44.

Anderson, K., and G. Peters (2016) 'The Trouble with Negative Emissions'. *Science* 354 (6309): 182–3.

Andrews-Speed, P. (2016) 'Applying Institutional Theory to the Low-Carbon Energy Transition'. *Energy Research & Social Science* 13: 216–25.

Ansar, A., B. L. Caldecott and J. Tilbury (2013) *Stranded Assets and the Fossil Fuel Divestment Campaign: What Does Divestment Mean for the Valuation of Fossil Fuel Assets?* Smith School of Enterprise and Environment, University of Oxford.

Ansuategi, A., P. Greño, V. Houlden, A. Markandya, L. Onofri, H. Picot, G.-M. Tsarouchi and N. Walmsley (2015) 'The Impact of Climate Change on the Achievement of the Post-2015 Sustainable Development Goals'. London: CDKN. https://cdkn.org/wp-content/uploads/2015/05/Impact-of-climate-on-SDGs-technical-report-CDKN.pdf.

Appadurai, A. (1990) 'Disjuncture and Difference in the Global Cultural Economy'. *Public Culture* 2(2): 1–24.

Arapostathis, S., and P. Pearson (2019) 'How History Matters for the Governance of Sociotechnical Transitions: An Introduction to the Special Issue'. *Environmental Innovation and Societal Transitions* (32): 1–6.

AREI (2015) Africa Renewable Energy Initiative (AREI). http://newsroom.unfccc.int/lpaa/renewable-energy/africa-renewable-energy-initiative-increasing-renewable-energy-capacity-on-the-african-continent/.

Arent, D., C. Arndt, M. Miller, F. Tarp and O. Zinaman (eds.) (2017) *The Political Economy of Energy Transitions*. Oxford: Oxford University Press.

Arndt, H. W. (1978). *The Rise and Fall of Economic Growth: A Study in Contemporary Thought*. Melbourne: Longman Cheshire.

Arranz, A. M. (2017). 'Lessons from the Past for Sustainability Transitions? A Meta-analysis of Socio-technical Studies'. *Global Environmental Change* 44: 125–43.

Arrighi, G. (2010) *The Long Twentieth Century: Money, Power, and the Origins of Our Times*. London: Verso.

Asheim, G., T. Fæhn, K. Nyborg, M. Greaker, C. Hagem, B. Harstad, M. Hoel, D. Lund and K. Rosendahl (2019) 'The Case for a Supply-Side Climate Treaty'. *Science* 365: 325–32.

Ayers, A. J. (2013) 'Beyond Myths, Lies and Stereotypes: The Political Economy of a "New Scramble for Africa"'. *New Political Economy* 18(2): 227–57.

Ayling, J., and N. Gunningham (2017) 'Non-state Governance and Climate Policy: The Fossil Fuel Divestment Movement'. *Climate Policy* 17: 131–49.

Ayres, R. (1984) 'Limits and Possibilities of Large-Scale Long-Range Societal Models'. *Technological Forecasting and Social Change* 25: 297–308.

Bachrach, P., and M. S. Baratz (1962) 'Two Faces of Power'. *American Political Science Review* 56: 947–52.

Bachram, H. (2004) 'Climate Fraud and Carbon Colonialism: The New Trade in Greenhouse Gases. *Capitalism, Nature, Socialism* 15(4): 1–16.

Baker, L., and B. Sovacool (2017). 'The Political Economy of Technological Capabilities and Global Production Networks in South Africa's Wind and Solar Photovoltaic (PV) Industries'. *Political Geography* 60: 1–12.

Baker, L., P. Newell, and J. Phillips (2014). 'The Political Economy of Energy Transitions: The Case of South Africa'. *New Political Economy* 19: 791–818.

Barry, J. (1999) *Rethinking Green Politics*. London: Sage.

(2018) 'A Genealogy of Economic Growth as Ideology and Cold War Core State Imperative'. *New Political Economy* 25: 1–12. 10.1080/13563467.2018.1526268.

Barry, J., and R. Eckersley (eds.) (2005) *The State and the Global Ecological Crisis*. Cambridge, MA: MIT Press.

Barry J., E. Geraint and C. Robinson (2008) 'Cool Rationalities and Hot Air: A Rhetorical Approach to Understanding Debates on Renewable Energy'. *Global Environmental Politics* 8(2): 67–98.

Bauwens, T., B. Huybrechts and F. Dufays (2019 online, 2020 journal issue) 'Understanding the Diverse Scaling Strategies of Social Enterprises as Hybrid Organizations: The Case of

Renewable Energy Cooperatives'. *Organization & Environment* 33(2): 195–219. https://doi.org/10.1177/1086026619837126.

Baynes, C. (2019) '"Utter Hypocrisy": Government Refuses to Stop Spending Billions on Fossil Fuel Projects across World'. *The Independent*, 2 October. www.independent.co.uk/environment/climate-change-fossil-fuels-uk-funding-environment-export-finance-a9129731.html.

Bazilian, M., M. Bradshaw, A. Goldthau and K. Westphal (2019) 'Model and Manage the Changing Geopolitics of Energy'. *Nature Comment*, 1 May. www.nature.com/articles/d41586-019-01312-5.

Becker, S., R. Byrne, D. Ockwell, N. Ozor, A. Ely and K. Urama (2013) 'Adapting the Innovation Histories Method for a Workshop on Solar Home Systems Uptake in Kenya'. https://steps-centre.org/wp-content/uploads/Innovation-Histories-briefing_S.pdf.

Beder, S. (1997) *Global Spin: The Corporate Assault on Environmentalism*. White River Junction, VT: Chelsea Green Publishing.

Begg, K., F. van der Woerd and D. L. Levy (eds.) (2005) *The Business of Climate Change: Corporate Responses to Kyoto* Sheffield: Greenleaf.

Belcher, O., P. Bigger, B. Neimark and C. Kennelly (2019) 'Hidden Carbon Costs of the "Everywhere War": Logistics, Geopolitical Ecology, and the Carbon Boot-Print of the US Military'. *Transactions of the Institute of British Geographers*.

Bellamy Foster, J. (1999). 'Marx's Theory of Metabolic Rift: Classical Foundations for Environmental Sociology'. *American Journal of Sociology* 105(2): 366–405.

Benford, R., and D. Snow (2000) 'Framing Processes and Social Movements: An Overview and Assessment'. *Annual Review of Sociology* 26: 611–39.

Bengtsson, M., E. Alfredsson, M. Cohen, S. Lorek and O. Schroeder (2018) 'Transforming Systems of Consumption and Production for Achieving the Sustainable Development Goals: Moving beyond Efficiency'. *Sustainability Science* 13: 1533–47.

Benney, T. (2019) 'Varieties of Capitalism and Renewable Energy in Emerging and Developing Economies'. *Journal of Economic Policy Reform*. 10.1080/17487870.2019.1637584.

Bergman, N. (2018) 'Impacts of the Fossil Fuel Divestment Movement: Effects on Finance, Policy and Public Discourse'. *Sustainability* 10(7): 2529.

Berkhout, F., D. Angel and A. J. Wieczorek (2009) 'Sustainability Transitions in Developing Asia: Are Alternative Development Pathways Likely?' *Technological Forecasting & Social Change* 76(2): 215–17.

Bernstein, S. (2000). *The Compromise of Liberal Environmentalism*. New York: Columbia University Press.

Besant-Jones, J. (2006) *Reforming Power Markets in Developing Countries: What Have We Learned?* Energy and Mining Sector Board Discussion Paper No. 19, September. Washington: World Bank Group.

Bickerstaff, K., G. Walker and H. Bulkeley (eds.) (2013) *Energy Justice in a Changing Climate*. London: Zed Books.

Bieler, A., and A. Morton (2018) *Global Capitalism, Global War, Global Crisis*. Cambridge: Cambridge University Press.

BIES (2019) 'The Future of Small-Scale Low Carbon Generation: A Consultation on a Smart Export Guarantee (SEG)'. https://beisgovuk.citizenspace.com/clean-electricity/small-scale-low-carbon-generation-seg/.

Bird, J., and K. Lawton (2009) *The Future's Green: Jobs and the UK Low-Carbon Transition*. London: IPPR.

Blondeel, M., and T. Van de Graaf (2018) 'Toward a Global Coal Mining Moratorium?' *Climatic Change* 150(1–2): 89–101.

BNP Paribas (2015) *Corporate Social Responsibility: BNP Paribas Commitments to the Environment.* https://group.bnpparibas/uploads/file/csr_commitments_1.pdf.

(2017a) *Coal-Fired Power Generation – Sector Policy.* https://group.bnpparibas /uploads/file/csr_sector_policy_cfpg.pdf.

(2017b) *Unconventional Oil And Gas – Sector Policy.* https://group.bnpparibas/uploads/ file/csr_sector_policy_unconventional_oil_and_gas_19_12_2017_v_standardized.pdf.

(2018) *BNP Paribas and the Exercise of Its CSR.* https://invest.bnpparibas.com/sites/ default/files/documents/bnp_paribas_and_the_exercise_of_its_csr_2018.pdf.

Boardman, B. (2012) *Achieving Zero: Delivering Future-Friendly Buildings.* ECI, Oxford. ISBN: 9781874370512. Supported by a grant from the Greenpeace Environmental Trust.

Boehmer-Christiansen, S. and J. Skea (1991) *Acid Politics: Environmental and Energy Policies in Britain and Germany.* Hoboken, NJ: John Wiley.

Böhm, S., and S. Dabhi (eds.) (2009) *Upsetting the Offset: The Political Economy of Carbon Markets.* Colchester: Mayfly Books.

Böhm, S., C. Jones, C. Land and M. Paterson (eds.) (2006) *Against Automobility.* Oxford: Blackwell.

Bond, P. (2005) 'Bankrupt Africa: Imperialism, Sub-Imperialism and the Politics of Finance'. *Historical Materialism* 12(4): 145–72.

(2012) *Politics of Climate Justice: Paralysis Above, Movement Below.* Scottsville, KY: KwaZulu-Natal Press.

(2015) 'Will BRICS Carbon Traders Bail Out the Bankers' Climate Strategy? Part I'. http:// triplecrisis.com/will-brics-carbon-traders-bail-out-the-bankers-climate-strategy-part-i/.

Bookchin, M. (1980) *Toward an Ecological Society.* Montreal: Black Rose Books.

Borras, S. M., P. McMichael and I. Scoones (2010). 'The Politics of Biofuels, Land and Agrarian Change: Editors' Introduction'. *Journal of Peasant Studies* 37: 575–92.

Boyce, M. (2009) 'G8 Climate Governance, 1975–2007'. Research Report. G8 Research Group, University of Toronto, May 2009. www.g7.utoronto.ca/evaluations/climate-boyce-090708.pdf.

Boyer, D. (2014) 'Energopower: An Introduction'. *Anthropology Quarterly* 87(2): 309–33.

Boyle, D. (2019) 'Five Questions on the Business of Rapid Transition'. Background Note for the Business of Rapid Transition workshop, London, May.

Bradshaw, M. (2010) 'Global Energy Dilemmas: A Geographical Perspective'. *Geographical Journal* 176: 275–90.

(2013) *Global Energy Dilemmas: Energy Security, Globalization and Climate Change.* Cambridge: Polity.

Brand, C., and B. Boardman (2008) 'Taming of the Few—The Unequal Distribution of Greenhouse Gas Emissions from Personal Travel in the UK'. *Energy Policy* 36(1): 224–38.

Bremmer, I., and R. Johnston (2009) 'The Rise and Fall of Resource Nationalism'. *Survival* 52(2): 49–158.

Brenner, N., and N. Theodore (2002) 'Cities and the Geographies of "Actually Existing Neoliberalism"'. *Antipode* 34(3): 349–79.

Bridge, G. (2014) 'Resource Geographies II: The Resource-State Nexus'. *Progress in Human Geography* 38(1): 118–30.

Bridge, G., and P. Le Billon (2013). *Oil.* Cambridge: Polity.

Bridge, G., S. Bouzarovski, M. Bradshaw and N. Eyre (2013) 'Geographies of Energy Transition: Space, Place and the Low-Carbon Economy'. *Energy Policy* 53: 331–40.

Bridge, G., S. Barr, S. Bouzarovski, M. Bradshaw, E. Brown, H. Bulkeley and G. Walker (eds.) (2018a) *Energy and Society: A Critical Perspective.* London: Routledge.

Bridge, G., B. Özkaynak and E. Turhan (2018b) 'Energy Infrastructure and the Fate of the Nation: Introduction to Special Issue'. *Energy Research & Social Science* 41: 1–11.

Brock, A. (2018) 'The Battle of Hambacher Forest'. *Red Pepper*, 20 September. www
.redpepper.org.uk/the-battle-of-hambacher-forest/.

Brock, A., and A. Dunlap (2018) 'Normalising Corporate Counterinsurgency: Engineering
Consent, Managing Resistance and Greening Destruction around the Hambach Coal
Mine and Beyond'. *Political Geography* 62(2018): 33–47.

Brockway, P. E., H. Saunders, M. Heun, T. Foxon, J. Steinberger, J. Barrett and S. Sorrell
(2017) 'Energy Rebound as a Potential Threat to a Low-Carbon Future: Findings from
a New Exergy-Based National-Level Rebound Approach'. *Energies* 10(1): 1–24.

Bromley, S. (1991) *American Hegemony and World Oil*. Cambridge: Polity.

(2005) 'The United States and the Control of World Oil'. *Government and Opposition* 40
(2): 225–55.

Bromley, P. (2016) 'Extraordinary Interventions: Towards a Framework for Rapid
Transition and Deep Emissions Reductions in the Energy Space'. *Energy Research
& Social Science* 22: 165–71.

Broto, V. C., and L. Baker (2018) 'Spatial Adventures in Energy Studies: An Introduction to
the Special Issue'. *Energy Research & Social Science* 36: 1–10.

Broto, V. C., L. Stevens, E. Ackom, J. Tomei, P. Parikh, I. Bisaga, L. S. To, J. Kirshner and
Y. Mulugetta (2017) 'A Research Agenda for a People-Centred Approach to Energy
Access in the Urbanizing Global South'. *Nature Energy* 2(10): 776–9.

Brummer, V. (2018) 'Of Expertise, Social Capital, and Democracy: Assessing the
Organizational Governance and Decision-Making in German Renewable Energy
Cooperatives'. *Energy Research & Social Science* 37: 111–21.

Buchan, A. (1972) 'Technology and World Politics'. In B. Porter (ed.) *The Aberystwyth
Papers: International Politics 1919–1969*. London: Oxford University Press.

Buck, D. (2006) 'The Ecological Question: Can Capitalism Prevail?' In L. Panitch and C. Leys
(eds.) *Coming to Terms with Nature*. Socialist Register 2007 London: Merlin Press, 60–72.

Bulkeley, H., and P. Newell (2010) *Governing Climate Change* Abingdon: Routledge.

(2015). *Governing Climate Change*, 2nd ed. Abingdon: Routledge.

Bulkeley, H., L. Andonova, K. Bäckstrand, M. Betsill, D. Compagnon, R. Duff, A. Kolk,
M. Hoffmann, D. Levy, P. Newell, T. Milledge, M. Paterson, P. Pattberg and
S. Vandeveer (2012) 'Governing Climate Change Transnationally: Assessing the
Evidence from a Database of Sixty Initiatives'. *Environment and Planning C:
Government and Policy* 30(4): 591–612.

Bulkeley. H., L. Andonva, M. M. Betsill, D. Compagnon, T. Hale, M. Hoffmann, P. Newell,
M. Paterson, C. Roger and S. VanDeveer (2014) *Transnational Climate Change
Governance*. Cambridge: Cambridge University Press.

Bulkeley, H., M. Paterson and J. Stripple (eds.) (2016) *Towards a Cultural Politics of Climate
Change: Devices, Desires and Dissent*. Cambridge: Cambridge University Press.

Bumpus, A., and D. Liverman (2008). 'Accumulation by Decarbonization and the
Governance of Carbon Offsets'. *Economic Geography* 84(2): 127–55.

Bumpus, A., J. Tansey, L. Perez Henriquez and C. Okereke (eds.) (2015) *Carbon
Governance, Climate Change and Business Transformation* Abingdon: Routledge.

Burke, M., and J. C. Stephens (2017) 'Energy Democracy: Goals and Policy Instruments for
Sociotechnical Transitions'. *Energy Research & Social Science* 33: 35–48.

Burningham, K., and S. Venn (2017) 'Moments of Change: Are Lifecourse Transitions
Opportunities for Moving to More Sustainable Consumption?' CUSP Working Paper
No. 7. Guildford: University of Surrey.

Butler, C., K. A. Parkhill and N. Pidgeon (2016) 'Energy Consumption and Everyday Life:
Choice, Values and Agency through a Practice Theoretical Lens'. *Journal of
Consumer Culture* 16(3): 887–907.

Butt, N., F. Lambrick, M. Menton and A. Renwick (2019) 'The Supply Chain of Violence'. *Nature Sustainability* 2(August): 742–7. 10.1038/s41893-019-0349-4.

Buttel, F. (1979) 'Social Welfare and Energy Intensity: A Comparative Analysis of Developed Market Economies'. In C. Unseld, D. Morrison, D. Sills and C. Wolfe (eds.) *Sociopolitical Effects of Energy Use and Policy* Washington: National Academy of Sciences, 297–327.

Buxton, N., and B. Hayes (2016) *The Secure and the Dispossessed: How the Military and Corporations Are Shaping a Climate-Changed World*. London: Pluto Press.

Buzan, B. (1994) 'The Interdependence of Security and Economic Issues in the New World Order'. In R. Stubbs and G. Underhill (eds.) *Political Economy and the Changing Global Order*. Basingstoke: MacMillan, 89–103.

Cafaro, P. (2011). 'Beyond Business as Usual: Alternative Wedges to Avoid Catastrophic Climate Change and Create Sustainable Societies.' In D. Arnold (ed.) *The Ethics of Global Climate Change*. Cambridge: Cambridge University Press, 192–215.

Caldecott, B., O. Sartor and T. Spencer (2017) *Lessons from Previous 'Coal Transitions': High-Level Summary for Decision-Makers*. Paris: IDDRI and Climate Strategies.

Caldwell, M., and J. Woolley (1976) 'Energy Policy and the Capitalist State'. In J. Hammarlund and L. Lindberg (eds.) *The Political Economy of Energy Policy: A Projection for Capitalist Society* IES Report 70. University of Wisconsin-Madison: Institute for Environmental Studies, 110–54.

Calvert, K. (2015) 'From 'Energy Geography' to 'Energy Geographies'. *Progress in Human Geography* 40: 105–25.

Caney, S. (2016) 'Climate Change, Equity and Stranded Assets'. Oxfam America Research Backgrounder Series.

Capstick, S., I. Lorenzoni, A. Corner and L. Whitmarsh (2015) 'Prospects for Radical Emissions Reduction through Behavior and Lifestyle Change'. *Carbon Management*. 10.1080/17583004.2015.1020011.

Carbon Action Tracker (2019) Transformation Points: Achieving the Speed and Scale Required for Full Decarbonisation. https://climateactiontracker.org/documents/516/CAT_2019_04_03_DecarbSeries_TransformationPoints.pdf.

Carbon Brief (2019) 'CORSIA: The UN's Plan to "Offset" Growth in Aviation Emissions after 2020.' 4 February. www.carbonbrief.org/corsia-un-plan-to-offset-growth-in-aviation-emissions-after-2020.

Carbon Tracker Initiative. (2013). *The Unburnable Carbon 2013: Wasted Capital Stranded Assets*. London: Carbon Tracker Initiative and Grantham Research Institute on Climate Change and the Environment.

Carlsson, C. (2015) 'Nowtopians'. In G. D'Alisa, F. Demaria and G. Kallis (eds.) *Degrowth: A Vocabulary for a New Era* London: Routledge, 182–4.

Carmody, P. (2011) *The New Scramble for Africa*. Cambridge: Polity.

Carrell, S. (2020) 'Greenpeace Faces Hefty Fine after Admitting Defying Court Order'. *The Guardian*, 24 February. www.theguardian.com/environment/2020/feb/24/greenpeace-faces-hefty-fine-after-admitting-defying-court-order.

Carrington, D. (2020) 'Heathrow Third Runway Ruled Illegal over Climate Change'. *The Guardian*, 27 February. www.theguardian.com/environment/2020/feb/27/heathrow-third-runway-ruled-illegal-over-climate-change.

Carruthers, B., and A. Stinchcombe (1999) 'The Social Structure of Liquidity: Flexibility, Markets, and States'. *Theory and Society* 28(3): 353–82.

Carver, T. N. (1924) *The Economy of Human Energy*. New York: MacMillan.

Casillas, C., and D. Kammen (2010) 'The Energy–Poverty–Climate Nexus'. *Science* 330: 1181–2.

Castellano, A., A. Kendall, M. Nikomarov and T. Swemmer (2015) 'Powering Africa'. McKinsey. www.mckinsey.com/industries/electric-power-and-natural-gas/our-insights/powering-africa.

CAT (2019) 'Transformation Points: Achieving the Speed and Scale Required for Full Decarbonisation'. Decarbonisation Series. April. climateactiontracker.org.

CDP (Carbon Disclosure Project) (2020) www.cdp.net/en/info/about-us/what-we-do.

Corporate Europe Observatory (CEO), Food & Water Europe, Friends of the Earth Europe and Greenpeace EU (2019) *Big Oil and Gas Buying Influence in Brussels: With Money and Meetings, Subsidies and Sponsorships, the Oil and Gas Lobby Is Fuelling the Climate Disaster*. Fossil Free Politics, October 24, Brussels. https://corporateeurope.org/sites/default/files/2019-10/FFP%20Research%20Briefing%20Oct%202019.pdf.

Cerny, P. (1995) 'Globalization and the Changing Logic of Collective Action'. *International Organization* 49(4): 595–625.

Ćetković, S., and A. Buzogány (2016) 'Varieties of Capitalism and Clean Energy Transitions in the European Union: When Renewable Energy Hits Different Logics'. *Climate Policy* 16(5): 642–57.

Chapman, A. (2018) *Community Energy in the UK*. October Green European Foundation.

Chatterjee, P., and M. Finger (1994) *The Earth Brokers: Power, Politics and World Development*. London: Routledge.

Cheon, A., and J. Urpelainen (2017) *Targeting Big Polluters: Understanding Activism Against the Fossil Fuel Industry*. Oxford: Oxford University Press.

Cherp, A., J. Jewell and A. Goldthau (2011) 'Governing Global Energy: Systems, Transitions, Complexity'. *Global Policy* 2(1): 75–88.

Cherp, A., V. Vinichenko, J. Jewell, E. Brutschin and B. K. Sovacool (2018) 'Integrating Techno-economic, Socio-technical and Political Perspectives on National Energy Transitions: A Meta-theoretical Framework'. *Energy Research & Social Science* 37: 175–90.

Chomsky, N., and R. Pollin (2020) *The Climate Crisis and the Global Green New Deal*. London: Verso.

Choucri, N. (1976) *International Politics of Energy Interdependence* London: Lexington Books.

Church, C., and A. Crawford (2018) *Green Conflict Minerals: The Fuels of Conflict in the Transition to a Low Carbon Economy*. Winnipeg: IISD.

Clark, J. (1990) *The Political Economy of World Energy: A Twentieth Century Perspective*. London: Harvester Wheatsheaf.

Clark, D. (2011) 'Google Discloses Carbon Footprint for the First Time'. *The Guardian*, 8 September. www.theguardian.com/environment/2011/sep/08/google-carbon-footprint.

Coe, N., and H. W. Yeung (2019) 'Global Production Networks: Mapping Recent Conceptual Developments'. *Journal of Economic Geography* 19: 775–801.

Colgan, J. (2013) *Petro-aggression: When Oil Causes War*. Cambridge: Cambridge University Press.

(2014) 'The Emperor Has No Clothes: The Limits of the OPEC in the Global Oil Market'. *International Organization* 68(3): 599–632.

Colgan, J., R. Keohane and T. Van de Graaf (2012) 'Punctuated Equilibrium in the Energy Regime Complex'. *Review of International Organizations* 7: 117–43.

Coll, S. (2012) *Private Empire: ExxonMobil and American Power*. Harmondsworth: Penguin.

Collett-White, R. (2019) 'COP25: Over 40 Gulf State Delegates Are Current or Former Employees of Fossil Fuel Companies'. 13 December. www.desmog.co.uk/2019/12/13/cop25-over-40-gulf-state-delegates-are-current-or-former-employees-fossil-fuel-companies.

Collier, P., and A. J. Venables (2015) 'Closing Coal: Economic and Moral Incentives'. *Oxford Review of Economic Policy* 30(3): 492–512.

Comeau, L., and D. Luke (2018) 'Climate Stability, Worker Stability: Are They Compatible?' Working Paper 202, University of New Brunswick.

Conca, K. (2005) 'Old States in New Bottles? The Hybridization of Authority in Global Environmental Governance'. In J. Barry and R. Eckersley (eds.) *The State and the Global Ecological Crisis*. Cambridge, MA: MIT Press, 181–207.

Costanza, R. (ed.) (1991) *Ecological Economics: The Science and Management of Sustainability*. New York: Columbia University Press.

Cottrell, F. (1955) *Energy and Society*. New York: McGraw-Hill.

Cox, R. (1983) 'Gramsci, Hegemony and International Relations: An Essay in Method'. *Millennium: Journal of International Studies* 12(2): 162–75.

   (1987) *Production, Power and World Order*. New York: Columbia University Press.

   (1993). 'Structural Issues of Global Governance: Implications for Europe'. In S. Gill (ed.) *Gramsci, Historical Materialism and International Relations*. Cambridge: Cambridge University Press, 259–90.

Cox, E., P. Johnstone and A. Stirling (2016) 'Understanding the Intensity of UK Policy Commitments to Nuclear Power'. *SWPS 2016–16*. http://dx.doi.org/10.2139/ssrn .2837691.

Crawford, N. (2019) 'Pentagon Fuel Use: Climate Change and the Costs of War'. Brown University https://watson.brown.edu/costsofwar/files/cow/imce/papers/Pentagon% 20Fuel%20Use%2C%20Climate%20Change%20and%20the%20Costs%20of% 20War%20Revised%20November%202019%20Crawford.pdf.

Crouch, C. (2011) *The Strange Non-death of Neoliberalism*. Cambridge: Polity.

Crouzet, F. (1972) *Capital Formation in the Industrial Revolution*. London: Methuen.

Cummins, C., and N. Aden (2014) Connecting Corporate Emission Targets with Climate. www.wri.org/blog/2014/05/connecting-corporateemissions-targets-climate-science.

Dale, G. (2012) 'The Growth Paradigm: A Critique'. *International Socialism* 134. http://isj .org.uk/the-growth-paradigm-a-critique/.

Das, K., H. van Asselt, S. Droege and M. Mehling (2018) 'Making the International Trade System Work for Climate Change: Assessing the Options'. Climate Strategies, 1–58. https://climatestrategies.org/wp-content/uploads/2018/07/CS-Report-_Trade-WP4.pdf.

Dauvergne, P. (2008) *The Shadows of Consumption: Consequences for the Global Environment*. Cambridge, MA: MIT Press.

Davidson, J. (2020) 'ExxonMobil Lobbyist Tried to Water Down European Green Deal'. *EcoWatch*, 9 March. www.ecowatch.com/european-green-deal-exxon-lobbyists -2645438998.html.

Depledge, J. (2008) 'Striving for No: Saudi Arabia in the Climate Change Regime'. *Global Environmental Politics* 8(4): 9–35.

Desai, R. (2013) *Geopolitical Economy: After US Hegemony, Globalization and Empire*. London: Pluto Press.

Descheneau, P., and M. Paterson (2011) 'Between Desire and Routine: Assembling Environment and Finance in Carbon Markets'. *Antipode* 43(3): 662–81.

DeSmog (2019) 'UK Government Agency's Annual Support for Overseas Fossil Fuel Projects Rises to £2bn'. 27 June. www.desmog.co.uk/2019/06/27/ukef-fossil-fuel-support-2bn-2018–2019?amp&__twitter_impression=true.

Dietz, T., G. Gardner, J. Gilligan, P. Stern and M. Vandenbergh (2009) 'Household Actions Can Provide a Behavioral Wedge to Rapidly Reduce US Carbon Emissions'. *Proceedings of the National Academy of Sciences* 106(44): 18452–6.

Di Muzio, T. (2012). 'Capitalizing a Future Unsustainable: Finance, Energy and the Fate of Market Civilization'. *Review of International Political Economy* 19(3): 363–88.

(2015). *Carbon Capitalism: Energy, Social Reproduction and World Order*. London: Rowman and Littlefield.

Di Muzio, T., and J. Ovadia (eds.) (2016). *Energy, Capital and World Order*. Basingstoke: Palgrave.

Dobson, A. (1990) *Green Political Thought*. London: Routledge.

Dore, J., and R. de Bauw (1995) *The Energy Charter Treaty: Origins, Aims and Prospects*. London: Royal Institute of International Affairs.

Douthwaite, R. (1996) *Short Circuits: Local Economies in an Unsustainable World*. Totnes: Green Books.

Doyle, M. (1986) 'Liberalism and World Politics'. *American Political Science Review* 80 (4): 1151–69.

Dubash, N. K., and S. Chella Rajan (2001) 'Power Politics: Process of Power Sector Reform in India'. *Economic & Political Weekly* 36(35): 3367–90.

Dubash, N., K. Sunila, S. Kale and R. Bharvirkar (eds.) (2018) *Mapping Power: The Political Economy of Electricity in India's States*. New Delhi: Oxford University Press.

Dubois, G., B. K. Sovacool, C. Aall, M. Nilsson, C. Barbier, A. Herrmann, S. Bruyère, C. Andersson, B. Skold, F. Nadaud, F. Dorner, K. R. Moberg, J. P. Ceron, H. Fischer, D. Amelung, M. Baltruszewicz, J. Fischer, F. Benevise, V. R. Louis and R. Sauerborn (2019) 'It Starts at Home? Climate Policies Targeting Household Consumption and Behavioral Decisions Are Key to Low-Carbon Futures'. *Energy Research & Social Science* 52: 144–58.

Dunlap, A. (2018) 'Counterinsurgency for Wind Energy: The Bíi Hioxo Wind Park in Juchitán, Mexico'. *Journal of Peasant Studies* 3: 630–52.

Dütschke, D., and J. P. Wesche (2018) 'The Energy Transformation as a Disruptive Development at Community Level'. *Energy Research & Social Science* 37: 251–4.

Eckersley, R. (2004) *The Green State*. Cambridge, MA: MIT Press.

Ediger, V., and J. Bowlus (2018) 'A Farewell to King Coal: Geopolitics, Energy Security and the Transition to Oil 1989–1917'. *Historical Journal* 1–23.

Ehrlich, P. (1975) *The Population Bomb*. Minneapolis, MN: Rivercity Press.

EJOLT (2020) www.ejolt.org/.

ECT (Energy Charter Treaty) (1994) The Energy Charter Treaty 14 July 2014 https://docs.pca-cpa.org/2016/01/Energy-Charter-Treaty.pdf.

Erickson, P., M. Lazarus and G. Piggot (2018) 'Limiting Fossil Fuel Production as the Next Big Step in Climate Policy'. *Nature Climate Change* (8): 1037–43.

Erickson, P., H. van Asselt, D. Koplow, M. Lazarus, P. Newell, N. Oreskes and G. Supran (2020) 'Why Fossil Fuel Producer Subsidies Matter'. *Nature* 578 www.nature.com/articles/s41586-019-1920-x.

Ervine, K. (2018) *Carbon*. Cambridge: Polity.

European Commission (2015) 'Revised Emissions Trading System Will Help EU Deliver on Climate Goals'. 15 July. http://ec.europa.eu/clima/news/articles/news_2015071501_en.htm.

Evans, G. (2010) *A Just Transition to Sustainability in a Climate Change Hot-Spot: From Carbon Valley to a Future Beyond Coal*. Saarbrücken: VDM.

Falkner, R. (2014) 'Global Environmental Politics and Energy: Mapping the Research Agenda'. *Energy Research & Social Science* 1: 188–97.

(2018) 'Climate Change, International Political Economy and Global Energy Policy'. In A. Goldthau, M. F. Keating and C. Kuzemko (eds.) *Handbook of the International*

Political Economy of Energy and Natural Resources. Cheltenham: Edward Elgar, 77–91.

Farand, C. (2018) 'Polish Coal Company Announced as First Sponsor of UN Climate Talks in Katowice'. 27 November. www.desmogblog.com/2018/11/27/polish-coal-company-announced-first-sponsor-un-climate-talks-katowice.

Faure, M., and W. Hui (2003) 'The International Regimes for the Compensation of Oil Pollution Damage: Are They Effective?' *Review of European, Comparative & International Environmental Law* 12(3): 242.

Felli, R. (2015) 'Environment, Not Planning: The Neoliberal Depoliticisation of Environmental Policy by Means of Emissions Trading'. *Environmental Politics* 24 (5): 641–60.

Feola, G. (2019) 'Capitalism in Sustainability Transitions Research: Time for a Critical Turn?' *Environmental Innovation and Societal Transitions*. https://doi.org/10.1016/j.eist.2019.02.005.

Fine, B. (2017) 'The Material and Culture of Financialisation'. *New Political Economy* 22 (4): 371–82.

Fine, B., and Z. Rustomjee (1997) *The Political Economy of South Africa: From Minerals-Energy Complex to Industrialisation*. London: C. Hurst & Co.

Finley-Brook, M., and C. Thomas (2011) 'Renewable Energy and Human Rights Violations: Illustrative Cases from Indigenous Territories in Panama'. *Annals of the Association of American Geographers* 101(4): 863–72. doi: 10.1080/00045608.2011.568873.

Firestone, J., and H. Kirk (2019) 'A Strong Relative Preference for Wind Turbines in the United States among Those That Live Near Them'. *Nature Energy*. https://doi.org/10.1038/s41560-019-0347-9.

Flavelle, C. (2020) 'Global Financial Giants Swear Off Funding an Especially Dirty Fuel'. *New York Times*, 12 February. www.nytimes.com/2020/02/12/climate/blackrock-oil-sands-alberta-financing.html?smid=tw-nytclimate&smtyp=cur.

Florini, A., and B. K. Sovacool (2009) 'Who Governs Energy? The Challenges Facing Global Energy Governance'. *Energy Policy* 37: 5239–48.

(2011) 'Bridging the Gaps in Global Energy Governance'. *Global Governance* 17: 57–74.

Foster, J. B., and H. Holleman (2014) 'The Theory of Unequal Ecological Exchange: A Marx-Odum Dialectic'. *Journal of Peasant Studies* 41(2): 199–233.

Foster Report (2019) No. 3246, Week Ending 26 April.

Fouquet, R. (2010) 'The Slow Search for Solutions: Lessons from Historical Energy Transitions by Sector and Service'. *Energy Policy* 38(10): 6586–96.

(2016a) 'Historical Energy Transitions: Speed, Prices and System Transformation'. *Energy Research & Social Science* 22: 7–12.

(2016b) 'Lessons from Energy History for Climate Policy: Technological Change, Demand and Economic Development'. *Energy Research & Social Science* 22: 79–93.

Fouquet, R., and P. Pearson (2012) 'Past and Prospective Energy Transitions: Insights from History'. *Energy Policy* 50: 1–7.

Foxon, T. (2003) 'Inducing Innovation for a Low Carbon Future: Drivers, Barriers and Policies'. London: Carbon Trust.

Freese, B. (2006) *Coal: A Human History*. London: Arrow Books.

Friedman, M. (2009 [1962]) *Capitalism and Freedom, 40th anniversary ed.* Chicago: University of Chicago Press.

Furby, L., P. Slovic, B. Fischhoff and R. Gregory (1988) 'Public Perceptions of Electric Power Transmission Lines'. *Journal of Environmental Psychology* 8(1): 19–43.

Gale, F., and M. M'Gonigle (eds.) (2000) *Nature, Production and Power: Towards an Ecological Political Economy*. Cheltenham: Edward Elgar.

Galeano, E. (1997) *Open Veins of Latin America: Five Centuries of the Pillage of a Continent*, anniversary ed. New York: Monthly Review Press.

Gallagher, K. (ed.) (2005) *Putting Development First: The Importance of Policy Space in the WTO and International Financial Institutions*. London: Zed Books.

Gallagher, K. (2018) 'China's Global Energy Finance: Poised to Lead'. *Energy Research & Social Science* 35: 15–16.

Garvey, N., and P. Newell (2004) 'Corporate Accountability to the Poor? Assessing the Effectiveness of Community-Based Strategies'. *Development in Practice* 15(3–4): 389–404.

GCI (Global Commons Institute) (2018) http://gci.org.uk/.

GDR (2018) http://gdrights.org/.

Geddes, A., T. S. Schmidt and B. Steffen (2018) 'The Multiple Roles of State Investment Banks in Low-Carbon Energy Finance: An Analysis of Australia, the UK and Germany'. *Energy Policy* 115: 158–70.

Geels, F. W. (2002) 'Technological Transitions as Evolutionary Reconfiguration Processes: A Multi-level Perspective and Case Study'. *Research Policy* 31(8/9): 1257–74.

   (2005) *Technological Transitions and System Innovations: A Co-evolutionary and Socio-technical Analysis*. Cheltenham: Edward Elgar.

   (2010) 'Ontologies, Socio-technical Transitions (to Sustainability), and the Multi-level Perspective'. *Research Policy* 39(4): 495–510.

   (2014) 'Regime Resistance against Low-Carbon Transitions: Introducing Politics and Power into the Multi-level Perspectives'. *Theory, Culture & Society* 31(5): 21–40.

   (2018) 'Disruption and Low-Carbon System Transformation: Progress and New Challenges in Socio-technical Transitions Research and the Multi-Level Perspective'. *Energy Research & Social Science* 37: 224–31.

   (2019) 'Socio-technical Transitions to Sustainability: A Review of Criticisms and Elaborations of the Multi-Level Perspective'. *Current Opinion in Environmental Sustainability* 39: 187–201.

Geels, F. W., and J. Schot (2007) 'Typology of Sociotechnical Transition Pathways'. *Research Policy* 36: 399–417.

Georgescu-Roegen, N. (1971) *The Entropy Law and the Economic Process*. Cambridge, MA: Harvard University Press.

Gerasimchuk, I., and J. Roth (2018) 'The French Lesson on Climate Policy President Emmanuel Macron Is Showing that Failing to Engage with the Public Invited the Mass Protests across the Country'. US News, 7 December. www.usnews.com/news/best-countries/articles/2018-12-07/commentary-emmanuel-macrons-mistake-was-not-consulting-with-the-public.

Gereffi, G., J. Humphrey and T. Sturgeon (2005). 'The Governance of Global Value Chains'. *Review of International Political Economy* 12(1): 78–104.

GGON (2019) *Oil, Gas, and Climate: An Analysis of Oil and Gas Industry Plans for Expansion and Compatibility with Global Emissions Limits*. www.ciel.org/wp-content/uploads/2019/12/oilGasClimateDec2019.pdf.

Gifford, R. (2008) 'Psychology's Essential Role in Alleviating the Impacts of Climate Change'. *Canadian Psychology/Psychologie canadienne* 49(4): 273–80.

Gill, S. (ed.) (1993) *Gramsci, Historical Materialism and International Relations*. Cambridge: Cambridge University Press.

Gill, S. (1995) 'Globalization, Market Civilisation and Disciplinary Neoliberalism'. *Millennium: Journal of International Studies* 24(3): 399–423.

   (2008) *Power and Resistance in the New World Order*. Basingstoke: Palgrave.

GIZ (2019) 'Towards Decarbonising Transport 2018 – A Stocktake on Sectoral Ambition in the G20'. www.changing-transport.org/publication/towards-decarbonising-transport-2018.

Global Commission on the Economy and Climate (2018) *The New Growth Agenda*. https://newclimateeconomy.report/2018/wp-content/uploads/sites/6/2018/09/NCE_2018_NEW GROWTH-AGENDA.pdf.

Global Witness (2017) *Defenders of the Earth*. London: Global Witness.

(2019) *Overexposed: How the IPCC's 1.5°C Report Demonstrates the Risks of Overinvestment in Oil and Gas*. London: Global Witness.

(2020) *In Aid of Who? The Obscure Investment Fund Using UK Aid Money to Finance Climate Change around the World*. London: Global Witness.

Gockelen-Kozlowski, T. (2020) '"2020 Is a Turning Point": Top Corporates Urge Boris Johnson to Accelerate Climate Action'. *BusinessGreen*, 9 March. www.businessgreen.com/news/4012013/2020-point-corporates-urge-boris-johnson-accelerate-climate-action.

Goldthau, A. (2012) 'From the State to the Market and Back: Policy Implications of Changing Energy Paradigms'. *Global Policy* 2(2): 198–210.

Goldthau, A., and N. Sitter (2015) *A Liberal Actor in a Realist World. The European Regulatory State and the Global Political Economy of Energy*. Oxford: Oxford University Press.

Goldthau, A., and J. M. Witte (2009) 'Back to the Future or Forward to the Past? Strengthening Markets and Rules for Effective Global Energy Governance'. *International Affairs* 85(2): 373–90.

Goldthau, A., and J. M. Witte (eds.) (2010) *Global Energy Governance: The New Rules of the Game*. Washington, DC: Brookings Press.

Goldthau, A., M. F. Keating and C. Kuzemko (eds.) (2018) *Handbook of the International Political Economy of Energy and Natural Resources*. Cheltenham: Edward Elgar.

Goldthau, A., K. Westphal, M. Bazilian and M. Bradshaw (2019) 'How the Energy Transition Will Reshape Geopolitics'. *Nature* 569: 29–31.

Gore, C. (2017) *Electricity in Africa: The Politics of Transformation in Uganda*. London: James Currey.

Goron, C. (2017) 'Climate Revolution or Long March? The Politics of Low Carbon Transformation in China (1992–2015)'. PhD Thesis, University of Warwick.

Gramsci, A. (1971) *Selections from the Prison Notebooks*, edited and translated by Q. Hoare and G. Nowell Smith. New York: International Publishers.

Grant, W., D. Matthews and P. Newell (2000) *The Effectiveness of EU Environmental Policy*. Basingstoke: MacMillan.

Green, F. (2018) 'Anti-fossil Fuel Norms'. *Climatic Change* 150: 103–16.

Green, F., and R. Dennis (2018) 'Cutting with Both Arms of the Scissors: The Economic and Political Case for Restrictive Supply-Side Climate Policies'. *Climatic Change* 150: 73–87.

Green New Deal Group (2008) *A Green New Deal*. London: Green New Deal Group.

Greenpeace (2019) *How Government Should Address the Climate Emergency*. London: Greenpeace.

Grubler, A. (2012) 'Energy Transitions Research: Insights and Cautionary Tales'. *Energy Policy* 50: 8–16.

Grubler, A., C. Wilson and G. Nemet (2016) 'Apples, Oranges and Consistent Comparisons of the Temporal Dynamics of Energy Transitions'. *Energy Research & Social Science* 22: 18–25.

Haas, T. (2019). 'Struggles in European Union Energy Politics: A Gramscian Perspective on Power in Energy Transitions'. *Energy Research & Social Science* 48: 66–74.

Haigh, M. S., J. Hranaiova and J. A. Overdahl (2007) 'Hedge Funds, Volatility, and Liquidity Provision in Energy Futures Markets'. *Journal of Alternative Investments* 9(4): 10–38.

Hall, T. (1986) *Nuclear Politics: The History of Nuclear Power in Britain*. London: Penguin.

Hall, P., and D. Soskice (2001) *Varieties of Capitalism: The Institutional Foundations of Comparative Advantage*. Oxford: Oxford University Press .

Hamilton, K. (2009) *Unlocking Finance for Clean Energy: The Need for 'Investment Grade' Policy*. Energy, Environment and Development Programme Paper 09/04, December. London: Chatham House.

Hammarlund, J. (1976) 'The International Implications'. In J. Hammarlund and L. Lindberg (eds.) The Political Economy of Energy Policy: A Projection for Capitalist Society. IES Report 70. University of Wisconsin-Madison: Institute for Environmental Studies, 154–98.

Hammarlund, J. R. and L. L. Lindberg (eds.) (1976) *The Political Economy of Energy Policy: A Projection for Capitalist Society*. IES Report 70. University of Wisconsin-Madison: Institute for Environmental Studies.

Harks, E. (2010) 'The International Energy Forum and the Mitigation of Oil Market Risks'. In A. Goldthau and J. M. Witte (eds.) *Global Energy Governance: The New Rules of the Game*. Washington, DC: Brookings Press, 247–67.

Harnesk, D., and S. Brogaard (2017) 'Social Dynamics of Renewable Energy: How the EU's Renewable Energy Directive Triggers Land Pressure in Tanzania'. *Journal of Environment and Development* 26(2): 156–85.

Harrison, G. (2004) *The World Bank and Africa: The Construction of Governance States*. London: Routledge.

Harvey, D. (1981) The Spatial Fix: Hegel, von Thünen and Marx. *Antipode* 13(3): 1–12.

(2003). *The New Imperialism*. Oxford: Oxford University Press.

(2005) *A Brief History of Neoliberalism*. Oxford: Oxford University Press.

Hasanov, M., and C. Zuidema (2018) 'The Transformative Power of Self-Organization: Towards a Conceptual Framework for Understanding Local Energy Initiatives in The Netherlands'. *Energy Research & Social Science* 37: 85–93.

Haynes, P. (2009) 'Al-Queda, Oil Dependence and US Foreign Policy'. In D. Moran and J. Russell (eds.) *Energy Security and Global Politics: The Militarization of Resource Management*. Abingdon: Routledge, 62–74.

Healy, N., J. C. Stephens and S. A. Malin (2019). 'Embodied Energy Injustices: Unveiling and Politicizing the Transboundary Harms of Fossil Fuel Extractivism and Fossil Fuel Supply Chains'. *Energy Research & Social Science* 48: 219–34.

Heaton, H. (1937) 'Financing the Industrial Revolution'. *Business History Review* 11 (1): 1–10.

Hedegaard, C. (2011) 'European Commissioner for Climate Action Climate Protection Is Not Deindustrialisation, but Reindustrialisation: Doing Things Smarter and More Efficiently!'. European Commission. https://ec.europa.eu/commission/presscorner/detail/en/SPEECH_11_780.

Heede, R. (2014). 'Tracing Anthropogenic Carbon Dioxide and Methane Emissions to Fossil Fuel and Cement Producers, 1854–2010'. *Climatic Change* 122(1–2): 229–41.

Heglar, M. (2019) 'I Work in the Environmental Movement. I Don't Care if You Recycle. Stop Obsessing over Your Environmental "Sins". Fight the Oil and Gas Industry Instead'. 4 June. www.vox.com/the-highlight/2019/5/28/18629833/climate-change -2019-green-new-deal.

Helleiner, E. (1994) 'From Bretton Woods to Global Finance: A World Turned Upside Down'. In G. Underhill and R. Stubbs (eds.) *Political Economy and the Changing Global Order*. Basingstojke: MacMillan, 163–75.

Helm, D. (2017) *Burn Out: The Endgame for Fossil Fuels*. New Haven, CT: Yale University Press.

Hess, D. J. (2018) 'Sustainability Transitions: A Political Coalition Perspective'. *Research Policy* 43: 278–83.

Hess, D. J., and M. Renner (2019) 'Conservative Political Parties and Energy Transitions in Europe: Opposition to Climate Mitigation Policies'. *Renewable and Sustainable Energy Reviews* 104: 419–28.

Heubaum, H., and F. Biermann (2015) 'Integrating Global Energy and Climate Governance: The Changing Role of the International Energy Agency'. *Energy Policy* 87: 229–39.

Hildyard, N. (2019) *Licencia para Saquear: Infraestructura y extracción financiera en el Sur Global*. Buenos Aires: Oilwatch Latinoamérica.

Hill, F. (2004) *Energy Empire: Oil, Gas and Russia's Revival*. London: FPC.

Hill, T., and J. Murray (2019) 'Coal Addicts: G20 Governments Have Doubled Support for Coal Power Plants, Report Finds'. www.businessgreen.com/bg/news/3077857/coal-addicts-g20-governments-have-doubled-support-for-coal-power-plants-report-finds.

Hillier, D. (2018). 'Facing Risk: Options and Challenges in Ensuring that Climate/Disaster Risk Finance and Insurance Deliver for Poor People' (Oxfam Briefing Paper). https://oxfamilibrary.openrepository.com/handle/10546/620457.

HM Government (2008) *Building a Low Carbon Economy: Unlocking Innovation and Skills*. London: DEFRA.

Hochstetler, K. (2021) *Political Economies of Energy Transition: Wind and Solar in Brazil and South Africa*. Cambridge: Cambridge University Press.

Hochstetler, K., and G. Kostka (2015) 'Wind and Solar Power in Brazil and China: Interests, State–Business Relations, and Policy Outcomes'. *Global Environmental Politics* 15 (3): 74–94.

Hoffmann, C. (2018) 'Beyond the Resource Curse and Pipeline Conspiracies: Energy as a Social Relation in the Middle East'. *Energy Research & Social Science* 41: 39–47.

Hoffmann, M. (2011) *Climate Governance at the Crossroads: Experimenting with a Global Response After Kyoto*. Oxford: Oxford University Press.

Holloway, J., and S. Picciotto (eds.) (1978) *State and Capital: A Marxist Debate*. London: Edward Arnold.

Hopf, T. (2018) 'Change in International Practices'. *European Journal of International Relations* 24(3): 19–20.

Hopkins, R. (2019) *From What Is to What If? Unleashing the Power of Imagination to Create the Future We Want*. London: Chelsea Green.

Hornborg, A. (1998) 'Towards an Ecological Theory of Unequal Exchange: Articulating World System Theory and Ecological Economics'. *Ecological Economics* 25(1): 127–36.

(2013) 'The Fossil Interlude: Euro-American Power and the Return of the Physiocrats'. In S. Strauss, S. Rupp and T. Love (eds.) *Cultures of Energy: Power, Practices, Technologies*. Walnut Creek, CA: Left Coast Press, 41–60.

Howe, C. (2015) 'Latin America in the Anthropocene: Energy Transitions and Climate Change Mitigations'. *Journal of Latin American and Caribbean Anthropology* 20(2): 231–41.

Huber, M. (2008) 'Energizing Historical Materialism: Fossil Fuels, Space and the Capitalist Mode of Production'. *Geoforum* 40: 105–15.

(2013) *Lifeblood: Oil, Freedom and the Forces of Capital*. Minnesota: University of Minnesota Press.

Hudson, M. (2018) Enacted Inertia: Incumbent Resistance to Carbon Pricing in Australia 1989–2011, PhD Thesis, University of Manchester.

Hudson, R., and D. Sadler (1987) National Policies and Local Economic Initiatives: Evaluating the Effectiveness of UK Coal and Steel Closure Area Re-industrialisation Measures. *Local Economy* 2(2): 107–14.

Hume, N. (2020) 'Glencore Chief Dismisses BP's Net Zero Goals'. *Financial Times*, 19 February, 14.

Hume, N., D. Sheppard and H. Sanderson (2019) 'Glencore Vows to Cap Global Coal Production: Trading and Mining Group Has Faced Investor Pressure over Polluting Fossil Fuel'. *Financial Times*, 20 February. https://on.ft.com/2DTXRQs.

ICAP (2019). *Emissions Trading Worldwide: Status Report 2019*. Berlin: ICAP.

ICLEI (2019) 'New York City Moves to Divest Pension Funds from Billions of Dollars in Fossil Fuel Reserves'. http://icleiusa.org/nyc-divestment/.

ICTSD (2011). 'China to End Challenged Subsidies in Wind Power Case'. *Bridges Trade BioRes* 11(11, June): 13.

IEA (2018) 'Global Energy Demand Grew by 2.1% in 2017, and Carbon Emissions Rose for the First Time since 2014'. www.iea.org/newsroom/news/2018/march/global-energy-demand-grew-by-21-in-2017-and-carbon-emissions-rose-for-the-firs.html.

(2019) *World Energy Outlook*. Paris: IEA.

(2019a) *World Energy Investment*. Paris: IEA.

(2020a) *The Oil and Gas Industry in Energy Transitions*. World Energy Outlook Special Report Fuel Report – January.

(2020b) 'Building a "Grand Coalition" to Bridge the Gap between Energy and Climate Goals'. Press Release, 12 February. www.iea.org/news/building-a-grand-coalition-to-bridge-the-gap-between-energy-and-climate-goals.

IEA, IRENA, UNSD, World Bank, WHO. (2020) *Tracking SDG 7: The Energy Progress Report*. Washington, DC: World Bank.

Ikenberry, G. J. (1986) 'The Irony of State Strength: Comparative Responses to the Oil Shocks in the 1970s'. *International Organization* 40(1): 105–37.

IMF (International Monetary Fund) (2015) *IMF Survey: Counting the Cost of Energy Subsidies*. www.imf.org/external/pubs/ft/survey/so/2015/NEW070215A.htm.

Inikori, J. (1987) 'Slavery and the Development of Industrial Capitalism in England'. *Journal of Interdisciplinary History* 17(4): 771–93.

IPCC (2018) *Global Warming of 1.5°C: An IPCC Special Report on the Impacts of Global Warming of 1.5°C above Pre-industrial Levels and Related Global Greenhouse Gas Emission Pathways*. IPCC.

IRENA (2017) *Rethinking Energy 2017: Accelerating the Global Energy Transformation*. Abu Dhabi: International Renewable Energy Agency.

(2019) *A New World: The Geopolitics of the Energy Transformation*. Abu Dhabi: IRENA.

Isakson, S. (2015) 'Derivatives for Development? Small-Farmer Vulnerability and the Financialization of Climate Risk Management'. *Journal of Agrarian Change* 15(4): 569–80.

Jacobson, M., and M. Delucchi (2009) 'A Pathway to Sustainable Energy by 2030'. *Scientific American* November: 58–65.

Jagers, S., M. Paterson and J. Stripple (2005) 'Privatising Governance, Practicing Triage: Securitization of Insurance Risks and the Politics of Global Warming'. In D. Levy and P. Newell (eds.) *The Business of Global Environmental Governance*. Cambridge, MA: MIT Press.

Janssen, M., and J. Rotmans (1995) 'Allocation of Fossil CO2 Emission Rights: Quantifying Cultural Perspectives'. *Ecological Economics* 13: 65–79.

Jarbandhan, V. D. B., N. Komendantova, R. Xavier and E. Nkoana (2018) 'Transformation of the South African Energy System: Towards Participatory Governance'. In P. Mensah, D. Katerere, S. Hachigonta and A. Roodt (eds.) *Systems Analysis Approach for Complex Global Challenges*. Cham: Springer.

Jarzabkowski, P., K. Chalkias, D. Clarke, E. Iyahen, D. Stadtmueller and A. Zwick (2019) *Insurance for Climate Adaptation: Opportunities and Limitations*. Rotterdam; Washington, DC: Global Commission on Adaptation. www.gca.org.

Jasanoff, S. (2018) 'Just Transitions: A Humble Approach to Global Energy Futures'. *Energy Research & Social Science* 35: 11–14.

Jessop, B. (2002) *The Future of the Capitalist State*. Cambridge: Polity.

 (2010) 'Cultural Political Economy and Critical Policy Studies'. *Critical Policy Studies* 3 (3–4): 336–56.

Jevons, W. S. (1906) *The Coal Question*, 3rd ed. London: Macmillan.

Jewell, J., D. McCollum, J. Emmerling, C. Bertram, D. Gernaat, V. Krey, L. Paroussos, L. Berger, K. Fragkiadakis, I. Keppo, N. Saadi Failali, M. Tavoni, D. Vuuren, V. Vinichenko and K. Riahi (2018) 'Limited Emission Reductions from Fuel Subsidy Removal except in Energy-Exporting Regions'. *Nature* 554: 229–33. 10.1038/nature25467.

Jewell, J., V. Vinichenko, L. Nacke and A. Cherp (2019) 'Prospects for Powering Past Coal'. *Nature Climate Change* 9: 592–7.

Johns, H. (2015) *Energy Revolution; Your Guide to Repowering the Energy System*. East Meon: Permanent Publications.

Johnstone, P., and S. Hielscher (2017) 'Phasing Out Coal, Sustaining Coal Communities? Living with Technological Decline in Sustainability Pathways'. *Extractive Industries and Society* 4: 457–61.

Johnstone, P., and P. Kivimaa (2018) 'Multiple Dimensions of Disruption, Energy Transitions and Industrial Policy'. *Energy Research & Social Science* 37: 260–5.

Johnstone, P., and C. McLeish (2020) 'The Role of War in Deep Transitions: Exploring Mechanisms, Imprints and Rules in Sociotechnical Systems'. SPRU Working Paper Series (SWPS), 2020–04.

Johnstone, P., and P. Newell (2018) 'Sustainability Transitions and the State'. *Environmental Innovation and Societal Transitions* 27: 72–82.

Johnstone, P., and A. Stirling (2020) 'Comparing Nuclear Trajectories in Germany and the United Kingdom: From Regimes to Democracies in Sociotechnical Transitions and Discontinuities'. *Energy Research & Social Science* 59: 101245.

JTA (Just Transition Alliance) (2011) 'About the Just Transition Alliance'. www.jtalliance.org/docs/aboutjta.html.

Jungk, R. (1979) *The Nuclear State*. London: John Calder Publications.

Kaldor, M., L. T. Karl and Y. Said (eds.) (2007) *Oil Wars*. London: Pluto Press.

Kanger, L., and J. Schot (2018) 'Deep Transitions: Theorizing the Long-Term Patterns of Socio-technical Change'. *Environmental Innovation and Societal Transition*. https://doi.org/10.1016/j.eist.2018.07.006.

Karlsson-Vinkhuyzen, S. (2010) 'The UN and Global Energy Governance: Past Challenges, Future Choices'. *Global Change, Peace and Security* 22(2) June: 175–95.

Kartha, S., S. Caney, N. Dubash and G. Muttitt (2018) 'Whose Carbon Is Burnable? Equity Considerations in the Allocation of a "Right to Extract"'. *Climatic Change* 1–13. 150. 10.1007/s10584-018-2209-z.

Kasser, T. (2016) 'Materialistic Values and Goals'. *Annual Review of Psychology* 67: 489–514.

Kassler, P., and M. Paterson (1997) *Energy Exporters and Climate Change*. London: RIIA.

Katz-Rosene, R., and M. Paterson (2018) *Thinking Ecologically about the Global Political Economy*. Abingdon: Routledge.

Keary, M. (2016), 'The New Prometheans: Technological Optimism in Climate Change Mitigation Modelling'. *Environmental Values* 25: 7–28.

Kelly, P. (1994) *Thinking Green! Essays on Environmentalism, Feminism and Non-violence*. Berkeley, CA: Parallax Press.

Kelsey, N., and J. Meckling (2018) 'Who Wins in Renewable Energy? Evidence from Europe and the United States'. *Energy Research & Social Science* 37: 65–73.

Kenner, D. (2019) *Carbon Inequality: The Role of the Richest in Climate Change*. Abingdon: Routledge.

Kern, F. (2011) 'Ideas, Institutions and Interests: Explaining Policy Divergence in Fostering 'System Innovations' towards Sustainability'. *Environment and Planning C: Government and Policy* 29(6): 1116–34.

Kern, F., and J. Markard (2016) 'Analysing Energy Transitions: Combining Insights from Transitions Studies and International Political Economy'. In T. Van de Graaf, B. K. Sovacool, A. Ghosh, F. Kern and M. T. Klare (eds.) *The Palgrave Handbook of the International Political Economy of Energy*. Basingstoke: Palgrave, 391–429.

Kern, F., and K. Rogge (2016) 'The Pace of Governed Energy Transitions: Agency, International Dynamics and the Global Paris Agreement Accelerating Decarbonisation Processes?'. *Energy Research & Social Science* 22: 13–17.

(2018) 'Harnessing Theories of the Policy Process for Analysing the Politics of Sustainability Transitions: A Critical Survey'. *Environmental Innovation and Societal Transitions* 27: 102–17.

Kirk, K. (2020) 'Fossil Fuel Political Giving Outdistances Renewables 13 to One'. *Yale Climate Connections*. www.yaleclimateconnections.org/2020/01/fossil-fuel-political -giving-outdistances-renewables-13-to-one/.

King, D., M. Rees, J. Browne, R. Layard, G. O'Donnell, N. Stern and A. Turner (2015) *A Global Apollo Programme to Combat Climate Change*. www.cser.ac.uk/media/ uploads/files/Global_Apollo_Programme_Report.pdf.

Kirshner, J., and M. Power (2015) 'Mining and Extractive Urbanism: Post-Development in a Mozambican Boomtown'. *Geoforum* 61: 67–78.

Kivimaa, P., S. Laakso, A. Lonkila and M. Kaljonen (2021) 'Moving beyond Disruptive Innovation: A Review of Disruption in Sustainability Transitions'. *Environmental Innovation and Societal Transitions* 38: 110–26.

Klare, M. (2009) 'Petroleum Anxiety and the Militarization of Energy Security'. In D. Moran and J. Russell (eds.) *Energy Security and Global Politics: The Militarization of Resource Management*. Abingdon: Routledge, 39–62.

Klein, N. (2007) *The Shock Doctrine*. London: Penguin.

(2019) *On Fire: The (Burning) Case for a Green New Deal*. New York: Simon & Schuster.

Knaus, C. (2020) 'Fossil-Fuel Industry Doubles Donations to Major Parties in Four Years, Report Shows'. *The Guardian*, 12 February. www.theguardian.com/environment/2020/ feb/12/fossil-fuel-industry-doubles-donations-to-major-parties-in-four-years-report-shows?CMP=share_btn_link.

Knuth, S. (2018) '"Breakthroughs" for a Green Economy? Financialization and Clean Energy Transition'. *Energy Research & Social Science* 41: 220–9.

Koch, M. (2012) *Capitalism and Climate Change: Theoretical Discussion, Historical Development and Policy Responses*. Basingstoke: Palgrave.

Köhler, J., F. Geels, F. Kern, J. Markard, A. Wieczorek, F. Alkemade, F. Avelino, A. Bergek, F. Boons, L. Fuenfschilling, D. Hess, G. Holtz, H. Sampsa, K. Jenkins, P. Kivimaa, M. Martiskainen, A. McMeekin, S. Mühlemeier, B. Nykvist and P. Wells (2019) 'An

Agenda for Sustainability Transitions Research: State of the art and Future Directions'. *Environmental Innovation and Societal Transitions* 31: 1–32. 10.1016/j.eist.2019.01.004.

Kolk, A., and J. Pinkse (2005) 'Business Responses to Climate Change: Identifying Emergent Strategies'. *California Management Review* 47(3): 6–20.

Konoplyanik, A., and T. Wälde (2006) 'Energy Charter Treaty and Its Role in International Energy'. *Journal of Energy and Resources Law* 24(4): 523–59.

Koplow, D. (2014). 'Global Energy Subsidies: Scale, Opportunity Costs, and Barriers to Reform'. In A. Halff, B. K. Sovacool and J. Rozhon (eds.) *Energy Poverty Global Challenges and Local Solutions*. Oxford: Oxford University Press, 316–37.

Kotch, A. (2020) 'Members of Congress Own Up to $93 Million in Fossil Fuel Stocks'. *Sludge*. https://readsludge.com/2020/01/03/members-of-congress-own-up-to-93-million-in-fossil-fuel-stocks/.

Krabbe, O., G. Linthorst, K. Blok, W. Crijns-Graus, D. van Vuuren, N. Höhne, P. Faria, N. Aden and A. Pineda (2015) 'Aligning Corporate Greenhouse-Gas Emissions Targets with Climate Goals'. *Nature Climate Change* 5(12): 1057–60.

Kumar, A. (2015) 'Cultures of Lights'. *Geoforum* 65: 59–68. 10.1016/j.geoforum.2015.07.012.

Kungl, G. (2015) 'Stewards or Sticklers for Change? Incumbent Energy Providers and the Politics of the German Energy Transition'. *Energy Research & Social Science* 8: 13–23.

Kuzemko, C. (2013) *The Energy Security-Climate Nexus: Institutional Change in the UK and Beyond*. Basingstoke: Palgrave.

Kuzemko, C., M. Keating and A. Goldthau (2015) *The Global Energy Challenge: Environment, Development and Security*. Basingstoke: Palgrave.

Kuzemko, C., M. Lockwood, C. Mitchell and R. Hoggett (2016) 'Governing for Sustainable Energy System Change: Politics, Contexts and Contingency'. *Energy Research & Social Science* 12: 96–105.

Kuzemko, C., M. Keating and A. Goldthau (2018) 'Nexus Thinking in International Political Economy: What Energy and Natural Resource Scholarship Can Offer International Political Economy'. In A. Goldthau, M. F. Keating and C. Kuzemko (eds.) *Handbook of the International Political Economy of Energy and Natural Resources* Cheltenham: Edward Elgar, 1–19.

Kuzemko, C., A. Lawrence and M. Watson (2019) 'New Directions in the International Political Economy of Energy'. *Review of International Political Economy* 26(1): 1–24.

Labban, M. (2008) *Space, Oil and Capital*. London: Routledge.

Lachapelle, E., and M. Paterson (2013) 'Drivers of National Climate Policy'. *Climate Policy* 13(5): 547–71.

Lachapelle, E., R. MacNeil and M. Paterson (2017) 'The Political Economy of Decarbonisation: From Green Energy 'Race' to Green 'Division of Labour''. *New Political Economy* 22(3): 311–27.

Lakhani, N. (2020) 'Major Blow to Keystone XL Pipeline as Judge Revokes Key Permit'. *The Guardian*, 16 April. www.theguardian.com/environment/2020/apr/15/keystone-xl-pipeline-montana-judge-environment.

Lamb, N., and D. Fugere (2014) 'Exxon Mobil's Commitment to Carbon Asset Risk Is Just the Beginning'. *The Guardian*, 24 March. www.theguardian.com/sustainable-business/exxon-mobil-carbon-asset-risk-pressure-oil-gas-investors.

Lane, R. (2015) The Nature of Growth: The Postwar History of the Economy, Energy and the Environment. PhD Thesis, University of Sussex.

Langford, E. (2020) 'Government Set to Reverse Cameron-Era Ban on Onshore Wind Farm Subsidies'. *Politics Home*, 2 March. www.politicshome.com/news/uk/environment/news/110288/government-set-reverse-cameron-era-ban-onshore-wind-farm-subsidies.

Larsson, J., A. Elofsson, T. Sterner and J. Åkerman (2019) 'International and National Climate Policies for Aviation: A Review'. *Climate Policy* 19(6): 787–99.

Lawhon, M., and J. T. Murphy (2012) 'Socio-technical Regimes and Sustainability Transitions: Insights from Political Ecology'. *Progress in Human Geography* 36(3): 354–78.

Lazarus, M., P. Erickson and K. Tempest (2015). 'Supply-Side Climate Policy: The Roaid Less Taken'. SEI Working Paper No. 2015–13.

Leach, M. (2010) *The Pathways Approach of the STEPS Centre*. STEPS Briefing. Brighton: IDS.

Leach, M., and I. Scoones (eds.) (2015) *Carbon Conflicts and Forest Landscapes in Africa*. Abingdon: Routledge.

Leal-Arcas, R. (2018) 'Unconventional Sources of Fossil Fuel in the European Union and China: Perspectives on Trade, Climate Change and Energy Security'. In P. Hefele, M. Palocz-Andresen, M. Rech and J.-H. Kohler (eds.) *Climate and Energy Protection in the EU and China*. Cham: Springer Verlag, 129–42.

Le Billon, P. (2007) 'Geographies of War: Perspectives on "Resource Wars"'. *Geography Compass* 1(2): 163–82.

Leggett, J. (2014) *The Energy of Nations*. London: Routledge/Earthscan.

Lehtonen, M., and F. Kern (2009) 'Deliberative Socio-technical Transitions'. In I. Scarse and G. MacKerron (eds.) *Energy for the Future: A New Agenda*. Basingstoke: Palgrave, 103–23.

Leipprand, A., and C. Flachsland (2018) 'Regime Destabilization in Energy Transitions: The German Debate on the Future of Coal'. *Energy Research & Social Science* 40: 190–204.

Lenferna, G. (2018) 'Can We Equitably Manage the End of the Fossil Fuel Era?'. *Energy Research & Social Science* 35: 217–23.

Lennon, M. (2017) 'Decolonizing Energy: Black Lives Matter and Technoscientific Expertise amid Solar Transitions'. *Energy Research & Social Science* 30: 18–27.

Lesage, D., T. Van de Graaf and K. Westphal (2009) 'The G8's Role in Global Energy Governance Since the 2005 Gleneagles Summit'. *Global Governance* 15(2): 259–77.

(2010) *Global Energy Governance in a Multipolar World*. Aldershot: Ashgate.

Lettenmeier, M., L. Akenji, V. Toivio, R. Koide and A. Amellina (2019) *1.5-degree Lifestyles: Targets and Options for Reducing Lifestyle Carbon Footprints*. Helsinki: Erweco.

Levi-Faur, D. (2005). 'The Global Diffusion of Regulatory Capitalism'. *Annals of the American Academy of Political and Social Science* 598: 12–32.

Levy, D., and P. Newell (2002) 'Business Strategy and International Environmental Governance: Toward a Neo-Gramscian Synthesis'. *Global Environmental Politics* 2 (4): 84–101.

Levy, D., and P. Newell (eds.) (2005) *The Business of Global Environmental Governance*. Cambridge, MA: MIT Press.

Lewis, J. (2014) 'The Rise of Renewable Energy Protectionism: Emerging Trade Conflicts and Implications for Low Carbon Development'. *Global Environmental Politics* 14 (4): 10–35.

LINGO (2018) http://leave-it-in-the-ground.org/exploration-moratorium/.

Lipow, G. (2014) 'Zombie Carbon Trading's Latest Resurrection'. http://grist.org/article/zombie-carbon-tradings-latest-resurrection/.

Lockwood, M. (2015). 'Fossil Fuel Subsidy Reform, Rent Management and Political Fragmentation in Developing Countries'. *New Political Economy* 20(4): 475–94.

Lockwood, M., C. Kuzemko, C. Mitchell and R. Hoggett (2016) 'Historical Institutionalism and the Politics of Sustainable Energy Transitions: A Research Agenda'. *Environment and Planning C: Government Policy* 35(2): 312–33.

Lofoten Declaration (2017) www.lofotendeclaration.org/.

Lohmann, L. (2006) *Carbon Trading: A Critical Conversation on Climate Change, Privatisation and Power*. Dorset: The Corner House.

Lohmann, L., and N. Hildyard (2014) *Energy, Work and Finance*. Dorset: The Corner House.

Longmate, N. (1971) *How We Lived Then*. London: Hutchinson.

Loorbach, D. (2007) *Transition Management: New Mode of Governance for Sustainable Development*. Utrecht: International Books.

Loorbach, D., N. Frantzeskaki and R. Lijnis Huffenreuter (2015) 'Transition Management: Taking Stock from Governance Experimentation'. *Journal of Corporate Citizenship* 2015(58): 48–66.

Lotka, A. J. (1922) 'Contribution to the Energetics of Evolution'. *Proceedings of the National Academy of Science* 8: 147–55.

Lovell, H., and D. MacKenzie (2011) 'Accounting for Carbon: The Role of Accounting Professional Organisations in Governing Climate Change'. *Antipode* 43(3): 704–30.

Lovins, A. (1977) *Soft Energy Paths*. Cambridge, MA: Harpers Business.

Lund, C., and W. Biswas (2008) 'A Review of the Application of Lifecycle Analysis to Renewable Energy Systems'. *Bulletin of Science, Technology & Society* 28(3): 200–9.

Macalister, T. (2016) 'More than Half of Jobs In UK Solar Industry Lost in Wake of Subsidy Cuts'. *The Guardian*, 11 June. www.theguardian.com/environment/2016/jun/10/uk-solar-power-industry-job-losses-government-subsidy-cuts-energy-policy.

Mackay, M. (2020) 'Greenpeace Prepared for Court Battle over Rig Occupation'. *The Press and Journal*, 24 February. www.pressandjournal.co.uk/fp/news/aberdeen/2036331/greenpeace-prepared-for-court-battle-over-rig-occupation/.

MacKenzie, D., D. Beunza, Y. Millo and J. P. Pardo-Guerra (2012) 'Drilling through the Allegheny Mountains: Liquidity, Materiality and High-Frequency Trading'. *Journal of Cultural Economy* 5(3): 279–96.

Malm, A. (2016) *Fossil Capital: The Rise of Steam Power and the Roots of Global Warming*. London: Verso.

Mann, G., and J. Wainwright (2018) *Climate Leviathan: A Political Theory of Our Planetary Future*. London: Verso.

Mardani A., D. Streimikiene, F. Cavallaro, N. Loganathan and M. Khoshnoudi (2019) 'Carbon Dioxide (CO2) Emissions and Economic Growth: A Systematic Review of Two Decades of Research from 1995 to 2017'. *Science of the Total Environment* 649 (February): 31–49.

Markard, J., R. Raven and B. Truffer (2012) 'Sustainability Transitions: An Emerging Field of Research and Its Prospects'. *Research Policy* 41(6): 955–67.

Markkanen, S., and A. Anger-Kraavi (2019) 'Social Impacts of Climate Change Mitigation Policies and Their Implications for Inequality'. *Climate Policy*. 10.1080/14693062.2019.1596873.

Markova, A. (2018) *A False Promise of Prosperity: An Analysis of UK Prosperity Fund Support to the Oil And Gas Industry*. London: Platform.

Marx, K. (1974) *Capital*. London: Lawrence and Wishart.

   (1981) *Capital, vol. III*. New York: Vintage.

Mason, A. (2013) 'Cartel Consciousness and Horizontal Integration in Energy Industry'. In S. Strauss, S. Rupp and T. Love (eds.) *Cultures of Energy: Power, Practices, Technologies*. Walnut Creek, CA: Left Coast Press, 126–39.

Mason, S. (2019) 'UK Trade Unions and Climate Change: Can They Ever Be at the Vanguard for a Green and Fair Future?'. Seminar Sussex University, 5 February, Policy Officer at the Public and Commercial Services (PCS) Trade Union.

Mathiesen, K. (2019) 'Coal Phase-Out Will Increase German Need for Gas, Says Merkel'. 23 January. www.climatechangenews.com/2019/01/23/coal-phase-will-increase-german-need-gas-says-merkel/.

Mazzucato, M. (2011) *The Entrepreneurial State*. London: Demos.

Mazzucato, M., and G. Semieniuk (2018) 'Financing Renewable Energy: Who Is Financing What and Why It Matters'. *Technological Forecasting and Social Change* 127: 8–22.

McCarthy, N. (2019) 'Oil and Gas Giants Spend Millions Lobbying to Block Climate Change Policies'. *Forbes*, 25 March. www.forbes.com/sites/niallmccarthy/2019/03/25/oil-and-gas-giants-spend-millions-lobbying-to-block-climate-change-policies-infographic/?sh=4af361637c4f.

McCully, P. (1996) *Silenced Rivers: The Ecology and Politics of Large Dams*. London: Zed Books.

McDonald, D. (2009) *Electric Capitalism: Recolonising Africa on the Power Grid*. London: Earthscan.

(2013) 'Discourses of Climate Security'. *Political Geography* 33: 43–51.

McGlade, C., and P. Ekins, (2015) 'The Geographical Distribution of Fossil Fuels Unused When Limiting Global Warming to 2°C'. *Nature* 517(7533): 187–90.

McKibben, B. (2012) 'Global Warming's Terrifying New Math'. *Rolling Stone*, 19 July. www.rollingstone.com/politics/news/global-warmings-terrifying-new-math-20120719.

(2018) 'At Last, Divestment Is Hitting the Fossil Fuel Industry Where It Hurts'. *The Guardian*, 16 September. www.theguardian.com/commentisfree/2018/dec/16/divestment-fossil-fuel-industry-trillions-dollars-investments-carbon.

McKinsey (2008) Quarterly Report, October.

McLoughlin, N., A. Corner, J. Clarke, L. Whitmarsh, S. Capstick and N. Nash (2019) *Mainstreaming Low Carbon Lifestyles*. Oxford: Climate Outreach.

Meckling, J. (2011) *Carbon Coalitions: Business, Climate Politics, and the Rise of Emissions Trading*. Cambridge, MA: MIT Press.

Meckling, J., N. Kelsey, E. Biber and J. Zysman (2015) 'Winning Coalitions for Climate Policy'. *Science* 349(6253): 1170–1.

Meadowcroft, J. (2005) 'Environmental Political Economy, Technological Transitions and the State'. *New Political Economy* 10(4): 479–98.

(2009) 'What about the Politics? Sustainable Development, Transition Management, and Long Term Energy Transitions'. *Policy Sciences* 42: 323–40.

Mercure, J.-F., F. Knobloch, H. Pollitt, L. Paroussos, S. Scrieciu and R. Lewney (2019) 'Modelling Innovation and the Macroeconomics of Low-Carbon Transitions: Theory, Perspectives and Practical Use'. *Climate Policy*. 10.1080/14693062.2019.1617665.

Metze, T., and J. Dodge (2016) 'Dynamic Discourse Coalitions on Hydro-fracking in Europe and the United States'. *Environmental Communication* 10(3): 365–79.

Mey, F., and M. Diesendorf (2018) 'Who Owns an Energy Transition? Strategic Action Fields and Community Wind Energy in Denmark'. *Energy Research & Social Science* 35: 108–17.

Midttun, A., and T. Baumgartner (1986) 'Negotiating Energy Futures: The Politics of Energy Forecasting'. *Energy Policy* 14(3): 219–41.

Mikler, J., and N. Harrison (2012) 'Varieties of Capitalism and Technological Innovation for Climate Change Mitigation'. *New Political Economy* 17(2): 179–208.

Miliband, R. (1969) *The State in Capitalist Society*. New York: Basic Books.

Milman, O. (2015) 'Zuckerberg, Gates and Other Tech Titans Form Clean Energy Investment Coalition'. *The Guardian*, 30 November. www.theguardian.com/environment/2015/nov/30/bill-gates-breakthrough-energy-coalition-mark-zuckerberg-facebook-microsoft-amazon.

Mitchell, T. (2011). *Carbon Democracy: Political Power in the Age of Oil*. London: Verso.

Mitchell, T., and S. Maxwell (2010) 'Defining Climate Compatible Development'. CDKN Policy Briefing, November.

Mittelman, J. (1998) 'Globalisation and Environmental Resistance Politics'. *Third World Quarterly* 19(5): 847–72.

Moberg, K., C. Aall, F. Dorner, E. Reimerson, J. P. Ceron, B. Sköld, B. K. Sovacool and V. Piana (2019) 'Mobility, Food and Housing: Responsibility, Individual Consumption and Demand-Side Policies in European Deep Decarbonisation Pathways'. *Energy Efficiency* 12: 497–519.

Mol, A. (2003) *Globalization and Environmental Reform: The Ecological Modernization of the Global Economy*. Cambridge, MA: MIT Press.

Moll, H., K. Noorman, R. Kok, R. Engström, H. Throne-Holst and C. Clark. (2005) 'Pursuing More Sustainable Consumption by Analyzing Household Metabolism in European Countries and Cities'. *Journal of Industrial Ecology* 9(1–2): 259–75.

Monbiot, G. (2000) *Captive State: The Corporate Takeover of Britain*. Basingstoke: Macmillan.

Moore, J. (2015a) 'Ecological Footprints and Lifestyle Archetypes: Exploring Dimensions of Consumption and the Transformation Needed to Achieve Urban Sustainability'. *Sustainability* 7(4): 4747–63.

Moore, J. W. (2015b) *Capitalism in the Web of Life: Ecology and the Accumulation of Capital*. London: Verso.

Moran, D., and J. Russell (eds.) (2009) *Energy Security and Global Politics: The Militarization of Resource Management*. Abingdon: Routledge.

Morena, E., D. Krause and D. Stevis (2019) *Just Transitions Social Justice in the Shift Towards a Low-Carbon World*. London: Pluto Press.

Mori, A. (2018) 'Socio-technical and Political Economy Perspectives in the Chinese Energy Transition'. *Energy Research & Social Science* 35: 28–36.

Moss, J. (2018) 'Exporting Harm' in *Climate Change and Justice*. Cambridge: Cambridge University Press, 73–89.

Mulvaney, D. (2013) 'Opening the Black Box of Solar Energy Technologies: Exploring Tensions Between Innovation and Environmental Justice'. *Science as Culture* 22(2): 230–7.

Mulvaney, D. (2014) 'Are Green Jobs Just Jobs? Cadmium Narratives in the Life Cycle of Photovoltaics'. *Geoforum* 54: 178–86.

Mumford, L. (1967 [1934]) *Technics and Civilisation*. New York: Harcourt, Brace and World.

Mundaca, L., H. Busch and S. Schwer (2017) '"Successful" Low-Carbon Energy Transitions at the Community Level? An Energy Justice Perspective'. *Applied Energy* 218: 292–303.

Nakhooda, S. (2011) 'Asia, the Multilateral Development Banks and Energy Governance'. *Global Policy* 2(1): 120–32.

Neale, J. (2001) 'The Long Torment of Afghanistan'. In J. Rees (ed.) Imperialism: Globalisation, the State and War, Special Issue *International Socialism* 93: 31–59.

Neslen, A. (2019) 'Majority of European Firms Have No CO_2 Reduction Targets'. *The Guardian*, 19 February. www.theguardian.com/environment/2019/feb/19/majority-of-european-firms-have-no-co2-reduction-targets?CMP=share_btn_link.

Newell, P. (2000) *Climate for Change: Non-state Actors and the Global Politics of the Greenhouse*. Cambridge: Cambridge University Press.

(2001) 'Managing Multinationals: The Governance of Investment for the Environment'. *Journal of International Development* 13(7): 907–19.

(2005a) 'Citizenship, Accountability and Community: The Limits of the CSR Agenda'. *International Affairs* 81(3): 541–57.

(2005b) 'Race, Class and the Global Politics of Environmental Inequality'. *Global Environmental Politics* 5(3): 70–94.

(2007) 'Trade and Environmental Justice in Latin America'. *New Political Economy* 12 (2): 237–59.

(2008) 'Civil Society, Corporate Accountability and the Politics of Climate Change'. *Global Environmental Politics* 8(3): 124–55.

(2009) 'Varieties of CDM Governance: Some Reflections'. *Journal of Environment and Development* 18(4): 425–35.

(2011) 'The Governance of Energy Finance: The Public, the Private and the Hybrid'. *Global Policy* 2(1): 94–105.

(2012) *Globalization and the Environment: Capitalism, Ecology and Power*. Cambridge: Polity.

(2014) 'The Politics and Political Economy of the CDM in Argentina'. *Environmental Politics* 23(2): 321–38.

(2015) 'The Politics of Green Transformations in Capitalism'. In I. Scoones, M. Leach and P. Newell (eds.) *The Politics of Green Transformations*. London: Routledge, 68–86.

(2016) 'The Political Economy of (Climate) Change: Low Carbon Energy Transitions under Capitalism'. In T. Di Muzio and J. Salah Olvadia (eds.) *Energy, Capitalism and World Order: Toward a New Agenda in International Political Economy*. Basingstoke: Palgrave, 127–45.

(2018) 'Trasformismo or Transformation? The Global Political Economy of Energy Transitions'. *Review of International Political Economy* 26(1): 25–48.

(2019) *Global Green Politics*. Cambridge: Cambridge University Press.

(2020a) 'Race and the Politics of Energy Transitions'. *Energy Research & Social Science* 71. a101839 1–5. ISSN 2214-6296. https://doi.org/10.1016/j.erss.2020.101839.

(2020b) 'The Business of Rapid Transition'. *WIREs Climate Change*. 10.1002/wcc.670.

(2020c) 'Towards a Global Political Economy of Transitions: A Comment on the Transitions Research Agenda; Commentary'. *Environmental Innovation and Societal Transitions* 34: 344–5.

Newell, P., and H. Bulkeley (2016) 'Landscape for Change? International Climate Policy and Energy Transitions: Evidence from Sub-Saharan Africa'. *Climate Policy* 17: 650–63.

Newell, P., and A. Bumpus (2012) 'The Global Political Ecology of the CDM'. *Global Environmental Politics* 12: 49–67.

Newell, P., and P. Johnstone (2018) 'The Political Economy of Incumbency'. In J. Skovgaard and H. Van Asselt (eds.) *The Politics of Fossil Fuel Subsidies and Their Reform*. Cambridge: Cambridge University Press, 66–80.

Newell, P., and R. Lane (2016) 'The Political Economy of Carbon Markets'. In T. Van de Graaf, B. K. Sovacool, F. Kern and M. Klare (eds.) *The Palgrave Handbook of the International Political Economy of Energy*. London: Palgrave, 247–69.

(2018) 'A Climate for Change? The Impacts of Climate Change on Energy Politics'. *Cambridge Review of International Affairs* 33(3): 347–64.

Newell, P., and A. Martin (2020) *The Role of the State in the Politics of Disruption & Acceleration*. London: Climate KIC.

Newell, P., and D. Mulvaney (2013) 'The Political Economy of the Just Transition'. *Geographical Journal* 179(2): 132–40.

Newell, P., and M. Paterson (1998) 'Climate for Business: Global Warming, the State and Capital'. *Review of International Political Economy* 5(4): 679–704.

(2010) *Climate Capitalism: Global Warming and the Transformation of the Global Economy*. Cambridge: Cambridge University Press.

Newell, P., and J. Phillips (2016) 'Neoliberal Energy Transitions in the South: Kenyan Experiences'. *Geoforum* 74: 39–48.

Newell, P., and D. Phylipsen (2018) 'Implications of the IPCC Special Report on 1.5 Degrees for Scaling Up NDCs'. *Climate Strategies 1.5 Insight Brief*. https://climatestrategies.org /wp-content/uploads/2018/10/P2933_CS_Newell_Phylipsen_PRINT.pdf.

Newell, P., and A. Simms (2019) 'Towards a Fossil Fuel Non-proliferation Treaty'. *Climate Policy*. 10.1080/14693062.2019.1636759.

Newell, P., and O. Taylor (2020) 'Fiddling While the Planet Burns? COP25 in Perspective'. *Globalizations*. www.tandfonline.com/doi/full/10.1080/14747731 .2020.1726127.

Newell, P., N. Jenner and L. Baker (2009a) 'Governing Clean Development: A Framework for Analysis'. *Development Policy Review* 27(6): 717–41.

Newell, P., J. Timmons Roberts, E. Boyd and S. Huq (2009b) 'Billions at Stake in Climate Finance: Four Key Lessons'. IIED Briefing, November. London: IIED.

Newell P., J. Phillips and D. Mulvaney (2011) 'Pursuing Clean Energy Equitably'. Research Paper for the UNDP *Human Development Report* 2011/03 November.

Newell, P., J. Phillips, A. Pueyo, E. Kirumba, N. Ozor and K. Urama (2014) 'The Political Economy of Low Carbon Energy in Kenya'. IDS Working Paper 445. Brighton: IDS.

Newell, P., H. Bulkeley, K. Turner, C. Shaw, S. Caney, E. Shove and N. Pidgeon (2015) 'Governance Traps in Climate Change Politics: Re-framing the Debate in Terms of Responsibilities and Rights'. *WIREs Climate Change*, 6: 535–40.

Nisbet, M. (2019) 'Climate Philanthropy and the Four Billion (Dollars, That Is)'. *Issues in Science and Technology*. https://issues.org/wp-content/uploads/2019/01/Nisbet-Sciences-Publics-Politics-34–36-Winter-2019.pdf.

Nixon, R. (2011) *Slow Violence and the Environmentalism of the Poor*. Cambridge, MA: Harvard University Press.

Nye, J., and R. Keohane (eds.) (1972) *Transnational Relations and World Politics*. Cambridge, MA: Harvard University Press.

O'Boyle, M. (2018) 'Investment-Grade Policy: De-risking Renewable Energy Projects'. *Forbes*, 12 November. www.forbes.com/sites/energyinnovation/2018/11/12/invest ment-grade-policy-de-risking-renewable-energy-projects/#55764f624e77.

OCI (Oil Change International) (2017) *Oil Change International Cross Purposes: After Paris, Multilateral Development Banks Still Funding Billions in Fossil Fuels*. Washington, DC: OCI.

Ockwell, D., and R. Byrne (2017) *Sustainable Energy for All: Technology, Innovation and Pro-poor Green Transformations*. Pathways to Sustainability Series. Abingdon: Taylor & Francis.

Ockwell, D., P. Newell, S. Geall, K. Mbeva, W. Shen and A. Ely (2017) 'The Political Economy of State-Led Energy Transformations: Lessons from Solar PV in Kenya and China'. STEPS Working Paper 92. Brighton: STEPS Centre.

O'Connor, J. (1973) *The Fiscal Crisis of the State*. New York: St. Martin's Press.
    (1991) 'On the Two Contradictions of Capitalism'. *Capitalism, Nature, Socialism* 2(3): 107–9.
Odell, P. (1981) *Oil and World Power*. London: Penguin.
OECD (2011) *Towards Green Growth*. Paris: OECD.
Okereke, C., B. Wittneben and F. Bowen (2012) 'Climate Change: Challenging Business, Transforming Politics'. *Business & Society* 51(1): 7–30.
Okonta, I., and O. Douglas (2001) *Where Vultures Feast: Shell, Human Rights, and Oil in the Niger Delta*. San Francisco: Sierra Club Books.
O'Meara, D. (2014). 'Companies Respond to Shareholder Activism on Carbon Risks'. *Financial Post*, 10 April.
Overy, N. (2018) *The Role of Ownership in a Just Energy Transition*. Cape Town: Project 90 by 2030.
Painter, D. (1986) 'Oil and the American Century: The Political Economy of U.S. Foreign Oil Policy, 1941–1954'. *Journal of American History* 73(4): 1070.
Palan, R. (2003) *Offshore World*. Ithaca, NY: Cornell University Press.
Parker, M. (1994) *The Politics of Coal's Decline: The Industry in Western Europe*. London: RIIA.
Parson, E. (1995) 'Integrated Assessment and Environmental Policy Making: In Pursuit of Usefulness'. *Energy Policy* 23(4/5): 463–76.
Parson, E., and K. Fisher-Vanden (1997) 'Integrated Assessment Models of Global Climate Change'. *Annual Review of Energy and the Environment* 22: 589–628.
Parthan, B., M. Osterkorn, M. Kennedy, St. J. Hoskyns, M. Bazilian and P. Monga (2010) 'Lessons for Low-Carbon Energy Transition: Experience from the REEEP'. *Energy for Sustainable Development* 14: 83–93. 10.1016/j.esd.2010.04.003.
Patel, R., and J. Moore (2017) *A History of the World in Seven Cheap Things: A Guide to Capitalism, Nature and the Future of the Planet*. Berkeley: University of California Press.
Paterson, M. (2001) 'Risky Business: Insurance Companies in Global Warming Politics'. *Global Environmental Politics* 1(3): 18–42.
    (2006) *Automobile Politics*. Cambridge: Cambridge University Press.
    (2009) 'Resistance Makes Carbon Markets'. In S. Böhm and S. Dabhi (eds.) *Upsetting the Offset: The Political Economy of Carbon Markets*. Colchester: Mayfly Books, 244–54.
    (2010) 'Legitimation and Accumulation in Climate Change Governance'. *New Political Economy* 15(3): 345–68.
    (2012) 'Who and What Are Carbon Markets for? Politics and the Development of Climate Policy'. *Climate Policy* 12(1): 82–97.
Paterson, M., and J. Stripple (2010) 'My Space: Governing Individuals' Carbon Emissions'. *Environment and Planning D: Space and Society* 28(2): 341–62.
Patterson, W. (1984) *The Plutonium Business and the Spread of the Bomb*. London: Paladin Books Granada Publishing.
    (2015) *Electricity vs Fire: The Fight for Our Future*. Amersham: Walt Patterson.
Pearce, F. (2018) *Fallout: A Journey through the Nuclear Age from the Atomic Bomb to Nuclear Waste*. London: Granta.
Pearson, P., and T. Foxon (2012) 'A Low Carbon Industrial Revolution? Insights and Challenges from Past Technological and Economic Transformations'. *Energy Policy* 50: 117–27.
Peck, J., and A. Tickell (2002) 'Neoliberalizing Space'. *Antipode* 34(3): 380–404.
Peet, R., P. Robbins and M. Watts (eds.) (2011) *Global Political Ecology*. London: Routledge.

Pegels, A. (ed.) (2014) *Green Industrial Policy in Emerging Countries*. London: Routledge.

Pegels, A., G. Vidican-Auktor, W. Lütkenhorst and T. Altenburg (2018) 'Politics of Green Energy Policy'. *Journal of Environment and Development* 27(1): 26–45.

Perez, C. (2002) *Technological Revolutions and Financial Capital: The Dynamics of Bubbles and Golden Ages*. Cheltenham: Edward Elgar.

    (2013) 'Unleashing a Golden Age after the Financial Collapse: Drawing Lessons from History'. *Environmental Innovation and Societal Transitions* 6: 9–23.

Pettifor, A. (2019) *The Case for the Green New Deal*. London: Verso.

Phillips, J., and P. Newell (2013) 'The Governance of Clean Energy in India: The Clean Development Mechanism (CDM) and Domestic Energy Politics'. *Energy Policy* 59: 654–62.

Piggot, G. (2017). 'The Influence of Social Movements on Policies that Constrain Fossil Fuel Supply'. *Climate Policy*: 1–13.

Pinkse, J., and A. Kolk (2009) *International Business and Global Climate Change*. Abingdon: Routledge.

Pirani, S. (2018) *Burning Up: A Global History of Fossil Fuel Consumption*. London: Pluto Press.

Plumwood, V. (2002) *Environmental Culture: The Ecological Crisis of Reason*. London: Routledge.

Podobnik, B. (1999) 'Toward a Sustainable Energy Regime: A Long-Wave Interpretation of Global Energy Shifts'. *Technological Forecasting and Social Change* 62: 155–72.

    (2006) *Global Energy Shifts*. Philadelphia, PA: Temple University Press.

    (2010) 'Building the Clean Energy Movement: Future Possibilities in Historical Perspective'. In K. Abramsky (ed.) *Sparking a Worldwide Energy Revolution: Social Struggles in the Transition to a Post-Petrol World*. Oakland, CA: AK Press, 72–81.

Polanyi, K. (1957 [1944]) *The Great Transformation*. Boston, MA: Beacon Press.

Pollitt, M. (2012) 'The Role of Policy in Energy Transitions: Lessons from the Energy Liberalisation Era'. *Energy Policy* 50: 128–37.

Ponte, S. (2019) *Business, Power and Sustainability in a World of Global Value Chains*. London: Zed Books.

Ponting, C. (2007) *A New History of the World: The Environment and the Collapse of Great Civilisations*. London: Vintage.

Porritt, J., (1989) *Seeing Green: Politics of Ecology Explained*. Oxford: Wiley-Blackwell.

Poulantzas, N. (2014) *State, Power, Socialism*. London: Verso.

Power, M., and J. Kirshner (2018) 'Powering the State: The Political Geographies of Electrification in Mozambique'. *Environment and Planning C: Politics and Space* 37(3): 498–518.

Power, M., P. Newell, L. Baker, H. Bulkeley, J. Kirshner and A. Smith (2016) 'The Political Economy of Energy Transitions in Mozambique and South Africa: The Role of the Rising Powers'. *Energy Research & Social Sciences* 17: 10–19. 10.1016/j.erss.2016.03.007.

Princen, T., J. P. Manno and P. L. Martine (eds.) (2015). *Ending the Fossil Fuel Era*. Cambridge, MA: MIT Press.

Räthzel, N., and D. Uzzell (2013) *Trade Unions in the Green Economy: Working for the Environment*. New York: Routledge.

Raworth, K. (2017) *Doughnut Economics: Seven Ways to Think like a 21st-Century Economist*. London: Random House Business Books.

Rees, J. (2001). 'Imperialism: Globalization, the State and War'. Special Issue. *International Socialism* 93.

Rees, W. (2020) 'Ecological Economics for Humanity's Plague Phase'. *Ecological Economics* 169: 106519. 10.1016/j.ecolecon.2019.106519.

Renn, O., W. Köck, P. J. Schweizer, J. Bovet, C. Benighaus, O. Scheel and R. Schröter (2014). 'Public Participation for Planning New Facilities in the Context of the German "Energiewende"'. Policy Brief Edition, 1.

Rennkamp, B., S. Haunss, K. Wongsa, A. Ortega and E. Casamadrid (2017) 'Competing Coalitions: The Politics of Renewable Energy and Fossil Fuels in Mexico, South Africa and Thailand'. *Energy Research & Social Science* 34: 214–23.

Reyes, O. (2011) 'Zombie Carbon and Sectoral Market Mechanisms'. *Capitalism Nature Socialism* 22(4): 117–35.

Ribiero, C. (2006) *Investment Arbitration and the Energy Charter Treaty.*

Ricardo, D. (1817) *On the Principles of Political Economy and Taxation.* London: John Murray.

Risbey, J., M. Kandlikar and A. Patwardhan (1996) 'Assessing Integrated Assessments'. *Climatic Change* 34: 369–95.

Robbins, P. (2004) *Political Ecology: A Critical Introduction.* Oxford: Blackwell.

Robbins, P., J. Hintz and S. Moore (2010) *Environment and Society.* Oxford: Wiley Blackwell.

Roberts, J. T., and B. C. Parks (2008) 'Fuelling Injustice: Globalization, Ecologically Unequal Exchange and Climate Change'. In J. Ooshthoek and B. Gills (eds.) *The Globalization of Environmental Crises.* London: Routledge, 169–87.

Roberts, C., F. Geels, M. Lockwood, P. Newell, H. Schmitz, B. Turnheim and A. Jordan (2018) 'The Politics of Accelerating Low-Carbon Transitions: Towards a New Research Agenda'. *Energy Research & Social Science* 44: 304–11.

Rockström, J., W. Steffen, K. Noone, Å. Persson, F. S. Chapin III, E. F. Lambin, T. M. Lenton, M. Scheffer, C. Folke, H. J. Schellnhuber, B. Nykvist, C. A. de Wit, T. Hughes, S. van der Leeuw, H. Rodhe, S. Sörlin, P. K. Snyder, R. Costanza, U. Svedin, M. Falkenmark, L. Karlberg, R. W. Corell, V. J. Fabry, J. Hansen, B. Walker, D. Liverman, K. Richardson, P. Crutzen and J. A. Foley (2009) 'A Safe Operating Space for Humanity'. *Nature* 461: 472–5.

Rockström, J., O. Gaffney, J. Rogelj, M. Meinshausen, N. Nakicenovic and H. J. Schellnhuber (2017) 'A Roadmap for Rapid Decarbonization'. *Science* 355(6331): 1269–71.

Roddis, P., S. Carver, M. Dallimer, P. Norman and G. Ziv (2018) 'The Role of Community Acceptance in Planning Outcomes for Onshore Wind and Solar Farms: An Energy Justice Analysis'. *Applied Energy* 226: 353–64.

Rodrik, D. (2007) 'Industrial Policy for the Twenty-First Century'. In D. Rodrik (ed.) *One Economics, Many Recipes: Globalization, Institutions and Economic Growth.* Princeton, NJ: Princeton University Press, 99–145.

Rogge, K., and P. Johnstone (2017) 'Exploring the Role of Phase-Out Policies for Low-Carbon Energy Transitions: The Case of the German Energiewende'. *Energy Research & Social Science* 33: 128–37.

Rogelj, J., G. Luderer, R. Pietzcker, E. Kriegler, M. Schaeffer, V. Krey and K. Riahi (2015) 'Energy System Transformations for Limiting End-of-Century Warming to Below 1.5°C'. *Nature Climate Change* 5: 519–27. 10.1038/nclimate2572.

Romero, G. (2019) 'Riesgo ambiental e incertidumbre en la producción del litio en salares de Argentina, Bolivia y Chile'. In B. Fornillo (ed.) *Litio En Sudamérica: Geopolítica, Energía y Territorios.* Colección Chico Mendes. Buenos Aires: Editorial El Colectivo, 223–60.

Roodhouse, M. (2007) 'Rationing Returns: A Solution to Global Warming?'. *Policy Papers, History & Policy,* 1 March. www.historyandpolicy.org/policy-papers /papers/rationing-returns-a-solution-to-global-warming.

Rosa, E., G. Machlis and K. Keating (1988) 'Energy and Society'. *Annual Review of Sociology* 14: 149–72.

Ross, M. (2012) *The Oil Curse: How Petroleum Wealth Shapes the Development of Nations*. Princeton, NJ: Princeton University Press.

Rostow, W. (1960) *The Stages of Economic Growth*. Cambridge: Cambridge University Press.

Rowell, A., (1996) *Green Backlash: Global Subversion of the Environment Movement*. London: Routledge.

Royston, S., J. Selby and E. Shove (2018) 'Invisible Energy Policies: A New Agenda for Energy Demand Reduction'. *Energy Policy* 123: 127–35.

Rubio, M., and M. Folchi (2012) 'Will Small Energy Consumers Be Faster in Transition? Evidence from the Early Shift from Coal to Oil in Latin America'. *Energy Policy* 50: 50–61.

Rüdinger, A. (2019) *Participatory and Citizen Renewable Energy Projects in France – State of Play and Recommendations*. Paris: IDDRI.

Rupert, M. (1995) *Producing Hegemony: The Politics of Mass Production and American Global Power*. Cambridge: Cambridge University Press.

Rutherford, J., and S. Jaglin (2015) 'Introduction to the Special Issue – Urban Energy Governance: Local Actions, Capacities and Politics'. *Energy Policy* 78: 173–8.

Said, E. (1978) *Orientalism*. London: Penguin Books.

Sanchez, T. (2010) *The Hidden Energy Crisis: How Policies Are Failing the World's Poor*. Rugby: Practical Action.

Satia, P. (2018) *Empire of Guns: The Violent Making of the Industrial Revolution*. London: Penguin.

Saurin, J. (2001) 'Global Environmental Crisis as the "Disaster Triumphant": The Private Capture of Public Goods'. *Environmental Politics* 10(4): 63–84.

SBTi (2017) 'Science-Based Target Setting Manual'. Version 3.0, 19 July. https://science basedtargets.org/wp-content/uploads/2017/04/SBT-Manual-Draft.pdf.

Scarse, I., and A. Smith (2009) 'The Non-politics of Managing Low Carbon Socio-technical Transitions'. *Environmental Politics* 18(5): 707–26.

Schmelzer, M. (2016) *The Hegemony of Growth: The OECD and the Making of the Economic Growth Paradigm*. Cambridge: Cambridge University Press.

Schmitz, H. (2017) 'Who Drives Climate-Relevant Policies in the Rising Powers?' *New Political Economy* 22: 521–40.

Schneider, L., and A. Kollmuss (2015) 'Perverse Effects of Carbon Markets on HFC-23 and SF6 Abatement Projects in Russia'. *Nature Climate Change* 5(12): 1061–3.

Schot, J., L. Kanger and G. Verbong (2016) 'The Role of Users in Shaping Transitions to New Energy Systems'. *Natural Energy* 1(5): 16054–7.

Schumacher, E. F. (1974) *Small Is Beautiful*. London: Abacus.

Scoones, I., M. Leach and P. Newell (eds.) (2015) *The Politics of Green Transformations*. London: Routledge.

Scoones, I., A. Stirling, D. Abrol, J. Atela, L. Charli-Joseph, H. Eakin, A. Ely, P. Olsson, L. Pereira, R. Priya, P. van Zwanenberg and L. Yang (2018) 'Transformations to Sustainability'. STEPS Working Paper 104. Brighton: STEPS Centre.

Scott, A. (2017). 'Making Governance Work for Water–Energy–Food Nexus Approaches'. CDKN Working Paper (July). London: CDKN.

Scott, J. C. (1998) *Seeing like a State: How Certain Schemes to Improve the Human Condition Have Failed*. New Haven, CT: Yale University Press.

Scott, A. (2017). 'Making Governance Work for Water–Energy–Food Nexus Approaches'. *CDKN Working Paper* (July). London: Climate and Development Knowledge Network.

SE4ALL (2019) www.seforall.org/.

Seabrooke, L., and D. Wigan (2017) 'The Governance of Global Wealth Chains'. *Review of International Political Economy* 24(1): 1–29.

Seel, B. (1997) 'Strategies of Resistance at the Pollok Free State Road Protest Camp'. *Environmental Politics* 6(4): 108–39.

SEI (2018) 'Aligning Fossil Fuel Production with the Paris Agreement'. Insights for the UNFCCC Talanoa Dialogue, March, Authors: Verkuijl, C. et al.

SEI, IISD, ODI, Climate Analytics, CICERO, and UNEP (2019). *The Production Gap: The Discrepancy between Countries' Planned Fossil Fuel Production and Global Production Levels Consistent with Limiting Warming to 1.5°C or 2°C.* http://productiongap.org/.

Selby, J. (2019) 'The Trump Presidency, Climate Change, and the Prospect of a Disorderly Energy Transition'. *Review of International Studies* 45(3): 471–90.

Seyfang, G., and A. Haxeltine (2012) 'Growing Grassroots Innovations: Exploring the Role of Community-Based Initiatives in Governing Sustainable Energy Transitions'. *Environment and Planning C: Government and Policy* 30: 381–400.

Seyfang, G., J. Park and A. Smith (2012) *Community Energy in the UK.* 3S Working Paper 2012–11. Norwich: Science, Society and Sustainability Research Group.

Seyfang, G., S. Hielscher, T. Hargreaves, M. Martiskainen and A. Smith (2014) 'A Grassroots Sustainable Energy Niche? Reflections on Community Energy in the UK'. *Environmental Innovation and Societal Transitions* 13: 21–44.

Shackley, S., and B. Wynne (1995) 'Integrating Knowledges for Climate Change; Pyramids, Nets and Uncertainties'. *Global Environmental Change* 5(2): 113–26.

Shen, W., and M. Power (2017) 'Africa and the Export of China's Clean Energy Revolution'. *Third World Quarterly* 38(3): 678–97.

Shenoy, B. (2010) *Lessons Learned from Attempts to Reform India's Kerosene Subsidy.* Winnipeg: IISD.

Shmelev, N., and V. Popov (1989) *Turning Point: Revitalizing the Soviet Economy.* New York: Doubleday.

Shove, E. (2003) *Comfort, Cleanliness and Convenience: The Social Organization of Normality.* London: Berg.

   (2010) 'Beyond the ABC: Climate Change Policy and Theories of Social Change'. *Environment and Planning A* 42(6): 1273–85.

Shove, E., M. Pantzar and M. Watson (2012) *The Dynamics of Social Practice.* London: Sage.

Simms, A. (2005) *Ecological Debt: The Health of the Planet and the Wealth of Nations.* London: Pluto Press.

   (2009) *Ecological Debt: Global Warming and the Wealth of Nations*, 2nd ed. London: Pluto Press.

   (2010) 'Growth Isn't Possible: Why We Need A New Economic Direction'. *New Economics Foundation*, 1–148. https://neweconomics.org/uploads/files/f19c45312a905d73c3_rbm6iecku.pdf.

   (2013) *Cancel the Apocalypse: New Pathways to Prosperity.* London: Little, Brown.

   (2015) 'We Need Honesty from Business to Tackle Climate Change'. *The Guardian*, 26 May. www.theguardian.com/sustainable-business/2015/may/26/we-need-honesty-from-business-to-tackle-climate-change.

   (2018) 'Smog Day Fell as Pollution Rose & One of Europe's Worst Air Quality Countries Holds Climate Talks'. www.newweather.org/2018/12/06/smog-day-fell-as-pollution-rose-one-of-europes-worst-air-quality-countries-holds-climate-talks/.

Simms, A., and P. Newell (2017) *How Did We Do That? The Possibility of Rapid Transitions.* Brighton: STEPS Centre.

Simms, A., and P. Newell (2018). 'We Need a Fossil Fuel Non-proliferation Treaty – and We Need It Now'. *The Guardian*, 23 October. www.theguardian.com/commentisfree/2018/oct/23/fossil-fuel-non-proliferation-treaty-climate-breakdown.

Sinn, H.-W. (2012). *The Green Paradox: A Supply-Side Approach to Global Warming.* Cambridge, MA: MIT Press.

Skovgaard, J., and H. Van Asselt (eds.) (2018) *The Politics of Fossil Fuel Subsidies and Their Reform.* Cambridge: Cambridge University Press.

Smil, V. (1994) *Energy in World History* Boulder, CO: Westview Press.

(2000) 'Perils of Long-Range Energy Forecasting: Reflections on Looking Far Ahead'. *Technological Forecasting and Social Change* 65: 251–64.

(2016) 'Examining Energy Transitions: A Dozen Insights Based on Performance'. *Energy Research & Social Science* 22: 194–7.

Smith, A. (1776 [2014]) *The Wealth of Nations.* London: Shine Classics.

(2008) 'Civil Society in Sustainable Energy Transitions'. In G. Verbong and D. Loorbach (ed.) *Governing the Energy Transition: Reality, Illusion or Necessity?* London: Routledge, 180–202.

(2014) 'Socially Useful Production'. STEPS Working Paper 58. Brighton: STEPS Centre.

Smith, A., A. Sterling and F. Berkhout (2005). 'The Governance of Sustainable Sociotechnical Transitions'. *Research Policy* 34: 1491–1510.

Smith, A., M. Fressoli, D. Abrol, E. Arond and A. Ely (2016a) *Grassroots Innovation Movements.* Abingdon: Routledge.

Smith, A., T. Hargreaves, S. Hielscher, M. Martiskainen and G. Seyfang (2016b) 'Making the Most of Community Energies: Three Perspectives on Grassroots Innovation'. *Environment and Planning A: Economy and Space* 48(2): 407–32. https://doi.org/10.1177/0308518X15597908.

Smith, J. (2000) *Biofuels and the Globalization of Risk: The Biggest Change in North-South Relations since Colonialism.* London: Zed Books.

Smits, M. (2009) *South-East Asian Energy Transitions: Between Modernity and Sustainability.* Aldershot: Ashgate.

Söderbaum, P. (2000) *Ecological Economics.* London: Earthscan.

Soddy, F. (1912) *Matter and Energy.* Oxford: Oxford University Press.

Sørensen, B. (2011) *Life Cycle Analysis of Energy Systems: From Methodology to Application.* Cambridge: Royal Society of Chemistry.

Sorrell, S., B. Gatersleben and A. Druckman (2020) 'The Limits of Energy Sufficiency: A Review of the Evidence for Rebound Effects and Negative Spill overs from Behavioural Change'. *Energy Research & Social Science* 64 June. https://doi.org/10.1016/j.erss.2020.101439.

Sovacool, B. K. (2014) 'What Are We Talking about Here? Analysing Fifteen Years of Energy Scholarship and Proposing a Social Science Research Agenda'. *Energy Research & Social Science* 1(1): 1–29.

(2016) 'How Long Will It Take? Conceptualizing the Temporal Dynamics of Energy Transitions'. *Energy Research & Social Science* 13: 202–15.

(2017) 'Reviewing, Reforming and Rethinking Global Energy Subsidies: Towards a Political Economy Research Agenda'. *Ecological Economics* 135: 150–63.

(2019) 'The Precarious Political Economy of Cobalt: Balancing Prosperity, Poverty, and Brutality in Artisanal and Industrial Mining in the Democratic Republic of the Congo'. *Extractive Industries & Society* 6(3) July: 915–39.

Sovacool, B. K. and M. C. Brisbois (2019) 'Elite Power in Low-Carbon Transitions: A Critical and Interdisciplinary Review'. *Energy Research & Social Science* 57: 101242.

Sovacool, B. K., and M. Dworkin (2014) *Global Energy Justice: Problems, Principles and Practices.* Cambridge: Cambridge University Press.

Sovacool, B. K., and F. Geels (2016) 'Further Reflections on the Temporality of Energy Transitions: A Response to Critics'. *Energy Research & Social Science* 22: 232–7.

Sovacool, B. K., and S. Griffiths (2020) 'Culture and Low-Carbon Energy Transitions'. *Nature Sustainability*. https://doi.org/10.1038/s41893-020-0519-4.

Sovacool, B. K., and J. Scarpaci (2016) 'Energy Justice and the Contested Petroleum Politics of Stranded Assets: Policy Insights from the Yasuní-ITT Initiative in Ecuador'. *Energy Policy* 95: 158–71.

Sovacool, B. K., M. Tan-Mullins, D. Ockwell and P. Newell (2017) 'Political Economy, Poverty, and Polycentrism in the Global Environment Facility's Least Developed Countries Fund (LDCF) for Climate Change Adaptation'. *Third World Quarterly* 38 (6): 1249–71.

Sovacool, B. K., B. Turnheim, M. Martiskainen, D. Brown and P. Kivimaa (2020) 'Guides or Gatekeepers? Incumbent-Oriented Transition Intermediaries in a Low-Carbon Era'. *Energy Research & Social Science* 66: 101490.

Spencer, H. (1980) *First Principles*. New York: A.L. Burt.

Sperling, K. (2017) 'How Does a Pioneer Community Energy Project Succeed in Practice? The Case of the Samsø Renewable Energy Island'. *Renewable Sustainable Energy Review* 71:884–97.

Spratt, S. (2015) 'Financing Green Transformations'. In I. Scoones, M. Leach and P. Newell (eds.) *The Politics of Green Transformations*. London: Routledge, 153–69.

Stahel, W. (2016) 'Circular Economy'. *Nature* 531: 435–8.

Steckel, J., and M. Jakob (2018) 'The Role of Financing Cost and De-risking Strategies for Clean Energy Investment'. *International Economics* 155: 19–28.

Steen, N. (1994) *Sustainable Development and the Energy Industries*. London: RIIA/ Earthscan.

Steffen, W., P. J. Crutzen and J. R. McNeill (2007) 'The Anthropocene: Are Humans Now Overwhelming the Great Forces of Nature?'. *Ambio* 36(8): 614–21.

Steffen, W., W. Broadgate, L. Deutsch, O. Gaffney and C. Ludwig (2015) 'The Trajectory of the Anthropocene: The Great Acceleration'. *Anthropocene Review* 2(1): 81–98.

Stephan, B., and R. Lane (eds.) (2015) *The Politics of Carbon Markets*. New York: Routledge.

Stephenson, J., B. Barton, G. Carrington, D. Gnoth, R. Lawson and P. Thorsnes (2010) 'Energy Cultures: A Framework for Understanding Energy Behaviours'. *Energy Policy* 38(10): 6120–9.

Sterl, S., M. Hagemann, H. Fekete, N. Höhne, J. Cantzler, A. Ancygier, M. Beer, B. Hare, K. Wouters, Y. Deng, K. Blok, C. Cronin, S. Monteith, D. Plechaty and S. Menon (2017) 'Faster and Cleaner 2: Kick-Starting Global Decarbonization: It Only Takes a Few Actors to Get the Ball Rolling'. www.climateworks.org/wp-content/uploads/ 2017/04/Faster-and-Cleaner-2-Full-Technical-Report.pdf.

Stern, N. (2006) *The Stern Review on the Economics of Climate Change*. London: HM Treasury.

Stern, R. (2015) 'De-risking Climate-Smart Investments'. 12 January. http://blogs .worldbank.org/climatechange/de-risking-climate-smart-investments.

Stevenson, H., and J. Dryzek (2014) *Democratizing Global Climate Governance*. Cambridge: Cambridge University Press.

Stevis, D., and R. Felli (2015) 'Global Labour Unions and Just Transition to a Green Economy'. *International Environmental Agreements: Politics, Law and Economics* 15(1): 29–43.

Stirling, A. (2005) 'Opening Up or Closing Down? Analysis, Participation and Power in the Social Appraisal of Technology'. In M. Leach, I. Scoones and B. Wynne (eds.)

Science and Citizens: Globalization and the Challenge of Engagement. Claiming Citizenship. London: Zed Books, 218–31.

(2011) 'Pluralising Progress: From Integrative Transitions to Transformative Diversity'. *Environmental Innovation and Societal Transitions* 1(1): 82–8.

(2014a) 'Emancipating Transformations: From Controlling 'the Transition' to Culturing Plural Radical Progress'. STEPS Working Paper 64. Brighton: STEPS Centre.

(2014b) 'Transforming Power: Social Science and the Politics of Energy Choices'. *Energy Research & Social Science* 1(1): 83–95.

(2018) 'How Deep Is Incumbency? Introducing a "Configuring Fields" Approach to the Distribution and Orientation of Power in Socio-material Change'. SPRU Working Paper SWPS 2018–23, University of Sussex, September.

Stoll, C., L. Klaaßen and U. Gallersdörfer (2019) 'The Carbon Footprint of Bitcoin'. *Joule* 3 (7): 1647–61.

Strange, S. (1988) *States and Markets: An Introduction to International Political Economy*. London: Pinter.

(1996) *The Retreat of the State: The Diffusion of Power in the World Economy*. Cambridge: Cambridge University Press.

Strauss, S., S. Rupp and T. Love (eds.) (2013) *Cultures of Energy: Power, Practices, Technology*. Walnut Creek, CA: Left Coast Press.

Sullivan, R., and A. Gouldson (2013) 'Ten Years of Corporate Action on Climate Change: What Do We Have to Show for It?' *Energy Policy* 60: 733–40.

Swilling, M., and E. Annecke (2012) *Just Transitions: Explorations of Sustainability in an Unfair World*. South Africa: UCT Press.

Swyngedouw, E. (2010) 'Apocalypse Forever? Post-Political Populism and the Spectre of Climate Change'. *Theory, Culture and Society* 27(2–3): 213–32.

(2015) *Liquid Power: Contested Hydro-modernities in Twentieth-Century Spain*. Cambridge, MA: MIT Press.

Szulecki, K., P. Pattberg and F. Biermann (2011) 'Explaining Variation in the Effectiveness of Transnational Energy Partnerships'. *Governance* 24(4): 713–36.

Taylor, I. (2006) 'China's Oil Diplomacy in Africa'. *International Affairs* 82(5): 937–59.

Tellam, I. (ed.) (2000) *Fuel for Change: World Bank Energy Policy – Rhetoric and Reality*. London: Zed Books.

Thaler, R., and C. Sunstein (2009) *Nudge: Improving Decisions about Health, Wealth and Happiness*. London: Penguin.

The Economist (2008) 'The New Colonialists'. Lead article, 13 March.

Thomson, F., and S. Dutta (2018) *Financialisation: A Primer. Technical Report*. Amsterdam: Transnational Institute (TNI).

Tienhaara, K., and C. Downie (2018) 'Risky Business? The Energy Charter Treaty, Renewable Energy and Investor State Disputes'. *Global Governance* 24(3): 451–71.

Tilley, L., and R. Shilliam (2018) 'Raced Markets: An Introduction'. *New Political Economy* 23(5): 534–43.

Tomain, J. (2017) *Clean Power Politics: The Democratization of Energy*. Cambridge: Cambridge University Press.

Topham, G. (2020) 'Virgin Atlantic to Seek Millions in State Aid amid Covid-19 Slump'. *The Guardian*, 27 March. www.theguardian.com/business/2020/mar/27/virgin-atlantic-to-seek-millions-in-state-aid-amid-covid-19-slump?CMP=Share_iOSApp_Other.

Trainer, T. (1996) *Towards a Sustainable Economy: The Need for Fundamental Change*. Oxford: Jon Carpenter.

Transitions Network (2017) 'Transition Initiatives Directory'. https://transitionnetwork.org /?s=transition+initiatives+directory.

Trexler, M., and A. Schendler (2015). 'Science-Based Carbon Targets for the Corporate World: The Ultimate Sustainability Commitment, or a Costly Distraction'. *Journal of Industrial Ecology* 19(6): 931–3.

Truffer, B. (2012) 'The Need for a Global Perspective on Sustainability Transitions'. *Environmental Development* 3: 182–3.

Turnheim, B., and F. Geels (2012) 'Regime Stabilisation as the Flipside of Energy Transitions: Lessons from the History of the British Coal Industry (1913–1997)'. *Energy Policy* 50: 35–49.

UNEP (2015) *The Financial System We Need*. Nairobi: UNEP.

   (2017) *Emissions Gap Report 2017*. United Nations Environment Programme, Nairobi, Kenya. http://uneplive.unep.org/theme/index/13#egr.

   (2018) *Emissions Gap Report 2018*. Executive Summary. United Nations Environment Programme, Nairobi, Kenya.

   (2020) *Emissions Gap Report 2020.* Nairobi, Kenya.

UNEP BNEF (2019) *Global Trends in Renewable Energy Investment 2019*. Frankfurt School-UNEP Centre/BNEF. www.fs-unep-centre.org.

United Nations (2015) Transforming Our World: The 2030 Agenda for Sustainable Development. New York: United Nations.

Unruh, G. C. (2000) 'Understanding Carbon Lock-In'. *Energy Policy* 28: 817–30.

Vailles, C., and C. Métivier (2019) 'Very Few Companies Make Good Use of Scenarios to Anticipate Their Climate-Constrained Future'. Climate Brief No. 61. Paris: I4CE (Institute for Climate Economics).

Van Asselt, H. (2014) 'Governing the Transition Away from Fossil Fuels: The Role of International Institutions'. Stockholm Environment Institute Working Paper, 7.

Van de Graaf, T. (2013) *The Politics and Institutions of Global Energy Governance*. Basingstoke: Palgrave.

Van de Graaf, T., and B. K. Sovacool (2020) *Global Energy Politics*. Cambridge: Polity.

Van de Graaf, T., B. K. Sovacool, A. Ghosh, F. Kern and M. Klare (eds.) (2016) *The Palgrave Handbook of the International Political Economy of Energy*. London: Palgrave.

Van de Kroon, B., R. Brouwer and P. J. H. van Beukering (2013) 'The Energy Ladder: Theoretical Myth or Empirical Truth? Results from a Meta-analysis'. *Renewable and Sustainable Energy Reviews* 20: 504–13.

Vandenbergh, M. P., and B. K. Sovacool (2016) 'Individual Behaviour, the Social Sciences and Climate Change'. In *Elgar Encyclopedia of Environmental Law*. Cheltenham: Edward Elgar, 92–102.

Van Gelder, S. (2017) *The Revolution Where You Live*. Oakland, CA: Berrett-Koehler.

Van Veelen, B., and D. van der Horst (2018) 'What Is Energy Democracy? Connecting Social Science Energy Research and Political Theory'. *Energy Research & Social Science* 46: 19–28.

Vaughan, A. (2018) 'Plastic Bans Worldwide Will Dent Oil Demand Growth, Says BP'. *The Guardian*, 20 February. www.theguardian.com/business/2018/feb/20/plastic-bans-worldwide-will-dent-oil-demand-growth-says-bp.

Verbong, G., and D. Loorbach (eds.) (2012) *Governing the Energy Transition: Reality, Illusion or Necessity?* Abingdon: Routledge.

Vernon, R. (1971) *Sovereignty at Bay: The Multinational Spread of US Enterprises*. New York: Basic Books.

Vidal, J. (2008) 'Not Guilty: The Greenpeace Activists Who Used Climate Change as a Legal Defence'. *The Guardian*, 11 September. www.theguardian.com/environment/2008/sep/11/activists.kingsnorthclimatecamp.

Victor, D., M. Thurber and D. Hults (2012) *Oil and Governance: State-Owned Enterprises and the World Energy Supply*. Cambridge: Cambridge University Press.

Wade, R. (2003) 'What Strategies Are Viable for Developing Countries Today? The WTO and the Shrinking of Development Space'. In J. Timmons Roberts and A. Bellone Hite (eds.) *The Globalization and Development Reader*. Oxford: Wiley-Blackwell.

Walenta, J. (2019 online, 2020 journal issue) 'Climate Risk Assessments and Science-Based Targets: A Review of Emerging Private Sector Action Tools'. *WIRES Climate Change* 11(2): e628. 10.1002/wcc.628.

Walker, G., and H. Bulkeley (eds.) (2006) 'Geographies of Environmental Justice'. *Geoforum* 37(5): 655–9.

Walker, G., S. Hunter, P. Devine-Wright, B. Evans and H. Fa (2007) 'Harnessing Community Energies: Explaining and Evaluating Community-Based Localism in Renewable Energy Policy in the UK'. *Global Environmental Politics* 72(2): 64–82.

Waterson, J. (2020) 'Guardian to Ban Advertising from Fossil Fuel Firms'. *The Guardian*, 29 January. www.theguardian.com/media/2020/jan/29/guardian-to-ban-advertising-from-fossil-fuel-firms-climate-crisis.

Watson, J. (2009) 'Technology Assessment and Innovation Policy'. In I. Scarse and G. MacKerron (eds.) *Energy for the Future: A New Agenda*. Basingstoke: Palgrave, 123–47.

Watt, H. (2017) 'Hinkley Point: The "Dreadful Deal" behind the World's Most Expensive Power Plant'. The Guardian, 21 December. www.theguardian.com/news/2017/dec/21/hinkley-point-c-dreadful-deal-behind-worlds-most-expensive-power-plant.

Watts, J. (2007) 'Riots and Hunger Feared as Demand for Grain Sends Food Costs Soaring'. *The Guardian*, 4 December. www.theguardian.com/world/2007/dec/04/china.business?CMP=share_btn_link.

(2015) 'Uruguay Makes Dramatic Shift to Nearly 95% Electricity from Clean Energy'. *The Guardian*, 3 December. www.theguardian.com/environment/2015/dec/03/uruguay-makes-dramatic-shift-to-nearly-95-clean-energy.

(2020) 'BP's Statement on Reaching Net Zero by 2050 – What It Says and What It Means'. *The Guardian*, 12 February. www.theguardian.com/environment/ng-interactive/2020/feb/12/bp-statement-on-reaching-net-zero-carbon-emissions-by-2050-what-it-says-and-what-it-means?CMP=share_btn_link.

Watts, M. (2008) *The Curse of the Black Gold*. New York: Powerhouse Press.

(2009) 'Oil, Development and the Politics of the Bottom Billion'. *MacCalaster International* 24(Summer): 79–130.

WBGU (2013) *World in Transition: A Social Contract for Sustainability*. Berlin: Heinrich Böll Foundation.

(2018) *Just & In-Time Climate Policy: Four Initiatives for a Fair Transformation*. Berlin: WBGU.

WCA (World Coal Association) (2021) 'Improving Access to Energy'. www.worldcoal.org/sustainable-societies/improving-access-energy.

WEC (2012) *World Energy Dilemma: Time to Get Real – The Case for Sustainable Energy Policy*. London: World Energy Council.

Weitz, N., C. Strambo, E. Kemp-Benedict and M. Nilsson (2017) 'Closing the Governance Gaps in the Water-Energy-Food Nexus: Insights from Integrative Governance'. *Global Environmental Change* 45: 165–73.

Wesselink, A., J. Paavola, O. Fritsch and O. Renn (2011) 'Rationales for Public Participation in Environmental Policy and Governance: Practitioners' Perspectives'. *Environment and Planning A* 43(11): 2688–2704.

White, L. (1943) 'Energy and the Evolution of Culture'. *American Anthropologist* 45(3): 335–56.

Whitley, S., J. Thwaites, H. Wright and C. Ott (2018) *Making Finance Consistent with Climate Goals*. London: ODI. www.odi.org/sites/odi.org.uk/files/resource-documents/12557.pdf.

Whitmarsh, L. (2009) 'Behavioural Responses to Climate Change: Asymmetry of Intentions and Impacts'. *Journal of Environmental Psychology* 29: 13–23.

Whitmarsh, L., S. O'Neill and I. Lorenzoni (eds.) (2011) *Engaging the Public with Climate Change: Behaviour Change and Communication*. London: Earthscan.

WHO (World Health Organization) (2014) '7 Million Premature Deaths Annually Linked to Air Pollution'. WHO, 25 March. www.who.int/mediacentre/news/releases/2014/air-pollution/en/.

Wilde, R. (2019) 'The Development of Banking in the Industrial Revolution'. 23 May. www.thoughtco.com/development-of-banking-the-industrial-revolution-1221645.

Wilhite, H. (2013) 'Energy Consumption as Cultural Practice: Implications for the Theory and Policy of Sustainable Energy Use'. In S. Strauss, S. Rupp and T. Love (eds.) *Cultures of Energy: Power, Practices, Technology*. Walnut Creek, CA: Left Coast Press, 60–72.

Wilkinson, R., and L. Pickett (2009) *The Spirit Level: Why Equality Is Better for Everyone*. London: Allen Lane.

Williams, E. (1994 [1944]) *Capitalism and Slavery*. Chapel Hill, NC: University of North Carolina Press.

Williams, M. (1994) *International Economic Organisations and the Third World*. London: Harvester Wheatsheaf.

Willis, R. (2020) *Too Hot to Handle? The Democratic Challenge of Climate Change*. Bristol: Bristol University Press.

Wilson, C. (2018) 'Disruptive Low-Carbon Innovations'. *Energy Research & Social Science* 37: 216–23.

Wilson, C., and D. Tyfield (2018) 'Critical Perspectives on Disruptive Innovation and Energy Transformation'. *Energy Research & Social Science* 37: 211–15.

Wilson, E. (1987) 'World Politics and International Energy Markets'. *International Organisation* 41(1): 125–49.

Wilson, J. (2015) 'Multilateral Organisations and the Limits to International Energy Cooperation'. *New Political Economy* 20(1): 85–106.

Winther, T., M. N. Matinga, K. Ulsrud and K. Standal (2017) 'Women's Empowerment through Electricity Access: Scoping Study and Proposal for a Framework of Analysis'. *Journal of Development Effectiveness* 9(3): 389–41.

Wood, E. (2002) *The Origin of Capitalism: A Longer View*. London: Verso.

World Bank (2010) *World Development Report 2010: Development and Climate Change*. World Bank: Washington, DC.

(2012) *Inclusive Green Growth: The Pathway to Sustainable Development*. World Bank: Washington, DC.

(2014) '73 Countries and Over 1,000 Businesses Speak Out in Support of a Price on Carbon'. World Bank, 22 September. www.worldbank.org/en/news/feature/2014/09/22/governments-businesses-support-carbon-pricing.

World Future Council (2012) 'Proposal for a High Commissioner/Ombudsperson for Future Generations: Reflections on the Negotiation Process'. http://sdg.iisd.org/commentary/guest-articles/proposal-for-a-high-commissionerombudsperson-for-futuregenerations-reflections-on-the-negotiation-process/.

Wright, C. (2011) 'Export Credit Agencies and Global Energy: Promoting National Exports in a Changing World'. *Global Policy* 2: 133–43.

Wright, C., and D. Nyberg (2015) *Climate Change, Capitalism and Corporations: Processes of Create Self-Destruction.* Cambridge: Cambridge University Press.

Wrigley, E. (2010) *Energy and the English Industrial Revolution.* Cambridge: Cambridge University Press.

Yadav, K. (2010) 'Nepal's Right to Energy Movement'. 4 May. www.indiaenvironmentportal .org.in/content/304914/nepals-right-to-energy-movement-lessons-for-super-grids-of-the-future/.

Yergin, D. (1991) *The Prize: The Epic Quest for Oil, Money and Power.* New York: Simon & Schuster.

York, R., and S. Bell (2019) 'Energy Transitions or Additions? Why a Transition from Fossil Fuels Requires More than the Growth of Renewable Energy'. *Energy Research & Social Science* 51: 40–3.

Zehner, O. (2012) *Green Illusions: The Dirty Secrets of Clean Energy and the Future of Environmentalism.* Lincoln: University of Nebraska Press.

Zelli, F., K. Bäckstrand, N. Nasiritousi, J. Skovgaard and O. Widerburg (2020) *Governing the Climate-Energy Nexus: Challenges to Coherence, Legitimacy and Effectiveness.* Cambridge: Cambridge University Press.

Index